Ambitious Brew

ALSO BY MAUREEN OGLE

All the Modern Conveniences:
American Household Plumbing, 1840–1890

Key West: History of an Island of Dreams

MAUREEN OGLE

Ambitious Brew

The Story of American Beer

HARCOURT, INC.

Orlando   Austin   New York   San Diego   Toronto   London

www.HarcourtBooks.com

Library of Congress Cataloging-in-Publication Data
Ogle, Maureen.
Ambitious brew: the story of American beer/Maureen Ogle.
p.   cm.
Includes bibliographical references and index.
1. Beer—History.   2. Brewing—History.
3. Brewing industry—United States.   I. Title.
TP577.O46   2006
663'.420973—dc22   2006011377
ISBN-13: 978-0-15-101012-7   ISBN-10: 0-15-101012-9

Text set in Perpetua
Designed by Linda Lockowitz

Printed in the United States of America
First edition

A C E G I K J H F D B

CONTENTS

INTRODUCTION

I N THE EARLY SPRING of 2001, I had recently finished writing a book and was trying to think of a topic for my next one. I knew that there was no point in pressing the issue: Writers don't find ideas; the ideas present themselves, and do so in unexpected ways.

One morning, I headed out on a shopping expedition to a small Italian grocery for sausage and pancetta. This store, named after the family that has owned it for over a century, sits in the heart of the city's oldest neighborhood, a relic of the long-gone days when dwellings and families shared their streets with pharmacies and hardware and grocery stores. Painted across the building in huge letters that can be seen several blocks away is the store's name, GRAZIANO BROS., and its founding date, 1912.

I was eyeing the sign and wondering what the shop looked like a century ago when a truck rolled across the street and into my line of vision. It was a very shiny, very red truck, and it was emblazoned with a single word: BUDWEISER.

Wham! That was it. I would write a history of beer in America.

I spent the next several weeks reading what few books there were on the subject and telling everyone I saw about my great new idea. I was fascinated and surprised by their responses. Invariably, they said one of two things: Did I want some help with the "research" (a joke usually accompanied by a wink and a nudge)? Or they talked—ranted is more like it—about what an embarrassment American beer was, thanks to the giant corporate breweries that had ruined it.

I laughed at the jokes, but the humor revealed genuine unease and discomfort. We Americans have an ambivalent relationship with alcohol. On one hand, we drink because we enjoy the way beer and wine taste with food, or for relaxation and sociability. On the other hand, we fear that even a single drink will damage our ability to work and "produce." Think what happens when someone orders a beer at lunchtime: The bottle or glass arrives, and so does a raised eyebrow of disapproval or a ribbing about not getting much work done the rest of the day.

The complaints about corporate brewers were more troubling. At the time, I knew nothing about beer—historical or other-wise—short of what I learned downing plastic cups of the stuff during dime beer hour at the Vine in Iowa City back in college. To my surprise, however, my ignorance placed me in a minority. It seemed as if everyone I ran into already knew the history of beer in America, and they were more than happy to fill me in on the facts, which went something like this:

> Back in the old days, Americans enjoyed an abundance of fine, local beers from thousands of breweries that were arti-san workshops where skilled brewers crafted ales using only four ingredients: malt, hops, yeast, and water.
>
> Prohibition ended that halcyon age. When beer came back in the 1930s, hundreds of breweries opened their doors. Most were owned by old brewing families who were deter-mined to brew only the finest and purest of beers. Alas, their dreams died aborning, thanks to the conniving of a handful of corporate behemoths—most notably Anheuser-Busch, Schlitz, Pabst, and Miller.
>
> These Big Brewers scorned honest beer in favor of wa-tery swill brewed from cheap corn and rice. The Big Brewers

added insult to injury by using crass commercials, linked mostly to professional sporting events, to sell their foul brew to working-class people. By the 1970s, only a handful of brewers remained and American beer was a thin, yellow concoction with no flavor and even less body.

Baby boomers to the rescue. In the 1960s and 1970s, young Americans backpacked through Europe and there discovered "real" ales and stouts. They returned eager to try their hand at making those beers at home. In the 1980s, some of the homebrewers opened microbreweries and brewpubs. These new artisans crafted beer of the purest and most flavorful sort—and so real beer was rescued from the evil corporate dragons.

I started to wonder: Did the world really need a rehash of this apparently well-known story? Was there anything new to tell about beer in America?

My fears were for nought. As I dug through archives and old trade journals, I discovered that almost every aspect of that oft-told tale of skullduggery, greed, and woe was false and that the truth was considerably more interesting and complex.

Beer's history, I learned, embodies the essence of what it is to be American: our ambivalent attitude toward alcohol, our passion for invention and creativity, and our seemingly limitless ability to take old ideas and things and remake them in our uniquely American image. But beer's history is also a tale of gamblers and entrepreneurial visionaries, as well as the cultural clashes that are inevitable in a democracy where ideas and values are freely debated.

It is the tale of Frederick Pabst, a sea captain who entered the beer business when he married a brewer's daughter and, forty years later, helmed the world's largest brewery. Of Ken Grossman, a California bicycle repairman and home brewer who built a brewery with his own hands and transformed that small start into the nation's ninth largest beer-making establishment. Of Howard Hyde Russell and Wayne Wheeler, who founded the organization that produced Prohibition and shut down thousands of breweries. Of Carl Conrad, who imagined an American version of a Bohemian beer, one that he called Budweiser, and Otto Lademan, the St. Louis brewer who tried to steal it from him. Of Charlie Papazian, a home-brewing enthusiast with no business background, whose zeal for beer inspired him to found not one but two national brewing groups. Of the Busch, Yuengling, and Leinenkugel families, who have kept their breweries alive from one generation to the next for decades on end, and in one of the most competitive and volatile of industries.

What I found was a truly American tale of ambition and passion populated by a cast of remarkable human beings. Here is their story.

CHAPTER ONE

German Beer,
American Dreams

L ATE SUMMER, 1844. Milwaukee, Wisconsin Territory. Phillip
Best elbowed his way along plank walkways jammed with
barrels, boxes, pushcarts, and people. He was headed for
the canal, or the "Water Power," as locals called it, a mile-long
millrace powered by a tree-trunk-and-gravel dam on the Milwaukee River. Plank docks punctuated its tumbling flow and small
manufactories—a few mills, a handful of smithies and wheel-
wrights, a tannery or two—lined its length. Best was searching
for a particular business as he pushed his way past more carts and
crates, and dodged horses pulling wagons along the dirt street and
laborers shouldering newly hewn planks and bags of freshly
milled grain. He had been in the United States only a few weeks,
and Milwaukee's bustle marked a sharp contrast to the drowsy
German village where he and his three brothers had worked for
their father, Jacob, Sr., a brewer and vintner.

Phillip finally arrived at the shop owned by A. J. Langworthy,
metalworker and ironmonger. He presented himself to the proprietor and explained that he needed a boiler—a copper vat—
for his family's new brewing business. Would Langworthy fabri-
cate it for them? The metalworker shook his head no. "I [am]

familiar with their construction," he explained to Best, ". . . but I [dislike] very much to have the noisy things around, and [I do] not wish to do so."

Wrong answer. Best possessed what the historian of his brewery later called a "fiery" personality and an irresistible fount of aggressive determination. Best cajoled Langworthy, argued with him, badgered, and perhaps even begged. The metalworker may have been surprised at the passion that poured from the otherwise unassuming man before him, a slender twenty-nine-year-old of medium height, whose prominent ears and blond hair framed deep-set gray eyes and a ruler-straight nose. Overwhelmed and overrun by the man's persistence, Langworthy finally consented.

That obstacle behind him, Best prodded Langworthy to hurdle the next: lack of materials. Milwaukee, frontier town of seven thousand souls, contained only two sheets of metal. Langworthy needed eight or nine plus a bucket of rivets. Left to his own devices, he might have abandoned the commission; with Phillip Best breathing down his neck, that was impossible. Langworthy headed south, first to Racine, then to Kenosha, and finally on to tiny Chicago. It was an exercise in frustration: He could not find enough material for even one section of the boiler. There was nothing for it but to dispatch an order to Buffalo, New York.

Eventually the goods arrived, and Langworthy and his employees set to work transforming metal sheets and rivets into an oversized pot. They worked on a nearby dock, where what the metalworker called the "music of riveting"—racket is more like it—drew an enormous crowd. "[A]ll came to see it," said Langworthy, "and I think if the roll had been called at that time that every man, woman, and child except the invalids, would have answered 'here.'" The finished product was a squat rotund vat, about four feet in diameter and four feet high, big enough to hold three to four hundred gallons of water.

When the boiler was completed, Phillip returned to the iron-monger's shop, this time lugging a cloth bundle of coins—so many that the two men spent more than an hour tallying the value. The task revealed the truth: Best did not have enough money. He explained that his family had spent nearly all of their funds—two hundred dollars—on a piece of property on Chestnut Street, where they planned to build their brewhouse. Phillip had commissioned the vat in expectation of a forthcoming loan, but the money had failed to materialize. The bundle of coins represented his family's only remaining cash. Phillip asked Langworthy to keep the boiler until he could scrounge up the balance.

What happened next is a credit to A. J. Langworthy's generosity and Phillip Best's integrity. Langworthy was but a few years older than Phillip. Like Phillip, he had left the security of the familiar—in his case, New York—for the adventure and gamble of a new life on the frontier. Perhaps he glanced through the door at the mad rush of people and goods flowing past unabated from daylight to dusk. He was no fool; he understood that business out in the territories would always be more fraught with risk than back in the settled east. But what was life for, if not to embrace some of its uncertainty?

He eyed the man standing before him. He knew about the family's decision to sell their winery and brewery and venture to the new world. He had come to understand that Best's "love for dramatic speech and action" stemmed not from swaggering braggadocio, but from the depths of a "born leader." The debt would never be paid until Best made some money, and the boiler was useless unless filled with steaming malt and hops.

Take the boiler and get busy, he told Phillip, and pay the balance when you can. Langworthy recalled years later that the man "was filled with great joy, and ever after my most ardent friend." Best promised his creditor not just the family's first keg of beer, but free brew for the rest of Langworthy's life. (The promise out-lived Best himself. On his deathbed in 1869, Phillip reminded his wife of the pact and charged his sons-in-law with the task of up-holding the family's end. In 1896, Langworthy, well into his eight-ies, was still drinking free beer.)

It's not clear how Phillip transported his treasure the half mile or so from Langworthy's shop to the family's brewhouse. Perhaps his new friend provided delivery. Perhaps Phillip persuaded an idling wagoner to haul the vat with the promise of free beer. Per-haps one or more of his three brothers accompanied him, and they and their burden staggered through Kilbourntown—the German west side of Milwaukee—and up the Chestnut Street hill. But eventually the vat made its way to the Bests' property—the location of Best and Company, and the foundation of their American adventure.

OVER THE NEXT FEW YEARS, Phillip Best would lay the ground-work for what stood, fifty years later, as the largest brewery in the world. But in 1844, he was just one anonymous drop in a stream of humanity that poured into the United States in the mid-nineteenth century. A mere 600,000 immigrants landed during the 1830s, but starting in 1840, that trickle swelled like a creek in early spring: 1.7 million in the 1840s and another 2.6 million the following decade. Seventy-five percent were Irish and German (the rest hailed mostly from England and non-German northern Europe). Many of the Germans were cut from the same mold as the Bests: They arrived in possession of a bit of money and a craft that would earn them more. Most of the Irish, however, were im-poverished peasants fleeing the famine that destroyed that sad is-land's main source of food and, before it ended, killed a million people. The million or so who survived the trip across the At-lantic (many succumbed to the vomit, feces, and filth of steerage) were mostly peasants, uneducated, unskilled, and carrying nothing more than the clothes on their backs.

The Bests had emigrated from a village called Mettenheim, where a Marley-like chain of war and poverty, taxes and regulations, shackled their ambitions. In the early 1800s, warfare and political turmoil left German-speaking Europeans, whether Prussian, Bavarian, Rhenish, or Austrian, exhausted, disabled, or angry. Explosive population growth and bad harvests added deprivation and poverty to the mix. Tyrannical princes and dukes suppressed political expression and individual ambition. Phillip and his countrymen yearned for a "true" Germany, a people united under one government that granted its citizens basic freedoms. No one believed it would happen anytime soon. The chain's grip tightened in the 1830s, when the price of coffee and tea plummeted, and customers abandoned beer for the intoxicating novelty of caffeine. Others embraced potato-based *schnaps,* a throat-burning, alcoholic jolt that was cheaper than beer. Hundreds of brewers emptied their vats, damped their fires, and shut their doors.

So it was that in the early 1840s, Jacob Best, Sr., and his sons decided that it was time to choose: German Europe with tyrants and oppression, or the United States, where angels blessed the ambitious? Sometime between 1840 and 1842, Phillip traveled to New York, intent on developing the contacts needed to export the Bests' wine to the United States. He failed in that mission and returned home so the family could plot its next move. By early 1843, Jacob, Jr., and Frederick (known around town as Carl) had settled in Milwaukee and opened a small vinegar manufactory, a common side venture of vintners everywhere.

The success of that experiment convinced them that their future lay in America. Carl retraced his steps, helped sell the Bests' Mettenheim properties, and by mid-1844 was on his way back to Milwaukee with the rest of the family in tow.

They landed in New York and boarded steamboats that chugged up the Hudson River to the Erie Canal. For several days the travelers glided along its waterway, the scenery dominated by tidy farms and grain mills. At Buffalo, they trooped to the harbor, there to board one of the dozens of ferries that plied the Great Lakes between New York and the West—across Lake Erie, up the sliver of water that separated eastern Michigan from the jagged southern tip of Ontario, up Lake Huron, and down Lake Michigan to journey's end, Milwaukee.

The nation where the Bests made their new home stretched from the Atlantic seaboard fifteen hundred miles to the Mississippi, from there hundreds more miles to the Rocky Mountains, and on to the border of unclaimed territory that included what are today Washington and Oregon. Within a few years of the Bests' arrival, Americans would lay claim to that contested terrain and to another vast expanse that included what would become California and Texas.

In Mettenheim, the land's potential might have remained cocooned in a web of restraints, dominated by lords and princes and worked by peasants burdened by illiteracy, heavy taxes, and impossible rents. Not so in the United States. Compared to people in the rest of the world, white Americans enjoyed extraordinary personal liberty and a short history: At the time Phillip commissioned his vat, the Revolution was still living memory for the oldest Americans. The nation was young in more ways than one: In 1830, to pick one year, about a third of the nation's twelve million people were under the age of ten, and the median age was seventeen. The federal government did little more than manage the public lands and deliver the mail. Taxes were few, land was abundant and cheap, and the political system was stable. Several million black-skinned humans endured the agony of the "peculiar institution," but already the paradox of slavery in the midst of such freedom had roused the forces that would eradicate that shame.

Americans even derived inspiration from the obstacles they faced: Overland travel over such enormous distances destroyed farmers' and merchants' hopes of profit; and, youthful energy and a parade of immigrants notwithstanding, there weren't enough people to do the nation's work. New Yorkers devoted the first half of the 1820s to constructing one grand solution to the transportation problem: the 350-mile Erie Canal, which linked New York City's harbors, the Hudson River, and the Great Lakes. In one swoop, the canal lopped weeks off the journey from east to west and dollars off the cost. That experiment's success launched canal mania: Between 1825 and 1840, Americans built three thousand miles of waterways, including one that ran from Chicago to the Illinois River and so connected that city—and thus Milwaukee— to the Mississippi. Canals proved a short-lived wonder, as other investors plowed their money into iron rails and steam locomotives. By 1840, three thousand miles of rails connected city and canal, canal and hinterland, hinterland and harbor. Over the next decade, Americans laid another six thousand miles of rail, and, in 1845, began stringing telegraph wire alongside the tracks.

Immigrants provided much of the labor for laying the rails and digging the canals, disseminating their ambitions and energy deep into the frontier, but Americans also invented their way out of the labor shortage, unencumbered by the guild and apprentice systems that hindered innovation in Europe. Cyrus McCormick's reaper, to name just one example, allowed one farmer to do the work of many hands. Talented artisans and tinkerers scattered along the eastern seaboard designed machines that replaced skilled craftsmen, such as automated devices that cut gunstocks or ax handles and so reduced the time and money needed to manufacture goods. In 1800, a New England clockmaker built perhaps a half dozen clocks in a year: fifty years later, a single factory turned out 150,000 clocks a year and at a price nearly any family could afford.

A man could make a fortune on Monday and lose it all by Friday. No matter. The era's byword—progress—rolled off every tongue. There was room for everyone and every idea. True, the pace of industrial change ground slow and uneven: In densely populated and increasingly urban Massachusetts, young women and immigrants operated clattering machinery that wove millions of yards of fabric each year, while in Milwaukee, A. J. Langworthy could not lay hands on enough metal for one brewing vat and Phillip Best employed a horse to grind his malt. But by mid-century, Americans enjoyed the highest standard of living in the world.

Critics complain about its uneven distribution—the wealthy few possessed an oversized chunk of the bounty—but no one could deny that in the United States, even a common laborer ate meat every day and owned a change of clothes, two facts that left his European counterpart gaping in awe. The young men and women who tended machines and shops—unmarried and still unfettered by responsibility—invested their meager wages in fine caps and jaunty jackets, beribboned bonnets and factory-made dresses. Immigrants watched and yearned as Americans in the burgeoning middle class devoted their cash to comfort: Oilcloth floor coverings gave way to rich woolen carpets; iron stoves replaced pots hung over open flame. Families scrabbling for a living on the frontier crowded into country stores to trade corn and homemade whiskey for hair ribbons and top hats, tea sets and button boots. Singer's sewing machine allowed women to transform machine-made fabrics into dresses and shirts. All of it—the hats and shoes, John Deere's plows and Samuel Colt's revolvers, factory-made clocks and soaps, wallpaper and candles—provided pleasure twice: first in the buying and then in the using.

No surprise, émigré letters to family back home praised an otherwise unimaginable paradise. "[O]ne cannot describe how good it is in America," reported one awestruck transplant. "In

America one knows nothing about taxes. Here one does not need to worry about beggars as we do in Germany. Here a man works for himself. Here the one is equal to the other. Here no one takes off his hat to another. We no longer long for Germany." "Every day," he added, "we thank the dear God that he has brought us . . . out of slavery into Paradise," a sweet fate he hoped to share with the millions still suffering, still living back in Germany "as if under lions and dragons, fearing every moment to be devoured by them." Another new arrival spoke for thousands when he wrote, "We sing: 'Long live the United States of America.'"

The Bests' new home provided inspiration aplenty. Milwaukee sat out in the frontier in what was still a territory rather than a state, but in the decade since the town had been founded, the American passion for converting land into profit had transformed a moribund trading post of a few hundred into a lively metropolis, vibrant testimony to the infinite possibility of America in the 1840s.

To the north and west of the family's Chestnut Street property lay a thick forest that stretched for miles. Concealed beneath the leafy mass, crude wagon tracks led away from the town and into the western hinterland, where dwindling forest eventually gave way to rolling hills and then the vast grassy sweep of the Iowa Territory, acres of soil that could be planted with barley. To the south and east lay the town itself, visible from atop the Chestnut Street ridge as a mosaic of roofs, chimneys, and steeples, their textures and colors interlaced with a mortar of muddy streets that teemed with people, horses, and wagons. "A fellow . . . can hardly get along the sidewalk," grumbled one visiting farmer. "[E]very kind of Mechanism is a going on in this place from street hawking to Manufacturing steam Engines and every kind of citizens [sic] from the rude Norwegian to the polished Italian."

Carpenters, metalworkers, and bricklayers hustled from one job to another, busy converting the city's vacant lots into hotels, houses, law offices, workshops, and taverns. Farmers, shoppers, and newly arrived émigrés thronged the plank walkways that bordered muddy thoroughfares. Lawyers bustled in and out of the courthouse, signing contracts and settling land claims. Carts laden with produce, building supplies, and grain rumbled through the streets. A clatter of languages and dialects filled the air: German, Irish, Italian, Norwegian, and Welsh; the New Englander's flat, clipped twang; the southerner's softer drawl.

Thanks to its location on the shore of Lake Michigan, Milwaukee was one of the most accessible of the nation's far western settlements. In the 1840s, it served as a gateway through which migrants passed on their way to the vast stretch of rich soil in the territories beyond, or to find work in the Wisconsin Territory's booming mining and timber industries. Every day, steamers spewing gritty clouds of black smoke and cinder chips belched human cargo onto the wharves.

The lake itself could not be seen from the Chestnut ridge, thanks to the sharp ascent of the Milwaukee's eastern bank. But when Phillip climbed the steep bluff that hugged the lake's edge, he marveled at the vast sheet of rippling gray silk that stretched as far as the eye could see. Here and there, jagged tripods of canvas-draped uprights sliced the horizon. Closer at hand, a jumble of masts cluttered the harbor. Bundles of wheat and timber dangled from the slender arms of cranes, then disappeared into waiting hulls. Grunting stevedores trundled carts filled with the multifarious tools needed to convert a wilderness of river and forest into a respectable example of American civilization: plowshares, iron plates, and saddles; boots, stationery, and shawls; casks filled with raisins, nuts, and oils; crates containing bottles of wine from France and porter and stout from England; dictionaries and primers; gloves, yarn, and fabric.

"The public houses and streets are filled with new comers and our old citizens are almost strangers in their own town," marveled the editor of one of the city's newspapers. "One hundred persons, chiefly German, landed here yesterday," another resident wrote to his brother during the summer of 1842. And more were on the way: In the early 1840s, Germans poured into the territory. Some came after reading a pamphlet published in 1841 by a German-speaking visitor who praised the climate, soil, and opportunity. Those first settlers in turn wrote laudatory letters of their own back home, which fueled still more migration to Wisconsin. By the time the Bests arrived, about one-third of the town's population spoke German.

In September of 1844, with Langworthy's copper vat installed, Phillip and the two Jacobs, father and son, began brewing, likely with recipes and yeast carried with them to their new home. They had been winemakers back in Germany, but Americans drank almost no wine and so the United States had no tradition of viniculture. Beer would provide the substance of their American dream.

They followed the practices of most German brewers of that time, relying on strong backs and shoulders to brew by hand rather than machine. At the new brewery, an L-shaped, one-story brick structure that also served as the family's residence, they trundled wheelbarrows of grain, either purchased in town from a farmer at market or ordered from Buffalo, into the shop and dumped it into a capacious wooden steeping vat to soak for a day or two. Then they spread the sodden grain on the floor and waited for the kernels to sprout. The acrospire, the quarter-inch sprout that emerged from the base of each kernel, contained the enzymes (diastase) that would convert barley's starch into sugar. Germination typically required two or three days, depending on the humidity and the age and quality of the grain. Phillip kept close watch on the pile, stirring and tossing it regularly to add new oxygen and ensure that all the heads sprouted at more or less the same time. A fruity aroma filled the brewhouse (much like the odor of rotten apples, critics complained) as nature conducted the business of turning barley into malt.

When each kernel had sprouted, the men shoveled the malt onto the drying floor, an elevated platform stationed above a kiln. They fed the firebox a steady diet of wood, watching the flames and testing the heat, aiming for a temperature somewhere between 160 and 170 degrees, hot enough to dry the malt but not burn it. With its moisture evaporated, the malt weighed less for the next go-round of shoveling, this time into a storage bin, where it was left to age a few weeks.

When Jacob, Sr., declared ripe both the grain and the time, he and his sons hauled the malt to the grinder. While the horse dragged a heavy stone over the grain, the brothers filled their precious copper boiler with water, heated it to about 130 degrees, and added the ground malt. As it cooked, they stirred it with long paddles, waiting for the enzymes to transform starch into sugar and the water into syrupy wort. When the sugar had dissolved, the brothers drained the wort, rinsed the vat to remove every bit of the syrup, and began cooking the wort again, this time adding hops, the cone-shaped flower of the *Humulus lupulus.* Hops added flavor, aroma, and bitterness to the beer and acted as a preservative, too, by inhibiting the growth of bacteria. In 1844, the Bests most likely relied on hops imported (like the metal for the brewing vat) from Buffalo. Much of the beer's character and taste emerged from this phase of the operation, and the men heated the mix slowly, constantly monitoring it and the fire's flames.

After several hours, they drained the wort into large flat pans, there to cool to about 45 degrees, no easy feat in an age when "refrigeration" depended on cold weather or blocks of ice. Luckily, Milwaukee in December and January offered plenty of both. Phillip and his brothers transferred the wort to a fermenting tub and added the yeast—"pitched" it, in brewing parlance—then held their breaths and waited. This was make-or-break time. Assuming the yeast had survived the trip from Europe and was alive and healthy, soon white foam would crawl across the wort's surface. If none appeared, their work was in vain.

To their relief and joy, about ten hours after the first pitch, a thin band of foam appeared. Some ten or twelve hours later, froth covered the entire surface. It dissipated and drifted down to the bottom of the vat, where it continued to work, turning the wort into beer. The brew fermented in its tub for seven to ten days. Then, leaving the yeast behind, the men drained the beer into pitch-lined barrels (the pitch protected the beer from the taint of wood) and transferred the kegs to a cellar beneath the brewery, where the beer aged in cool temperatures.

Now the waiting began—anywhere from two to six months, during which the beer's flavor mellowed and the yeast precipitated. Jacob and his sons passed the time converting barley, wine, and cider into whiskey and vinegar, tasks that required less labor and time than did brewing. In February 1845, they introduced (or, in the case of the vinegar, reintroduced) Milwaukeeans to the Best family of products in advertisements in the city's German-language newspaper: "Best & Company, Beer Brewery, Whiskey Distillery & Vinegar Refinery . . . on the summit of the hill above Kilbourntown. Herewith we give notice to our friends that henceforth we will have bottom fermentation beer for sale." The family promised to provide its "worthy customers" with "prompt and satisfactory service."

Best and Company was in business.

THEY WERE NOT ALONE. Everywhere that Germans went in the 1840s, beer flowed close at hand, and several hundred immigrant brewers opened their doors during the decade. New York and Philadelphia claimed the lion's share, with forty breweries founded in Philadelphia and several dozen in New York. But beer also foamed freely in other cities where Germans congregated in large numbers: St. Louis, Cincinnati, Buffalo, Brooklyn, Chicago, and, of course, Milwaukee, where ten brewers set up shop during the decade. (For years, beer historians have credited John Wagner of Philadelphia with introducing lager to the United States, but the title of first lager brewer probably belongs to émigrés Alexander Stausz and John Klein, who founded a tiny outfit in Alexandria, Virginia, in 1838.) Like the Bests, these other pioneering German-American brewers cultivated a local market, selling beer to customers who lived around the corner or a few blocks away.

The Bests were not their city's first German brewers. That honor belonged to Simon (sometimes called Herman) Reutelshofer. According to one of the laborers who helped build the brewshop, the proprietor tapped his first keg in May 1841. It was nearly his last, presumably because he lacked either the skill or the customers. Within months his business teetered on the brink of collapse. The would-be beer baron went hunting for an infusion of cash, and, to his everlasting regret, found salvation in the person of one John B. Meier (sometimes spelled Meyer), also a German émigré. Reutelshofer wanted a mortgage, but Meier presented him with a contract to buy the property. Reutelshofer, who either ignored the fine print, could not read a document that may have been written in English, or was illiterate, unwittingly signed away his livelihood.

Meier ordered Reutelshofer to vacate the premises. The brewer, still unaware that he no longer owned the shop, resisted. Meier grabbed his dupe and "then and there with divers sticks and clubs and with his fists gave [him] . . . many blows and strokes about his head, face, breast, back, shoulders, arms, [and] legs." Not content with his handiwork, Meier hurled Reutelshofer to the ground "with great force and violence" and "kicked, struck and . . . choked him."

Poor Reutelshofer recovered neither pride nor property. He sued his attacker, demanding $2,000 in damages and the return of the brewery. A judge ordered Meier to pay a mere $150 and dispatched a sheriff to seize the building and its contents and return them to their original owner. Nothing doing. Meier had already deeded not only the brewery but everything else he owned to his father-in-law, Franz Neukirch. Reutelshofer's claims against Meier fell into the category of lost causes. He never collected the monies due him, never regained possession of his brewshop, and dropped out of sight not long after the Best family arrived in Milwaukee.

Had he known, Reutelshofer might have taken comfort in numbers. His failure typified the experience of most brewers who set up shop in the 1840s (except, we hope, in the matter of the trickery and violence that separated him from his brewery). Many failed after a few years, likely due to inexperience or poor management. Others limped along for a decade or two before being bought by new owners who changed the name.

But successful or not, and whether located in New York or the Wisconsin Territory, the first immigrant brewers introduced a new kind of beer to the United States: lager. In the early nineteenth century, the only beer Americans knew was English-style ale, brewed in the states since colonial days but never as popular as either cider or spirits. The differences between British ale and German lager were apparent to both eye and tongue. Ale sat dark, heavy, and "still" in a tankard, brown in color and thick in body. Lager seemed nearly buoyant in contrast, thanks to its lighter body and color, and lower alcohol content. The yeast accounted for part of the difference between the two: Ale's organisms worked on the wort's surface; lager yeast foamed and then drifted to the bottom of the vat, there to spin its magic in the dark.

But there was another, greater divide between the two kinds of beer: temperature and fermentation time. Ale fermented at room temperature, it required no aging, and was ready to drink in a matter of days. That also meant that it turned sour and nasty as soon as a man turned his back on it. Wise drinkers edged toward a mug of ale, taking a delicate first sip in order to find out whether the tankard contained sweet beer or sour; a thick, yeasty pleasure or a rank broth with the taste and texture of muddy water. Those who could afford it turned up their noses at local ales in favor of bottles of imported porter or stout from more proficient British brewers.

Lager required more time and care. Brewers stored—or "lagered," from the German verb *lagern,* meaning "to rest"—the beer in capacious wooden puncheons that held hundreds of gallons, stacking these in their "caves," or underground caverns, at near-freezing temperatures for two or three months. As the lager rested, remnants of yeast and other solids drifted to the bottom of the barrel as harmless sediments. The brew mellowed and its flavors ripened. Most important, the combination of rest and cold endowed the beer with greater longevity than ale. Assuming all went well, tapping day produced a malty, amber lager with the heft and sustenance of liquid bread. Then the brewer transferred the beer from the fermenting kegs into smaller barrels, usually sized to hold thirty-one gallons. Because even lager began to decay once it left its cold berth, brewers kept the beer in underground storage until it was sold.

Nowadays, brewers ship their beer long distances on paved highways, but the 1840s were a time of few roads or rails and reliable cold storage was limited to underground caverns. A lager brewer sold nearly all of his beer within a mile or two of his brewhouse, cultivating the goodwill of nearby tavern owners, Germans for the most part who had set up shop in order to supply beer to other immigrants. But both the tavern owners' and the brewers' market was driven by their clientele: In the first ten years of German-American brewing, lager was consumed almost exclusively by German-speaking immigrants.

There was a reason that beer and taverns followed on the heels of German immigration. Brewing and beer had been part of Germanic culture for centuries. Ancient northern sagas, among them the *Kalevala* and the *Edda,* memorialized fermented beverages as gifts from the gods and as the source of poetry. For centuries, Germanic tribes prized ale as food, and as the centerpiece of the drinking fests that preceded and followed warfare. By the fourteenth century, beer—fermented barley cooked with hops as a preservative—had become central to German culture. To drink with friends was to celebrate life and its bounty. People affirmed wedding vows, settled arguments, and sealed contracts with glasses of beer, which served in those cases as a sacramental offering to the event. As a result, brewing was a craft that was deeply entrenched among the German-speaking peoples of northern Europe. But in the 1840s, it was a rare "American"—an English-speaking native—who embraced the beverage.

By 1847, THE BEST FAMILY was selling thirty barrels of beer a week to saloons in and around Milwaukee. Three horses crowded the small yard on Chestnut Street; two powered the grinding stone and a third pulled the brewery's delivery wagon. The men hoped to add a fourth animal soon, a necessity now that the family was carrying beer to the outlying villages that dotted the Milwaukee and Menomonee river valleys.

Their success was not hard to understand. Milwaukee behaved like a living creature, a boisterous infant to be precise, whose insatiable appetite fueled seam-ripping growth. The town's population numbered seven thousand when Phillip arrived in 1844: it topped ten thousand in 1846, and would race past twenty thousand in 1850. The Bests found customers for their lager among the third that was German-speaking. But the Bests' success rested on more than Phillip's salesmanship. A young man who tasted the family's brew in the late 1840s described it as "the most delicious lager," worth a trek up the hill, and already ranked among Milwaukee's finest.

In the summer of 1851, Phillip and brother Jacob opened a beerhall in downtown Milwaukee and a second, smaller, tavern above the remodeled brewery. Then, in 1852, the brothers embarked on a new, riskier expansion. Chicago had become one of the great marvels of the nation, growing at a pace that astonished even the most optimistic of boosters: Four thousand residents in 1840 mushroomed to thirty thousand just ten years later. The city's few brewers could not keep pace, especially as German immigrants arrived to grab their share of the city's bounty. Phillip and Jacob seized the opportunity and began shipping their lager to Chicago by ferry, an easy day's trip, two thousand barrels' worth in 1852 and a thousand more the next year.

Then came the summer of 1854—so agonizingly hot and humid that brewers in both St. Louis and Chicago ran out of lager. "Something must be done," complained the editor of the *Chicago Journal*. "Germans disconsolate and haggard wander from hall to hall, and as yet there is no beer."

The Best brothers, already established in Chicago's market, capitalized on the moment, expanding production to keep pace with this venture into long-distance shipping. They continued to send beer to Chicago by ferry, and then, after 1855, by the rail line that linked the two cities. Lager bound for St. Louis traveled to Chicago first, and then by canal to the Illinois River, and from there to the city blossoming on the Mississippi River. By the late 1850s, a railroad shortened the journey and reduced its cost.

Nothing says more about Phillip's ambition and business acumen than this decision to venture into distant markets. Both Chicago and St. Louis contained a solid German presence, which meant that Best beer competed with lagers from other immigrant brewers. But he brewed an exceptional beer, and it was on this that he based his gamble. The maneuver catapulted Best Brewing out of the ordinary and set it on its course toward greatness. "I could never have imagined," marveled Phillip, "that [the business] could develop as far in ten years as it is now." But he was quick to credit the real source of his success. "In Germany," he wrote to his wife's family, "no one knows how to appreciate the liberty to which every human being is entitled by birth, only here in America can he experience it." His bustling brewery, Milwaukee's relentless growth, and the heated competition among the town's brewers exemplified the nature of the United States, a place where liberty nurtured ambition, and ambition fostered success.

TRUE, PARADISE SUFFERED from a few flaws here and there. "[N]obody has any idea of '*plaisir*'," lamented one discouraged émigré, "but just business, business, business, day out and day in; so that one's life is not very amusing." Americans talked of nothing but business and money. They lived to turn every inch of land and every minute of each day to profit. As for leisure, they "played" at quilting bees and barn-raisings—work disguised as pleasure. The nation's cities sprouted factories and shops, mills and warehouses—but no parks or pleasure gardens. In most towns, cemeteries provided residents with their only green spaces. Land devoted to pleasure? What was the point?

One need only watch the nation at table to discover the people's priorities: Americans hunched over their plates and gobbled their food. No time to waste on idle chitchat. No time to savor flavors and textures; just gorge and run. Sometimes they did not even bother to sit, choosing instead to stand and feed "like an animal," as one shocked German traveler put it, racing through meals as if they were endurance tests or some form of gastronomic torture (and, given the quality of most American food—heavily salted meats, undercooked pastries, breads fried in pools of fat—perhaps theirs was a wise strategy).

Americans drank furtively, greedily, and with no thought of pleasure. A typical American tavern, complained another German, contained "neither bench nor chair, just drink your schnaps and then go." Who wanted to linger? Dingy and devoid of sunlight, floors decorated with spit and cigar butts, the air laced with ribbons of thick smoke and the nose-wrinkling perfume of stale whiskey, the tavern was not a place to relax, and definitely no place to take women and children. Even when Americans sat to drink, they were less interested in enjoying the company or the moment than in testing one another's generosity and capacity for booze. Germans recoiled from the national practice of "treating" or "buying rounds." Once a fellow bought you a drink, common courtesy and good sense dictated that you stick around until it was your turn to buy, but you could be topsy by the time your round came—especially if the group was tossing back shots of hard liquor.

German émigrés concluded that they would have to create their own pleasure. The artistically inclined organized orchestras, singing societies, opera clubs, and theater groups. Others introduced the old country tradition of sharpshooting, and Phillip Best supported one group by setting up a shooting gallery out back of the brewery. Club members took turns displaying their marksmanship and sipping Best's fine lager. Young men organized *Turnvereine*, clubs aimed at promoting both physical fitness and intellectual well-being, where they practiced the accoutrements of German manhood: gymnastics, shooting, debate, and singing.

The Turners wore their military-inspired uniforms to outings at the city's new German beerhalls, many of which had been opened and were operated by brewers like the Bests. Jacob and Phillip served cheese and German wine, and of course their lager, which, they informed readers of the town's several German newspapers, "bubbles as fresh and clear as ever—for our benefit and the good and refreshment of thirsty mankind." The Bests' advertising also included a snappy jingle (probably written by Jacob, who was a bit of a wit): "When the glasses loudly ring,/All the waiters quickly spring,/Serving promptly all the guests/With the 'bestest' of the Bests." But theirs was a German-inspired house of amusement, and felt more like the old country than the new one. Light poured through large windows. In the evening, young couples and families congregated for music, dancing, food, and the house lager. Men met there each morning for gatherings devoted to chess or cards, literature and politics.

In warm weather, the city's Germans migrated to "pleasure gardens." In the evenings, and on Sunday, the week's one day of rest, crowds thronged the grassy lawns at Bielfeld's and Kemper's; Leudemann Park, perched on the bluff overlooking the lake; and the Ludwigsthal nestled on a small rise just north of Cherry Street. Proprietors wooed customers with flower beds, twinkling lanterns, and gravel paths that wound through leafy arcades. Visitors wandered the manicured grounds or claimed tables and chairs near the music. Waiters trooped through the crowds bearing trays laden with sausage and cheese, ice cream, lemonade, and wine, and, of course, mugs dripping with lager. The young flirted, the old danced, and the pungent aroma of lager nosed its way from table to table. Young and old alike waltzed and polkaed the evening away. Musicians strolled through the crowd, and patrons burst into song or rose to their feet in impromptu dance, their hearts filled with the exquisite pleasure of being a German in free America.

The beer gardens and halls allowed Phillip Best and other German immigrants to infuse their new homeland with old-world pleasure, but in so doing, the brewers and their fellow émigrés collided head-on with an incontrovertible fact of life in the United States: A multitude of Americans scorned those who made and drank alcohol, and stood ready to prevent both.

————

THAT HAD NOT ALWAYS been the case. The men and women who first settled the colonies shared the view of Increase Mather, who described alcohol as "a good creature of God" and treated drink as a necessary component of daily life—in moderation and so long as its use did not interfere with God's other creatures: worship, work, and the pursuit of wealth.

But the colonists who carried beer from England to North America in the early seventeenth century promptly abandoned it, early evidence of the new world's uncanny ability to inspire new modes of behavior. Settlers devoted every waking minute to the demands of survival: They girdled and burned trees, scratched furrows in the thin, rocky soil, and cultivated meager crops of wheat and corn. Given the amount of labor needed to produce a season's worth of food, only a fool wasted time fiddling with luxuries like barley or hops. Southern settlers could grow just about anything, but their steamy climate worked a weird magic that turned ale to swill. Far easier, colonists decided, to plant apple and pear trees, which demanded minimal attention and produced plenty of fruit for cider and brandy.

Rum took care of the rest. In the late seventeenth century, West Indian and Caribbean plantation owners flooded the North American colonies with molasses and rum, the waste byproducts of their sugar cane mills. Mainland colonists developed a passion (more like an addiction, critics sniffed) for rum's intoxicating allure. They drank it straight or mixed it with water, fruit juice, or milk to create slings, sloes, punches, and toddies. They drank it hot; they drank it cold; they drank it morning, noon, and night.

The age of rum ended when the colonies rebelled against England and the price of molasses soared. No matter. Rum represented royalty and repression. In the wake of independence, the citizenry streamed west, up into and beyond the Alleghenies and Appalachians, buying cheap land whose rich soil yielded more grain than a farm family could consume or ship overland to the urban coast. Farmers cobbled together crude stills, converted their grain surpluses into hard liquor, and doused the nation with cheap, potent whiskey.

Like rum, whiskey warmed body and soul; eased digestion of the piles of greasy food that dominated mealtimes; and tempered the frantic pace of life in young America. Every occasion, from breakfast to dinner, birthings to funerals, weddings to barn-raisings, unfolded to the accompaniment of copious amounts of whiskey. Americans' appetite for spirits stupefied and astounded foreigners. "I am sure," wrote an English visitor, "the American can fix nothing without a drink. If you meet you drink; if you part you drink; if you make an acquaintance you drink. They quarrel in their drink, and they make it up with a drink." And woe be to those who resisted. A Methodist minister riding the Ohio River valley circuit found that it was he who had to pay the price of con- version. One of his would-be followers stated the terms of the bargain with the powerful simplicity of a biblical verse: "[I]f I did not drink with him," the cleric reported, "I was no friend of his, or his family, and he would never hear me preach again."

By the early nineteenth century, fourteen thousand distillers were producing some twenty-five million gallons of whiskey each year, or, in more digestible terms, some seven or eight gallons per adult per capita. Compared to the seduction of a tot of whiskey, beer had all the allure of an aging maiden aunt. A mere two hun- dred or so breweries produced English-style ale.

But starting in the 1820s, the passion for drink collided with a moment of national doubt and self-reflection. The rambunc- tious half century that followed the Revolution had produced independence—meaning a free market and plenty of it; self- governance, and damned little of that—that proved as intoxicat- ing as cheap whiskey. But the burgeoning economy also prompted an orgy of speculation and consumption. Bidding wars for west- ern land created fortunes overnight. A new breed of chap, the "confidence man"—con man for short—spun outrageous schemes from thin air, each one designed to part fools and their money. A host of "capitalists," as men with money termed themselves, harvested a cornucopia of objects and ideas, each one a seed sown in hopes of reaping a crop of cash. Those who weren't selling were buying. Americans reveled in *things*, glorious *things*, the less useful the better.

Eventually, the niggling ghosts of the Puritan forefathers interrupted the lunatic frenzy of free-market self-indulgence. In the 1820s, as if awakening from a bad hangover, millions of Americans turned their gaze on themselves and each other, and cringed at the sight. Was getting rich truly the mission for which the founding fathers had sacrificed? Was money the be-all and end-all of this great experiment in human liberty? Had Mammon become the god to which Americans prayed?

Self-doubt and self-examination inspired action. In the 1820s and 1830s, hordes of well-meaning crusaders launched a multi-armed effort to reform and perfect the American character, to woo it away from self-indulgence and toward rectitude, and thereby ensure the nation's future. Campaigners railed against every conceivable national ill, from dueling and spitting to bad architecture and masturbation. Others campaigned for exercise and well-chewed food, cold baths and better ventilation. While the crackpots and fanatics jostled for attention, the high-minded crusaded for abolition, female suffrage, and free education.

But the jewel in reform's thorny crown was temperance. Nothing before or since has matched the passion with which ordinary folk waged war on wicked whiskey, which they regarded as the devil's spawn and the root of the nation's ills. The temperance crusade began in earnest in the 1820s as an army of anti-liquor zealots preached, prayed, and sang the evils of whiskey and rum, all in the name of converting their countrymen away from excess and toward moderation, sobriety, and good citizenship.

"Intemperance," thundered Lyman Beecher, the Billy Graham of his day, "is a national sin carrying destruction from the centre [sic] to every extremity of the empire . . ." An enormous cross-section of Americans agreed, and campaigned against drinking and drunkenness, which they regarded as a "gangerous [sic] excrescence, poisoning and eating away the life of the community." Their logic was simple: Alcohol and its partner intoxication hindered the progress of "Capital,—Enterprise,—Industry,—Morals,— and Religion." Alcohol wasted mind and body, destroyed ambition, and laid asunder marriages and families. It spawned murder, prostitution, and gambling; deprived the poor man's family of food; and led young men into degeneracy. Allowed to flow unchecked, the liquid terrors threatened the future of the republic itself. Eliminate drink and most of the nation's ills would vanish as well.

The crusade against alcohol has erupted with predictable regularity since that time, although each subsequent generation has stamped the effort with its own rationale. The early-nineteenth-century campaigners took seriously then, as we perhaps do not now, the mission to make tangible the founding fathers' dream of life, liberty, and the pursuit of happiness. They took as a personal charge the need to prove to skeptics that ordinary people possessed the wisdom necessary to make democracy live. The momentary pleasures of intoxication interfered with the demands of this great moment in human history. Between 1820 and 1850, millions of Americans pledged to abstain from drink, and among people age fifteen or older, alcohol consumption fell from seven gallons per capita in 1830 to three gallons in 1840. By the time Phillip Best arrived in the United States, Americans downed less than two gallons per year.

More important, that first generation of anti-drink crusaders infused the manufacture, sale, and consumption of alcohol with a stain of disrepute that has never gone away. God's good creature had become the devil's handmaid, and respectable folk were, by definition, ones who abstained. The flip side of that equation was obvious: Those who trafficked in alcohol, whether by making, selling, or drinking it, were people of dubious repute. In the 1840s, taverns were dark and dreary because most Americans regarded them as houses of shame.

No surprise, the casual embrace of alcohol by German and Irish immigrants clashed with the American disdain for drink and drink-makers. A temperance leader in Cincinnati denounced the Irish and German "liquor power" as "unquestionably the mightiest power in the Republic," one that must be destroyed. Neal Dow, the mayor of Portland, Maine, argued that the only people who drank to the point of danger were "working people" like the Irish. Remove alcohol, he argued, and the poor would have more money to spend on their basic needs; "they [would] earn more, enjoy more, and save more than they ever did before" and so become good citizens.

Dow's words inspired his state's legislators to pass the nation's first prohibition act. The Maine law, as it was called, banned the sale, manufacture, and consumption of alcohol. Maine's legislation electrified the temperance movement and a prohibition crusade fifty years before the better-known eruption. Between 1850 and 1855, legislators in two territories and eleven of the thirty-one states followed Maine's lead.

But where prohibition prevailed, violence erupted as mobs challenged the alcohol bans, or exacted revenge on the "pestilent . . . foreign swarms" whom they blamed for inspiring the laws. Such was the case in Chicago after voters filled city hall with pro-temperance, anti-immigrant officials and the new mayor ordered a ban on Sunday drinking. The mostly native-born police force closed the city's foreign-owned beer gardens, beerhalls, and taverns but turned a blind eye to "American" taverns that stayed open in violation of the law. As the accused, most of them German, went on trial, six hundred men and boys, also mostly German, stormed the courthouse and battled police in the streets. The Lager Beer Riot ended when both sides fired shots; one man died, many were injured, and scores were arrested.

A few weeks later, it was Cincinnati's turn. Violence erupted on an election day in April, as a mob attacked German voting stations and destroyed more than a thousand ballots. Germans barricaded the bridge leading to the city's "Over the Rhine" Germantown, but their opponents, armed with a cannon and muskets, stormed the defenses. The conflict dragged on for three days, leaving many dead and wounded on both sides.

During the "Bloody Monday" riots in Louisville in August 1855, Germans, Irish, and nativists armed with muskets, bayonets, and cannons roamed the streets firing on each other and passers-by. Nineteen men died in that rampage. Violence erupted even in Portland, Maine, where Neal Dow bragged that prohibition had eradicated crime: Rumors spread that Dow had purchased liquor and sold it to the state for medicinal purposes. A mob gathered outside the Portland liquor agency and Dow ordered a local militia group to the scene. When rioters broke into the building, Dow commanded the troops to fire. Their bullets killed one person and injured seven others.

The temperance campaign rent the fabric of Milwaukee. When the state legislature passed a bill that imposed new restrictions on alcohol sales, an angry crowd filled the streets in the town's business district. Crowds of men and boys lit bonfires and fired rifles, blew horns and pounded on pans. Eventually a mob of about three hundred surrounded the house of John Smith, Milwaukee's state representative and president of a local temperance society, and pelted it with rocks and bricks, smashing windows and terrifying the four children and two servants inside.

From Phillip Best's perspective, this was bad news indeed. He had built both a thriving business and a reputation as a man of honor and an honest entrepreneur trusted by Germans and

Americans alike. A mob scene like the one at Smith's house damaged the reputation of all Germans, but it hurt the brewers most of all. The city's moralists would be quick to charge the crowd with drunkenness, and if the crowd was mostly German, they would have been drunk on only one thing.

So it went around the country, as prohibition laws inadvertently and unexpectedly sparked the crime and chaos they had been designed to eliminate. This turn of events troubled many Americans, and by the mid-1850s, some who had once supported prohibition began to reject this extreme solution to the nation's drinking problem. But even as the riots raged, the temperance crusaders found themselves under attack from another quarter.

In the 1850s, the most contentious issues facing the nation involved not drink but land and slavery. Politicians longed to open the nation's vast western territories—nearly everything west of the Missouri River—to settlement and statehood. Every American thrilled to the prospect of all that land waiting to be plowed, planted, and built, but no hearts beat faster than those of southern slave owners. To the west, they realized, lay a magnificent opportunity to expand slavery beyond the Deep South. That same prospect terrified white northerners. Once slavery ensnared the West, would it conquer the North, too? Would slaves invade northern factories and farms, their free labor eliminating the need to pay a white man's wages?

Those questions trumped the debate over drink. No one could see that more clearly than the leaders of the nation's two major parties, the Whigs and the Democrats. The Whigs hated slavery and immigrants but loved prohibition, a combination that repelled German and Irish voters. The Democrats welcomed immigrants and lager lovers alike. Unfortunately the party also supported slavery, and men like Phillip Best had not fled Europe's oppression in order to join hands with politicians who ignored the distinction between free labor and slavery. Laborers and fields hands shied away, too, fearful that Democratic victories would deposit slavery on factory floors and northern farms.

In March 1854, a group of Wisconsin men frustrated with the Whigs' anti-immigrant message and the Democrats' pro-slavery stance organized a new political party devoted first and foremost to the end of slavery. Prohibitionists tried to clamber aboard the new bandwagon. Nothing doing. The Republicans, as the new party's leaders called themselves, shoved them right back off: They planned to win elections, and to do so, they had to woo voters. They understood that prohibition, which alienated immigrants and urbanites, had become a political liability. There was no place in the new party's agenda for a divisive crusade against drink.

And if the lesson was lost on some, a Milwaukee man hastened to set the record straight. "[N]early all the Germans of this city," he announced in a letter published in a local newspaper, were prepared to cast their lot against slavery and with the new party, but they refused to bow to the dictates of "fanatic and zealous temperance men." They would even support a "teetotaller" candidate, as long as he promised to stand against slavery. But Germans would not vote for prohibition or a prohibition man. "Can you expect of a brewer that he will tear down, with his own hands, his brewery?" he demanded. Or ask a laborer, after a "hard day's work . . . paving your streets," to "throw away" his "wholesome and nourishing Lagerbeer," to "sacrifice his comfort for the sake of restricting slavery"? Go ahead, he added, punish the drunk. Close the beerhalls on election day. But if the Republicans wanted German support, they had to steer clear of the "fanaticism" of prohibition.

Lawmakers in Madison got the message. In early 1855, Wisconsin's governor vetoed a flimsy prohibition law. Jacob Best, Jr., hung a "veto pen" in pride of place at the brothers' beerhall, and

Milwaukee's young men celebrated the freedom to drink lager by marching from beerhall to beerhall, lighting bonfires and shooting fireworks.

CAUGHT BETWEEN the rock of slavery and the hard place of immigration, the temperance crusade collapsed. But this short-lived battle over drink produced an unintended, profound consequence that shaped brewing's next fifty years. On one hand, even the zealots were forced to acknowledge that prohibition created more problems than it solved. On the other hand, most Americans sincerely believed that drink posed a genuine threat to the nation's future. Where, many wondered, was the middle ground between the two?

The answer lay close at hand, and among the very people and beverage formerly accused of degrading American morals: Germans and their lager. Weary of the temperance movement and the conflict that it sparked, native-born Americans latched onto lager and the German model of sociable drinking as a compromise that allowed them to avoid the two extremes of prohibition and drunkenness.

The violence that accompanied the short-lived prohibition effort had drawn attention to the German lifestyle, to the beer gardens that welcomed families, and, of course, to lager itself. But the spotlight revealed what many Americans had been loath to admit: German-Americans lived respectably and moderately. They had prospered and assimilated into the American mainstream. They had built churches, and many owned their own businesses. Their homes were well kept and orderly. And they had accomplished this in spite of their lager.

The staff at the *St. Louis Republican* quantified the point. Between March and mid-September of 1854, they calculated, St. Louisians had consumed some eighteen million glasses of lager. "And yet," they mused, Germans "contributed the smallest ratio to the sick list [and] the smallest number of convicts or criminals." More to the point, the Germans "prosper[ed] in health, worldly goods and happiness." The point was clear: Temperance crusaders insisted that alcohol led to degradation and crime, vice and decay, but Germans stood as living proof that it was possible to combine alcohol and respectability, pleasure and decency. A Buffalo newspaper editor chimed in with a possible explanation for the conundrum: American drinkers drank to get drunk and swilled "liver-eating gin, and stomach-destroying rum." But Germans sipped lager as an accompaniment to other pleasures, such as singing and dancing and card-playing, and enjoyed lager's yeasty heft as more of "a kindly sedative than a stimulus."

Juries in several cities confirmed the growing belief that lager beer posed no threat to the nation's future. In February 1858, one George Staats, a Brooklyn brewer and proprietor of a lager garden, went on trial on charges of violating the city's Sunday drink law. Staats's lawyer offered an ingenious defense: His client was innocent because lager beer was not intoxicating.

Men of science took the stand to explain that, at 3 percent alcohol content, lager could intoxicate only if consumed in extraordinary quantities. Or, as a reporter for the *New York Times* explained, "if it takes a pail-full of bier to make a person drunk, and the same person could get drunk on an eighth the quantity of rum, then lager is not an intoxicating drink, but may be a wholesome beverage." Men of more practical experience agreed. Witness after witness testified to drinking excruciating quantities of lager—twenty to ninety pints a day—with no ill effects. The jury retired, debated the case for three hours (presumably without the benefit of lager to clear their minds), and returned to declare both Staats and lager not guilty.

Three months later, an identical case unfolded before a judge in Manhattan. Physicians took the stand to defend George Maurer against a charge of selling intoxicants on Sunday. One analyzed lager at three different New York breweries and concluded that, when consumed in moderate quantities, lager could not and did not intoxicate. Another reported that he had watched men imbibe as many as sixty glasses of lager without any evidence of intoxication. A third informed the jury that "he was in the habit of ordering [lager] for females after their confinements, and with good results."

Professionals of another kind followed them to the stand, among them a portly German who volunteered the information that he regularly drank more than one hundred glasses of lager a day and never got drunk. In fact, he added, in case the jurors doubted his word, he had consumed twenty-two glasses that very morning before reporting to the courtroom. And so it went during four days of testimony. The jury retired, contemplated the facts for over seven hours, and reported they could not agree on a verdict. The judge, perhaps longing for a glass of lager, sent them and Mr. Maurer home.

The editors of *Harper's Weekly* provided further evidence for lager's benefits: "Good lager beer is pronounced by the [scientific] faculty to be a mild tonic, calculated, on the average, to be rather beneficial than injurious to the system." The editor of the La Crosse, Wisconsin *Union* concurred: "There is no denying the fact," he wrote, that under the regime of "total abstinence American women are sadly degenerating," adding that one "good, rollicking fast-liver could clean out a regiment" of temperance types "in ten minutes." Queen Victoria drank beer on a regular basis, he pointed out, as did German women, and they were "as robust as any women in the world."

Even the editors of the *New York Times,* who groused that lager had become "a good deal too fashionable for . . . the morals of young citizens," conceded that it was better than the alternative. When that state's legislature passed a bill banning the sale of wine and spirits, Americans flocked to lager beer gardens. A reporter's investigation revealed the truth: Many New Yorkers formerly "in the habit of drinking one or more glasses of rum, gin or brandy, every day" now consumed lager instead, evidence, he claimed, of people's willingness to forgo "the stronger [alcoholic] beverages" in favor of the "very weakest."

So it went around the country, as non-German Americans rendered their own verdict: Lager was both good and safe. By the late 1850s, "lager bier" saloons lined the streets of cities large and small, and a profusion of new summer gardens dotted leafy suburbs. There men and women danced to German bands, thrilled to the exquisite voices of German choral groups, enjoyed opera and dancers and comics, and relaxed over glasses of fresh lager. In Buffalo, families that once picnicked at Forest Lawn cemetery— the only green space in town—now thronged Westphal's Garden to enjoy lager and music. Respectable businessmen and artisans learned that they need not endure the humiliation of slipping furtively into a grimy tavern for beer; they could stroll Westphal's greenery with wife on arm and children straggling behind. Every-one—German, Irish, American—looked forward to that city's St. John's Day Festival. "A German festival is always full of life, spirit and fun," commented one local newspaper editor.

So, too, in Cincinnati, where one man marveled at the change: Lager beer, he informed readers of his guide to that city, "forms refreshment to one-half of our native population . . . [and] is driving out the consumption of whiskey . . ." A Richmond, Virginia, man agreed. "Lager has gone ahead of all other beverages," he claimed, and Germans were that city's "gayest citizens," ones who knew how to "enjoy their hours of relaxation." Thanks to the émigrés, American life had entered a "new and pleasant phase."

An Englishman who spent the 1850s in the United States also testified to the change in tastes. "A dozen years ago," he wrote in 1862, at the conclusion of his stay, "brandy and whiskey were the popular drinks; now they have, in a great measure, given place to this lager-bier, with its three per cent. of alcohol . . . [N]obody liked it at first," but now "everybody . . . everywhere" drank it in "immense quantities." Americans had embraced the pleasures of café life, and he advised the temperance crowd to come up with other "wholesome, palatable, and invigorating drinks, which people could drink and talk over . . . The use of lager-bier proves the practicability of this course."

LAGER'S NEW POPULARITY among Americans of all backgrounds and ethnicities spurred the growth of breweries nationwide, nearly all of them owned by Germans who hoped that lager mania would pave their way to wealth. Ten new breweries opened in Milwaukee alone during the 1850s.

Among the newcomers was Valentin Blatz. He had trained as a brewer in his native Bavaria before emigrating to Milwaukee in the 1840s, where he began his American life working for another beermaker, John (or Johann) Braun. But Blatz wanted more, and in 1851 he pitched the first yeast in his own brewing vat. He revealed the expanse of his ambition a few months later when Braun died in an accident: Blatz married the man's widow and took control of his brewery. Like the Bests, he had devoted the 1850s to expansion, building a larger brewhouse and more extensive malthouse. Unlike the Bests, Blatz paid for the projects by pilfering the estates of the children of his now-deceased former employer. Blatz arranged for a lawyer friend to be appointed as legal guardian to the children and their inheritance; the friend opened the door to the money and Blatz helped himself.

August Krug, too, longed for a larger operation. In 1849 he had added a brewery to the restaurant and saloon he owned on Chestnut Street, and an opportunity for growth presented itself a year later, when his father arrived from Germany bearing eight hundred dollars in gold coin and Krug's eight-year-old nephew, August Uihlein (pronounced E-line). Krug placed the boy in school and invested the coin in the brewery. He purchased more land and excavated a 150-barrel lagering vault, a clear signal that he planned to run on the same turf as Phillip Best. Krug could manage the brewery and restaurant, but he needed help keeping an eye on the numbers. In 1855, he hired a bookkeeper named Joseph Schlitz.

But in December of that year, Krug tumbled down a hatchway and landed hard on the floor below; a few days later he died, leaving his estate to his wife. Schlitz wasted no time in offering the widow his life savings in exchange for a partnership. In 1858 he sealed the deal by marrying her, hiring August Uihlein as the new bookkeeper, and changing the company name to Joseph Schlitz Brewing Company.

Phillip Best's brother Carl suffered a different kind of loss. He had not joined the family brewery, preferring to stick with the vinegar factory he had founded. But in 1849 he sold that, and he and a business partner purchased land for a new brewery three miles west of Milwaukee in the relatively unpopulated Menomonee Valley. They christened their venture the Plank Road Brewery, named for the wooden roadway that ran past their door (today's State Street). The partners hoped to sell part of their output to the farmers who hauled grain into town one way on Plank Road and supplies back the other. When the partner ran the brewery into debt and then absconded, Carl and younger brother Lorenz carried on until young Lorenz died; Carl, either bereft or inept, let the brewery slide into bankruptcy.

Thirty-year-old Frederick Miller, who had emigrated to the United States a few months earlier, leased the property in 1855, then purchased it outright a year later and set about to make his family's American fortune. He had begun training as a brewer fifteen years earlier, and by the time he arrived in the United States had achieved the status of brewmaster and managed his own brewhouse. Another century would pass before the small outfit he helmed joined the ranks of the world's great breweries, but in the late 1850s, his talents earned a good living for his family. He lured Milwaukeeans to his relatively distant location with a garden filled with tables, shade trees, and a multicolored, aromatic array of formal flower beds that cascaded down the sides of the bluff behind the brewery. Customers enjoyed homemade breads and cakes and specially prepared hams. Women sipped a house specialty, mocha coffee, while men clutching beer steins thronged the bowling alley. Children romped to the strains of orchestras and choruses that performed under the roof of the open-air pavilion. Miller would succeed where Carl Best failed, and today all that remains to memorialize Carl's efforts is a section of his lager cave, now the last stop on the visitors' tour at Miller Brewing Company.

PHILLIP AND JACOB JUNIOR enjoyed the competition, which only spurred their own ambitions. By the late 1850s, the modest brewhouse on the hill, symbol of their émigré hopes and the limits of their original capital, had outlived its usefulness. In 1857, the pair plowed their profits—some $20,000 a year (over $400,000 in today's dollars)—into a new plant: an imposing two-story brick complex adorned with turrets and Gothic windows, with a life-sized statue of lager-swilling Gambrinus, the mythical inventor of lager, perched on top. The new brewery could be seen from almost everywhere in the city, testimony to Phillip and Jacob's ambitions and to the importance of lager to Milwaukee's economy. But its crowning glory lay hidden from sight: The "vaults," or lager cellars, consisted of several blocks of flagstone corridors surmounted by arched brick ceilings and lined with hundreds of rows of puncheons sized to hold thirty barrels, or about one thousand gallons, of lager.

The decision to expand forced them to live with stomach-wrenching risk. In order to earn a return on their investment, they had to operate at full capacity. Milwaukee's growth continued apace, but the contest for customers grew more heated each year. Chicago's growth was, if anything, even more astonishing, and the brothers could count on selling several thousand barrels there each year to taverns around that bustling city. But even that outlet bristled with uncertainty: They had to buy or rent real estate in Chicago, both for their office and for warehousing the beer. And they had to hire a reliable agent to manage their Chicago affairs—lining up customers, ordering ice, and hiring teams and drivers to deliver the beer. All of it—the new plant, the larger vats, the Chicago branch, the soaring payroll—forced the men to the edge of their means.

What is most remarkable about this moment in the history of what would become the world's largest brewery is that Phillip and Jacob played their hand just as the nation's economy skittered into a two-year recession. The so-called Panic of 1857 spawned a string of bankruptcies and foreclosures that reached from the urban coast to the rural frontier. The impact crashed across the Midwest, where investors in Wisconsin, Illinois, and Iowa had dumped millions into railroad projects, using loans from chronically wobbly banks that crumpled under the impact of first recession, then depression. In Milwaukee, beer sales plunged: The 100,000 barrels produced by the city's brewers in 1857 fell to 42,000 in 1859.

That may explain why, just a year after building the new brewhouse, the brothers parted ways, Phillip claiming the brewery and Jacob the real estate—a couple of lots and a large brick building—that they owned in downtown Milwaukee. Years later, an aging Milwaukee saloonkeeper claimed that the brothers rolled dice to determine the division of property. According to this account, Phillip won the toss and opted to keep the brewery, betting, apparently, that good times would return and so would the demand for his beer.

It's hard to imagine so shrewd a businessman as Phillip Best risking so much on chance. On the other hand, he never lost touch

with the hard-driving roustabout within. On more than one occasion, he galloped his horse down East Water Street and charged
through the doorway of the Menomonee Saloon, one of the city's
most popular watering holes. As the men draped across the bar or
slouched in chairs watched, whooped, and hollered, the equally
amused barkeeper shooed Best out the door. Phillip tied his horse
at the rail outside and then strolled back inside, shouting an order
to "'set 'em up' for the house."

As with the dice-rolling partnership split, there's no way to
know if the horse tale is apocryphal. But both have a ring of truth:
If we know anything about Phillip Best and the handful of brewers who laid the foundations of fortunes in those early days of the
brewing industry, it is that they embraced risk. After all, Phillip
had turned thirty the year he left Europe for the United States.
By the late 1850s, he'd long since passed the first flower of youth
and understood that this gamble might not pay off, especially
given the number of players who crowded the table. Like him,
ambitious brewers in New York, Chicago, St. Louis, and other
cities were busy adding steam engines and larger vats to their
brewhouses. Also like him, they relished the competition from
the hundreds of new breweries that had opened to accommodate
Americans' new passion for lager.

Phillip's choice, like his earlier decision to risk his adulthood
on America, paid off. By the time he gained sole ownership of the
brewery, he could measure his American success by more than his
company's profits. A Democratic governor honored his contributions to Wisconsin politics by granting him a commission in the
Milwaukee Dragoons militia company, and a grateful Republican
governor elevated him to the rank of brigadier general in a division of the state militia.

In 1857, Phillip reigned as Prince during Milwaukee's first
Lenten-season Carnival. He presided over a lavish reception on
opening night and sat enthroned on the lead wagon of a parade

that sashayed through the city's streets the next day. Behind him marched horn-tooting musicians and beribboned stallions carrying local dignitaries. A river of wagons flowed behind, loaded with men and women attired in ornate costume and mask: A majestic King Gambrinus waved to the delighted onlookers; Bacchus greeted his subjects; two "apostles of Temperance" perched on another wagon, and the crowd roared when one fell off and into the muddy street.

By any measure, German or American, Phillip had succeeded. Among the city's two dozen or so brewers, only Val Blatz produced more lager, and Best Brewing lagged by fewer than two hundred barrels. As the decade turned, the landscape that Phillip surveyed from his hilltop empire contrasted dramatically with the one he had first seen back in 1844. Then, he looked down on a sea of leafy green on one side and a small town on the other. Now Milwaukee, population forty-five thousand, sprawled in all directions. Rippling layers of forest had given way to houses and roads. Phillip owned not just two small lots, but several city blocks. And beneath his feet lay thousands of barrels of German lager, the stuff of his American dreams.

CHAPTER TWO

"I Must Have Nothing But the Very Best"

L IKE MILWAUKEE, St. Louis began life as a frontier settlement, and, also like Milwaukee, it thrived in the heady
go-go atmosphere that permeated mid-nineteenth century
America. Its growth, too, boggled the imagination: 20,000 people
in 1840; nearly 160,000 in 1857.

St. Louis shared another property with its Wisconsin cousin:
Germans, thousands of them, arrived during the 1840s and
1850s. The city was "inundated with breweries, beer houses,
sausage shops, Apollo gardens, Sunday concerts, Swiss cheese,
and Holland herrings." And, too, as in Milwaukee, lager flowed
free. Nor, by the late 1850s, did most regret that fact. Nowhere,
claimed one observer, had "the German influence been more . . .
beneficially felt, than in the introduction of beer," a beverage "well
nigh universally adopted by the English speaking population; and
the spacious bier halles and extensive gardens nightly show that
the Americans are as fond of the Gambrinian liquid as are those
who have introduced it."

This was the city where eighteen-year-old Adolphus Busch
decided to make his fortune. The beer baron later claimed that he
loafed his way through the first few weeks after his arrival in St.

Louis in 1857. In truth, Busch likely never idled a day in his life. Educated, multilingual, charming, and intelligent, he was an attractive asset to any employer, and he immediately found sales work at a commission house. But the young man had not come so far to work for another. In 1859, a scant two years after arriving in the United States, he and a partner opened their own brewing supply company, a shrewd move in a German-rich city whose forty breweries produced 200,000 barrels of beer each year and consumed a half million dollars' worth of barley, hops, and other materials.

Busch's foray into sales and supplies provided him with an opportunity to learn the business of brewing. Presumably he called on the men who operated the city's smallest outfits—shops like Fortuna and Hickory, Pacific and Laclede, where the owners counted production in hundreds rather than thousands of barrels. But he focused his charm and salesmanship on the city's success stories. On Second Street was St. Louis's oldest lager brewhouse, Western Brewery, owned by Adam Lemp and his son William. Lemp had opened his doors in the early 1840s with a tiny twelve-barrel vat. During the next decade he purchased an otherwise undistinguished parcel of land whose main virtue was an extensive natural cave that eased the storage burden at his cramped facility. By the 1850s, the Lemps were making about five thousand barrels a year.

But Lemp's operation was dwarfed by that of Julius Winkelmeyer, whose Union Brewery ranked as one of the nation's largest. Winkelmeyer's twenty employees brewed about fifteen thousand barrels of beer each year. His brick buildings filled much of Market Street between Seventeenth and Eighteenth Streets. Beneath lay an extensive series of lagering caves. A mile or so south on Eighteenth stood the Phoenix Brewery, the city's second-largest operation, where twenty-five employees crafted thirteen thousand barrels of lager a year.

A short stroll across Market Street from Winkelmeyer's took Busch to Joseph Uhrig's Camp Spring Brewery. Uhrig's fifteen hands and forty-horsepower steam engine made only about twelve thousand barrels, but the operation included a popular beerhall and a dance room. Uhrig's profits had already purchased nine acres and a palatial summer home in Milwaukee, as well as regular visits to Germany.

Busch also met Eberhard Anheuser, owner of the much-troubled Bavarian Brewery on the city's far south side. Anheuser acquired the Bavarian in 1859 as payment for debts owed him by its previous owners. It is not clear why he decided to hang on to the place. It's not as if, at age fifty-four, he needed the headache of a failed brewery, not when the soap factory that he had co-owned for nearly two decades had made him rich. Perhaps soap had lost its charms and he longed for a new challenge. Perhaps he yearned for the security of diversity. Or perhaps he was simply swept up in the spirit of the times, when new factories sprouted as if by magic and fortunes hung ripe for the picking. Whatever the reason, Anheuser took charge of the Bavarian. Presumably he possessed what the previous owners lacked: enough cash to keep the place going.

In 1860, he and a partner sold some three thousand barrels of beer. Whether, in the normal course of events, Anheuser would have survived the still shaky economy and the dominance of Winkelmeyer and Uhrig, is an unanswerable question. And a moot one, because in November of that year, "normal" fell by the wayside. Americans elected Abraham Lincoln president. A few weeks later, a convention of South Carolinians voted to secede from the Union.

Tension rattled St. Louis, a city divided against itself in a state wracked with conflict. Missouri had entered the Union as a slave state, and many residents owned slaves and identified with the Confederate cause. The core of Union support centered on the Germans living in and around St. Louis; they abhorred slavery as a threat to individual rights. President Lincoln understood that if Missouri fell to the Confederacy, he and his army would lose control of the Mississippi River, the main highway running deep into Confederate territory. He and his generals had to hold Missouri, and that meant keeping a grip on St. Louis with its wharves, warehouses, and vital rail links to the eastern United States.

Over the next few months, Union officials struggled to maintain order in a city riven by loathing and hatred. "I see nothing but ruin and starvation," lamented one Confederate sympathizer, "and when it will end God only knows, our City is encompass'd with armed *Goths* and *Vandels* [*sic*], for they are Dutch [*Deutsch,* or Germans] or Poles that cannot speak our language and they are searching every carriage as it passes, and every house in the environs of the City for arms and ammunition . . ." Eberhard Anheuser surely sighed with relief when federal troops seized control of the arsenal, a hulking structure filled with gunpowder and weapons that sat just two blocks from his brewery.

Amidst the turmoil, Adolphus Busch played the kind of hand that Joseph Schlitz and Valentin Blatz would have recognized: In March, he married Anheuser's daughter Lilly (Adolphus's older brother Ulrich, who also lived in St. Louis, married another Anheuser daughter on the same day). With that union, Busch committed himself to his adopted home.

He made a good choice at a good time. The war proved a godsend to the city's beermakers: St. Louis swarmed with troops headed into or out of enemy territory, and with an endless stream of prisoners, wounded soldiers, refugees, escaped and freed slaves, and other bits of human flotsam and jetsam. Military clerks trudged from warehouse to wharf, from butcher shop to bakery, in search of supplies. Bricklayers, stonemasons, blacksmiths, and carpenters arrived. Soldiers guarded wharves, warehouses, and the arsenal, as well as the ring of fortifications that dotted the city's western fringes. Everyone needed beer. "I never saw a city where there is as much drinking of liquor as here," marveled a physician stationed with the Union army. *"Everybody*—almost— drinks. Beer shops and gardens are numerous." No fan of drink, drinkers, or Catholics, the good doctor blamed the city's sorry state on the Germans, who, he reported, clung "to their meer- schaums & beer, and their miserable faith . . ."

His disdain was lost on the multitudes. This was a war fought with beer. Military commanders banned intoxicants from camp and field, leaving lager—officially nonintoxicating—as the troops' choice of drink. Military supply clerks contracted with hundreds of brewers to supply men with lager, which traveled better and lasted longer than ale. Hundreds of thousands of sol- diers forged friendships and built camaraderie over tin cups of lager, an experience they carried home when the war ended.

Lager even received a stamp of approval from the United States Sanitary Commission, a civilian organization that moni- tored the troops' health. A USSC physician who studied camp diets reported that lager drinkers suffered less from diarrhea than did non–beer drinkers. Lager, he noted, "regulates the bowels, prevents constipation, and becomes in this way a valuable substi- tute for vegetables" (a food in short supply). "I encourage all the men," added the doctor, to drink lager.

Good news for the nation's brewers, another thousand of whom set up shop during the war. But old or new, they all paid a price for their success. In the summer of 1862, the cash-strapped Union Congress began taxing "luxury" items: billiard tables and playing cards, yachts and carriages, and liquor and beer. The leg- islation levied a tax of one dollar per barrel and required brewers to purchase a federal manufacturer's license (one hundred dollars annually for those who produced more than five hundred barrels; half that for smaller makers). Over the next three years, the new Internal Revenue Department collected $369 million in taxes, nearly eight million of it from beer.

The German lager brewers, anxious to affirm their loyalty and patriotism (and to defeat the hated Slave Power, as it was called by Union supporters), paid. But they recognized that once imposed, the levy would never go away. Less than a month after Lincoln signed the tax law, a few dozen eastern brewers convened in New York City to ponder the new regulations. The group persuaded Congress to lower the rate to sixty cents a barrel. As the war dragged on, lawmakers hiked the tax back to a dollar; still, the brewers learned a valuable lesson: better to cooperate than to resist; to educate the nation's lawmakers than to ignore them. That meeting in New York inspired the formation of the nation's first trade and lobby organization of any kind, the United States Brewers' Association.

In April 1865, Union and Confederate generals and their troops played out the final scene of the nation's sad drama in the woods and fields near Appomattox Courthouse, Virginia. In St. Louis, the lager-hungry supply clerks vanished and the troops mustered out. Refugees began the long journey south; masons and carpenters packed their tools and headed home.

Eberhard Anheuser's brewery might not have survived the downturn. His partner had jumped ship in 1864, leaving the old man to manage the place alone. Therein lay the problem: No one would ever accuse Anheuser of being a master brewer; he knew soap, but the mysteries of beer presented an entirely different challenge. Yankee troops and laborers had been willing to drink his beer, but the discriminating Germans of St. Louis turned up their noses at his brew. And rightly so; why settle for the mediocre when any one of a dozen other brewers in the same neighborhood turned out fine lager for the same price?

Eberhard Anheuser had not succeeded in the rambunctious American economy because he was stupid. He knew that he needed help and he needed it now. And he knew just what form that help ought to take: his talented and charismatic son-in-law, who could charm the skin off a snake and sell it back to its owner. In 1865, Adolphus Busch purchased a share of the company. Nobody knew it then, but the changing of the guard had begun. One of the giants of American brewing had just stepped into place. Together, he and a handful of other titans were about to reinvent the industry.

ADOLPHUS BUSCH grew up in Mainz, Germany, on the Rhine River, where his wealthy father, Ulrich, owned thousands of acres of vineyards and forests. The second-youngest of twenty-two children, he received a fine formal education at several prestigious schools. But Busch preferred action to theory. He left school in his early teens for two apprenticeships, first working as a poleman helping move timber downriver for his father and then as a helper at an uncle's brewery.

He was a quick study and forgot nothing, a fact that he would still demonstrate late in life. One evening during a visit to Frankfurt, Germany, in 1895, Busch hosted a dinner for two St. Louis friends who were also vacationing there. Afterward the three men set out for a tour of the city. When they reached the banks of the Main, Busch noticed that a raft-jam had halted river traffic. He jumped out of the carriage and leapt onto the nearest raft. As his startled companions watched, the sixty-two-year-old brewer strode from craft to craft until he reached the one that he had identified as the source of the clog. He poled it free, broke the jam, and then returned to his guests. "I spent my early life in rafting on the Rhine and Main," he explained to them, "and I am familiar with the ways of rafts and raftsmen."

That episode summed up the man. Busch was a natural leader, thanks to what one friend described as "assertiveness and good-natured aggressiveness" and an optimistic arrogance rooted in intelligence, self-confidence, and charisma. He stood but mid-height—about five feet, five inches—but his stocky frame, ramrod posture, and elegant dress commanded attention. So did his voice, booming and articulate. When he spoke, he hypnotized his audience with sweeping gestures. "He wills and does," a reporter for a brewing trade paper once observed. "His power over men is great, yet he does not seem to know or realize it." He competed relentlessly, and assumed and believed that winners deserved their success. "I love work," he said, "[and] find much pleasure and agreeable recreation in it, especially when I see that my efforts are crowned with success."

In a lesser man, these qualities might have spawned resentment, jealousy, and enemies. But Busch tempered his dominance with kindness, an abiding passion for fair play, and generous respect for those who earned it. "I am an eternal optimist," he once said, "[and] never lean in the least to the other side, and I am always coming out right." He believed in "the ultimate good of man," and he enjoyed nothing so much as identifying the deserving and nurturing their careers. At the brewery he captained for nearly fifty years, he expected everyone, including family, to start at the bottom—as he had—and work their way up. All of his supervisory and managerial employees, he once boasted, had started as laborers because men of modest beginnings were "more ambitious and industrious" than those from privileged backgrounds. His advice for any employer was to promote employees "according to their merits," a tactic that he believed inspired and nurtured ambition.

As BUSCH settled into one St. Louis brewery, August Uihlein prepared to leave another. Uihlein, a quiet man of stocky build and cherubic face, had left Milwaukee and his uncle Schlitz's brewhouse in 1860, moving to St. Louis to work at Joseph Uhrig's Camp Spring Brewery. Uhrig was lucky to get him. Uihlein had studied bookkeeping at a Milwaukee business school, earned room and board by keeping the books at Schlitz's brewery, and supplemented his education with a year's unpaid apprenticeship at the mostly German-owned Second Ward Bank, whose directors included Phillip Best and other brewers. The young man, a "delightful companion and a lovable character" whose "word was as good as gold," impressed his supervisors with his industry and honesty. Uihlein worked his way up to general manager at Uhrig's in only two years.

But Uihlein's talents were not enough to trump ties by marriage. When the war ended, Uhrig offered a partnership to his new son-in-law, twenty-four-year-old Otto Lademan. Lademan had emigrated to the United States from Prussia in 1856, landing at New Orleans and then heading to St. Louis, where he worked as a clerk and salesman for a number of merchants. After four years fighting for the Union cause, he returned to St. Louis and married Joseph Uhrig's daughter. Uihlein stuck it out in St. Louis for another three years and then wrote to his uncle Schlitz: Was there room at the brewery for himself and brothers Henry, Alfred, and Edward, all of whom had also emigrated to the United States? There was. And so the Uihlein brothers returned to Milwaukee and Walnut Street. August became company secretary, and Henry, who possessed practical brewing experience, took charge of the brewhouse.

A quarter century later, Schlitz Brewing would be the third largest brewery in the world, and August and his brothers among the nation's wealthiest citizens, so rich that they made money faster than they could give it away. Just after the turn of the century, Henry Uihlein attempted to shrug off his wealth, with the goal of living on $75,000 a year ($1.5 million in today's dollars). He gave his stock to his children and set up a million-dollar trust fund for each. It was not enough. A few years later, his remaining holdings had so increased in value that he doled out another $2.5 million. The Uihleins earned such riches in part because, unlike the flamboyant and equally wealthy Adolphus Busch, they practiced a "deep seated . . . modesty" and disdained overt displays of wealth or success. They were also more reclusive than the gregarious Busch, preferring the company of but a few close friends and their own families, whose members numbered well into the dozens. As a result, we know less about them than about the other two major nineteenth-century beer barons—except for the salient fact of their astounding success.

But the wealth came from more than just beer: The brothers believed in property, and August and Edward, the family's chief land scouts, steered the company into hundreds of real-estate investments, especially in Chicago. August also profited from his foray into horse breeding, and at century's end he would own one of the country's largest, most respected, and most profitable stud farms. But all that lay in the future. For now, the brothers headed to Milwaukee to join their equally driven uncle Schlitz at the brewery on Walnut Street.

THE UIHLEINS arrived back in Milwaukee not long after Phillip Best launched his retirement by leaving for a long vacation in Germany. The years at the brewery had broken his health, and he lacked the energy to keep pace with his competition. But he was leaving his empire in the hands of his capable son-in-law: twenty-nine-year-old Frederick Pabst, former waiter, cabin boy, and sea captain, and as of early 1864, partner in Best and Company.

Pabst, born in 1836, grew up in Saxony in what is now eastern Germany. His father, Gottlieb Pabst, managed a sizable estate near a small village. It's not clear why he abandoned that position for the uncertainty of America, but in August of 1848, Gottlieb, wife Frederika, and twelve-year-old Frederick landed in New York. From there the family headed first to Milwaukee, where some friends lived, and then to Chicago. Pabst's mother died the following year in the great mid-century cholera epidemic, and father and son found employment at the Mansion House hotel, the father as a cook and the son as a waiter.

Young Frederick's restless ambition drove him toward the water. He found work as a cabin boy on one of the many steamers that plied the waters of Lake Michigan; by 1857 he commanded and owned shares in his own vessel. At some point in the 1850s, he moved back to Milwaukee. There he made the acquaintance of August Uihlein, who described Pabst as an "open hearted, congenial man" who was "the most popular man sailing the west shore of Lake Michigan." Another lifelong friend described the "Captain," as he was known to all, as "a hale fellow well met, genial and popular among all his associates." Albert Blatz, Valentin's son, pronounced his competitor "one of nature's noblemen. Generous, kind hearted, with a good word for every one he met."

Affable. Likable. Kind. Generous. Frederick Pabst routinely inspired such accolades. Just over six feet in height, he had heavy-lidded, lively eyes balanced by a prominent nose and full lips. Like Adolphus Busch, Pabst commanded any room he entered. But if Busch's charisma issued from his flamboyant self-assurance, Pabst's flowed from a quieter self-confidence, although he, like Busch, possessed a kind nature and generous warmth. Unlike Busch, Frederick Pabst had little if any formal education. He more than compensated for that, however, with an astonishing intellect and what one Milwaukee businessman and longtime friend described as a "remarkable genius for organization."

Where and when Frederick Pabst met Phillip Best is not known. Their German heritage would have brought them together socially, but Best may have encountered the Captain during one of the brewer's trips to Chicago. In any case, three days before his twenty-sixth birthday, in March 1862, Frederick Pabst married Best's oldest daughter, nineteen-year-old Maria.

The union benefited both men. Just three of Best's seven children had survived infancy, and his only son, Henry, was but ten years old. Presumably Phillip and Frederick discussed the possibility of Pabst leaving the water for beer. Bad luck forced the issue. On December 16, 1863, a ferocious storm pounded Lake Michigan. Pabst was on a regular run, his beloved *Sea Bird* filled with passengers and crew. Faced with the possibility that vessel and passengers might not survive the onslaught of waves and wind, Pabst beached the steamer, a maneuver that damaged it but saved everyone's life. It would cost $20,000 to repair the *Sea Bird*'s broken hull. A few weeks later, Frederick Pabst reported for work at the brewery on Chestnut Street.

Another of Phillip's sons-in-law, Emil Schandein, soon joined Pabst at the helm. Schandein had trained as an engineer before he emigrated to Philadelphia in 1856, at age sixteen. There he tended bar, a position that surely disappointed him intellectually and financially. A year or two later, he headed west to Illinois for the life of a traveling salesman. That work carried him to Watertown, Wisconsin, where he met the Best family. He married Phillip's daughter Lisette in the spring of 1866 and went to work for his father-in-law soon after. As vice-president of Best Brewing, he complemented Pabst's lack of education with his own scientific and technical expertise. But Schandein suffered from frail health—induced, perhaps, by the heavy drinking that provided an escape from an unhappy marriage (Lisette conducted a long affair with their son-in-law). He spent much of his time in restorative travel, during which he visited the company's branch offices and spied on the competition.

IN THE MID-1860s, Pabst and Schandein, Busch, and the Uihleins were just a few brewers among many, their brewhouses barely distinguishable from thousands of others. Each boasted a dozen or so employees, a steam engine, some wagons, and a few teams. Each served up about four thousand barrels of beer, or one-third of the output of what were then the country's biggest brewhouses. Forty years later, these men helmed the three largest breweries in the world, sprawling factories whose output topped or neared the million-barrel mark.

Historians today generally scorn the idea of the "great man," but these émigrés who became the giants of the American brewing industry were made of rare and precious materials; were, in their own way, great men who ranged through their days oblivious to indecision or failure, dismissive of doubt and human frailty. Where some men edged their way toward change, Frederick Pabst dived headfirst. What some condemned as recklessness, Adolphus Busch embraced as lifeblood. August Uihlein seized the chance from which other men shrank. Their personalities differed, but circumstances and a passion for competition linked their futures.

So did another fact, one so obvious that it's easy to overlook: Each fell into the industry by accident rather than design. True, Adolphus Busch worked briefly—less than a year—at an uncle's brewery, but his real training in the business, and that of the other great brewers, only began after he had sealed a partnership with a relative. Like the nation they adopted as home, these men were wedded to the future, not the past, and so entered their careers unburdened by stone-etched ideas about how a brewery ought to run and who its customers should be. Nor were they brewmasters, and so came to the brewhouse without any firm ideas about how the beer ought to look or taste. Their breweries sat before them as lumps of clay, raw potential on which each man's ambition could work its will.

In that respect these four matched the times. In the thirty-five years after Appomattox, Americans masterminded one of the greatest economic and social transformations in history, and theirs became the leading industrial nation in the world. The heady 1840s and 1850s proved a mere appetizer for the main course, a late-century feast of automated production and gargantuan factories. Ravenous manufacturing operations devoured the labor of nearly twelve million new immigrants, and the hundreds of thousands of Americans who migrated to town and factory, refugees from farms where McCormick's reapers and Deere's plows rendered their labor obsolete. The owners of the Amoskeag Manufacturing Company in Massachusetts, the world's largest textile mill, required the services of seventeen thousand people to manage and operate their clanking bobbins and looms. Cyrus McCormick's fifteen hundred hands built fifty thousand reapers a year.

Other manufacturers cranked out typewriters and copper tubing, railroad tracks and ready-made clothes. Mechanical rocking chairs and porcelain toilets. Thousands of miles of electrical wire to carry millions of telegraphic messages. Gears and bolts and nails and drills tumbled out of factories large and small. Saddles and whips and machine-made doilies. Canned soups and bottled condiments—fifty-seven varieties from the Heinz Company alone. Boxes of crunchy Uneeda Biscuits to replace barrels of anonymous general-store crackers. Enough velvet upholstery and drapery fabric to reach the moon. Machine-rolled cigarettes and two-story Corliss steam engines. The American landscape would never be the same, and Americans would wait a hundred years before they negotiated another such moment of transformation.

When the nation celebrated the hundredth anniversary of independence in 1876, the centerpiece of the Philadelphia Centennial Exhibition was Machinery Hall, a massive structure filled with fourteen acres of every kind of labor-saving and automated device then known to man. The building's "tremendous iron heart" was a 1,400-horsepower Corliss steam engine that stood forty feet tall, weighed six hundred tons, boasted a three-hundred-foot driveshaft, and drove the full mile of shafting that powered exhibits such as mechanical icemakers and refrigerators, presses, lathes, and looms. So important was the Corliss engine that President Ulysses Grant formally opened the Exhibition by cranking the handle that set into motion this "athlete of steel and iron."

But the products of the factories and the sweatshops were useless without buyers. They were there, too, thanks to investors like Jay Gould and Jay Cooke—manipulators, some called them—who transformed what had been single, scattered rail lines into vast railroad empires that linked coast with coast and carried goods over vast distances. Between 1865 and 1893, crews of Irish and Chinese laborers laid 150,000 miles of railroad tracks. Unlike the rails of an earlier age, these were steel, the core of the new economy. In 1870, Americans produced just 850,000 tons of steel, at that time a revelatory new material—an inexpensive process for making large batches was developed only in the late 1850s. By 1900, with steel-manufacture technology perfected, more than ten million tons of the magic material rolled out of enormous fiery altars tended by thousands of men sweating through the brutality of ten- and twelve-hour shifts.

The era's potential sprawled ripe and full at Americans' feet, ready for the picking by men of vision and energy. That some were corrupt or rapacious—Jay Gould and John D. Rockefeller come to mind—was never the point. What mattered was that J. P. Morgan and Charles Schwab, Thomas Edison and John Roebling, Peter Cooper and Gustavus Swift understood how to transform incandescent potential into substance and heft. Could turn a split second of inspiration—the light bulb—into a vast network of dynamo and wire and alter night's landscape. Could fashion a skein of steel into that majestic ribbon of grandeur, the Brooklyn Bridge. Could weave ambition and daring (and greed and deceit) into personal fortunes, as Jay Gould would do time and again. Could extract billions of gallons of petroleum from the Pennsylvania hills and enrich men like Rockefeller and his partner Henry Flagler beyond imagination.

BUSCH, PABST, AND the Uihleins belong in that pantheon. They dived into the age, gambling on new and untested technologies: artificial refrigeration, pressurized carbon injection, pasteurization, and automated bottling machines. They built state-of-the-art laboratories and staffed them with European scientists who explored the manufacture and manipulation of yeasts and bacteria. Henry Ford usually gets credit for pioneering the concept of assembly-line production, but his factories came nearly forty years after these brewers transformed what had been small-batch, labor-intensive workshops into sprawling factories devoted to automation, efficiency, and profit.

They also enjoyed the luck of good timing: All of them entered brewing at a heady moment for the industry. In the five years after the Civil War, another thousand brewers set up shop nationwide, testimony to returning soldiers' fondness for lager and to the steady westward movement of population. San Francisco, offspring of the great gold rush of the early 1850s, boasted a dozen or so breweries. A fistful of others lay scattered across the plains and mountains, from Montana to Texas, where men dreamed of another gold rush or herded cattle toward eastern markets.

Over all these towered New York City. The combined output of Milwaukee and St. Louis was a mere drop in the ocean of beer that poured out of Manhattan's brewvats in the nineteenth century. Brewers there benefited from relentless population growth that transformed Manhattan's rocky, wooded terrain into a tidy grid of paving and brick, each block crammed with buildings, each of those stuffed to suffocation with humanity. The city's half million people in 1850 swelled to 814,000 by 1860 and 1.2 million in 1880.

In the 1870s, one of those New Yorkers, George Ehret, reigned as the king of American brewing. Ehret, a trained brewer, emigrated in 1857, the same year as Adolphus Busch. He found work at an established brewery, but like so many of his fellow émigrés, he chafed under another man's lead. In 1866 he opened the doors at his own brewhouse, situated on what was then a rural area north of the city but is today the northern reaches of Manhattan's Upper East Side. Eight years later his Hell Gate Brewery, named after a particularly vicious stretch of the East River, surpassed the 100,000-barrel mark. Like the Uihleins, Ehret believed in diversifying his assets. When he died in 1927, he was the city's second-largest landowner (bested only by the John Jacob Astor estate), claiming title to a Fifth Avenue mansion, large holdings in the Wall Street area, a corner lot abutting Columbus Circle, and chunks of Harlem, in the late nineteenth century a posh neighborhood for the city's upper middle class.

Just south of Ehret's brewery stood the outfit belonging to Jacob Ruppert, Sr. In 1867, Ruppert cleared the timber on a lot on what is now Third Avenue between Ninety-first and Ninety-second streets and brewed his first beer. He lagged behind Ehret by some fifteen thousand barrels, but even at that pace he was forced to build a new plant in 1874. So, too, a mile or so to the south at East Fiftieth Street and Fourth Avenue (today's Park Avenue), the Schaefer brothers, Frederick and Maximilian, struggled to keep pace with demand. They'd built a four-story building in 1848, grand and imposing for its day, but outgrew it almost as soon as the last brick was laid. By the time Ehret and Ruppert opened shop, the Schaefer brewery had devoured several blocks, and that despite the fact that the Schaefers produced only about 44,000 barrels a year.

Although none of the New York brewers knew it at the time, the city's teeming multitudes would prove both a boon and a burden: No matter how many brewvats Ehret or Ruppert added, no matter how large the Schaefers' malthouse, New Yorkers devoured every drop. As a result, brewers in Manhattan, Brooklyn, and Newark, New Jersey, never had to seek new markets; never tested the treacherous waters of long-distance shipping; never built networks of salesmen and agents, warehouses and depots. The ready market fostered a complacency that would eventually prove near-fatal.

Pabst and Schandein faced different challenges on their march toward greatness. They demonstrated their intent—and their mettle—in those first few years after the war when Phillip Best, trusting their judgment, retired to Germany to nurse his poor health. The pair apprised their father-in-law of their efforts in letters detailing purchases of malt and hops and the progress of employees new and old. "Dear father, last Saturday we burnt coal and noticed that this is cheaper for us than purchasing wood," Pabst told Best in the summer of 1867. He calculated that they could save three dollars a day by switching from wood to coal, and reported that Blatz had surrendered most of his Chicago trade to Schlitz, and Pabst knew why: "His beer is bad."

Pabst and Schandein tracked their pennies because they needed each one in order to finance their plans for growth. Phillip Best died in the summer of 1869, so he did not live to see his sons-in-law launch their journey toward brewing history. A year later, Pabst and Schandein borrowed $100,000 to buy the South Side Brewery, a large, well-equipped plant left idle by the death of its owner. The acquisition offered a feast of opportunities: Besides its brewkettles, maltkilns, cellars, and steam engines, the property included a substantial dock on the Menomonee River, pathway to Lake Michigan and points south and east, as well as rail sidings whose tracks fed into two major lines. Together with the original plant on Chestnut, the new property provided the men with a capacity of about ninety thousand barrels a year, a universe of production away from the five or six thousand barrels their father-in-law had brewed in a good year.

The maneuver also represented a gamble of the first order, because the burden of debt would crush them unless they filled the vats at both plants. Luck paid a visit. The Chicago fire of 1871 destroyed two million dollars' worth of brewing real estate. Reconstruction would take months.

Pabst and Schandein moved in for the kill. Running the Empire and South Side breweries at capacity, they ordered new vats, boilers, and engines, and tripled the number of employees and teams dedicated to filling Chicago's lager vacuum. Day and night, hot wort streamed into flat cooling pans and then into fermenting tubs.

The production outstripped the capacity of the old brick-lined lagering caves. Construction crews built a new kind of "refrigerator": a windowless, vertical brick shell divided horizontally by iron floors. Racks stacked with puncheons of beer filled the first and second floors, or "cellars," as the brewers still called them, even though the chambers stood above ground. Chilled air streamed down to the beer through vented sidewalls thanks to a twenty-foot heap of ice that covered the top floor.

The company consumed some fifteen thousand tons of ice annually. Icehouses lined riverbanks and the shores of upstate lakes and ponds. In January, February, and March, dozens of harvesting teams guided horse-drawn cutters back and forth over the surface, slicing a grid of six- to ten-inch trenches into the glistening white expanse. After scoring the ice, the harvesters pried huge sheets free from the larger mass, and then sawed and hacked those into blocks about twenty-two inches square and ten to thirty inches thick. Winch arms swung some of the blocks to a loading chute for storage in the icehouse. Workers loaded part of the frigid cargo directly onto wagons headed to the brewery; waiting rail cars devoured the rest, transforming the cars into crude refrigerators.

Problems could slow the progress. In February 1872, a fire at the Chestnut Street facility destroyed the cooper house and everything in it. Two weeks later, a boiler exploded at the South Side plant. The vessel, five feet in diameter and eighteen feet long, blasted through the roof. The detonation ripped the eighty-horsepower steam engine from its bed, blew out windows and gaslights, and unleashed a downpour of brick, plaster, and metal on the neighborhood.

All in a day's work for the bold and ambitious. Pabst and Schandein rebuilt the cooper house and ordered a new boiler and engine. In early 1873, Best Brewing's output topped 100,000 barrels. Six years later, the upstarts temporarily toppled George Ehret from his throne, a stunning achievement for two men who had entered the industry with little business experience and even less knowledge of brewing. In between, they built a ninety-thousand-bushel malt elevator at South Side as well as a third set of tracks from that plant to the city's main rail yards; began shipping to Colorado; and established a branch operation in New York City that included a capacious icehouse, several teams, and two agents.

The move to New York was particularly bold. But it was prompted by need as much as by ambition: In order to make their investment pay, the men had to brew at capacity. Milwaukee could not begin to drink all the beer they produced; hence the decision to try to grab a slice of the huge market in the fast-growing urban Northeast. Still, much of the company's business centered on Chicago, where customers consumed about one thousand kegs of Best lager each day, so Pabst and Schandein enlarged their depot there; the new building held three thousand barrels and six hundred tons of ice. The company's officers— Pabst, Schandein, and Charles Best (son of Carl and nephew of Phillip)—tracked the movement of materials, shipments, and agents by means of telegraph lines that ran from each of the breweries to the Western Union office downtown.

The men drove the fact of their success home in the spring of 1875 when they staged an elaborate procession through the streets of Milwaukee. Early May marked the unofficial opening of the new beer season in the United States, the moment when brewers tapped their first kegs of winter-brewed lager and unleashed the pleasures of malt-rich bock. On this occasion, Best employees decorated their horses with ribbons and their wagons with bunting and flags. Cockades sprouted from the teamsters' hats. Poles lashed to the wagons' sides anchored banners that flapped in the breeze, the company's name emblazoned on each. As jolly Gambrinus, who still sat on his perch atop the archway leading to the loading yard, watched, twenty teams and wagons paraded along Chestnut Street toward the rail yards downtown, each bearing a small pyramid of lager-filled kegs destined for Chicago, a jubilant celebration of success and a blatant challenge to the rest of the city's brewers.

TEN DAYS EARLIER, Joseph Schlitz had headed for Stuttgart and a sharpshooting tournament aboard the steamer *Schiller.* Just off the coast of England, the vessel's captain lost his way in dense fog and heavy seas. As Best Brewing's teamsters paraded toward the rail yard, the *Schiller* smashed into the Retarriere ledge near Bishop's Rock, a jagged mass southeast of Land's End, England. Only a handful of the nearly four hundred on board survived.

Schlitz would have enjoyed the challenge posed by the colorful cavalcade. After running a consistent fourth among the city's brewers during the 1860s, he and the Uihleins greeted the new decade by setting sail on the hazardous seas of large-scale brewing. In 1870, the men razed what was left of the old Krug brewhouse, purchased the rest of the block at Third and Walnut, and launched themselves toward fame with a new brewhouse and 125-barrel kettle. A 64,000-square-foot icehouse cooled two storage racks and expanded cellars. All told, they could lager seven thousand barrels.

The storage capacity lasted a mere two years. In 1873, Schlitz built a second, larger icehouse; a year later, laborers excavated a new six-thousand-keg cellar. "Schlitz has loomed into prominence . . . within the past year," commented a reporter for the local newspaper. Indeed, and not just in Milwaukee. Schlitz and the Uihleins had been shipping to Chicago for several years, but that market no longer satisfied their ambitions. By the time Schlitz's body drifted to the floor of the Celtic Sea, he had shipped small quantities of his beer throughout the Midwest and Deep South, and to California, Tennessee, New York, Mexico, Brazil, and parts of South America. The beer traveled in corked bottles and only small quantities made any one trip—as much as could be packed into a wooden, ice-filled cask. But as for Pabst and Schandein, it was these first few forays into long-distance shipping, more than any of the new buildings and larger vats in which Schlitz invested, that laid the foundation for the brewery's growth.

Down in St. Louis, Adolphus Busch embraced his new venture with equal parts fervor and imagination. When he joined Anheuser & Co. in 1865, the brewery contained one twenty-five-horsepower engine and produced, in a good year, about four thousand barrels of mediocre lager. But Busch knew that even if he improved the beer, St. Louis represented a small market. To satisfy his ambition, he had no choice but to develop a clientele far beyond that city. Milwaukee's brewers already controlled Chicago, its hinterlands, and the shores of Lakes Michigan and Erie. Rather than muscle his way into that crowded pack, Busch cast his canny eye in another direction: He would conquer the Southwest.

The decision was at once both daring and logical, and typical of the man. During the Civil War, the demands of conflict had hindered ready access to the Mississippi River and routes south to New Orleans, as well as the rail lines that carried beer to Chicago and other eastern locations. Forced to adapt to these closed doors, St. Louis merchants and manufacturers had developed new relationships in the growing Southwest as an alternative market for their goods. By the late 1860s, they controlled lucrative routes that stretched from St. Louis to Nebraska and down into Texas. In the early 1870s, a group of businessmen pooled their funds and laid a rail line across Missouri and through the sparsely populated hills and plains of Kansas and Oklahoma to a terminus in Texas.

Adolphus Busch, as brilliant an entrepreneur as brewing or any other industry would ever know, recognized the opportunity immediately. There were already small breweries in Texas, thanks to German settlements founded there back in the 1840s. But the state was vast and the breweries were small. Here was an opportunity to capture and hold a wide-open market.

Striking into that distant territory posed considerable risk. It was one thing for, say, Pabst to ship beer to Chicago, a short day's trip away, or for Joseph Schlitz to supplement his local sales with a few bottles sent hither and yon. It was another matter to gamble a brewery's future and reputation on regular, large-scale shipping and to send beer, a fragile product with a relatively short life, on a thousand-mile journey.

That didn't faze Busch, who never met a challenge, scientific innovation, or labor-saving device he didn't like. He also never lost his passion for learning, and his curiosity led him far afield from brewing. He co-founded a Crop Improvement Bureau in Chicago, monitored developments in agricultural science and farming, and bred a particularly fine strain of chicken. He read scientific literature in English, French, and German, and could provide any listener with detailed assessments of the latest inventions, patents, and technologies. He would conquer the risk with technology and science.

Busch planned to ship some of the beer in wooden kegs, as was standard for brewers at the time, but he calculated that bottled beer would provide greater profit and enhance his reputation as well. As he knew, one glass of beer looked like any other, so unscrupulous saloonkeepers routinely purchased barrels of cheap draft swill and passed it off to unwitting customers as the more expensive lager of a superior brewhouse. They could not do that with a bottle, whose label announced the brewer's name in bold lettering, simultaneously advertising and protecting the brewery's good name. He decided to embark on large-scale, assembly-line bottling (and was first among American beermakers to do so), and nothing says more about the man's ambition, entrepreneurial genius, and passion for gambling than this foray into the unknown.

But between idea and reality lay obstacles. Brewers had bottled some of their stock for years, using primitive equipment: a hand-held siphon tube and a hand-operated cork tamper. Busch had to hire an engineer to design and build automated equipment that would permit large-scale bottling. He had to find a manufacturer willing and able to produce enough glass, a feat in itself given the limitations of manufacturing technology.

And large-scale, long-distance shipping depended on more than bottling. Busch also had to protect the beer during its long journey south, through frigid temperatures in winter and blistering heat in summer. He turned to science, and Louis Pasteur's discovery that heat killed bacteria. Busch, fluent in French, had read Pasteur's work in the late 1860s, and so knew of the Frenchman's discovery. He tackled the task of translating that theory into practice, systematizing the task of heating the beer and bottles so that he could process enormous quantities each day.

By 1872, Busch and Anheuser were shipping pasteurized bottled beer to the Southwest, making them the first Americans to exploit the commercial possibilities of Pasteur's ideas. It's not clear who designed and built their first bottling equipment, or "line," as brewers called it, but it was a pioneering piece of machinery. Thanks to it, eighty employees and two stories of automated equipment cranked out forty thousand bottles of beer a day, an unprecedented achievement in brewing. Keg beer traveled with the bottles, thanks to another Busch innovation: refrigerated rail cars, which he introduced to the company sometime around 1874 or 1875, shortly before meatpacker Gustavus Swift, typically credited as the godfather of refrigerated rail shipping, began using them.

In between, Busch equipped his father-in-law's brewery with the latest, newest, and most efficient machinery. In his first few years, he installed a mechanized barley cleaner, a 450-bushel malt hopper, new brewvats, and above-ground cold storage. By 1879, the newly renamed Anheuser-Busch Brewing Association was shipping its products to every state in the union and in small quantities to India, Japan, Central and South America, Mexico, the West Indies, Hawaii, Germany, England, and France. Anheuser-Busch beer had won competitions in Philadelphia, St. Louis, Texas, and Paris. The brewery filled seven acres of south St. Louis, and forty-year-old Busch, his mostly-retired father-in-law, and 250 employees produced more than 100,000 barrels of a half dozen or so styles of lager.

THE TITANS' AMBITIONS exacted a toll on those around them, as Charles Best discovered in early 1884, when his nervous disposition and frail health collided with the weight of his responsibilities as secretary of Phillip Best Brewing Company. His employer and cousin-by-marriage, Frederick Pabst, had glanced at a piece of his correspondence on its way to the out-box and, finding some sentence, some word, or some bit of punctuation out of order, had grabbed the letter and scrawled on it comments of a "humiliating nature." Furious at this assault on his competence and the intrusion into his realm, Best penned an angry letter of his own: "To Fred Pabst President Phillip Best Brewing Company: I do not know whether it was your intention to humiliate me like a schoolboy before my subordinates in the office, . . . but whether intentional or not, you surely have done it and in the most remarkable manner." Charles reminded Pabst that his duties as secretary left him "pushed & rushed" to that point that many days he simply could not find the time to dot every "i" and cross every "t." "[M]any a night I have left here with a burning head glad only to have the letters go away . . . If . . . you desire to sign the mail hereafter & to permanently assume the management of this office, be kind enough to say so in plain & direct words . . ."

Best, the nephew of brewery founder Phillip Best, had worked for Pabst and Schandein since 1872, first as cashier, now as secretary. In the early years, he arrived at work at four A.M. to tally beer kegs as the drivers hoisted them onto delivery wagons. These days he settled in at the office at eight and remained there until at least six o'clock, six days a week, keeping the brewery's complicated books and managing its voluminous correspondence. He took "an extraordinary interest" in the company's affairs, dithering over every dot and comma, fretting over every unaccounted-for penny, and agonizing over every expensive new machine. It is not surprising that the self-imposed pressure created "a worried, vexed & troubled state of mind."

Pabst routinely urged Best to avoid seeing only "the dark side of everything." "You make nothing better with it," he scolded, "and only make yourself unhappy." He, too, worked long hours, but somehow the weight of the grind lay lighter on his shoulders. When the company needed an infusion of cash, for example, he simply wrote overdrafts at his bank (of which he was also a director) and paid the interest when it was convenient. "Don't worry Charles," he would say with his typical flourish of underlinings, "it will not help you a bit. Take matters as they come."

On this occasion, Pabst, no master of grammar, spelling, or punctuation, scrawled a fast reply: "My dear Sir! I think you was a little excited when you wrote that letter[.] Tomorrow morning when you are cooled of [sic] a little I will talk with you. But of one thing I can assure you: The Remarks in the Letter were *not* intented [sic] to hurt anybodys [sic] Feelings particularly not yours. . . . Very Respectfully Yours Fred Pabst without the President."

Whatever the two men said the next day is lost to us, but it was not enough. Three months later, Best wrote Pabst another letter, this one a measured but devastating attack on his old friend. "What I desire to say to you," Charles began, "has been worrying me for a long time, and in connection with the unceasing trouble in our business has caused me to become so nervous that I am often almost unable to attend to my daily duties." For many years, he had devoted all his "heart and will" to the company's interests, but he could no longer ignore the consequences of Pabst's "false ambition to be the greatest brewer in the land . . ."

Best charged that Pabst had endangered the brewery's health by "investing and accumulating all the profits in the plant of the Company and by increasing its capacity far beyond [its] legitimate earnings, on borrowed money, causing us to be more and more involved in debt from year to year." Many times Best had pointed out the "danger" of Pabst's policies, but for the most part, Pabst merely "laughed," pronounced Best a "black see-er," and continued his march down the path to ruin. "Had you . . . followed my well meant and oft repeated advice," Charles added, the company might be smaller but at least it would be debt-free and "running to its full capacity." Instead, Best found himself nearly ill from the "continual embarrassment and worry."

And then the harried secretary unleashed the full measure of his grievances: "We have a large overgrown establishment on our hands, the capacity of which exceeds sales by nearly 150,000 Bbls. per annum, are carrying an enormous load of debts, and our manufacturing expenses are greater than those of our competitors . . ." Best had hoped that his employers "would entirely drop the idea of investing any more money" in the brewery, but alas, Pabst's recent "movements and remarks" had led Charles to the sad conclusion that the brewer planned to "follow the examples" of his competitors, "a very dangerous, even suicidal policy" as long as Best Brewing Company was "so heavily indebted." Not being in a "position to offer any objection to such a course," Charles concluded, "I desire to sever my connection with the Brewing Company at the earliest possible moment . . ."

Again, what happened next is long lost to us, but we can assume that Pabst wooed rather than raged, shining the full light of his charm and good humor on his fretful cousin. Charles retracted his resignation and stayed another five and a half years, finally leaving in December 1889, one year after Emil Schandein's death and ten months after Frederick Pabst replaced the word "Best" with "Pabst" on the brewery letterhead.

One fact is undeniable: During his twelve years with the company, Charles Best had watched Pabst and Schandein engineer a series of maneuvers that transformed a small brewhouse of ten thousand barrels into a behemoth that produced more than 374,000 the year of Best's outburst. The age demanded such devil-may-care daring, and if the Charles Bests developed headaches, the Frederick Pabsts prospered beyond imagination. By the turn of the decade, the breweries of Pabst and Schandein, the

Uihleins, and Adolphus Busch dwarfed most others. In 1880, half of the nation's 2,271 beermakers produced fewer than one thousand barrels a year, and 75 percent sold fewer than four thousand, disposing of most of it at saloons within a mile or so of their brewhouses. Best Brewing Company's 200,000 barrels in that year, an output surpassed only by George Ehret in New York City, appeared nearly grotesque in comparison. Bergner & Engel of Philadelphia ranked third, and behind them stood the Uihleins with 195,000 barrels and Adolphus Busch with 141,000.

As Charles Best rightly observed, the foray into large-scale brewing was freighted with uncertainty: Expansion necessitated not just debt, but risk of another sort. In order to make the debt pay, the brewery had to produce at capacity. But Milwaukee and St. Louis could not begin to absorb the vast swell of lager that poured from Best Brewing or Anheuser-Busch. The men had no choice but to push their beer into distant markets, and therein lies the brilliance behind the mechanical innovations and investments of Pabst and Schandein, the Uihleins, and Busch: They grew not by trundling their brew down the street and around the corner to neighborhood taverns, as did Ehret, Bergner & Engel, and other mammoth brewing houses in New York City and Philadelphia, but by taking their beer on the road, creating vast networks of markets that ranged from their own backyards to the Deep South, from tony company-owned hotels in New York and Dallas to dozens of foreign countries, and consisted of agglomerations of storage depots, agencies, salesmen, managers, and saloons. Nowadays, of course, manufacturers assume the existence of a national or even international market, but in the 1870s and 1880s, the notion of selling Milwaukee beer in, say, San Francisco was still new and untested. It is a measure of the genius of Adolphus Busch and the others that they not only envisioned such a market but created and succeeded in it.

But the brewers' success also rested on what is too often over-looked by those eager to condemn the era's industrialists: Captains of industry like Busch and Uihlein amassed their wealth during decades of hard work. Pabst "knew more about the details" of his company, claimed one of his agents, "than any other [brewer] in the business." The brewer earned that knowledge. He left the house, which stood on the same grounds as the brewery until the early 1890s, each day before breakfast to tour the plant and check on the day's work. That round completed, he returned home for a quick meal and then hustled back to the office, where, except for a lunch break, he stayed until six o'clock. "He knew the different bottling machines just as well as the men operating them," an employee once said, "and he took a pride in making a personal inspection" daily.

Adolphus Busch never claimed to be a "practical brewer"—indeed, almost none of the century's titans possessed formal training as a brewmaster—but few men in the business knew as much as he did about making lager, and he deserves recognition as one of the great American brewmasters. He analyzed and mastered every detail of the work, including "the various ways of brewing and the manipulation of the material, the boiling of the beer, fermenting and storing and especially the preparation of the malt," which he regarded as "one of the most significant factors in making fine beers." Study inspired confidence. "I am the maltster [and] superintendent of the malt-house," he once explained, ". . . and I am the buyer of the barley and the hops and I keep a general superintendence of the brewing process, fermenting process and stirring process." Each day, he said, "I examine the barley" and visit "the malt houses with my various foremen and give them orders how I want everything done; . . ."

He also became a superb judge of hops and personally selected those needed for the brewery. Woe to the dealer who submitted "mouldy" or "watery" samples, or ones "miserably picked, full of leaves and stems" that would taint beer with "a disagreeable and bitter taste." "You hop men," he told his brother August, a German hops merchant, "do not consider what harm you do if a brewer wants a certain fine hop and is willing to pay for it, and does not get it." "I wish it understood," he informed one dealer, "that I must have nothing but the very best and finest picks." To another, he wrote: "*What I said about stems and vines, I meant in dead earnest.* . . . Why should I pay duty and freight on an article that is absolutely worthless and injures our product besides?" It's not likely the agent made that mistake again.

Nor was the man surprised to hear from Busch himself. Corporations today are managed by layers of specialized bureaucrats and university-credentialed "experts," but late-nineteenth-century Americans were just learning how to construct managerial flowcharts and chains of command. Busch and Pabst captained enormous enterprises, but they relied largely on tiny in-house staffs, often consisting mostly of members of their own families. Charles Best, to name one beleaguered example, shouldered a burden of detail and tasks that would be shared among several dozen employees in one of today's corporations. The owners pitched in, corresponding regularly with their salesmen out on the road and making personnel decisions that a modern CEO would dismiss as trivial.

THE ATTENTION the men paid to their beer was particularly critical, and in the late 1860s and early 1870s, they realized that they needed to modernize it as they had modernized their breweries. In part, that decision was based on supply and demand. Lager's growing popularity strained farmers' ability to produce enough barley for the nation's three thousand beermakers, shortages exacerbated in the early 1870s by several years of bad weather. But there was another reason to rethink traditional all-malt beer.

American six-row barley, which was what most brewers used to make their malt, was exceptionally rich in protein. Lagering precipitated much of it, but dregs remained as unsightly globs that formed haze, soured the beer, and shortened the lager's life. Put another way, the decision to brew traditional all-malt Bavarian beer using American six-row barley produced an unstable beer with a relatively short life. If brewers could eliminate excess proteins, the beer would be more stable and durable; they could ship it even longer distances and so expand their markets. And if they could brew with some grain other than barley, they would ease the stranglehold of high prices caused by crop shortages.

In the late 1860s, many American brewers began experimenting with corn in their mashing tuns. Like barley, corn is rich in starch that can be converted to sugar, but unlike barley, it contains little protein. Mixing corn into the mash added an extra helping of starch that absorbed barley's excess proteins and, as a bonus, "stretched" the grain, much the way a cook might add pasta to a pound of hamburger to make it go farther. And thanks to mechanical reapers and better plows, corn yields were high and bushel prices low.

What sounded good on paper turned sour in practice. Corn oil infused the lager with an unctuous, rancid flavor. Brewery employees could eliminate much of the oil by grinding the corn to remove the husk and kernel, but doing so added another layer of expense to the process. And that was just one of the many puzzles of what beermakers called "adjunct" brewing, or making beer using grains other than barley. What was the best ratio of corn to barley? Should the corn be cooked separately and then added to the mash, or added at the outset and cooked with the barley? How long should it be boiled, and at what temperature? Only time and trial taught brewers how to incorporate corn into the mashing tun. Every move cost money—and when something went wrong, the entire mess had to be dumped. Put another way, the effort to keep pace with production when barley was scarce cost plenty.

Given the difficulties, adjunct-based brewing might have limped along for years before it became an integral part of the American brewery. Only some compelling reason, some irresistible benefit, could have induced brewers to expend the time and money necessary to overcome its liabilities.

In the early 1870s, the irresistible presented itself in the form of growing resistance to all-malt beer on the part of Americans themselves, as more non-Germans among them embraced lager as a nonintoxicating beverage. Brewers noticed what had not been obvious back in the 1850s, when lager's audience consisted almost entirely of German-speaking immigrants: When it came to beer, an enormous divide separated Europeans and Americans. Germans, deck of cards or chess set in one hand and pipe in another, plunked themselves in front of a frothy mug and nursed it for hours. Americans wanted to *drink*—and they didn't want to imbibe a brown broth that hit the stomach like a seven-course meal any more than they had wanted English ale.

Perhaps the difference stemmed from nothing more than scarcity and abundance: German beer culture was born and raised in a place that was overcrowded and where food was often in short supply. For centuries, Germans and other Europeans had prized beer as food—liquid bread. But the American experience relegated that idea to antiquity's dustbin. The United States was the land of liberty, high crop yields, and protein-rich diets. No one need drink beer for food. No surprise, then, that Americans preferred a beer that sat light on the stomach, a beer more suited to the American way of life.

John E. Siebel, the science editor for one of the first brewing trade journals, *Western Brewer,* and founder of the first American brewing school, understood this point. The old-world crowd would always prefer the "nourishing qualities" of full-bodied

Bavarian lager, he reminded his readers, but Americans drank in order "to pass time pleasantly in jovial society." They disdained old-world lager as too heavy, too filling, and entirely too brown, and demanded instead a light sipping beer, one that fell somewhere between "light wine and the heavy Bavarian lager." Brewers who planned to stay in business had to adjust to the times and the place.

Thus the great wave of experimentation with beer styles. Improvement-minded inventors obtained patents on new methods of brewing with corn and other cereals in hopes of creating a lager that allowed brewers to cope with chronic shortages of grain and satisfy the tastes of non-German Americans. But in the early 1870s, the nation's brewers encountered the answer to both problems: Bohemian lager, a light-bodied, low-alcohol, lemon-colored, translucent brew. On the tongue, it tasted and felt as different from Bavarian lager as lager did from English ale. Many brewers recognized that this style of beer would appeal to an American audience.

The brew originated in the early 1840s in Pils, a city in the Bohemia region of the Austrian Empire, and spread across the Empire and Europe. Because most German-American brewers hailed from and trained in the brewing traditions of Bavaria and Prussia, Bohemian-style lagers took longer to arrive in the United States. A handful of New York liquor wholesalers imported some of it in the 1850s, though few people noticed, thanks to its high price.

But Bohemian lager's stars aligned in 1873 at the Vienna International Exposition, one of many such events in the second half of the nineteenth century. Starting with the Crystal Palace Exhibition at London in 1851 and culminating in the spectacular World's Columbian Exposition at Chicago in 1893, millions of people toured these grand fairs. Part sideshow, part trade show, 100 percent entertainment, the expositions spotlighted national progress through displays of food, crops, clothing, machinery, engineering, art, and architecture.

The expositions also featured brewing exhibitions and contests where brewers competed for medals and trophies. At the 1873 Vienna Exposition, Bohemian beers stole the show and captured top prizes. There is limited evidence that Adolphus Busch was there, but if he missed the event, he heard about it from Otto Lademan, who traveled to Vienna as the state of Missouri's official representative. There Lademan tasted Pilsener and another lemony yellow Bohemian lager from Budweis (Ceské Budějovice), an ancient Bohemian city where an "official" court brewery produced the "Beer of Kings" (a slogan Adolphus Busch would later invert). Like Pilsener, Budweis contained Saaz hops and Moravian barley. But a slightly different mashing method and the unique local water resulted in a lager that was a shade lighter in color and slightly more effervescent than its Pils counterpart.

Lademan, Busch, and other brewing entrepreneurs had seen the future and it was Bohemian. They began fiddling with recipes and tinkering with malts and mashes in an effort to replicate this sparkling lager. Almost immediately, however, every brewer who attempted to duplicate Pilsener or Budweis collided with an incontrovertible truth: It was impossible. Or, more accurately, it was impossible using protein-rich American six-row barley. Bavarian lager's amber, almost opaque, color and heavy body hid six-row's deficiencies. A glass of sparkling, translucent Bohemian lager, however, functioned as a klieg light that illuminated every blob of unprecipitated protein, every tendril of undissolved yeast. Every flaw, every jot of unidentifiable *stuff*, hung there for all the world to see.

Anton Schwarz to the rescue. Bohemian-born Schwarz studied brewing at the Polytechnic Institute in Prague. His mentor there, Karl Balling, an influential nineteenth-century brewing chemist, recognized that Bohemia's brewers labored under two handicaps: scarce land and low crop yields, both of which forced up the price of brewing materials. Balling thus focused his research on the use of adjuncts, which he believed would enable brewers to maximize their resources. Under Balling's tutelage, Schwarz received solid technical training in the science and practice of adjunct-based brewing.

In late 1868, twenty-nine-year-old Schwarz emigrated to the United States and took a position writing technical and scientific papers for *American Brewer,* the nation's first brewing trade journal, including ones that provided explicit instruction in how to create mashes using adjuncts. From Schwarz, American brewers learned how to fashion an American version of Bohemian beer by mixing either white corn (less oily than the yellow varieties) or rice into the barley mash. Rice worked particularly well: Like corn, it is rich in starch and low in protein, but unlike corn, it contains almost no oil.

But whether made from corn or rice, the result was a new and, because it contained adjuncts, a uniquely American beer and a triumph of brewing technique: The new lagers were yellow in color with a brilliant sheen, light-bodied with a foamy head, and a rich, almost creamy flavor. They cost more to make than conventional Bavarian all-malt beers, but as brewers soon learned, the new creations pleased American palates.

Some brewers, German themselves and fond of heavy all-malt lagers, scorned the new brew as a fad, but Adolphus Busch recognized that he was now an American brewer, and that in his adopted country, the era of heavy amber Bavarian beer had ended. He tackled this new opportunity with his usual thorough enthusiasm, studying the matter in books and the trade press and consulting with men who had worked in Bohemian breweries. He and his brewmaster, Irwin Sproule, created a new beer that they called "St. Louis Lager." Sproule modeled the brew after the "highly esteemed" beer from Pils, using rice instead of corn. Then he and Busch created a second Bohemian beer, this one for Busch's friend Carl Conrad, a St. Louis dealer of imported wines and liquors. Conrad knew nothing about making beer, but he knew a market trend when he saw one and asked Busch to create a "very pale, fine beer." Busch would develop the recipe and brew the lager; Conrad would bottle and sell it under his own label.

By the mid-1870s, many brewers had succumbed to Pilsener fever, so Conrad, hunting for a way to make his product stand out in an increasingly crowded field, decided to model it after the style of Bohemian beer brewed in Budweis, a lager of which he was particularly fond. Neither Busch nor Conrad had visited Budweis, but they had toured Bohemia during trips to Europe in the late 1860s and early 1870s and tasted Budweis beer in other German and Austrian cities, including Mainz and Geisenheim. Conrad asked Busch to use imported barley if possible. He also wanted Busch to use hops from Saaz, a region of Bohemia known for the fine character and quality of its hop plants, which imbued the beer with an "exquisite aroma" and "special . . . bouquet." But, he added, if those were not available, well, Busch was to make do. Conrad mainly cared that the final result look, taste, and feel on the tongue like the lovely lager he had drunk in Europe.

After some months of experimentation, Busch and brew-master Sproule settled on a combination of technique and ingredients. They began with a mixture of high-grade North American barleys, germinating the grain for six days at temperatures ranging from 55 to 60 degrees and then roasting it for forty-two hours at 144 degrees Fahrenheit. To make the wort, brewery employees soaked the grain for about an hour in hot water. Then they transferred the mash to a second tub, boiled it, and returned it to the first vat. The mash contained about eight pounds of rice to every five bushels of barley, but it's not clear when they added the rice or how long it cooked. Nor were Busch and Conrad inclined to reveal the details of what they regarded as a priceless trade secret. When questioned, Busch would only say that after the initial soak, "we take the malt & water out of the first mash & put it into a tank & boil it for a certain time—the length of time depends upon the malt[;] then we let it go back to the first mash." He was less reluctant to explain his reasoning: "Taking [the grain] out of the water mash & boiling it & putting it back in the water mash again makes a much better mash, & gives the Beer a better flavor."

When the wort was ready, the brewmaster added Saaz hops, about twenty to twenty-four ounces of hops per barrel—less than the thirty or so ounces used in the company's other beers— and pitched the lager with another import, a Bohemian yeast that gave the beer "a peculiar, fine flavor." Beechwood strips lined the bottoms of the aging vats, rough-textured traps for impurities and bits of flock or yeast that drifted their way. Then workers transferred the beer to special kegs coated with an "aromatic" pitch made from fitchen pine; this, claimed Busch, endowed the beer with yet another "special characteristic."

The result, which Conrad named after its place of origin, was a masterpiece of brewing prowess. Budweiser "is . . . very fine and elegant," he once boasted. "It has a very pretty flavor, it sparkles better [than other lagers] & [is] not so heavy." He also decided to bottle the beer rather than sell it in barrels. The label would advertise the beer and protect its reputation and his from crooked tavern owners who might otherwise try to sell another brewer's inferior lager under the Conrad Budweiser name. It's not clear what the original label looked like, but the man who created and printed Conrad's second label claimed that the first version included the word "champagne." That would not be surprising, because effervescent Budweiser looked more like Champagne than it looked like other beers. At least Conrad thought so, because he fostered the comparison by corking the lager in Champagne bottles. Alas, the point was lost on customers: The glass was so dark that they could not see and enjoy the beer's sheen and brilliance. About a year after Budweiser's 1876 debut, Conrad switched to a translucent green bottle.

Whether Budweiser, St. Louis Lager, or some other brand, the new brew changed the face of American brewing for all time and did so almost overnight. Pabst and Schandein learned that lesson the hard way. Their brewmaster, Phillip Jung, launched the brewery's experiments with rice and corn in late 1873 and early 1874, mixing the adjunct grains with barley imported from Italy. But Jung's considerable skill and ambition outweighed his loyalty to the company, and in late 1879 he left to open his own brewery. His first replacement lasted less than a year. The next man, August Olinger, knew how to make old-style, dark Bavarian, but floundered when it came to lighter Bohemian lager. Olinger slashed the amount of corn and added more barley, with disastrous results. In Chicago, customers deserted Best's too-dark beer in favor of competitors' offerings. "Can't you give us a paler, purer beer," pleaded the branch manager. "Our customer Shaughnessy out on Graceland Road, sent us word he could not use our beer any longer, it being so dark."

Pabst penned a note of his own to Olinger and his assistant. "There is no doubt in my mind if that kind of beer keeps on, we will lose a great deal of trade which had cost us a great deal of trouble and money to get . . . We surely furnish everything necessary to make good beer," he pointed out, "and I can only look at this as either carelessness or not the necessary knowledge of the business." "I want to be understood," he added, in case his employees had missed the point, "that we cannot afford to have anything of this kind repeated . . ."

Olinger either ignored the warning or, more likely, lost his footing under pressure. In March 1882, the manager at Best Brewing's Kansas City branch received a shipment of Bohemian-style beer that had turned hazy in transit. He refused to send it out with his salesman and complained to Pabst. "Now Charley, I believe you are wrong!," Pabst replied. "The Beer is undoubtedly all right. . . . Take your Beer give it the right Temperature & I'm satisfied you will find it all right. . . . I never felt so confident of good Beer as I do now. We have the best we ever had, we use the best Material we could buy, & we have taken every Precaution to make good Beer and you will find it so."

Pabst's soothing words belied the turmoil back home. Olinger had left, although whether for the firmer footing of greener pastures or because fired is not clear, and his replacement, John Metzler, would not start until April. Metzler brought European training and considerable skill to the brewhouse, but two years later, he, too, departed Milwaukee.

This time Pabst and Schandein asked for help. Charles Best penned one of his meticulous letters to Anton Schwarz in New York, requesting recommendations. Schwarz dispatched salvation in the form of J. F. "Fritz" Theurer, one of the most important names in late-century American brewing, a skilled and imaginative man who created superb beer and invented a string of money- and time-saving technologies. These included a yeast-pitching machine, filters, various beer coolers, and a barley washer. His most important contribution to brewing, however, was the creation of a new way to krausen beer. When brewers krausen, they add fresh, still-fermenting wort to already fermented lager. The young wort generates a secondary fermentation and enlivens the lager with natural carbonation. Unfortunately, the fresh wort often contained impurities that contaminated the beer. Theurer developed a method of capturing the carbon dioxide that generates during the initial fermentation, scouring it to remove impurities, and then injecting it under pressure into the beer in cask.

Two years later, Pabst and Schandein supplemented Theurer's talent with the addition of Otto Mittenzwey, a German-trained chemist hired to explore the possibilities of hard science, and especially the cultivation of "pure" yeast strains developed in a laboratory specifically for beer. Pabst also ensured that his successors, sons Gustav and Fred Junior, would enjoy what he and Schandein had not: formal training in the art and science of brewing. He sent both boys off to New York to study with Schwarz. It was decisions like these that separated Pabst—and Busch and the Uihleins—from most other brewery owners, who relied on brewmasters schooled in trial-and-error rather than science.

Carl Conrad fared better with his new beer, thanks to the meticulous care and skill of Anheuser Brewing's Irwin Sproule. Conrad sold 250,000 bottles of the lager in just twelve months, and two years after its debut on the market, Busch and Sproule had brewed six thousand barrels of Budweiser. "I never found a business so easy as this Budweiser," raved one of Conrad's agents, and that despite its being "sold at a higher price than any other Beer in the country."

Easy to sell and easy to steal. It is a measure of Budweiser's superb flavor and character that, almost immediately, someone tried to capitalize on Conrad's investment. In April 1878, Conrad received disturbing news from a brother who lived in New Orleans: Another version of Budweiser had arrived in town bearing a label virtually identical to the one Conrad used on his beers. The mock-Budweiser label was blue and white rather than red, but, like Conrad's original, consisted of two parts: a rectangular main label and a bow tie around the bottle's neck. The latter featured a diamond-shaped knot, crowns in the neckbands, an oblong laid over the bow, and the words "The World Renowned Budweiser Lager Beer." Diamond and rectangle both sported a manufacturer's trademark: "B. B. B.," a near-duplicate of the "C. C. C." on Conrad's label. By that time Conrad had identified the perpetrator of the insult: Otto Lademan, president of Joseph Uhrig Brewing Company.

Lademan had been brewing the new style beer for several years, but he had discovered the power of Budweiser in particular a year or so earlier during a trip to Denison, Texas, where he maintained an agent and a sales outlet. A bartender there tried to pass off Conrad's brew as an imported Budweiser to the tune of a dollar a bottle, a shockingly high price at a time when customers paid a nickel for a schooner (and more shocking still when translated into today's money: seventeen dollars). Lademan handed over his dollar, examined the label, took a sip, and informed the bartender that the stuff was a fake, an imitation of the foreign brew. Imitation or not, Otto Lademan recognized a good idea when he saw one.

Back in St. Louis, other reports trickled in. An Anheuser salesman working the Galveston territory ran into one of Lademan's travelers, a Mr. Lippenberg. When the conversation turned to Budweiser, Lippenberg boasted that he was the brains behind the Uhrig imitation. He had spotted Budweiser in California and promptly telegraphed his boss, urging him "to put up a similar label to Conrad's and make it look like Budweiser Beer."

More news, none of it good: V. H. Stum, Conrad's San Francisco agent, complained that his trade was being stolen by Uhrig's people, who promised barkeepers Budweiser at cheaper prices than Stum offered. Stum slashed his price by fifty cents, ran newspaper advertisements warning of the fraud, and devoted the rest of his time to trying to persuade beer drinkers that only his Budweiser was the real thing. The clientele at one bar also insisted on Conrad Budweiser, but when the owner tried to replenish his supply, he ended up with a case of triple-B. A customer took a sip, pronounced it a fraud, and refused to drink the rest of it.

Matters came to a head on a fine day in early May as Conrad and Adolphus Busch enjoyed a buggy ride through downtown St. Louis. Not far from the Union Depot (then located at Eleventh Street and Chouteau), they spotted Lademan in his buggy. Conrad hailed the man. "We stopped," Conrad reported later, "and com-menced talking about his imitation Budweiser Lager Beer. I told him that he was doing very wrong in making his imitation . . ." Lademan "indignantly repelled the accusation," pointing out that his triple-B trademark was "entirely different" from his rival's triple-C and that Conrad was not entitled to "claim the whole al-phabet." Whereupon Conrad warned that Lademan "would have to stand the consequences" of a lawsuit. Lademan told him to "go ahead and crack the whip." He, Lademan, "had as good right to manufacture Budweiser Beer as anybody in America." Conrad's was nothing more than a "counterfeit," he added, and his own Uhrig brand "was not any better."

On May 15, 1878, Carl Conrad filed suit, charging Joseph Uhrig Brewing Company with "pirating" the Budweiser label and name in order to defraud the public. Joseph Uhrig Brewing, in the person of Otto Lademan, denied the charge. The word "Bud-weiser" could not be trademarked, he argued, and if anyone was defrauding the public, it was Carl Conrad: His beer contained not one ounce of Saaz hops or Bohemian barley; it was not brewed "according to the Budweiser process"; and the beer's label perpe-trated those falsehoods for the sole and "fraudulent purpose of de-ceiving the public."

The parties met in court in late October. Today, such a case would drag on for months and require the services of a horde of lawyers and expert witnesses, but Conrad and Lademan were in and out of the courtroom in two days. Conrad marched to the witness stand first and bumbled his way through an explanation of why he chose the name "Budweiser"—"the Budweiser process makes the finest beer"—and why his beer differed from all oth-ers—its unique qualities rested on a bottling method known only to himself and his foreman. Adolphus Busch and Irwin Sproule followed him to the stand; both insisted that the Budweiser brew-ing process—based on double vats and mixed mash—was unique.

Over a dozen of Conrad's dealers and salesmen testified, too, each claiming that Lademan's inferior imitation damaged Conrad's business and reputation.

Lademan's lawyer called Lademan, William Lemp, and several other St. Louis brewers to the stand. One, the brewmaster for Wainwright and Co., summarized their collective testimony: "I don't know anything about any process called the Budweiser process of brewing—never heard of such a process until I heard of this case." Lademan was even more dismissive: "I know the process that was described by Mr. Busch this morning called the Budweiser process. It is a process used by everyone who uses rice in brewing. We make a water mash first, then a thick mash, & afterwards a water mash. It is no particular process at all."

Lademan should have tried harder. The jury ordered him to pay Conrad $4,175 in damages (approximately $73,000 today). Lademan appealed, but the new judge concurred with the original jury: Lademan, he said, intended to deceive, and did deceive; he ordered the brewer to stop using the copycat labels.

THAT LADEMAN WAS willing to risk so much speaks well not just of Budweiser, but of the new lager, which threatened to elbow all-malt lagers right out of existence. Beer aficionados today scorn lagers made with corn or rice as inferior to all-malt products, believing that brewers adopted the use of other grains only to save money. That was not true: It cost Adolphus Busch more to make his adjunct-based beers than his all-malt brews, and those lagers sold for higher prices than did their conventional Bavarian-style counterparts.

Nor were the beers inferior. If any one fact lies at the heart of the stunning success of Busch, Pabst, and the Uihleins, it is that by the 1880s, they were brewing some of the finest beers in the world, beers that stood up against competition with anything made in Europe. The Uihleins knew that: In the fall of 1880, they shipped some of their bottled Bohemian to relatives of a Schlitz employee in Zeitz, a city in north central Germany. The recipients took the beer to a local chemist for analysis. The man expressed astonishment at its purity. Its flavor and character, he reported, compared with the finest Bohemian lagers.

While that might be dismissed as salesmanship on the part of the Uihleins, it's not so easy to dismiss the grand gold prize that Anheuser Brewing won at Paris in 1878, where its beer faced off against one hundred other lagers and ales from France, Britain, Austria, Bavaria, and Bohemia. The brewery's St. Louis Lager generated an "immense sensation" among the competition's jurors, reported a correspondent for the *New York Times,* especially after the supervising chemist reported that the beer contained rice.

But the three great brewing concerns also succeeded where others failed because they recognized what is fundamental to any brewer's success: the need for consistency. Pabst and Schandein invested in a laboratory and a European-trained chemist because they knew that they could not afford to sell a single batch of bad beer. They employed prime ingredients, hired the finest brewmaster they could find, and spared no effort in creating fine malt and yeast, all for one end: so that each glass of their beer tasted the same every time, whether on tap or in a bottle; whether sold in Milwaukee, Chicago, or San Francisco.

Not all the other American brewers cared as much or understood brewing fundamentals. The fact is that much of the local beer sold in the nineteenth century was of poor quality, inconsistent, sour, or flavorless. And many of those other brewers never grasped the care, time, and money that stood behind the beers coming out of the titans' breweries. One of those lesser brewers inadvertently admitted as much, when in 1881 he wrote to the editor of *Western Brewer* to ask a question. How, he wondered, did Best Brewing give its beer such a sturdy, long-lived head? "We use bi-carbonate," he wrote, "but the beer won't carry like the Milwaukee." The editor's reply was a masterpiece of tact and restraint. Foamy head, he replied, "depends not so much on addition of foreign substances as on the quality of the malt, the mode of mashing," and a long, slow, secondary fermentation. Best Brewing's "superior article is due to the superior facilities which they enjoy in their manufacture."

But whether it was made in Milwaukee or St. Louis, New York or Cincinnati, nineteenth-century Americans embraced the new beer with open hearts—and mouths—because, explained a reporter for the *New York Times,* they disliked the "'sour' and 'bitter'" taste of all-malt beer, preferring instead the "sweeter" taste of light-bodied Bohemian brews. The nation's brewers, "recognizing the fact that one American beer-drinker consumes more, on an average, than three Germans look out to please the greatest number—particularly when it pays them the best." And as long as the "greater part" of the nation's beer "flow[ed] down American gullets," the mostly German-born and bred brewers had no choice but to "modify the flavor of their beer to suit American palates" rather than those of their fellow émigrés.

So the Schaefer brothers of New York discovered in 1875 when they "tried the experiment of sending out to their customers genuine old lager." Their effort to turn back the clock produced "a general growl over the hard, bitter, hoppy taste, and the absence of the rich, creamy broth" found in pale Bohemian beers. Americans had become "so accustomed to a light colored beer that a beer colored somewhat darkly is considered of inferior or indeed bad quality." One hundred years later, another group of innovators would turn back time with greater success. But the late nineteenth century belonged to pale, adjunct-based lager. The barons built their fortunes on the foundation of its golden broth.

CHAPTER THREE

"Masters of the Situation"

T HE GILDED AGE was an era of unrivaled wealth, obscene poverty, lung-scarring pollution, and epic struggles for power. But it was also the golden age of American public life, when men and women gathered at cafés and amusement parks, saloons and beer gardens, to enjoy dancing and dining, roller coasters and bowling. Back before the Civil War, the brewers' gardens and beerhalls had been snug affairs: The one Jacob and Phillip Best opened above their brewery accommodated perhaps fifty to seventy-five people, and in the green spaces behind the brewery wooden tables were crammed elbow-to-elbow if more than one or two hundred people gathered. But like so much else about that era of nearly theatrical extremes, beer gardens swelled to enormous proportion in the late nineteenth century and became playgrounds of unrivaled comfort and modernity, while the saloons served as havens for the era's masculinity, poverty, and corruption.

Consider the drama that unfolded in Milwaukee on a Sunday morning in the spring of 1880. Thousands of good folk passed the morning in church where they sat and listened, stood and sang, kneeled and prayed. But as the sun rose toward midday, the citizenry stashed its prayer books and spiritual obligations for another

week, and the various rivulets of Catholics, Lutherans, Metho-
dists, and Presbyterians merged into a river of humanity streaming
toward a single destination: Schlitz Park. This particular Sunday
marked the grand opening of Milwaukee's newest and most elaborate attraction, and no one wanted to miss the excitement.

Schlitz Park rose out of the ruins of Quentin's Park, a moth-
eaten seven-acre lot a few blocks northwest of the brewery. After
the Uihlein brothers purchased the land in July 1879, a small
army of carpenters, bricklayers, laborers, and landscapers had
refurbished the site, a $75,000 project designed to provide Mil-
waukeeans with a good reason to drink Schlitz beer.

Now it was time to see where the money had gone. Thousands of people pushed through the main gate, where a life-sized
statue of Joseph Schlitz surveyed the throng. Some strolled mean-
dering ribbons of gravel. Others lounged on the veranda of the
two-story building that housed a restaurant and lavatories outfitted with marble fixtures. Still others hunted for seats inside the
park's centerpiece, an octagonal pavilion that accommodated five
thousand people. A multifaceted glass ball hanging from the
twenty-eight-foot ceiling sparkled with the light reflected off the
horns and tubas in the twenty-five-piece orchestra seated below.
On this special day, the brothers Uihlein even allowed competitors' wares into the park, "all the leading brewers having contributed some of their choicest stock." With four bowling alleys,
a first-class restaurant, lighted fountain, sixty-foot lookout tower,
plenty of lawn where children could play, and Milwaukee's finest
lager, Schlitz Park offered something for everyone.

A reporter who ambled the grounds in search of a story rumi-
nated on the larger lessons of this particular day of rest. The
jostling crowd included many of Milwaukee's "best citizens," up-
standing men and women who scorned the old-fashioned idea that
it was "sinful to go out and enjoy the bright sunshine" on Sunday.
"There is no mistaking the fact," he observed, "that a more liberal

spirit pervades the mind of the public of the present day." He attributed this sea change to the city's large population of "foreigners" whose long years of respectability had convinced even "Orthodox Christians that Sunday may be A DAY OF REST and of harmless relaxation and recreation as well." Even the formerly puritanical "New Englander . . . now feels that his fellow citizen who sticks to his business through the week and gives three feet of honest measure to a yard, is NEITHER A HEATHEN NOR A TURK if he takes a few hours of innocent and instructive amusement on Sunday."

And not just on Sunday. Over the next twenty years, hundreds of thousands of Milwaukeeans flocked to Schlitz Park. In summer, they danced and watched polo matches, applauded operas and orchestras, rode the carousel, and howled at the antics of acrobats and vaudeville performers. In winter, they skated to the accompaniment of live music. One memorable January, the park's manager hosted a carnival. Colored lights and Chinese lanterns illuminated the parade that glided across the ice: ten horses adorned with ribbons and wreaths, an enormous boat, two icebergs, a troupe of clowns, and ten ornately attired elephants.

Not to be outdone, Frederick Pabst and Emil Schandein acquired Bielefeld Garden, a dilapidated mid-century vestige of a garden on North Third Street. They invested $30,000 transforming the site into a mirror image of Schlitz Park. A few years later, the partners bought seven oak-strewn acres on a bluff overlooking Whitefish Bay just north of Milwaukee, purchased an excursion steamer, laid trolley tracks between the park and the city, and welcomed the multitudes to their first-class resort.

So it went around the country. In New York City, rich and poor danced and drank at the Tivoli and the Bowery, the Teutonia and the Pacific—beer halls that accommodated fifteen hundred or more people. At one of the city's finest venues, Atlantic Garden, guests entered a vestibule lined on two sides by bars stocked with lager and wine, and food counters bulging with pretzels, cheese, sausage, and crackers. From there, they passed into a cavernous space filled with tables and benches. Massive chandeliers illuminated a vaulted ceiling decorated with painted panels and frescoes. Gothic windows lined two walls; a parade of faux columns and arches marched across another, the niches adorned with plaster scallops and fleur-de-lis. There customers danced and drank lager and Rhine wines; played at cards and dominoes, billiards and bowling.

Warm weather drew New Yorkers to outdoor venues—Bellevue or Jones' Woods, or the East River Gardens—where sunlight replaced chandeliers, and lush groves and arbors the beerhalls' frescoes and fleur-de-lis. In the mid-1880s, George Ehret spent $220,000 on an enormous estate in Weehawken, New Jersey, just across the Hudson River from Manhattan, and created there a public beer garden complete with ferry service from the city. Not to be outdone, rival Jacob Ruppert built his own posh garden on South Brother Island, a tiny chip of land nestled between the northern tip of Queens and the southern edge of the Bronx.

AT THE OTHER END of the drinking spectrum lay the saloons, most of them dimly lit holes-in-the-wall where the air sagged in layers of smoke and grease, and spittoons and sawdust littered the floors; where the beer cost a nickel and the lunch, cigars, and companionship were free. For every Atlantic Garden or Schlitz Park, there were a hundred saloons, 150,000 in 1880 and nearly 300,000 by 1900—and that was not counting the illegal unlicensed joints. Americans could not walk more than a half block in any business district in any city without passing a saloon. In the early 1880s, Milwaukee's 120,000 residents could chose from nine hundred saloons, one for every 130 people, and more than that per capita for their mostly adult male clientele. A single block of Howard Street in San Francisco contained twenty-one saloons, thirteen on one side of the street, eight on the other. In 1899, Chicago police estimated that half the city's population entered at least one saloon a day.

The era spawned the saloon. The new steel mills, textile factories, and machine shops devoured the labor of millions who fashioned lives out of twelve-hour days tending mechanical devices and too-short nights endured in sordid tenements and hovels. The rackety pace of factory and city fueled a desire to re-create some measure of comfort and community from rural lives and European homelands left behind. Just as New Yorkers and Parisians today congregate at cafés because they lack the space to entertain at home, so men fled the tedium of the factory and the cramped squalor of home for the warmth of the saloon. Male working-class camaraderie rested on a cornerstone of neighborhood beer joints, each one a quasi-public club presided over by the keeper and his bartenders. There, men convened meetings of clubs organized around bicycling, card-playing, rowing, politics, unions, and baseball. Political candidates wooed voters by shaking hands, slapping backs, and buying rounds for the house. Ward bosses conducted nominating conventions, harangued the undecided, and bestowed jobs on the loyal.

Industrialism affected women, too. For the most part they gathered in warm weather on tenement stoops, sending a child down the street with an empty pail to fetch a "growler" of lager. But many women left home each day to toil in sweatshops and factories, and the grind of labor eroded their ideas about propriety and the barriers between the sexes. Young Dorothy Richardson discovered that near the turn of the century, when she worked twelve hours a day, six days a week at a commercial laundry in Manhattan. One day a co-worker collapsed from "nausea and exhaustion." As the younger women helped her to her feet,

Mrs. Mooney, older and more worldly, scolded them, blaming the young woman's faint on "them rotten cold lunches you girls eat."

When the noon bell rang the next day, Mooney hauled the lot of them down the street to Devlin's saloon, where she ushered them through the "ladies entrance." In most saloons, this was a side or back entrance that opened off an alley directly into the back room. This was not, as it might seem, an indication of inferiority. Rather, this sheltered entry afforded women more privacy than the front door and, more important, enabled them to avoid the sometimes rowdy male horde congregated around the mahogany bar that dominated the saloon's main room. Unlike the front, the back room was quiet and relatively free of both smoke and the spittle that decorated the saw-dust strewn floor out front.

"Six beers with the trimmin's," Mooney demanded from the waiter, the "trimmin's" being the saloon's salty but hearty free lunch. "I who never before could endure the sight or smell of beer, found myself draining my 'schooner' as eagerly as Mrs. Mooney herself," Richardson recalled. Energized by the hefty meal, she vowed to return; by week's end she proudly identified herself as a Devlin's "regular" and a convert to beer.

Saloons devoured most of the breweries' output and provoked the brewers' worst headaches. At a time when spirits and bottled beer were expensive, the typical saloonkeeper earned most of his profit from lager on tap, and served the product of only one brewery. This "tied" system, as it was called, began emerging in the 1870s, as brewers, needing to pay for their remodeling projects, for the new and larger brewvats, for steam engines, malt hoppers, and icehouses, sought the security of guaranteed retail outlets for their beer.

At first the system consisted of gentlemen's agreements: A local tavern owner agreed to carry a favored brewer's brand and only his. That worked well enough in lager's early days, when saloonkeepers and brewers had stood as equals in the world of small-time entrepreneurship. But as men like Pabst and the Uihleins razed their relatives' comfortable brewhouses and replaced them with factories, a chasm opened between beermaker and beerseller. That became painfully obvious during a confrontation in Milwaukee in early 1874, when inflation and recession roiled the economy and drought sent crop prices sailing skyward. The city's brewers announced plans to raise prices by two dollars a barrel.

Saloonkeepers rebelled and convened a series of meetings to discuss the matter, but the ensuing "wailing and gnashing of teeth" among the "knights of the spigot" brigade had less to do with the price hike than with their resentment toward—and fear of—the changes roiling their world, thanks to the "bloated monopolists perched upon the hillsides of the city."

One old-timer recalled the days when "Papa Best set up his little brew-kettle and by dint of careful toil brewed the first lager for the pioneer" and turned a profit, too. Now that "little beginning" of Papa's was "worth a million of dollars," and his successors' pockets bulged with their profits, thanks to mechanization and brewing methods of a sort that Papa Best would not even recognize. Another speaker recounted the history of a local beer king who inherited a "business worth $23,000." Now the brewery's profits equaled those of a "diamond mine," and the owner's wealth belied his "lamentations" of poverty.

Ranting was about all the saloonkeepers could manage. The barkeeper who chaired the meetings detailed the results of his confrontation with Valentin Blatz, who owned his saloon. The white-aproned knight dispatched a letter to the Broadway brewing castle, announcing that he would pay ten dollars per barrel for Blatz's beer until May 1, and then just one dollar more. King Blatz rejected his subject's offer, whereupon the tavernkeeper removed the Blatz sign from his front door, offered a last free round on the house, and wrote to a Fond du Lac brewer asking for more lager. No doubt the upstate beermaker would oblige, but who knew at what price? The saloonkeepers, unable to hold out against warriors armed with better weapons and deeper pockets, finally agreed to a compromise: a price hike of one dollar until May 1, at which time the brewers would get their full two-dollar increase in the barrel price.

As competition accelerated and brewing's stakes—all that machinery to pay for—grew, brewers longed to keep their retailers on a tighter leash. In the 1880s, many began buying the saloons outright and leasing them to saloonkeepers, who, having become what amounted to company employees, had no choice about the beer they carried. As Frederick Pabst told one of his branch managers in the early 1880s, "[i]t strikes me that the right way to do a Thing of that Kind would be for us to take the Lease for a Number of years put in Tables Chairs Counter & Shelves. The Man who runs it should buy Glasses and *all* the fixtures which is necessary to run a No. 1 Place . . . Then we should have a Contract that at anytime when the Man don't attend to his Business or keeps the Place up he must get out at short Notice." Most important, Pabst added, "who ever runs the Place must . . . invest some Money. He should also pay interest for the Money invested by us."

The Uihleins worked the tied system as well as anyone, snapping up every street corner they could lay hands on. August Uihlein "was away from home every night," his son Erwin later recalled, ". . . out judging property and he became one of the best real estate judges in the country." The brothers funneled large chunks of their cash into saloons and hotels in Chicago and Milwaukee. By the turn of the century, Schlitz Brewing owned well over fifty saloons in Milwaukee and another sixty in Chicago. "In this manner," explained Edward Uihlein, "we not only reached higher sales figures, but we also insured our clients against competition. . . . When we rented to a merchant who handled our products exclusively we were very sure of his reputation and his compliance with all laws and ordinances . . . [O]ur policies," he added, "were not highly regarded by the competition."

Or by the saloonkeepers themselves. They expected brewers' salesmen to pay regular visits and buy rounds for the house. They expected free signs, coasters, and wall hangings. They expected free kegs at Christmas and New Year, and deep discounts when business was slow. Moreover, they rarely missed a chance to play one brewer off another, buying beer from Pabst in October and switching to Schlitz in December when that company's agent sidled through the back door with a better deal. A saloonkeeper need only hint that he might switch to another brand, and "Presto!" complained the editor of *Western Brewer.* "As if by magic, the wily saloon keeper has struck a bonanza. His place becomes the resort of a score of brewery 'agents.' Money is lavished upon him, wine flows in rivers, and the keen publican waxes fat." The exchange of pleasantries, money, and booze would drag on for a few weeks, perhaps a month, and then, "Presto!" again: "the badly fooled brewers and their 'agents' are informed by the sleek Boniface, that at present he will make no change in his brewer or his beer."

Every once in awhile the game backfired. Best Brewing's Chicago manager confronted a saloonkeeper who offered to provide the brewery with several more saloons in exchange for a 10 percent discount on the keg price. "I laughed at him," the manager wrote to the home office. The saloonkeeper told the Best agent that Schlitz's man had already agreed to the terms. Fine, Best's man told the saloonkeeper, go to Schlitz. To his surprise, the chagrined barkeeper stuck with Best. "It was no doubt a bulldozing operation," reported the manager. "I do not feel like complaining of our business here," he added, "but it is hell on earth as usual."

Then there was the bad-beer-refusal-to-pay trick. Brewers

lured saloonkeepers into their company's pen by loaning them start-up funds or fronting them kegs of beer on credit. The barkeepers then refused to pay up on grounds that the beer had gone sour. The practice confounded Charles Nagel, a St. Louis attorney who managed the legal affairs of Anheuser-Busch. He pleaded with his friend Adolphus Busch to read the fine print in the contract that bound brewer and saloonkeeper.

"[Y]ou will notice," Nagel explained to Busch, "that you are compelled to furnish merchantable beer in sufficient quantities . . . All the parties have to do therefore, is to keep your money, and to assert that your beer is not merchantable for one reason or another," refuse payment, and then turn around and make a similar deal with Schlitz or Pabst. The stratagem enabled the saloonkeeper to float on free beer for several weeks, leaving the Anheuser-Busch collector holding an empty money bag. "You would not think of giving this amount of money to any reputable man without security," added the exasperated Nagel. "Why would you give it to strangers who in asking it have to admit that they have not the necessary funds to carry on the business. . . . [T]his kind of loan system is the weakest spot in your whole business and subjects you to more losses, and to more expense and unsatisfactory litigation, than all your other business put together."

Nagel was right, although brewers couldn't see any way around the saloons, which had become indispensable components of their empires. Indispensable and problematic: These real-estate holdings, vast in the case of the largest breweries and intended to eliminate the aggravations of retailing, instead exacerbated them—and eventually would serve as a lightning rod for a new generation of temperance and prohibition crusaders.

It's easy to see why. Trying to squeeze profits out of their penny-ante saloons tied the brewers to a treadmill of woe. They wanted to lease saloons to reliable men who were willing to invest some of their own funds; wanted clean, honest saloons where the keeper banned prostitution, gambling, and sloppy drunks. More often than not, however, they settled for ne'er-do-wells, thieves, or dolts. The result was a string of sleazy saloons with the breweries' names plastered across them in large letters. August A. Busch, Sr., Adolphus's son and, by the 1890s, second vice-president of Anheuser-Busch, hated the whole mess. "[Brewers] were so anxious to sell their products," he complained some years later, "that if a brewery put a saloon on one corner, immediately three other brewers would buy the other three corners and put saloons there, and they would have to put in all sorts of disreputable devices and attractions, 'wild women,' and the like to draw trade."

Wild women, indeed. For every honest saloonkeeper who earned his living dispensing drinks and camaraderie, there were fifty who all but ignored the beer or whiskey in favor of more lucrative "sidelines" in the back room or upstairs: gambling, prostitution, pickpocket rings, and the like. A standard saloon-based vice operation consisted of a bar fronting the street. Prostitutes worked the room, soliciting for tricks, whom they took upstairs to one in a warren of curtained cubicles. A thick cloud of cigar smoke hung over the gaming tables and roulette wheels in the back room.

"Big Jim" O'Leary, son of Mrs. O'Leary of the Chicago cow-bucket-and-fire, owned such a place just opposite the city's stockyards. His Horn Palace contained baths, a barbershop, and a thousand-seat concert hall. There was a bar, of course, well stocked with lager, but its take was measly compared to the money O'Leary earned from his gambling room. There his customers placed bets on sporting events in New York or California, and then whiled away the hours at cards or roulette while they waited for the in-house "wire" to convey the results. Saloons near railroad stations provided a base of operations for organized theft, as painted women and skilled pickpockets hailed the rube off the train, accompanied him to the saloon for a (drugged) drink, and then rolled him, relieving him of cash and luggage. The saloon-keeper took a cut of the loot, and Mickey Finn and his wife earned national fame for the skill with which they separated their quarry from its money.

August Busch and other brewers well knew that many, perhaps even a majority, of the saloons tied to their beer profited less from lager than from larceny. When a well-known Chicago gambler declared bankruptcy not long after the turn of the century, he listed Anheuser-Busch as his main creditor. The Seipp Brewing Company advertised its saloons and beers in a guide to Chicago brothels. The brewers also understood that they were at least partly to blame for crime-ridden saloons: The barkeeper, leashed to his brewer, had no choice but to pay the brewer's prices, not least because he was already in debt to him for the price of the license, the fixtures, and perhaps his first month's rent. The only way an otherwise honest man could make a tied saloon profitable was by steeping himself in the dishonesty of gambling or prostitution.

Was every saloon a morass of illicit sex and organized theft? No. But there were enough of them that even the most respectable bars were tainted by association. Val Blatz found that out in 1884 when he announced plans to build a new saloon on a lot in a prosperous residential area. The news sparked an outcry from nearby property owners, and especially a group of developers who were planning to build $100,000 worth of new houses in the neighborhood (the equivalent of about $18 million today). Eighty residents signed a petition asking Blatz to back off. "Mr. Blatz," wrote the complainants, "would do better to establish his saloon, bowling-alley, etc., in some neighborhood where there is more demand for such an institution." Mr. Blatz obliged. The potential profits from the "club-house" were worth less than the headaches his antagonists would cause.

AT THE HEART OF the tied system, of course, was a brewer who needed to sell enough beer to recoup his investment in a sprawling plant filled with expensive machinery. Sell more beer every year: That was the brewer's goal. And if that forced him into retailing on one hand, it also prodded the largest among the beermakers to conquer markets far from home. The good people of St. Louis, for example, would never be able to drink as much beer as Adolphus Busch's ambition inspired him to brew. He had no choice, then, but to invest in long-distance shipping. But the larger his market grew, the more brewing capacity he needed; and the bigger his brewvats, the more beer he had to sell in order to make the investment in plant pay off.

That constant interplay between ambition and production in turn spun a vast web of warehouses, depots, train schedules, agents, and salesmen needed to move the beer from brewery to saloon to far-distant market. In the late 1880s, Busch, for example, built an agency depot in Fort Smith, Arkansas, complete with an icehouse, vault, bottling line, and stable. He opened an office in Toronto, constructed warehouses and bottling plants in Salt Lake City, and did the same in St. Augustine and Jacksonville, Florida, towns fast becoming posh winter resorts for the nation's newly wealthy. He staffed agencies in Chicago, New York, Philadelphia, New Orleans, and Savannah, and built and owned shares of breweries in Houston, Galveston, and San Antonio. The Uihleins saturated the upper Midwest with a string of warehouses and offices, and shipped tens of thousands of barrels of beer to California. So, too, Pabst, whose outlets ranged from the Dakotas to the Oklahoma Territory, and east to Pennsylvania and New York.

Saloons grabbed most of the headlines then, and much of the historical interest later, but the brewers like Pabst and Busch wanted their beers associated with tonier settings. Much of the barons' bottled beer ended up in brewery-owned hotels, theaters, and opera houses, swanky piles of marble, stone, and glass that featured high-tone bars where polite, white-aproned waiters dispensed company brew. The Uihleins' famous Palm Garden in their Schlitz Hotel in downtown Milwaukee featured a barrel-vault ceiling, Gothic-style stained-glass windows, an orchestra, and a forest of feathery potted palms. Busch and Pabst followed suit, Pabst most notably with his Manhattan properties: the Pabst Grand Circle, a theater and restaurant at Columbus Circle; Pabst Harlem, the world's largest restaurant, located in what was then a fashionable middle-class residential neighborhood, and the Pabst Hotel, a nine-story structure that stood at the heart of what is now Times Square and featured cuisine from the chef at Delmonico's, the nation's most famous restaurant.

Building the properties proved the easy part of long-distance shipping and sales. Acquiring and managing the necessary staff required finesse and patience. Emil Schandein spent much of his time on the road, wooing reputable beer dealers with promises of fine lager at low prices. In the spring of 1880, he visited Manchester, New Hampshire, where he courted the man who handled beers from George Ehret's brewery, hoping to persuade him to switch to Best products. The man was ready to listen, for Ehret's beer was "not as good" as it had been in past years and the agent was anxious to preserve his own reputation by selling only "good beer." Schandein accomplished his mission. "With this [new agent]," he crowed, he and Pabst had "crowded out [their] two biggest competitors" and rendered them "harmless" in the region.

If only it were always that easy. "[S]ecure such Men as you want to do the Work right at the KC. Branch," Pabst told his

Kansas City manager in 1882 with his usual flourish of emphatic underlinings, "& and we will then see what can be done with Redwitz but leave him down there until such time as we can dispose of him I don't want him here." Perhaps, he suggested, the manager could move Redwitz to Peoria, "because there is not a great deal to be done there." Pabst promised another salesman "a good warm overcoat" if he could sell "30 cars Bottled Beer to new trade" during September and October of 1880. An overcoat was a small price to pay: In 1888, that salesman soldiered through a staggering 350 days on the road, visiting saloons and buying rounds for the house, listening to bartenders' woes, wooing agents, and scolding recalcitrant customers in a sixteen-state territory that ran from New York and Pennsylvania to Montana, the Washington Territory, and California. His expenses averaged just over $16 a day (about $300 in today's money), which irritated the penny-wise Charles Best. "Danzinger uses money too freely," Best complained, and "has been talked to on this point."

At least Danzinger was honest. The same could not be said of Charles Best's brother Phillip, whom Charles hired in the mid-1870s to work in the company's office. Phillip repaid the favor with embezzlement, first in Milwaukee and then at the Kansas City branch, where he had been sent to make a fresh start. Upon being discovered, Phillip faked his suicide, a maneuver that distracted Charles, the local branch manager, and the police long enough for him to hop a train for Colorado. Pabst and Schandein absorbed the loss and moved on, but they had learned a lesson. In 1894, Pabst brought in the police after the manager of the company's Louisville office emptied the safe of $6,000.

The search for reliable men sometimes required dubious forms of enticement. "Concerning a suitable agent I regret to say that we have found none," Charles Best wrote to Joseph Billigheim, who managed sales in northern Wisconsin, suggesting that Billigheim pursue Miller Brewing's man in the region, a Mr.

Toepel. "Undoubtedly we would acquire in him a good, well-known and . . . well-liked agent and with him the Miller clientele and in this way drive our competitors out of the field." Best instructed Billigheim to offer Toepel $100 in cash and "a fine suit of clothes, or something of that sort (you understand)? . . . You can make it hot for him if you'll make him understand that otherwise we will give him colossal competition and that it would be a point of honor with us to crowd him out of his territory." Winning Toepel, Best added, would "immediately make us masters of the situation."

"MASTERS OF the situation." That described the baron's endgame: to make and sell the most beer, earn the most profit, and demolish the competition.

Gilded Age robber barons such as Carnegie, Rockefeller, and Gould demonstrated brilliance in creating and implementing new modes of business organization, but those accomplishments were overshadowed then (and for the most part still are) by the tactics they employed to control markets and crush competitors: They organized pools and cartels in order to fix prices. They forced railroads to offer rebates and special pricing, and created trust mechanisms that enabled them to skirt tax and incorporation laws.

So, too, the beer barons, who were as adept at such tactics as their more famous counterparts in steel, banking, and railroads, integrating vertically in order to reduce production costs and horizontally in order to absorb competitors. Pabst owned a power company that supplied energy to a theater, hotel, and office building that he owned in downtown Milwaukee. His stock farm provided the draft horses that hauled the brewery's beer wagons (which also functioned as rolling billboards). He and the Uihleins co-owned a barrel-making operation, the Delta Cooperage Company; the lumber came from 41,000 acres of timber the men held in Mississippi. Busch founded Manufacturers' Railroad, a small line that linked the brewery yard to the city's main rail line. His St. Louis Refrigerator Car Company supplied the company's cool cars. Bottles came from two company-owned glass factories or from a third in which Busch held shares. He owned all or part of coal mines, hotels, and banks.

Assets like these enabled Busch, the Uihleins, Pabst, and a handful of other giant brewers to integrate vertically and so reduce costs. But brewers also used price to maneuver and manipulate their markets, especially in the 1880s and 1890s, when they engaged in a series of price wars that ravaged the industry. When Uihlein or Pabst decided to invade new territory, he dispatched his advance guard—his agents—to scout the terrain. "[K]eep on the lookout," Fred Pabst, Jr., instructed his branch managers, "so that if you find that any of the shipping brewers [such as Schlitz or Anheuser-Busch] have taken trade from us, you can immediately report to us. In such instances we will make it our business to retaliate."

Translation: we'll lower our price. The operatives arrived armed with deeply discounted barrels—perhaps 50 percent less than the going rate in that town. Local brewers, smaller fry making only a few thousand barrels each year, lowered their price to match. The invader, armored by his giant beer factory and near-million-barrel capacity, lowered his again; the local lords replied with the same reduction. Sniffing the possibility of plunder, another baron's man charged into the fray, brandishing barrels priced even lower. Warfare ensued, lasting for weeks, sometimes even years. More often than not, the small local brewer gave up, leaving the titans to wage war amongst themselves.

In one contest, according to Adolphus Busch's grandson August "Gus" Busch, Jr., a group of small New Orleans brewers resisted Adolphus's efforts to control that city's trade. A prolonged struggle drove the barrel price well below the profit zone. Finally

Adolphus ended the conflict by informing the men that he planned to "control the price of beer for the next 25 years . . . whatever goddamn price I put on my beer, you go up [or down] the same goddamn price."

Gus, who claimed to have witnessed the encounter, re-counted the tale years later as evidence of his grandfather's wily ways and masterful control over lesser men. If the Busches invaded, say, Peoria, they could afford to wait out the competition; could afford to absorb the losses incurred by selling barrels at cost. Small local breweries could not. More often than not, the conqueror drove the conquered into bankruptcy.

The anecdote, though it captures the brutality of the struggle, is likely apocryphal. The most ferocious beer wars unfolded in the two decades prior to Gussie's birth in 1899. Adolphus's health failed in 1906, leaving him frail and wheelchair-bound; from then until his death in 1913, he spent most of his time in California or Europe. Even assuming the event took place as late as, say, 1910, when Gussie would have been eleven years old, Adolphus would not have been involved and his grandson would have been too young to comprehend the grownups' conversation, let alone re-member it accurately some seventy-five years later. More likely the tale evolved over the years as part of the mythology that sur-rounded a family of successful men with oversized personalities.

More to the point, Adolphus Busch was no fool and under-stood that price wars consumed time and energy better devoted to creating new markets or making fine beer. He laid part of the blame on salesmen, agents, and saloonkeepers. "The men we have to deal with," he argued, "are given to misrepresent facts . . . The traveling agents very often make false reports and try to get trade through misrepresentations and wrong statements; while they are out, they always endeavor to reduce prices . . ." Inevitably, he added, such false reports spawned "competition that helps to ruin the profits."

Besides, he argued in a letter written to Frederick Pabst in 1889, price wars were outmoded and the warriors "behind" the times. Instead of "fighting each other and running the profits down," he and other giant brewers ought to be "working in harmony" as manufacturers in other industries were doing. Busch overstated the extent to which harmony reigned elsewhere, but he was correct that in the 1880s and 1890s, many industrial magnates were experimenting with various forms of organization that allowed them to regulate competition and, in theory at any rate, avoid ruinous price wars. Pools, the most common form of association, were informal agreements among manufacturers of, say, salt, by which the members agreed on a single industry-wide price or established production quotas that enabled them to control supply and so artificially manipulate price—to their benefit rather than to that of consumers. Each member paid a sum into the pool's fund, monies they would forfeit if they violated the terms of this gentlemen's agreement. The set-ups never lasted long: One member, sniffing opportunity, would lower his price or raid another's markets, and a free-for-all would ensue.

"Now a perfect understanding between your good self, Schlitz, Lemp and myself ought to be reached [and] matters regulated," Busch suggested to Pabst. By "a concerted action, and interchange of courtesies, . . . we could easily fix and hold" prices and "realize a profit of a half million or even a million more" than was possible while the wars raged. "[Y]ou had better come down here," he urged, "so that we can talk matters quietly over . . . we are only hurting each other."

That was wishful thinking on the part of Busch. He, the Uihleins, Pabst, and other beermakers tried this system of price management, but late-century brewers' pools were no more successful than they'd been in other industries, lasting perhaps a few years at most. One or another member would violate the terms, launch an unprovoked attack on another member, or simply weary of the leash. Sometimes an effort to create a pool provoked the very warfare it was designed to constrain. That happened in Chicago. That city's brewers and outsiders who sold beer there, including, most likely, Pabst and Schlitz, agreed to form a pool. But one holdout, Manhattan Brewing Company, a small and recently founded firm, refused to join. The pool threatened to drop barrel prices down to three dollars, which they knew Manhattan Brewing could not match. Still the newcomer refused.

One morning, two Manhattan employees set off on their rounds delivering kegs to the saloons that carried the brewery's lager. An hour or so into the day, they realized that they were being followed by two men in a carriage. The Manhattan driver turned his buggy to block the street. He and the salesman jumped down from their wagon and confronted the other men—and learned that the pair had been hired by the pool to find out which saloons carried Manhattan's lager, with orders to report back so that the pool could pressure those saloonkeepers to drop Manhattan's beer. A "wordy altercation" ensued, which only ended when a passing policeman hauled all four off to jail. In that case, as in so many others, the pool collapsed soon after, and the ensuing price war provided Chicagoans with cheap beer for two years—until brewers called a truce and organized another pool. It, too, failed in short order.

Many small beermakers, bloodied by price wars and realizing that they could never fight the barons on equal terms, sought safety in numbers. Some relinquished their independence and banded together in "combinations," by which they traded their own stock for shares of the new single brewery forged from many small ones. The maneuver reduced the industry's numbers by hundreds, but in the end merely replaced shaky small independent outfits with only slightly less fragile medium-sized breweries.

Other brewers abandoned the fight altogether and sold out to syndicates of British capitalists, who arrived in the United States in the late 1880s seeking safe outlets for their money—safer, at any rate, than African mining operations, Mexican railways, and the boom-bubble-bust pyramid schemes of the sort lampooned in the novels of Anthony Trollope, more than one of which had parted plenty of Englishmen from their money. Some of the British investors bought flour or steel mills; others purchased cattle ranches. But the scent of lager proved the most intoxicating. Between 1888 and 1891, the outsiders snapped up dozens of breweries: seventeen in St. Louis alone, leaving Lemp and Anheuser-Busch as that city's only independents; nearly every brewery in the San Francisco Bay area; and most of the major Chicago brewers. In Detroit and Buffalo, Phoenix and Baltimore, Denver and Cincinnati, owners cashed in on the craze. Many of Milwaukee's smaller breweries closed their doors and reopened as cogs in the machinery of a syndicate. Valentin Blatz sold out for $3 million in stock (a staggering $60 million in today's dollars).

Not surprisingly, syndicate representatives hounded the barons, offering millions for their firms. In early 1890, the saloons and hotel bars of Milwaukee ran full with rumors that Pabst planned to sell for $10 million. The Captain was "very much annoyed" by the gossip. "It is the most foolish thing I ever heard," he told a reporter. His brewery was not for sale, nor, he insisted, would it be in the future. He added, "I am sick and tired to death of this whole syndicate business."

So read Pabst's public face. In private, he spoke otherwise. "There is no Piece [sic] from morning til night," he told Charles Best a year later. At times, he mused, "I think its [sic] a little foolish to trouble myself as I do, still I enjoy it, and will try it a while longer, anyway until I get ready to settle down on a good large farm where I can have a lot of land and water, that is where I could contend [sic] myself & be happy. I may by that time get ready to let the Englishmen have the Brewery. They are still after us, and have offered as high as 16,000,000$ still I refused, as I'm satisfied as things go, and not wanting to work for the Englishmen." The sum, he admitted, was "enough to make a man's hair stand on end," and tempting, too, if only because he was running out of steam. "I'm very glad of olden times," he confided to Best, "and like to think about how many pleasant hours we spend [sic] even if we did work hard." But, he added, "I should not like to go over it all again[.] [A]lthough I'm perfectly healthy & stoud [sic] I don't think I could stand the Racket again."

But the "Racket" was relentless, if only because, having made the decision to act on ambition and create one of the world's largest breweries, men like Pabst, Busch, and the Uihleins were forced to maintain constant vigilance, promoting and protecting the good name they had worked so hard to make famous. Every brewer engaged in salesmanship: Their saloons sported the company logos, which also adorned serving trays, glassware, and color posters. Souvenir books contained lithographic images of the brewery and its affiliated hotels, saloons, and gardens. Brewers sponsored *sangerfests,* the great German singing festivals held around the country. When Milwaukee hosted the twenty-third annual Encampment, or reunion, of the Grand Army of the Republic in 1889, Frederick Pabst funded the construction of a 35,000-seat amphitheater so that none of the veterans or their family members would have to pay the entry fee otherwise necessary to recoup the cost. That act earned him the gratitude of the tens of thousands of men attending the event, who altered their parade route so that it passed by the Pabst home and brewery on Chestnut Street.

No one understood salesmanship better than Adolphus Busch. Anyone who met him walked away with a penknife or deck of cards, a corkscrew or bottle opener, each decorated with the company's trademark eagle. The brewery furnished all of its saloons with a rotating collection of framed lithographs, the most famous of which was an engraved, and gruesome, depiction of *Custer's Last Fight*. All of this helped sell more beer, easy enough to do when the beer was so fine, but as Budweiser's popularity soared, Busch paid a price for his efforts.

Between March 1876 and December 1882, Carl Conrad had sold some twenty million bottles of Budweiser—a stunning achievement—but not enough to protect the liquor dealer from bad investments and his own inept management. In early 1883, Conrad filed for bankruptcy. While he weighed offers for what was left of his business and waded through a pile of overdue bills, he settled his debts with Anheuser-Busch by signing over to the brewery his remaining stock of Budweiser bottles and labels. Eventually Conrad decided to leave Budweiser in Busch's hands and the rest of his business in limbo. Three years later, however, having restored his financial health, he tried to reclaim his property.

Too late. Having tasted Budweiser's profit potential, Adolphus was reluctant to give it back. He and Conrad struggled over custody of the trademark for several years, and in January 1891, a year in which Busch sold fourteen million bottles of the beer, Conrad conceded defeat and granted Anheuser-Busch permanent rights to the Budweiser name. There was something of the inevitable in the acquisition. Since 1876, the beer had provided much of the profits earned by Anheuser-Busch and had made Busch and the brewery world famous: "I am very often greeted as 'Mr. Budweiser' instead of Mr. Busch," Adolphus was fond of remarking. His fame, his immense fortune, and his sons' futures all rested in large measure on the care he had taken with this one beer. To own it outright made that fortune and those futures that much more secure.

But as it had in the Lademan case back in 1878, Budweiser inspired dozens of imitators in the form of sometimes insipid lagers whose labels sported the same name. During the 1880s, Schlitz sold a version of Budweiser, as did the Budweiser Brewery in Brooklyn, Fred Miller Brewing of Milwaukee, Texas Brewing of Fort Worth, Prospect Brewing of Philadelphia, and the Westside Brewery in Chicago, to name just a few of the dozens of beer-makers who "borrowed" the name. Adolphus Busch disliked courtroom face-offs, but he despised those—whether it be the Uihleins or a two-bit brewer from Brooklyn—who tried to hitch a free ride on Budweiser's reputation. After Busch gained permanent rights to the trademark, he directed attorney Nagel to issue cease-and-desist letters to the usurpers. All but one of the brewers backed down. On May 20, 1893, Adolphus Busch filed suit against the last holdout: Fred Miller Brewing of Milwaukee.

Miller had earned a comfortable living selling beer to customers in surrounding states and operating a small distribution center in the Dakota Territory, but he never posed a serious threat to the barons. He did not introduce mechanical refrigeration until 1887, nearly a decade after Busch and Pabst had done so, and at the time of his death in June 1888, the brewery produced a mere 82,000 barrels a year, about what Fred Pabst brewed in a month.

Miller's sons, Ernest and Fred, Jr., wasted no time converting the cash inherited from their father's estate into new brewery equipment and buildings. The company had been selling bottled beer since 1883, but in 1889, Ernest Miller decided to add to his roster a beer brewed in the "Budweis" manner. Neither he nor his brewmaster had any idea how to make such a lager, so Miller wrote to Anton Schwarz, the New York brewing maven, requesting a recipe and detailed brewing instructions. When the materials arrived, he handed them over to his brewmaster and told him to get busy. Miller Budweiser was the result.

In 1893, Anheuser-Busch attorneys attacked on two flanks. They argued, first, that the St. Louis giant owned the name "Budweiser." In the 1890s, that was a risky maneuver: Trademark laws were a swamp of conflicting statutes and murky legal rulings, so proving ownership would be difficult, which was why Busch hired Rowland Cox, the nation's foremost trademark and patent lawyer. Cox also argued that Anheuser-Busch had invested millions of dollars to advertise Budweiser as an "exceptionally expensive, pure and superior product." The Miller brothers, in contrast, slapped Budweiser labels on an "ordinary" beer brewed with "very cheap and inferior" materials, and then sold the beer "for the express purpose of creating a false and fraudulent competition and unfair trade."

One fact emerged from the heaps of testimony presented in the case: Ernest Miller, a small-time, small-town brewer, was in over his head. His hometown newspaper described him as one of Milwaukee's "deepest, shrewdest, and ablest" and "most ambitious" businessmen. Perhaps that describes his acumen as a real-estate magnate—he and his brothers owned hundreds of saloons—but his testimony in the Budweiser lawsuit reveals a man who was either a first-class liar or a stunningly indifferent businessman, or both; a man, in fact, who knew next to nothing about beer and brewing. Rowland Cox had only to ask a few questions and then stand back and watch Miller dig his own legal grave.

What ingredients, asked Cox, differentiated Budweiser from the brewery's other lagers? Miller hemmed and hawed, and finally admitted that he couldn't answer the question. Cox reminded Miller that, according to the beer's label, Miller Budweiser contained "the best Bohemian barley." No, Miller responded; he never used imported barley. Perhaps in response to a look on Cox's face, Miller blamed the lithographer for the text. "I don't know whether [those words] are on the label at Budweis or not; probably that is the reason the lithographers put it on, I don't know."

"Do you mean to say," Cox responded, "it is possible your label was taken from a label used at Budweis, Bohemia?" "I say," Miller replied, "I don't know where that was gotten from . . . I don't know much about it." What about the label's color: red, the same as the Anheuser-Busch label. Was that a coincidence? Yes, replied the brewer. He and his brother "didn't care very much about the color" or, for that matter, anything else about the label. They had turned the entire matter of design—font, color, wording, everything—over to the lithographer.

Cox asked Miller to describe the technique used to brew Budweiser. Miller considered the request and finally replied that it was the same as any other brewing process. "You don't understand, do you," Cox retorted, "that the Budweiser process is materially different from the Pilsener process?" Well, replied Miller, perhaps there was some slight difference in fermentation, or perhaps in the mash or the temperature of the water. Perhaps.

Then how, Cox asked, could Miller be sure that his brewmaster was making Budweiser and not some other kind of beer? Because, the brewer replied, he had obtained information on the subject from Schwarz, the "greatest authority in the brewing business in America."

So Miller agreed that there was such a thing as the Budweiser process? "I am not quite sure as to that," responded an exasperated and perhaps exhausted Miller. "I am no brewer." He wanted to use the name Budweiser, and he had sent away for information, and he had told his brewmaster to make the beer, and as far as he, Ernest Miller, was concerned, that was that.

But why Budweiser?, Cox persisted. Why not some other name? Had Miller's clientele demanded a Budweiser beer? Did Miller know that Budweiser was popular with a "better class" of customers? "No sir," Miller responded. "Our customers asked for something different and we got it up." So the name is "just a matter of accident—is that what you mean to say?" queried Cox, who must have been weak-kneed from astonishment. "That is pretty near it, yes sir," replied Miller.

This was too much even for the unflappable Cox. "You did not know that the Anheuser-Busch Brewing Association were at the time you got up your beer selling millions of bottles of Budweiser annually? You didn't know that?" Miller responded with another verbal shrug: "Once in a while we heard of it up in this section, but it is not sold much." "I never traveled much down" toward Missouri, he explained. "I was only once in my life in that section of the country, and up in our section there was very little of Anheuser-Busch beer."

What about Chicago, Cox inquired. Surely Miller had seen or heard of Budweiser in a city where the Millers had sold beer for decades. "I know," insisted Miller, "it has only been sold there for a few years in medium quantities, and before that but very little." And, he added, as if to seal the point, he had laid eyes on a Budweiser bottle but one time. Miller Brewing had bought out the Anheuser-Busch agency in Duluth, including the agent's stock of Bud. Miller had taken a bottle back to Milwaukee and shipped it off for analysis, he explained in a statement that effectively undermined most of his previous testimony.

The addlepated Milwaukee David would never slay the self-assured St. Louis Goliath. "Miller Bros. are really of very little consequence now," Nagel wrote to Rowland Cox in late 1896. "They never were formidable competitors." He concluded, "As to the question, whether or not the case shall be finally pressed, we feel clear that really the main purpose of the suit has been accomplished; as competitors Miller Bros. sink into nothingness."

Nagel overstated the case, but on October 17, 1898, a judge ordered Fred Miller Brewing Company to stop using the name Budweiser. A century later, Miller Brewing would stand as Anheuser-Busch's most formidable competitor, but as far as Adolphus Busch and his crew were concerned in the 1890s, the enemy possessed all the menace of a housefly. Most interesting is what the case reveals about Adolphus Busch's understanding of the essence of entrepreneurial greatness. The threat in this case was not the Miller brothers' prowess—Busch's legal fees surely cost more than whatever piddling market share the Millers might have managed to steal—but the damage that a bottle of inferior Miller Budweiser might inflict on the reputation of Anheuser-Busch beer, which was among the finest in the world. The power and strength of the world's second-largest brewer, Adolphus Busch understood, lay not in the number of brewvats or refrigerated rail cars he owned, but in the public's perception of his beer. Only that mattered; only that guaranteed future prosperity.

BY THE EARLY 1890s, the brewing industry had sorted itself into three tiers: hundreds of tiny local independents; dozens of medium-sized American- or British-owned corporations, almost none of which would survive Prohibition; and a handful of family-owned behemoths: the world's three largest breweries, Pabst, Anheuser-Busch, and Schlitz, and slightly smaller but still huge giants like Ruppert, the Schaefers, and Ehert in the urban Northeast.

Frederick Pabst rested secure in his position as the largest beermaker in the world. He had much to show for a good life's work. "We have done & are doing a good deal of Building," he wrote to Charles Best in early 1891, "but we are in Shape now to sell 1,200,000 Bbls by only putting in 2 more kettles in the Brew House, which will be done this fall." "Our Sales this year will very likely reach 800,000 Bbls.," he added, a comment that no doubt provoked a shudder of apoplexy in Best, who would have calculated immediately the gap between capacity and actual sales. As it turned out, Pabst counted his barrels before they sold. "We will not quite reach the 800,000 Bbls," he told Best in December, "but will get within about 10,000 Bbls of it . . ." He blamed labor issues—striking brewery workers were boycotting Pabst-owned saloons. But the missed sales goal mattered less than the other, more important figure in the Pabst ledger books: "We will lead Busch over 100,000 Bbls."

The king of brewers ruled a brewhouse that dwarfed in every way the one he had first entered as a young man years earlier. Every remnant of Phillip Best's old brewery had vanished, replaced by a gargantuan fermentation factory where capital and labor paid homage to the gods of mechanization and automation, mass production and efficiency.

In the powerhouse stood fire-eating, smoke-breathing steam engines whose compressors, pulleys, and pistons harnessed more than a thousand horsepower. Their flywheels were sixteen feet in diameter, with three-foot-wide shaft belts and pulleys ten feet in diameter. The engines drove five, six, even seven thousand feet of shafting that coursed from floor to floor and building to building and powered the machinery that transformed barley into beer.

Mechanized hoists lifted the grain from street level to the upper reaches of three- and four-story elevators—massive upright brick rectangles that warehoused a quarter million bushels. Inside, conveyor belts transported it to machines whose gears, paddles, disks, and levers graded, separated, and ground the kernels. More belts and hoists whisked the barley from elevators to eight- and nine-story malthouses, where whirring mechanical arms washed and rinsed it, preparing it for germination. Atomizers sprayed jets of water over the golden heaps. Turning machines chugged along an endless loop of iron track: rectangular frames armed with giant screws whose threaded shafts burrowed into piles of grain, tossing and lifting the damp heaps, silent warriors that replaced the labor of dozens of men grown old before their time from the strain.

Conveyors fed the grain into the top floor of four-story kilns. Pumps spewed hot air that gently roasted it, and when it had partially dried, a solitary man cranked a handle fastened on the wall outside the drying room. Magic! The seemingly solid floor separated into ten-inch slats that rotated 90 degrees and dumped their loads onto a similar floor below, where more dry air flowed over the freshly turned grain. Massive grinding wheels—as large as old Phillip Best's first brewhouse—crushed the malt to a granular powder. Then to the brewhouse, a shrine of glass and light, gleaming copper and steel. Six or eight burnished brew kettles dominated the space, while another half dozen mash tubs stood sentry nearby. Ornate stair rails and balustrades guarded walkways that ran overhead and alongside the vats, all of it illuminated by enormous skylights and stained-glass windows.

As the wort simmered and the paddles, gears, and flywheels whirred, the temple's priests—university-trained chemists imported from Europe—worshipped at the altar of science. Their incantations produced pure yeasts that ensured the beer's stability or guaranteed a specific color or body. In the fermentation cellars, flywheels and pumps, gears and belts, transformed four- and five-story brick caverns into refrigerators fit for giants. This, the first successful application of mechanical refrigeration, freed brewers from the vagaries of weather and hulking mounds of expensive ice. It freed them, too, from the dank brick-and-flagstone caves that now lay empty save for bats and rats.

The crude "bottling" line of the 1870s—a handful of employees siphoning beer from vats into bottles—had been replaced by bottle-washing and capping machines, rackers and pasteurizers, siphon fillers and labelers, all of them automated. By the 1890s, bottles rattled through the washers' ninety-six spindles at a rate of 75,000 bottles an hour per spindle; Pabst needed nine hundred employees just to monitor the bottling operation, a far cry from the two hundred workers employed plant-wide twenty years earlier. Nine hundred barrels of beer flowed into the packaging department each day, and marched back out as orderly rows of bottled beer.

A century later, a new generation of beer enthusiasts would scorn "factory beer," but late-nineteenth-century Americans thrilled to the sights and sounds of the massive hulks that populated their landscape, whether steel mills, textile factories, or breweries, and found poetry in crankshafts and piston rods, cylinders and flywheels. Pabst and Schandein identified themselves not as brewers but as "manufacturers of lager beer." They and other beermakers advertised with "show cards," cardboard plaques that contained finely detailed images of their grand plants. These men prided themselves as much on the mode of making beer as on the beer itself. Their factories stood as monuments to their business acumen and to an era of unprecedented mechanical progress. True, many then (and now) also criticized the power and scope of the "machine," as if all the new factory tools, large or small, were appendages on the body of a sentient being intent on seizing control of humanity. But steel rails made it possible for families to migrate safely and quickly to cheaper western land, and machine-made clothes eased the housewife's burden.

The vast army of labor that toiled long days tending furnaces, lathes, and looms often resisted the factory's brutal regimen, lashing out at the growing power of white-collared owners and managers who toiled in clean, quiet offices. Millions of workers struck in the 1880s as employer and employee wrangled over the terms of engagement in the new economy. Brewery workers were among the highest-paid industrial employees in the country, but that did not stop them from calling strikes and boycotts, less over money than over their demands for union recognition and their brutally long working hours—as much as fourteen hours a day, seven days a week. As both sides knew, beermaking was a continuous process, and owners often granted concessions in order to keep the vats full. By the turn of the century, most brewery employees were working shorter hours and for more money than they had two decades earlier.

But the "Racket," as Pabst called it, required to build the monument had taken its toll. By the early 1890s, the empire-builders were tired. The life was hard, the hours long. Pabst had managed much of the burden of the hectic 1880s on his own, because Emil Schandein's health, never good, had deteriorated markedly in that decade, thanks in part to the scandal that ravaged his family.

During an 1874 trip to Germany, Emil and wife Lisette, daughter of brewery founder Phillip Best, met a sixteen-year-old named Jacob Heyl and invited him to return to Milwaukee with them. In 1886, Heyl married the Schandeins' oldest daughter, Louise, but Milwaukee gossips whispered that the union only provided a front for the affair between Mrs. Schandein and the young man.

In 1888, father and daughter died, both succumbing, perhaps, to broken hearts. Emil passed away while traveling in Europe and upon hearing the news, Lisette and Heyl set off across the Atlantic, ostensibly to arrange for the shipment of Emil's remains to the United States. They stayed six months. When the pair returned to Milwaukee, Lisette married Heyl off to her oldest living daughter, all but abandoned her other two children, and installed the newlyweds in her sprawling Grand Avenue mansion.

The ménage shocked Frederick Pabst and his family, but he and they had no choice but to endure the embarrassment: Emil's death elevated Lisette to company vice-president, and Heyl owned more shares of company stock than either Gustav or Fred Junior. "I often think," Frederick's wife, Maria, wrote in her creaky English to Lisette's daughter Ella, that Heyl, "the miserable one, should live in fear of your father's shadow in the house from which he pushes you children, like from the heart of your mother."

No doubt Frederick Pabst uttered a silent prayer of thanks that he had married a "good" Best. Maria; her father, Phillip; and her uncle and company secretary, Charles, had proved the few good seeds in a family otherwise gone very bad. Two of Charles's brothers were in prison; Lisette orchestrated not one but two sham marriages. Other Bests died young at their own hands. Henry Best, Phillip's only son, had long since taken his company shares and retired to a life of leisured wealth in Germany. Those familiar with the Best family history were not surprised when, less than a year after Schandein's death, Pabst persuaded the board of directors to abandon "Phillip Best Brewing Company" in favor of "Pabst Brewing Company."

Nor was Frederick Pabst about to let his own sons go awry. Gustav Pabst and his brother, Frederick Junior, had been prodded and pulled into the brewing life by a father who tempered discipline with trust and love. On Christmas Eve 1888, Frederick Senior gave Gustav, then twenty-two, $50,000 of company stock. "Now my dear Boy," he wrote in the letter that accompanied the gift, "you can be proud to be a Stockholder of the Ph. Best Brewing Co., and I hope you will use all your energy, to farther [sic] the interest, and promote the standing of the Company for which I have spend [sic] the best part of my life and whose Reputation is, as far as I know without Reproach. I wish you all Succes [sic] imaginable, and sincerely hope, that our feeling towards each other, and our Confidence in each other, will remain in the Future as they have been in the past. . . . [M]y dear Boy be reassured, and never forget that your Parents are allways [sic] your best Friends in time of Need or Trouble and never hesitate to come to us for advise [sic] or Consolation. . . . as ever your loving Papa."

Pabst tested his sons' ability to "promote the standing of the Company" with more than just stock. In the spring of 1890, he considered canceling a planned trip to Germany in order to oversee a necessary overhaul of the malthouse and extensive remodeling at two of his downtown Milwaukee properties, the St. Charles Hotel and the Opera House. Instead, the Captain seized the opportunity to test his sons.

"I made up my mind to go," he told Charles Best, "it was not necesary for me to go [*sic*]. But I wanted to know wether [*sic*] they could get along without me." The gamble paid off. "Now they do better without me. . . . It shows what men are made out of when you make them shoulder Responsibility, and I have long ago made up my mind the Business can be run without me. . . . I can begin to take it a little easier and still she goes." Time proved him right. "Everything is lovely," he observed a year later, "& the Goose hangs high," in part because of his beloved sons. "Gustav is out on the Road a great deal, I want him to get aquainted [*sic*] with the Trade. He seems to take hold very well and gives good Satisfaction. Fred. is in New York at Schwarzes [brewing school] and is doing very well."

Frederick Pabst was wise to confront head-on the occupational hazard of the self-made man: prodding sons raised in privileged ease to shoulder the burdens of the workingman's life. August Uihlein avoided the issue entirely: He amassed a fortune, but he required his children to work for their spending money. They reached adulthood well schooled in the relationship between work, money, and leisure. His brothers' sons chose nonbrewing careers, but August's three—Joseph, Robert, and Erwin— trained early for beer, studying beermaking at the Wahl-Henius Institute in Chicago and Carlsberg Laboratories in Denmark. Erwin topped off his formal education with a law degree, but that was not enough: August dispatched him and brother Robert on a study tour of breweries, sixty-eight of them in Europe and 134 in the United States. Each week the travelers cranked out a five-thousand-word report, an exercise that forced them to pay heed to even the smallest details of the firms they visited.

Adolphus Busch, in contrast, suffered excess of his own making: the love of his children. The Busch siblings grew up in unabated luxury, educated erratically by tutors or at posh private schools and vacationing in opulent surroundings. Of his three possible heirs, only one, Adolphus Junior, showed any inclination to follow his father's path. August A., the oldest surviving son (the eldest brother died young), was not above dirtying his hands and family name in an occasional barroom brawl, and in 1884, at age nineteen, unnerved his father by announcing his intention to abandon beermaking for the cowboy's life. Adolphus indulged that whim, and six months in the Southwest cured August of his passion. The young man returned to St. Louis to cast his lot with Anheuser-Busch; in 1889, both he and his brother Adolphus joined the board of directors.

Peter, the fourth born, preferred baseball, gambling, and drinking to work. At his father's prodding, the young man traveled the country checking on the company's distributors and dealers, but work played second to pleasure that too often spilled over into scandal. In 1898, Adolphus Senior cut him off, charging Charles Nagel with the mission of delivering the bad news. "Your father," the lawyer informed Peter, "declines to enter into further direction [sic] communication with you . . . He declines to be made responsible for you in any manner whatsoever. He denies any and all liability on account of anything that you may have done or may in the future do. He will not hesitate . . . to say this publicly." Busch softened the blow with a $25 weekly allowance, but, Nagel warned, "[h]e does not promise to continue this . . . [and] he will under no circumstances do more."

The St. Louis rumor mill claimed that Busch pinned his hopes for succession on Adolphus Junior. It was not to be: The old man's namesake died in the spring of 1898. That left August to carry the mantle, but the father struggled to corral this willful son. He demanded that August and family move into the Busch mansion next to the brewery, hoping, perhaps, to weave an umbilical cord of the plant's smells and sounds. August refused and settled his family several miles away at an acreage once owned by Ulysses S. Grant. There he built a palatial home that rivaled the minor castles of Europe and transformed its meadows and timber into a luxuriant landscape complete with swan pond and deer park.

The decision—and the expense—irked the old man. "I must repeat," Adolphus wrote, "that I am not at all pleased about it and feel sure it is going to divert your mind from business again, which is bad, because the brewery needs your whole attention and time." He pointed out that "everyone" who had purchased land on the fringe of St. Louis had "met with absolute failure," adding, "And I will tell you why; when anyone can afford to go away for the summer, they are not going to the outskirts of the city" to be "annoyed" by bad roads, "tramps, thieves and loiterers," "very bad neighbors" and "flies and mosquitoes." He concluded, "I do not want you to put any money in foolish improvements on this place. I am totally against it, and do not want it."

But August persisted. "Be moderate and sensible," his father pleaded. "It only hurts you to do this sort of thing. We have too big a business to take care of, and must keep our forces . . . together. We do not want to have it said that our brewery lost because the proprietors no longer gave it the attention it required, which they say of the Pabst and Lemp boys."

August Busch knew quite well that the Pabst "boys" were managing. (The Lemps were another story: William Lemp sired several sons, but none showed much inclination for the hard work needed to stay on top.) Still, Adolphus Busch had a point. Between them, the Busch and Pabst families owned the two largest breweries in the world (and elbowed each other in and out of first place every other year). They had arrived at that exalted status by marching a steep road lined with decades of ten- and twelve-hour days. They would only stay on top with more of the same. In that respect, the "boys" needed to be their fathers' sons—and more.

As THE SONS began managing their families' empires, the fathers turned to well-earned leisure and rest. August Uihlein devoted his time to travel and to horses. He owned one of the largest breeding operations in the United States, with stock farms at five locations scattered around the Milwaukee hinterland.

Frederick Pabst, too, feasted on the fruits of his labor. In 1892, he moved his family out of the old house that stood in the brewery's shadow and into a custom-built mansion on stylish Grand Avenue (now Wisconsin Avenue). Pabst spent nearly five million of today's dollars on the house and its furnishings, including linen and silk wall coverings, marble hearths, and oak and mahogany paneling. Pabst's cozy study included a built-in humidor, a faux-inlay ceiling decorated with German proverbs, and oak-paneled walls that concealed fourteen secret compartments.

The Pabsts also invested in livestock, which they kept at a 225-acre farm west of town. "It is grand out there," Pabst told Charles Best, "and I wish I could spend more time there." He and son Fred raised Percherons and Hackneys. Gustav devoted his leisure to hunting, which in turn fueled an interest in breeding and showing pointers and setters. Fred Junior developed a passion for scientific agriculture, and he bought fourteen hundred acres thirty miles west of the family farm in order to raise horses and Holsteins.

But as always, Busch outdid them all. His stable, surely one of the world's most ornate—it featured Tiffany stained-glass windows—housed a collection of Percherons and Mexican mules. The Busches exhibited the animals and their accessories—gold-plated harnesses and shiny red Anheuser-Busch beer wagons—at fairs around the country.

Adolphus and wife Lilly transformed Busch Place One, as they named the Victorian pile adjacent to the brewery, into "the most aristocratic" house in St. Louis. The family entertained presidents, senators, cabinet officers, and visiting royalty in the forty-foot-long Green or Rose rooms, each stuffed with velvet drapes and Aubusson carpets, ivory knicknacks and oil paintings, gilded tables and chairs, and ceilings slathered with angels and chariots.

Palms and miniature orange trees filled the conservatory; cloisonné and oversized vases the Chinese Room; pianos, stools, and mirrors the Music Room.

Busch's favorite residence, Ivy Wall, which he purchased in the early 1880s, sat amidst thirty acres of formal gardens in Pasadena, California. There he and Lilly entertained Theodore Roosevelt and President William Howard Taft, steel king Andrew Carnegie, and tea magnate Sir Thomas Lipton. Fourteen miles of paths wound through luxuriant grounds dotted with eucalyptus, willows, and oaks. Rare birds swooped through the trees. Busch spent well over a million dollars transforming the acreage into a child's playground imbued with myth and magic. Elves and gnomes stood sentry amongst the shrubs, and the parklands included a half-million-dollar replica of the Banbury Cross described in a nursery rhyme, complete with stream, waterfalls, waterwheel, and grinding stones.

Granddaughter Alice cherished "Rosy Wall," a three-room playhouse outfitted with upholstered wicker furniture, a kitchen and dining room, and a child-sized four-poster bed heaped with dolls. The "gnome house" delighted children and grownups alike. Busch would lead visitors through wooded paths, past a pond thick with water hyacinth and lilies, to a tiny round house nestled in fragrant shrubs. Guests knocked on the solid oak door and a voice called, "Come in." A collection of chairs circled the room within. "Little men," Busch would call, "send the table with the candy and cakes for my grand-child." Eyes widened as the floor rose up and out of the way, replaced by a table laden with sweets.

Most of the brewers had arrived from Germany as young men; as old ones, they renewed their ties with the homeland, returning in splendor to a land many had left penniless. Some purchased estates there and socialized with royalty. George Ehret's daughter, Anna, married a German baron, as did Helene Schmidt, daughter of Edward Schmidt, a Philadelphia brewer. Schmidt hosted the

$100,000 nuptials at his country estate, the aptly named "Baronial Hall."

Busch, too, reveled in the pleasures of European life and enjoyed first-name friendships with emperors, princes, and dukes. Three of his daughters married Germans. Clara Busch's union with Baron Paul von Gontard elevated her into the German aristocracy—she served as lady-in-waiting to the Empress Augusta Victoria—and strengthened Busch's relations with the royal family. That was as close as Prince Adolphus, as he was often called, ever got to becoming a real noble, but on formal occasions he adorned his chest with medals presented to him by German royalty: Kaiser Wilhelm granted him the Order of the Red Eagle and the Order of Philip the Good, while the Duke of Hesse bestowed the Order of Commercial Councilor.

EVEN AS THEY luxuriated in the leisure and splendor their wealth afforded them, the barons never lost sight of the main goal: to best each other, a task for which they still possessed plenty of fight. Pabst and Busch demonstrated their prowess in war at the 1893 World's Columbian Exposition, the last major engagement between the two grand old men of nineteenth-century brewing.

The Exposition, which commemorated the four-hundredth anniversary of Columbus's encounter with the new world, was the last and greatest of the nineteenth-century world fairs. During its run, from May 1 to October 31, twenty-seven million people visited the White City, as admirers called the array of buildings, pavilions, and plazas that housed an exhaustive and exhausting collection of exhibits demonstrating the latest advancements in industry and art: Caskets and toys; trains, plows, and cattle; George Ferris's wheel; zippers and cereal; an electric chair and Edison's kinescope all drew gawkers when the fair opened in May 1893.

Inside Agriculture Hall stood the "fermented beverages" exhibit, where the nation's brewers had installed displays such as the one constructed by Bartholomay Brewing Company of Buffalo: a four-foot-square mechanical model of the brewery's interior, complete with an eighteen-inch-tall ice machine and a twelve-inch-tall copper mash tub. "It is a working model in all respects," a journalist reported to his readers, "although owing to internal revenue regulations it is simply in motion at the Fair, and not brewing." Christian Moerlein of Cincinnati presented a pavilion that housed twelve life-sized figures, four representing the seasons, two each for the four major continents (Columbia and Pocahontas symbolized North America, Cleopatra and a servant, Africa). A full-sized statue of a horse bearing a life-sized image of "the standard bearer of the famous Bismarck regiment" reared up from the roof. Pocahontas, Cleopatra, and the rest of the figures, as well as pyramids of bottles, rotated, thanks to a two-horsepower engine hidden beneath the works. The more dignified horse and rider remained stationary.

But these were positively puny compared to the offerings from Pabst and Anheuser-Busch (the Uihleins set up a display, too, but in their usual modest fashion, made it so understated that it drew little attention). Adolphus Busch, who spent $15,000 on his installation, started with a twenty-five-foot-tall, gold-flecked iron and steel pavilion. Its soaring buttressed ceiling and arched open sides were lined with bottles of Anheuser-Busch beer and illuminated by light filtering through panes of glass positioned between steel ribs. Another row of bottles girdled the dome roof, and oversized winged nudes hoisting tankards of lager straddled a smaller arch at each corner. Inside the pavilion was a twenty-five-square-foot model of the brewery built by the company's architect, Edmund Jungenfeld. The model was "correct to the minutest detail," marveled a reporter from *Western Brewer*. It contained every building, brick, window, stack, and turret, as well as tiny horses and wagons; the Busch family's residence; the stable; the rail tracks complete with locomotive, freight, and refrigerator cars; and the streetcar system that ran alongside the plant.

Sadly, one feature of the Anheuser-Busch display can never be reconstructed: the look on Adolphus's face when he laid eyes on the Pabst exhibit. Frederick Pabst spent $20,000 on a terra-cotta pavilion that featured granite steps, tile floor, and gold-leaf decoration. A stained-glass dome rested on columns decorated with carved hop vines and topped with mythological figures supporting a frieze painted with scenes depicting the history of brewing. Enormous cherubim and other vaguely religious-mystical-medieval figures perched atop the roof, their various arms, legs, and wings dangling over the sides.

A mere roof, that pavilion, designed to shelter the wonder within: a detailed model of the brewery, thirteen feet square and plated in twenty-four-karat gold, for which Fred Pabst paid $100,000 ($1.9 million today). Three dozen Italian artisans devoted four months to sculpting and molding its pieces and parts. They carved tiny plaster-of-Paris reproductions of "every outline and detail of every building," fashioned wax molds from the carvings, and then cast the gold plates from the molds. "Nothing has been omitted," reported the awestruck correspondent, "from the figure of Gambrinus that crowns the arch over the Chestnut street [sic] entrance to the ornamental work about the top of the towering boiler house chimney." Streetcar and railroad tracks coursed gold-paved streets, and a tiny gold-plated train loaded with beer stood poised for departure from the shipping yard.

But the cherubim, marble, and models were mere overtures to the main event: the competition. Like the rest of the era's expositions, the Columbian lured exhibitors with the promise of awards, but the congressmen who created the 1893 fair envisioned an event loftier in tone than the century's other expositions. At this fair to end all fairs, exhibitors competed not against each other, but against a list of criteria that represented the standard of excellence for a particular category. Every entrant who met the standard would leave Chicago with a commemorative bronze medal and a parchment certificate. The White City's purity would thus remain unsullied by undignified brawls for grand prize and grubby scrimmages over medals and ribbons.

A noble goal indeed, and one that exhibitors, being not only human but seasoned combatants from capitalism's cruel wars, ignored. Nowhere was that more true than among the brewers, whose competition violated every official guideline laid down by Congress.

John Boyd Thacher, who chaired the Exposition's Committee on Awards, instructed the brewing judges to employ blind tests and rate the exhibits on purity, color, and flavor. Every exhibitor who scored eighty points or more out of the hundred possible would receive a commemorative Exposition medallion. Thacher warned the judges to keep track of points only as a guide, and otherwise to keep the numbers secret. Once a judge had deemed an exhibit worthy of award, he was to ignore the numerical scale and write a narrative describing that exhibit's "specific points of excellence."

Nothing doing, replied the five judges, all but one of whom were connected closely to either Frederick Pabst or Adolphus Busch. Instead, they told Thacher, they planned to award ranked prizes based on numerical scores, using a scale of their own creation: fifteen points for "brilliancy," twenty for flavor, forty-five for "chemical purity," and a final twenty for "commercial importance."

Twenty points for commercial importance? What did that mean? A reporter for *American Brewers' Review* nosed about the brewing gallery in search of an explanation. None of the Exposition officials could explain the category, but the other competitors drew their own conclusion. "We exhibitors have had some pretty lively meetings about the matter," announced the manager of Stroh Brewing of Detroit. "Nobody knows what the 20 points on 'commercial importance' are, unless to favor the large breweries over the little ones."

The judges defended their decision. A brewer who " 'march[ed] at the head of the procession' deserved credit for his achievements," explained a spokesman. A reporter arrived at the logical conclusion: The largest brewers—Pabst, Busch, Schlitz—would automatically earn twenty points. "Oh, no; by no means!," replied the judge. The reporter knew when he was beaten. The question of "commercial importance," he concluded, would remain "mysterious."

Harvey Wiley elevated the affair from the mysterious to the incomprehensible. Wiley, the chief chemist for the United States Department of Agriculture, supervised a temporary laboratory at the Exposition, where he and his staff analyzed every food-based exhibit. The chemist planned to test each beer entry against a standard sample he had brewed himself at the laboratory. Unfortunately, neither Wiley nor his employees knew how to brew beer, let alone analyze it, and the reference samples he and his staff concocted bore no resemblance to the expertly crafted lagers and ales submitted for judging.

In late October, as the fair drew to a close, the judges began affixing black-and-gold cards to the exhibitors' pavilions—temporary stand-ins for the bronze medals to be shipped later. Germany's Löwenbräu earned a medal for its bottled export lager, and Canada's John Labatt for his ale and porter. Adolph Coors, a small brewer who dominated the Denver beer market, received honors, as did three of the Uihleins' lagers. Between them, Pabst and Busch earned eleven awards for their various beers.

Through it all, the judges published the numbers. Flaunted the numbers. Tallied and coddled and fondled the numbers. Given the judges' passion for numbers, the exhibitors arrived at the only logical conclusion: He who racked up the most points won. Never mind that there was no grand prize. Never mind that each medal looked like every other medal, and nearly every exhibitor who showed up carried one home. The obsession with numbers spawned what a Milwaukee newspaper reporter described as "the hottest kind of rivalry" and the "bitterest fighting" between the world's two largest beermakers.

A Milwaukee newspaper claimed that Anheuser-Busch agents had been seen wooing judges and organizers with "suppers, banquets and less pretentious 'treats.'" One Chicago reporter claimed that some competitors had offered the beer jurors bribes—as much as a quarter million dollars. Another noted that many brewers had stayed home rather than deal with unjustified "self-puffing" and "manipulated" awards.

It's safe to assume that the gossip contained a kernel of truth. Only about two dozen of the nation's nearly two thousand brewers showed up at the White City. The judges' rejection of Thacher's rules oozed the odor of Busch, Pabst, or both. After all, if the jury followed the Exposition's official rules, Frederick Pabst would tote home the same medal as a two-bit brewer from Buffalo. If, on the other hand, the judges ignored official guidelines and insisted on awarding prizes based on point totals, the final numerical tally would enable the brewer with the highest score to pronounce himself the "winner." That said, there was no hard evidence then, and none now, of bribery or other pressure (not, of course, that there would be).

Skullduggery or not, Anheuser-Busch headed into the final round of judging with a two-point lead over Pabst. That was good enough for Adolphus Busch. On October 27, he posted an award placard at the front of his pavilion and placed announcements in the Chicago papers proclaiming ownership of a nonexistent grand prize and crowning himself "King of Brewers." "[B]y using the best barley and hops," Anheuser-Busch beers had "conquered the highest award" bestowed by a jury composed of "connoisseurs and chemists of the highest rank." Never mind that chemist Wiley had not completed his analyses or submitted his results. Never mind that the jury in this case consisted of a group of businessmen who knew nothing about beer and had neither declared a winner nor bestowed awards. Never mind, for that matter, that there was no winner to declare and no grand prize to bestow.

The Milwaukee contingent fought back. "The stuff published by Busch of St. Louis is rot of the worst kind," a judge friendly to Pabst informed a reporter. "It was simply presumption on his part" to anoint himself the winner. A reporter for the *Milwaukee Sentinel* claimed that the other brewers demanded to know "by what authority" Busch had been allowed to post the card. In a response every bit as disingenuous as Busch's bragging, the Director General replied that "he could not say." In fact, as he admitted later, he himself had provided Busch with the judges' numerical tallies and the certificate posted at the Anheuser-Busch pavilion.

The Exposition ended on October 31, and two days later, Wiley submitted the first of his analyses. Only three of the five judges were on hand to receive the results. They took one look at Wiley's numbers—and promptly changed them, claiming that Wiley had erred in his calculations. The new tally put Pabst ahead of Anheuser-Busch.

The two absent judges protested the move, arguing that they had neither read Wiley's report nor signed the scorecard. Thacher urged patience and calm, reminding them that Wiley had not finished his analyses and the tallies were not complete. But the rest of Wiley's scores only confused the issue, and in mid-November, the judges declared themselves deadlocked. A special supervisory committee voted to abide by the report that added the two points onto the Pabst score. Thacher announced the tallies (Pabst Brewing, 94.6 points; Anheuser-Busch, 94.3), declared the results final, and the brewing jury adjourned.

Frederick Pabst pronounced himself the grand prize winner and celebrated by draping his brewery in blue ribbon and giving his workers a day off. A nearly quarter-page ad appeared in the *Milwaukee Sentinel*: "PABST Milwaukee Beer WINS," read the headline. "A victory complete and absolutely unparalleled in the History of Expositions." Adolphus Busch pronounced himself robbed and filed a petition with the Exposition Court of Appeals. The hearing lasted five days, adjourning on November 28 so that the officers could "digest the voluminous evidence and arguments along with [their] Thanksgiving dinner."

Several days later, Harvey Wiley contacted Thacher and explained that back in October, one of the laboratory chemists had filed a report indicating salicylic acid in an Anheuser-Busch beer. That was an error, Wiley told Thacher. None of the company's samples contained acid and the judges should recalculate that score.

Skeptics no doubt see the hand of Adolphus Busch in this maneuver, and perhaps Busch prodded Wiley to contact Thacher. But it's doubtful that Busch did much more than prod. Wiley held a visible, responsible, and prestigious position as the nation's First Chemist. There was no reason for him to risk his reputation for a bribe. It's safe to assume that someone erred in the analysis of the Anheuser-Busch beer, since it's likely that most of the chemist's tests of two hundred beer and ale exhibits contained errors.

It's also unlikely that the Anheuser-Busch beer contained salicylic acid or any other additives. Adolphus Busch deserved his reputation as a maker of fine beers, which explains why he went to as much trouble over a phantom medal as he did over Miller Brewing's ersatz Budweiser: In the late nineteenth century, there were no laws governing advertising, so his competitors could broadcast the news about the mistaken analysis. A gullible public would swallow the story and lump the fine lagers of Anheuser-Busch in with the shoddy creations of lesser brewers, the kind who used bicarbonate of soda to produce a sturdy head of foam rather than long fermentation and quality materials. Busch insisted that Exposition commissioners clear his name.

On December 21, the players reassembled to hear the Appeals Committee's findings. If either Busch or Pabst expected a clear verdict, they were disappointed. The committee reminded the audience that there was no prize to be won, and anyone who claimed otherwise spoke in error. The appeals committee ordered Thacher to eliminate, destroy, and otherwise eradicate any and all evidence of numbers from the reports.

Those words fell on deaf ears. Busch continued to demand a public correction of the mistaken test results and a return of the five points deducted from his score. The Exposition's executive committee pondered his request, studied the chemical tests, and consulted with Wiley. Then, for reasons known only to themselves, they turned the whole messy affair over to Dr. Lichtenfeldt, a German who had served as one of the five brewing judges. Figure it out, they told him, and we will abide by your decision.

The indefatigable Busch departed for Europe to search for Lichtenfeldt, traveling from Berlin to Paris to Baden-Baden, where he nabbed his quarry and sat him down for some "fine diplomatic talk and 1862 wines . . . You have no idea," Busch told son August, "what tricks were resorted to. I found out things in Berlin which I never expected. Pabst wanted to win at all hazards and at any cost." So did Adolphus Busch. He emerged from the wine-and-dine with Lichtenfeldt's letter affirming the purity of Anheuser-Busch beer.

'Twas to no avail. By the time the document reached the United States, the members of the executive committee had performed another about-face: They refused to consider the letter and pronounced the matter closed. The delighted Frederick Pabst drew his own conclusion: He had won the nonexistent prize. More than a century later, Pabst Blue Ribbon labels still read "Selected as America's Best in 1893."

Busch, outraged at the loss and infuriated by the insult to his beer, refused to abandon the fight. Many months later, he won a small victory: a court order directing the officials of the World's Columbian Exposition to issue an amended score card that returned those five stolen points to their owner. Still, the episode soured Busch on medals and prizes, which, he told August, "are not given to the goods meriting same, but are secured by money and strategy."

BUT THE DAYS when the two titans had the energy for such conflict were dwindling. By the turn of the century, both Busch and Pabst had handed affairs over to their sons. To no one's surprise, they found it hard to let go. Even as he eased into full-time retirement, Frederick Pabst kept the brewery—and his sons—clipped to his leash. "You ask me Gustav do I want more details of the business?" he wrote from Wiesbaden in 1901. "I don't want little details. But I would like to know something about the Cuba Plant, how New York is doing, what are you doing in Chicago, are you building?" More than a month had passed since the directors' annual meeting, he complained, "and I haven't heard nor seen a particle of it." Such "negligence" on the part of the company secretary, Charles Henning, could not be tolerated. "I think a great deal of Henning as you *know* but he must wake up. Things *must* be kept up, and we must be alive, or take a back seat" and let others "run away" with the business.

Two years later, in January 1904, Frederick Pabst died at home in Milwaukee, surrounded by his family, succumbing to the diabetes, emphysema, and heart disease that gnawed at his health during the last years of his life. The entire city mourned a man much loved, not just for his kind heart and fine character, but for the thousands of jobs he had provided, for his countless acts of charity, for his spirit, and yes, his ambition. "I can truly say," remarked one of Pabst's old friends, "that I never met a man of who so many good things can be said, and who will be more genuinely regretted by every one in the city, rich or poor."

Adolphus Busch outlived his friend and competitor, although he, like Pabst, suffered from poor health in the last years of his life. From 1890 until his death in 1913, Busch spent little time in St. Louis. Most summers, he and various children, grandchildren, brothers, cousins, and assorted in-laws and hangers-on sailed to Europe to enjoy the majestic grounds at Villa Lilly, ten miles from the Rhine River at Langenschwalbach near Wiesbaden. Sometimes he loaded the family onto his private rail car, the *Adolphus,* for a sojourn at his residence on Otsego Lake near Cooperstown in upstate New York. "Let us meet in Cooperstown," Busch cabled Nagel in 1910. "We will go fishing and sailing, we will sing. Who does not love wine, woman, a fine dinner, a good cigar, cheerful company and song, shall not live a life long."

No surprise, Busch, like Pabst, wanted the best of both worlds. As he traded the working life for leisurely travel, he longed to enjoy his children's company even as he dictated to those children how to manage the brewery. In a 1903 letter, Busch demanded to know when son August would join him in Europe for hunting and horse-buying. "[Y]ou are such a daisy hunter and companion. I wish you could have arranged to come over if only for a couple of weeks. . . . I really would enjoy a [visit] from you if you can be spared from business, which I hope you can when everything is running smoothly." Given that the rest of the long missive consisted of demands for details about the brewery as well as a lengthy to-do list, August might well have wondered how he was supposed to maintain the "world wide fame" of Anheuser-Busch and live the gentleman's life, too.

But the brewery was not the only aggravation wrinkling the brow of Adolphus Busch during the last decade of his life. Frail and wheelchair-bound though he was, he was not too ill, nor too weary, to fret over the enemy massing at his empire's borders.

CHAPTER FOUR

The Enemy at the Gates

I N MAY 1893, the American stock market collapsed and launched the first great depression in American history. Before the year ended, five hundred banks and some sixteen thousand businesses had shut their doors.

In May 1893, the gates opened at the World's Columbian Exposition and brewers girded their brewvats for the contest over nonexistent prizes.

In May 1893, Anheuser-Busch Brewing Company, having sold about seven of the fourteen million bottles of Budweiser that customers would drink that year and anxious to protect its golden egg from cheap imitators, filed suit against Miller Brewing Company.

And in May 1893, Howard Hyde Russell launched the organization whose anti-drink campaign would end the manufacture and sale of alcohol in the United States—and American brewing's first golden age.

RUSSELL WAS BORN in 1855 to missionary parents. He spent his twenties working as a lawyer, drinking socially, and thinking of alcohol, if at all, only insofar as the making, selling, or drinking of it collided with the law. But in 1883, he attended a church revival and experienced a religious awakening. The Almighty guided him to divinity school at Oberlin College, an Ohio institution noted for its dedication to free thinking (as early as the 1830s, its faculty welcomed women, Native Americans, and African Americans) and, in the 1880s, a prime breeding ground for Christian activism. There Russell developed a passion for social reform in general and temperance and prohibition in particular.

He was not alone. In the 1880s and 1890s, an entire generation of Americans turned their attention toward remedying society's ills, of which, it seemed, there were entirely too many and mostly urban in nature. The number of cities and their size soared in the late nineteenth century, thanks to the combination of immigration—there were ten million newcomers between 1870 and 1900—and rapid industrialization. The nation's municipalities also served as the great laboratories of the age, where Americans first encountered electricity, mass transit, centralized water supply, and sewer systems.

The task of building the power plants, laying the trolley tracks and water and sewer pipes, and digging the tunnels for subway systems fell to immigrant laborers, who, along with factory and sweatshop workers, all of them underpaid and undernourished, crowded into tenements where disease and hunger made them old before their time and where one-quarter of babies died before their first birthdays. At the other end of the urban spectrum were the (mostly) men who designed the tenement buildings, sewer systems, and trolley cars, college-educated professionals for the most part, the offspring of a growing number of colleges that adjusted their curricula to meet the needs of the industrial age. New graduate and professional programs generated cadres of credentialed specialists—engineers, sanitarians, social workers, sociologists, and urban planners—to analyze, plan, and build industrial America. The job of dispensing the contracts for the work, however, landed in the hands of local politicians, who seized on the millions of dollars in fees and the thousands of jobs as means for lining their pockets and building armies of voters who expressed their gratitude on election day.

The result was an ugly collision of ambitions, agendas, poverty, pollution, and crime that inspired a new generation of reformers. Jane Addams founded Hull House in Chicago in 1889; dozens more "settlement" houses opened in other cities. There, middle-class men and women struggled to bring order to the chaotic neighborhoods around them. The morass of municipal corruption and cronyism inspired campaigns for "good government." The "goo-goos," as the skeptical called them, wanted to bring professional management to city hall; wanted to separate city governance from politics (in the nineteenth century, city officials ran on party tickets); and wanted a secret ballot, which would sever the link between the ward boss and the immigrant grateful for work. They wanted, in short, to make the city as efficient as the corporations that managed the nation's railroads and steel mills.

But the factories and railroads generated their own brand of activism. In 1881, workers challenged the tyranny of corporate overlords and the six-day workweek by organizing the American Federation of Labor, an association of unions of skilled workers in various trades who banded together in order to meet their employers as equals. They used strikes, walkouts, and slowdowns to achieve what they called "collective bargaining." The tactics sometimes worked, but the AFL's first two decades were marked by violence, as men like Andrew Carnegie and John D. Rockefeller refused to bargain, collectively or otherwise, and dispatched local police or armed company guards who battled the workers in combat that often turned deadly.

While workers struggled, a new breed of muckraking journalists detailed the crimes of corporate America. Rockefeller's Standard Oil became the poster child for growth gone wild. He persuaded, if that word can be used for the promise of destruction to those who refused to oblige, his competitors to surrender their company stock and independence for shares of a larger "trust," Standard Oil, of which—no surprise—Rockefeller held the largest chunk. By 1880, the trust controlled 95 percent of the nation's refining capacity. Its legal structure was more stable and inviolable than that of a pool, and so giants in other industries followed suit, and by the late 1890s, a host of industries were controlled by companies that held an oligopoly or monopoly over production.

Much good came from the reformers' welter of exposés, organizing, and agitation: the secret ballot and the eight-hour workday; statutes outlawing child labor and insurance fraud; city parks and potable water; railroad crossing signals and lower infant mortality rates; unemployment compensation and the minimum wage. Civil service laws replaced patronage positions with jobs earned by testing and merit.

These successes were not hard to understand: Like their counterparts fifty years earlier, the late-century middle class was sincerely concerned about the nation's future. Mostly educated, white, and Protestant, they believed that it was their duty as citizens to eradicate the ills that had beset a nation enduring the tumult of industrialization.

Not surprisingly, one group of reformers turned its attention to alcohol. Saloons and drink, they believed, plagued the nation, and like prostitution, urban poverty, and lynching, drink and its bedfellows were particularly overt and thus identifiable evils. By the early 1880s, the anti-alcohol movement, badly wounded by party politics before and during the Civil War, had regained its health and two groups of activists had emerged to carry the flag for a dry America.

The older of the pair was the National Temperance Society (NTS), an amalgam of church organizations and what was left of antebellum temperance groups. Determined to avoid the political morass that had injured dry efforts before the war, NTS members focused on education rather than direct political engagement, publishing two monthly magazines as well as a plethora of pamphlets and books. Thanks to hefty donations from J. P. Morgan, Rockefeller, and other wealthy benefactors who loathed the effects of drinking on the nation's workers, the NTS distributed the materials for free to any person or group who wanted them. Much of the literature ended up in churches, and especially Sunday school classrooms.

The second, and more powerful, group, the Women's Christian Temperance Union (WCTU), also emerged from Christian activism. In December 1873, a group of Hillsboro, Ohio, women, inspired by a speaker who had visited their town, decided to march against drink. One hundred or so women gathered at a church to pray and brace themselves for their work, then paraded into the streets and marched to the city's eight liquor retail outlets. At each stop, the women demanded that the male owners abandon their devilish business and prayed for their redemption. Over the next year, women in more than nine hundred towns in thirty-one (out of thirty-seven) states and the District of Columbia closed hundreds of saloons, persuaded thousands of people to sign pledges of abstinence, and then founded the WTCU.

By the early 1880s, the organization boasted more than 73,000 dues-paying members, with local units and paid staffs in nearly every state and territory. The WCTU, like the NTS, served up a hefty dose of anti-alcohol education, but coupled that with agitation for legal action that promoted a dry America. The women could not vote—except in a few school districts in a few states— but they persuaded nearly every state legislature to require public schools to provide pupils with "scientific temperance instruction." According to a standard textbook, "[t]he constant use of beer is found to produce a species of degeneration of most of the organism," causing "fatty deposits," poor circulation, and congestion. Many school districts ignored the law or adhered to it using textbooks that offered a neutral view of alcohol, but the WCTU's persistence kept the issues of temperance and prohibition in the public eye and on politicians' minds.

The combined efforts of the WCTU and the NTS produced results. In the 1870s and 1880s, eighteen states pondered the passage of prohibition amendments, and six approved them. In thousands of cities and counties, voters, boards of supervisors, and city councils refused to renew licenses for saloons and drugstores that sold alcohol. Municipal officials and police departments cracked down on long-ignored Sunday closing laws. In hundreds of locales, the "high license" movement raised the cost of operating a saloon from $50 to $500 or even $1,000, thereby running many saloonkeepers out of business—or, more typically, into the arms of beermakers who agreed to pay the license in exchange for "tying" the saloon to that brewer's beer.

The crusaders also used the "pure food" craze as a means of attacking brewers. As more and more food came from factories rather than local farms or backyard gardens, Americans had become increasingly unnerved by the possibility that giant food processors were more concerned about profits than about purity. A federal pure food and drug act, and *The Jungle,* Upton Sinclair's novel that spurred passage of the law, were still several decades away, but as early as the 1870s alarms were sounded over tainted oleomargarine, foul milk, and contaminated canned goods. Then George T. Angell, a Massachusetts lawyer and reform enthusiast whose interests ranged from preventing cruelty to animals to exposing the dangers of deleterious foods, added fuel to the fire by publishing his "reports" about the state of the nation's food supply. He purported to have studied the matter in depth, but his conclusions consisted of an amalgam of exaggeration, half-truth, and outright lies about maggotty meat, copper-tainted pickles, dyed pepper, and butter and cheese concocted from "the filthiest fats of diseased animals."

The nation's press, always delighted to regurgitate the sensational and provocative, printed his reports with gleeful abandon. Physicians, university chemists, and public health officials denounced Angell's research and pleaded for calm. But lurid and shocking trumped reasoned and measured, especially at a moment when the pace of change in the United States seemed to have ratcheted out of control. If John Rockefeller could control oil supplies, and if railroad magnates could sell watered stock to a gullible public, why not assume the worst about food manufacturers?

One of Angell's favorite bugaboos was glucose, a corn-based sweetener that had been widely used for decades to make candy, honey, and syrup. Manufacturers soaked corn, separated its starch, and then employed sulfuric acid to convert the starch into sugar. Angell claimed that glucose makers dumped filthy rags, floor sweepings, and acids into their vats, and the ghastly mixture was bottled as syrup or honey and passed on to consumers. Spurred by his nattering attacks, researchers at the National Board of Health, a short-lived federal agency, studied the stuff in minute detail. The analysts concluded there was nothing inherently dangerous about glucose, except, perhaps, to those with an insatiable sweet tooth.

Unfortunately, the NBH staff also reported that brewers added glucose to their mash as a cheap substitute for barley. It was true that some brewers did so, but their numbers were few and there was nothing harmful or dangerous about the beer they made. In one well-aimed fusillade, the NTS and WCTU grabbed this ammunition and charged brewers with selling dangerous beer laced with glucose and acid, a baseless accusation that any chemist could dismantle in the space of a minute, but one that rang alarm bells in the minds of a suspicious public.

The owner of a struggling Milwaukee newspaper in search of a scoop had used the moment to attack the city's beermakers. "It is well known," the investigating reporter informed readers, "that the brewers are a poor, struggling heaven-forsaken class" who, when faced with rising barley prices, turn to "cheaper substitutes." As proof, the reporter listed the amounts of corn and rice purchased recently by several of the city's brewers, starting with Phillip Best Brewing Company and ending with Fred Miller. Over the next few weeks, the newspaper blamed Milwaukee's high infant mortality rate on "spurious beer" and pointed out that the "oriental races," who subsisted on a diet of rice, were "dwarfed in features, body, morals and intellect." A local physician informed readers that beer brewed from rice caused diarrhea, upset stomach, and brain damage.

A second local newspaper, not to be robbed of this episode of high drama, had chimed in with charges that rice and corn beer caused "temporary insanity," presenting Emil Schandein as the main exhibit. According to the reporter who witnessed the event, during a night of drinking, Schandein (who had been arrested at least once on charges of being drunk and disorderly) had become violent while suffering the "temporary insanity" caused by "rice and corn beer." The witness claimed that Schandein railed against temperance do-gooders and nosey newspaper reporters but remained silent on the subject of his brewery's "secret drug store," where a "French practical chemist" was paid a "fancy salary" to teach Schandein the secrets of chemical adulteration.

Among the city's brewers, only Frederick Pabst had mounted a defense. "[W]e have constantly aimed," he explained in an interview with a reporter, "to provide an article suitable to the demands of trade which shall at the same time be wholesome and free from all impure or harmful ingredients." Pabst also dismissed the accusation that the city's brewers had abandoned barley in favor of cheaper adjuncts. Rice, he explained, cost fifteen or twenty cents more per bushel than barley. At Best Brewing, he added, "[w]e are not aiming to make the cheapest beer in the market; we are trying to make the best beer."

But the idea that beer made with anything other than barley constituted adulteration had taken hold of the public imagination. In the summer of 1881, the Business Men's Moderation Society (BMMS) of New York City submitted a detailed questionnaire to that city's brewers demanding to know if their lagers contained corn, rice, glucose, grape sugar, potato or corn starch, or molasses, and if so, why. The BMMS hounded New York brewers for more than a year, testing one beer after another until it finally found one that contained glucose. The *New York Times* dutifully printed the nasty exchange of letters that followed, as the brewers accused the BMMS of cheating, and the BMMS charged brewers with fraud. And nearly every article or letter that the *Times* published ran below a large-type headline that contained the words "brewers" and "adulteration."

Plenty of Americans already doubted the wisdom of imbibing alcohol; easy enough, then, to take the next step and imagine brewers as corporate crooks more concerned with profit than with the public's well-being, whose factories churned out millions of gallons of vile poison. Accusation spawned action. The New York State Board of Health authorized an investigation into that state's brewers, and legislators in several states contemplated statutes that would require brewers to use nothing but malt, hops, and yeast. In 1888, Harvey W. Wiley, chief chemist at the U.S. Department of Agriculture, published a report on fermented beverages that claimed that American brewers used salicylic acid as a preservative, an additive that was cheaper than pasteurization but one that caused "mental disturbance" and "violent delirium." Only a careful reader would notice that the study offered no proof of the presence of the acid in the samples tested. Why? Because the researchers had not found any. Still, the distorted results were widely reported in newspapers. "*Acid in the Beer,*" announced the headline above an article that informed readers that "beer is generally adulterated with acid poisonous and injurious to health."

HOWARD HYDE RUSSELL watched, listened, and learned. Ohio provided an excellent training ground for the fledgling reformer: The state's largest cities, heavily German in population, contained dozens of breweries and hundreds of saloons, providing ample opportunity for agitation. He fulfilled his seminary ministry in Brea, Ohio, where, combining his skills as preacher and attorney, he closed saloons with one hand and prosecuted drink-law violators with the other.

In late 1887, members of an Oberlin-based temperance group persuaded Russell to lead a campaign for a state local option law. Local option was fast becoming the temperance movement's most powerful weapon. It enabled voters to stamp "wet" or "dry" on individual precincts, wards, townships, municipalities, and counties, and so close saloons or ban retail sales of liquor in grocery stores or drugstores. Since a local option vote affected only a tiny and specific segment of the electorate—only the residents of a single precinct or town—dry campaigners needed to capture far fewer votes than they would to pass, say, a referendum on statewide prohibition. Under Russell's leadership, the campaign succeeded.

Upon graduating from Oberlin in 1888, the newly frocked Congregational minister headed west to Kansas City and service in an urban mission, then moved to Chicago and worked as director of the Armour Mission, a Christian-service foundation funded by the Armour meat family. There he became even more convinced that society's evils would end only when drink had been eradicated from the land.

But for every victory that the WCTU or the NTS achieved, for every local option law or high license fee, there were a half dozen failures, and Russell's experiences in the courtroom, pulpit, and statehouse led him to an uncomfortable conclusion: The American temperance movement was in trouble, crippled by in-fighting and fragmentation. One faction within the WCTU wanted to remain nonpartisan, but another wanted to fold the battle against drink into a larger crusade against prostitution, child labor, and insurance fraud. Some members of the Prohibition Party insisted on maintaining its independence; others longed to merge with the Republican Party. Russell concluded that power struggles and excessive democracy sapped the movement's energy and confused and distracted its foot soldiers.

In a stroke of genius inspired in part by the corporate organizations that had drawn so much of the reformers' fire, not least of them the giant breweries, Russell envisioned a new mode of fighting the liquid devil: an anti-drink organization structured like a modern corporation and operated as a dictatorship rather than a democracy, the former being more efficient than the latter. Full-time, paid directors would set policy and plan strategy; full-time, paid managers would carry them out. The dictator-leaders would generate one product and one product only: a campaign against the saloon. No hand-wringing over the horrors of prostitution, no detours into campaigns against child labor or for woman suffrage. One leadership. One issue.

And one goal: to eradicate the saloon and every other liquor and beer retail outlet. Russell's reasoning was elegant in its simplicity: As the number of places to buy liquor declined, so, too, would the number of Americans who imbibed. As customers vanished, so would distillers and brewers, and the nation would be freed of a terrible scourge.

Russell's genius lies partly in his conceptualization of what we know today as the single-issue interest group, but he deserves credit as well for his recognition of the pitfalls of political machinations. The group he envisioned would be strictly nonpartisan and support any candidate from any political party as long as he promised to vote against the saloon.

But the key to Russell's eventual success lay not so much in structural creativity as in his grasp of a single salient fact, one that had escaped other anti-drink crusaders: Americans were not ready for outright prohibition. The proof lay in the numbers: In the late 1870s and early 1880s, eighteen states considered prohibition amendments but only six had passed them, and one of those states, Rhode Island, had repealed the ban almost immediately. Perhaps the lessons of the 1850s were still fresh in some people's minds; perhaps Americans feared such excessive intrusion into otherwise private lives.

Whatever the case, Russell intuited that Americans would have to be led to the holy grail by small steps and only after years of education had paved the way. Any organization that campaigned overtly and directly for constitutional prohibition would lose. So Russell conceived of his campaign as not *for* prohibition, but *against* saloons, an easy target given their association with crime and given Americans' passion for cleaning up their cities. That limited and specific goal would satisfy the extremists, reassure the uncertain, guarantee a steady string of successes from the outset, and, most important, teach Americans to accept, eventually, Russell's final goal: constitutional prohibition.

IN MAY 1893, the executive board of the Oberlin Temperance Alliance adopted Russell's ideas and reorganized as the Ohio Anti-Saloon League. It appointed him as its first superintendent at a salary of $2,000 a year, about $40,000 today and a stunningly optimistic figure for an organization that had no other employees, no specific plan of operation, and, at that moment, a grand total of $513 on hand.

Russell hired a recent Oberlin graduate named Wayne Wheeler to be his second-in-command, and the pair charged forth, laboring eighteen hours a day, seven days a week. They wrote and delivered anti-drink sermons and lectures to Ohio's ministers, who spooned them out to their flocks on Sunday, which, persuaded of the League's value, paid for the pleasure by handing over the donations needed to keep the OASL in business and its printing press running. On the other six days of the week, the temperance faithful gathered at League-sponsored rallies and picnics, where they handed over still more money in exchange for food, (non)alcoholic drink, and more temperance rhetoric. "In those first few years," Wheeler later recalled, "we had all we could do to raise the money to pay actual expenses, railroad fare, rent, etc." But the well-plowed field returned a rich harvest: In the organization's first two years, Ohio voters ousted a wet state senator in a key legislative district and cast local option votes that closed four hundred saloons.

Anti-drink enthusiasts in other states sat up, astonished at the rapid transformation in Ohio, heretofore a bastion of lager and liquor. In December 1895, Russell traveled to Washington, D.C., to meet with temperance faithful from church groups, the WCTU, and the Prohibition Party, all of them eager to copy his methods. He and they agreed: "The Saloon Must Go!," and so was born the National Anti-Saloon League, later the Anti-Saloon League of America, and, to most Americans, simply the Anti-Saloon League, or ASL. The national office functioned as a parent organization that spearheaded the creation of smaller Leagues in every state, each of them modeled after Russell's "Ohio Plan," each of them pointed toward the same task: electing sympathetic politicians who would support local option, so that voters could eliminate the saloon. The orders flowed from the top down, and the money from the bottom up—tiny donations for the most part, collected at thousands of churches from millions of disciples. Organizers elected Russell as the first national superintendent and charged him with the task of rallying the supporters needed to create the separate state leagues. There he stayed until 1903, managing the details on which the crusade depended.

Chief among them was the League's printing plant, from which poured literature for the state leagues' campaigns, picnics, and rallies at the rate of forty tons a month: pageant scripts, stories, and poems for children; ready-made sermons for the convenience of finger-pointing, fist-shaking ministers whose pulpits linked the League's leaders to its foot soldiers and their money; and posters, pamphlets, and sheet music (crusaders marched to the cadence of "The Saloon Must Go": *I stand for prohibition / The utter demolition / Of all this curse of misery and woe; / Complete extermination / Entire annihilation / The saloon must go"*). The ASL also published several monthly magazines (including the *New Republic*) and the *American Issue,* a weekly compendium of news, essays, and exhortations mailed to dues-paying members and designed to inspire the troops and keep them on issue and on target.

"The Headquarters for Murderers," screamed the headline above one article, which argued, "The saloon is the resort of the underworld [whose] inhabitants swarm like maggots." Another essay linked the "twin evils" of saloon and brothel, and insisted that "every man who votes for the liquor traffic is indirectly voting to create conditions" that nurtured prostitution. "[W]hen the saloon comes to town," warned another writer, "the children are forced to stay out of school to work in support of a drinking father."

Statistics of dubious validity were sprinkled throughout the text to reinforce the anecdotes: Each year, alcohol killed 10 percent of the population, and saloons produced 80 percent of the nation's criminals and led sixty thousand young women astray. Drinkers contracted tuberculosis at twice the rate of nondrinkers. "Liquor is responsible for 19 percent of the divorces,

25 percent of the poverty, 25 percent of the insanity, 37 percent of the pauperism, 45 percent of child desertion and 50 percent of the crime in this country. And this is a very conservative estimate." The source of these "facts" was never given, and few of them had much connection to reality. But the constant barrage turned hyperbole into truth, at least in the minds of the men and women who grabbed the magazine from their mailboxes each week.

The rhetoric might sound to our ears like the overblown ranting of self-righteous crackpots. Alas, the nation's saloonkeepers, brewers, and distillers provided material that bolstered the most outrageous anecdote and flimsy statistic. In 1912, an ASL agent (most likely Wayne Wheeler) infiltrated the annual meeting of the Retail Liquor Dealers' Association of Ohio and heard a speaker urge the audience to "create the appetite for liquor in the growing boys." "Men who drink . . . will die," the speaker explained, "and if there is no new appetite created, our counters will be empty as well as our coffers. The open field for the creation of appetite is among the boys. Nickels expended in treats to boys now, will return in dollars to your tills after the appetite has been formed." The remarks appeared in the next *American Issue*. There was no evidence that brewers deliberately targeted boys, but again, once planted, the notion was hard to refute.

By 1902, the ASL boasted two hundred full-time employees and a budget of $250,000, and maintained offices in thirty-nine states and territories. Bolstered by grass-roots support and ample funding, the League's assault left a trail of battered victims. The ASL "is the most autocratic, the most dictatorial, as well as the most dangerous power ever known in the politics of this country," charged one opponent. An Alabama politician who had been "run over" by the League's "steam-roller" moaned that "[t]he good but gullible people of the churches permitted themselves to be humored and hoodwinked . . ." Politicians who "surrendered, saved themselves from slaughter." But he and others who resisted "were just swept aside to make room for the more susceptible."

BUT IF THE Anti-Saloon League's success rested on an underpinning of passionate support and Howard Hyde Russell's understanding of organizational dynamics, its eventual victory could not have happened without one other factor: lack of opposition. The League's natural opponents, the brewers and distillers, refused to acknowledge the enemy at the gates. Levies on liquor, beer, and wine constituted 20 to 40 percent of the nation's tax revenues, and the manufacturers of alcoholic beverages assumed that neither Congress nor the people would derail the money train. Moreover, federal officials regarded alcohol manufacturers as friends of the government. Revenue commissioners often spoke at industry conventions and worked for liquor and beer manufacturers after leaving government. "Uncle Sam is our partner," read the slogan on one liquor dealer's letterhead.

And, too, the ASL's initial successes came in the Far West and the Deep South. Big shipping brewers like Pabst and the Uihleins believed they could afford to lose a rural market here or there, as did the major northeastern beermakers—Jake Ruppert, the Schaefer brothers, and George Ehret—who shrugged at closures suffered by brother brewers in irrelevant Wyoming or Mississippi.

The distillers ignored the danger for another reason: They were not its main target. Since the 1850s, beer had outsold spirits by a wide margin, especially in the saloons that were the avowed target of the ASL's troops. In 1840, Americans had drunk about 2.5 gallons of spirits per capita; by 1896, they drank only about a gallon. Beer consumption, in contrast, had soared during the same period, from about one gallon in 1840 to fifteen gallons per capita. Distilleries were also large corporate conglomerates run by anonymous managers on behalf of stockholders, so liquor makers never developed the public face and fame that brewers and beer did. Nor did liquor makers operate "tied" houses. Indeed, virtually all of them sold liquor to wholesalers who in turn sold it to retailers, whose bottles of bourbon and rye gathered dust even as beer kegs ran dry as soon as they were tapped. In this new war on drink, public enemy number one was not the distiller but the men who brewed and sold the saloon's lifeblood: beer.

One of the few brewers who recognized that fact was the aging Adolphus Busch, who sensed the danger emanating from the "tyrrany [sic], idiocy, fanaticism and intolerance" that fed the ASL's legions. "There is something . . . that I do not like in the American man," not least his "hypocrisy," he told his old friend Charles Nagel. "He recommends and speaks for Prohibition and [condemns] the manufactures of all liquor while, at the same time, he drinks like a fish and becomes as drunk as a fool." Lunacy it might be, hypocritical, too, but Busch acknowledged the threat. "It is my aim to win the American people over to our side, to make them all lovers of beer and teach them to have respect for the brewing industry and the brewer. . . . It may cost us a million of dollars, and even more, but what of it if thereby we elevate our position?" he wrote to a business associate in 1905.

Busch did not expect to lose Missouri to the drys, but he feared that Texas might slip out of his hands. Since the 1870s, he'd invested considerable energy and money into building his Texas market. He sold much of his beer there and owned part or all of three other breweries in that state. But the ASL wanted Texas to go dry, and was busy funneling people, money, and time into the state.

Busch recognized that he and other brewers needed to mount their own campaign to promote the virtues of beer and the insanity of dry laws. But he knew, too, that Texans might eventually be asked to vote on statewide prohibition. Since the ASL supported dry politicians friendly to their cause, the beermakers had no choice but to use the same tactic, giving funds to ensure that wet politicians filled the Texas statehouse and that sympathetic judges, who might be asked to rule on election legalities, sat on court benches. He and the state's major beermakers organized the Texas Brewers' Association (TBA), which consisted of Anheuser-Busch, William J. Lemp Brewing, and seven Texas breweries, and each company deposited twenty cents per barrel in the organization's treasury. Even the United States Brewers' Association, otherwise slow to acknowledge the threat posed by the ASL, recognized that Texas was in danger, and assessed its six hundred–plus members one cent per barrel for the Texans' battle.

The money was not enough to wage war against the freshet of municipal and county elections spawned by the local option law. In August 1903, the president of a Houston brewery mailed a check for $250 to his dealer in Palestine, Texas, to fund an election campaign in Anderson County. "As you are aware," he reminded the agent, "the breweries are taxed with three or four elections . . . every month, and have been for the past year, and it has eaten up all of the profits and more." Still, the brewer knew that it was "impossible" to campaign without the money. "[H]ow it is spent," he added, "we do not want to know as long as it is spent for a good cause."

The TBA also bought votes when it could, slipping some of its precious funds into the hands of agreeable but indigent citizens so that they could pay the poll tax that stood between them and the voting booth. In the summer of 1903, a field agent spent a thousand dollars in just one county to pay the tax for fifteen hundred black men. Candidates cost even more. "We have about arranged with the ruling political party to allow us to name a Senator and Representative to the Legislature," reported an operative working for the San Antonio Brewing Association. "We are trying to get Judge Dean to run as Senator, and I believe he will go if paid for his time while away from his business." Dean's services would cost the TBA "at least $3,000," but the agent expected to offset the expense by acquiring another judge "without paying him anything."

But as Busch and others were slowly learning, the ASL's success rested on more than money. Americans were fed up with saloons. True, they had been prodded to that view by ASL propaganda, but there was no denying that beer joints poisoned civic harmony and order. The TBA's election manager in Freestone County admitted as much as he struggled to reconcile his job and his conscience with the reality of daily life in a community plagued by saloons. He reported that voters in one town demanded a local option election as a way to eliminate a particularly foul beerhouse, a gathering spot for "the young, lawless element who make nights hideous and when weary of raising hades in the house go out and shoot up the town." The marshal refused "to abate the trouble, and whenever there is any difficulty the new Sheriff always has a sick cow or calf down at his farm . . . Do you blame the people for calling a local option election?" asked the exasperated agent.

By 1907, the United States Brewers' Association had finally begun, albeit slowly and sporadically, to organize against the danger posed by the ASL and local option laws. But its field operatives discovered that persuading brewers to abandon self-interest was like asking Howard Hyde Russell to have a friendly drink. W. F. Schad, a USBA employee, ran up against that fact when he tried to organize Utah brewers and beer salesmen. Every saloon in Salt Lake City, he noted, contained slot machines and 20 percent of them were "low dives, catering for their trade to women of ill repute and the lowest class of men." The city's beermakers and brewery agents knew that. They knew, too, that they ought to close the dives and combat the Mormon prohibitionists (most of whom, Schad noted, "use stimulants quietly"). But one local beermaker explained to Schad that he would close his dens of iniquity only if the rest of the city's brewers did the same; until then, his tied houses would stay open. Worse yet, the manager of Salt Lake Brewing Company refused to have anything to do with any clean-up operation that involved Reilly, the local Lemp sales representative.

Schad hurried over to the Lemp office to investigate. It turned out that Reilly had handled Salt Lake Brewing's beer until wooed away by Lemp, and now he supplied Lemp lager to saloons formerly in Salt Lake Brewing's corral. Reilly assured Schad that he was willing to work with his former employer. Schad trotted back to Salt Lake Brewing, but his powers of persuasion crumbled in the face of its manager's recalcitrance: He refused to join any organization that included Reilly and neither Schad nor anyone else could change his mind. "The Salt Lake Brewing Company, being the largest Brewery in the State," Schad reported, "I of course failed to organize as contemplated."

This shortsighted self-absorption frustrated Charles Nagel. He pleaded with Adolphus Busch and son August to board the bandwagon of reality and push harder to get out their side of the story. Beer had become "the object of severest criticism" and brewers could not even "get a hearing in the public prints," he told August. And why? Because "the whole country is infested with disreputable saloons," and it was those that fueled public outrage against drinking, and, by extension, the brewing industry. Forced to choose between the "disreputable" saloon on the one hand and prohibition on the other, Americans would come down on the side of the "greatest . . . good to the general public"—and so against the brewers.

Chastened or inspired, in late 1907, August Busch announced that he and his father would cooperate in "the suppression of lawless saloons." "We do not expect great results in a day," Busch said. But "[s]how us a saloon or a club in which crime is bred and fostered, and if it belongs to our custom our support shall be withdrawn."

Fred J. Kern, the mayor of Belleville, Illinois, challenged Busch to make good on his words. Kern told a reporter that the town, which lay fifteen miles southeast of St. Louis, contained "110 saloons, of which 105 are decent." But the town's most in-decent places were owned by Anheuser-Busch, and the manager of the Budweiser Garden, the most notorious of the lot, had paid numerous fines for admitting minors to the attached dance hall. "[I]t is the rankest kind of hypocrisy," Kern charged, "for Gussie Busch to insist on law enforcement in the newspapers and then for his tenants and his agents . . . to denounce the public officials who demand some little respect for the decencies and the propri-eties . . . of orderly society."

"Gussie" wasted no time in responding. Twenty-four hours later, the manager turned out the lights and locked the doors; soon after, an Anheuser-Busch employee collected the keys.

But Charles Nagel was right: It was too little, too late. Few other brewers were willing to take the same step, and the Bud-weiser Garden was a mere drop in a gargantuan vat of saloons and dance halls. That puny effort could not divert the tide of public opinion from the channel dredged by the Anti-Saloon League. By late 1909, 46 million Americans—just over 50 percent of the total population—lived under some form of dry law. That included half of Chicago, long regarded as an impenetrable bulwark of booze. Voters in nine states had embraced outright prohibition, one of which, Oklahoma, had entered the Union two years ear-lier with a constitutional ban on liquor sales.

Saloons weren't the League's only targets in the march toward total prohibition. ASL operatives personalized the war by attack-ing the men behind the beer, easy enough to do at a time when muckraking journalists painted corporate magnates as sleazy crooks, and when tales of monied greed and scandal filled news-papers and magazines. Many brewers, especially the Uihleins,

Jake Ruppert, and George Ehret, had become famous in large part because of their wealth. But no beermaker drew more fire than flamboyant Adolphus Busch. A prohibitionist newspaper announced in early 1910 that the brewer had recently paid the highest price ever recorded for a second residence in Pasadena, not far from his beloved Ivy Wall. "[H]ow many thousands of homes of the patrons of his business have been mortgaged in order that Mr. Busch might enjoy the luxury of having the most 'palatial estate on the Pacific Coast,'" wondered the reporter.

Busch came in for another attack in early 1911 on the occasion of his fiftieth wedding anniversary. Lilly and Adolphus, he ill, frail, and wheelchair-bound, celebrated at Ivy Wall. Hundreds of bouquets and wreaths decorated the house, and two hundred strands of gold roses hung from the ceiling. On the morning of the great day, Adolphus opened the gift from his St. Louis employees, a solid gold block the size and shape of a telegram and engraved with sentiments of "devotion and love," and promptly collapsed—overcome by emotion and, perhaps, the sheer weight of the thing.

That evening Adolphus mustered the strength to join his wife and guests at dinner, where the thirty-eight attendees sat in gilded chairs, their places at the table marked by solid gold engraved souvenir plates. He presented Lilly with a gold tiara studded with diamonds and pearls. Heaps of beribboned gifts covered forty feet of table space and spilled over onto the floor. Among the treasures were three solid gold "loving cups," one each from Theodore Roosevelt, Kaiser Wilhelm, and the citizens of Pasadena. Adolphus's good friend William Howard Taft, president of the United States, sent one of the Saint-Gaudens twenty-dollar gold pieces pulled from circulation because they had been cast without the words "In God We Trust."

That last item caught the attention of Mrs. Sue F. Armstrong of Cedar Rapids, Iowa, who, like many Americans, read about the festivities in her local newspaper. She might have been able to swallow the notion of $200,000 tiaras and Americans accepting gifts from German emperors, but the idea of the nation's president consorting with purveyors of evil was more than she could stand. Mrs. Armstrong demanded an explanation from the White House. "I . . . wish to know," she wrote in a letter to Taft's office, "if the statement in regard to the president is true. Here in Iowa where we are trying to put out the saloons we should be glad to say that this report is untrue."

It's not clear whether Taft replied to her letter, but Sue Armstrong was not the only American demanding answers from the White House. A few months after the Busch anniversary, President Taft's agriculture secretary, James Wilson, accepted an invitation to serve as an honorary vice-president and speaker at the International Brewers' Congress in Chicago. The Anti-Saloon League organized a protest, and hundreds of clubs and associations bombarded the White House and Department of Agriculture with letters and telegrams. Arthur B. Farwell, president of the Chicago Law and Order League, urged Christians to pray for Wilson's misguided soul and begged the Agriculture Secretary not to "promote" the brewers' "schemes" or "stoop" to their morally repugnant level.

Wilson ignored the request. "If Mr. Farwell will call upon me, I would be only too glad to give him a few instructions in the art of praying," he told a reporter. "I have been a church member all my life and have been conscientious in everything I have done." Moreover, he had no plans to allow "criticism" from "so-called reformer[s]" or anyone else to interfere with his job. True to his word, Wilson attended the Brewers' Congress and delivered his speech. "[T]here was nothing else to do," he told Taft. "The prohibitionists have been threatening that they will take away votes from you in the coming campaign. The brewing people assure me that they will make good everything of that kind . . ."

Taft would need the support: As the 1912 presidential campaign kicked into gear, he backed away from what Anti-Saloon League leaders had interpreted as a commitment to their cause. One of the thorniest issues that the ASL faced was that of interstate transport of liquor. In 1911, it was legal for, say, a retailer in a dry city in Illinois to buy beer from a Wisconsin brewer, have it shipped to Illinois, and sell it there. This continent-sized loophole undermined local option laws and the League's dreams of a dry America. Early in his presidency, Taft had promised that if Congress passed a bill banning interstate shipments of liquor into dry areas, he would sign it. The League wrote such legislation, and maneuvered it into the Judiciary committees of both houses, but by 1911 it had become clear that Taft valued his reelection more than his earlier promise, and valued the financial contributions garnered from brewers and distillers more than the support of the ASL.

Adolphus Busch favored Taft's reelection bid, though Busch, like others of his ilk, would have voted Republican, the businessmen's party, no matter who was running. He also scoffed at Taft's opponent, Woodrow Wilson: "Well, they couldn't have done anything more stupid than to nominate the Weakest Candidate of the Bunch." "I have a kind of feeling," he said a few months later, "that the fellow is a prohibitionist . . . for that he ought to get another knock with the stick."

A YEAR LATER, at age seventy-four, Busch died at Villa Lilly, the family residence near Wiesbaden. Lilly Anheuser Busch and son August accompanied the body back to the United States, where a five-car train carried it and family and friends from New York to Missouri. Nagel and Missouri congressman Richard Bartholdt were on board, as was Carl Conrad, an old man himself now and bereft at the loss of his boon companion of some forty years.

Kaiser Wilhelm telegrammed his condolences and ordered a representative of the German embassy to attend the funeral and lay a wreath.

At a private service at One Busch Place, Nagel eulogized his old friend as a "giant among men," "a descendant of one of the great, vigorous and ancient gods." A mass of floral arrangements covered the grounds outside the house, and tens of thousands of people lined the streets of St. Louis to bid farewell and watch brewery employees escort the hearse to the gravesite. There Bartholdt memorialized a life lived full: "Our song to-day is in praise of . . . that ornament of creation, the self-made man." "Kings inherit their realms," he said, "statesmen are entrusted with their power by others, but our departed friend . . . built his own world, an empire of possessions extending . . . to the farthest corners of the globe."

Before Busch died, he saw his prediction fail. In November 1912, the "Temperance Crank," as Busch had mocked him, won the election. Woodrow Wilson owed his victory to third-party candidate Theodore Roosevelt, who ran as the candidate of the Progressive Party, a group of renegade Republicans who feared the incumbent Taft would sell his presidency to corporate America rather than fight for a reform agenda that would promote the interests of ordinary people. Roosevelt's exercise in political bravado siphoned votes from Taft and threw the election to Wilson.

Busch had been right to wonder where Wilson stood on the subject of prohibition. The new president entered the White House trailing a record of waffling and indecision. As a devoted Progressive, he favored cleaning up the saloons. As New Jersey governor, he supported local option, which he viewed as a tool that placed power in the hands of ordinary voters. As president-elect, he urged Congress to close the interstate loophole before he arrived in Washington. Yet once in office, he performed an about-face and refused to endorse outright prohibition, even statewide prohibition.

Soon it no longer mattered what the occupant of the White House wanted, said, or did. In early 1913, the lame-duck Taft Congress (in those days, presidential terms began in March), many of whom had lost their own reelection bids and no longer had to please constituents, ratified the Sixteenth Amendment, which introduced the income tax. This was a deadly blow to the brewers' cause: They assumed that as long as beer taxes poured into the treasury's coffers, national prohibition would never come to pass. The new income tax replaced alcohol as the main source of the government's revenue and whacked the legs out from under the wets' most forceful argument against prohibition.

A few days later, the House of Representatives approved the Webb-Kenyon Act, the single most important piece of pre-prohibition legislation. Webb-Kenyon, written and bulldozed through committee and onto the House floor by Wayne Wheeler, closed the hated interstate loophole. Local option and even statewide prohibition suddenly gained a clout and force they had lacked before, and brewers in dry locations who had kept their businesses alive by selling beer out of state understood that their ledger books had just suffered a fatal wound that would turn black ink to red. Taft took a break from packing his bags to veto the act, but the House and Senate overrode his action. "Prohibition is no longer a local issue," announced the editors of *American Brewers' Review.* "*Prohibition is a national danger.*"

In December 1913, just two months after the death of Adolphus Busch, a procession marched through the streets of the nation's capital; had Busch lived to witness it, he likely would have keeled over from apoplexy. One thousand members of the Woman's Christian Temperance Union and one thousand men affiliated with the Anti-Saloon League walked to the Capitol building, accompanied by another two thousand men, women, and children who serenaded passers-by with a boisterous rendition of "Onward, Christian Soldiers."

Senator Morris Sheppard of Texas and Representative Richmond P. Hobson of Alabama greeted them on the Capitol steps. As the thousands watched, two men stepped out of the ranks and handed the senator and congressman a draft of a proposed amendment to the Constitution that would ban the sale and manufacture of alcohol anywhere in the United States.

The moment that Howard Hyde Russell had envisioned back in 1893 had arrived. The push for constitutional prohibition had begun.

THE LEAGUE had traveled far in a short time, but Americans in 1913 were no more interested in outlawing alcohol than they are today. Prohibition was and is an extreme measure that smacks of coercion and invasion of privacy; resistance to both is the bedrock of Americans' DNA. Nor does the idea of amending the Constitution lay easy on the American mind. It is something we do rarely and with caution, and typically only to correct a perceived injustice: to outlaw slavery, or to define citizenship and voting rights.

So how did the League come to the Capitol steps so quickly? Part of the ASL's success can be attributed to the times themselves: Drastic measures seemed necessary in a society battered by the speed and intensity with which the industrial economy had taken hold. As one dry put it, "You may exercise your personal liberty only in so far as you do not place additional burdens upon your neighbor, or upon the State." Alcohol, many sensible people believed, did precisely that in terms of work hours lost, families harmed, wages wasted, health injured, and lives damaged beyond repair.

But the events of 1913 also stand as testimony to the tenacity, passion, and skill of the leaders of the nation's first single-issue lobbying group, the progenitor of so many that would follow. Its members, zealous and dedicated, had persuaded Americans to ban booze locally; now they stood ready to ask them to take this next, more extreme, step.

Had the electorate been asked to vote directly on the measure, it likely would have failed, but the mechanism of ratification worked to the ASL's advantage. The issue would never go before the voters themselves. Rather, ratification would fall to the members of state legislatures; only they would cast ballots yea or nay on the amendment.

The process would begin in Congress, where two-thirds of the House and Senate had to authorize submission of the amendment to the forty-eight states. Ernest Cherrington, the ASL official who devised the group's strategy, planned a test vote in Congress in 1914. The ASL would then devote 1915 and 1916 to electoral warfare, mowing down wet congressmen and replacing them with drys. If the plan went as plotted, a dry Congress would approve the amendment in 1918 and send it on to the states, where the League, having by then filled legislatures with sympathetic drys—or the easily coerced—expected no trouble in garnering the needed thirty-six votes.

Simple, but not necessarily easy. The League's near-impenetrable hide consisted of the rural Deep South, Far West, and Midwest. But its soft underbelly—and the wets' armor—lay in the nation's cities, where 45 percent of Americans lived. A mere nine heavily urban states commanded 196 votes in the House; wets needed only 146 to kill the amendment.

On paper, at any rate, the League's final campaign seemed lost before it began. And in the hands of other organizers, it might have been. But the foot soldiers launched themselves into this final phase of the war with renewed passion. A League official said later that ASL headquarters knew "the progress of every fight at every village crossroads. We were at all times intimately in touch with the battle on all fronts." Petitions, letters, and telegrams "rolled in by tens of thousands, burying Congress like an avalanche." League spies sent daily updates to headquarters so that League officials knew every move that the wets made.

And the League continued to benefit from the mystifyingly hapless, seemingly indifferent brewers. Just as it had been hard to muster a good reason to support the saloon, so the anti-amendment crowd was hard pressed to present a compelling case against constitutional prohibition. The one significant argument rested on what might be, on theory rather than fact. As one wet put it, a ban on booze would "breed deceit, hypocrisy, [and] disrespect of law, and encourage evasion, lying, trickery, and lawlessness." Enforcement would "require an army of United States officials, paid spies and informers . . ."

That of course turned out to be true, but in 1913, it was an argument that lacked teeth. The ASL made sure of that: Their newspapers, magazines, and press releases all touted the decrease in crime wherever local prohibition was already in effect. It was harder to broadcast the other side of the story: Local prohibition consistently gave rise to "blind pigs," as illegal retail outlets were called, and to bootlegging.

And so the campaign for consitutional prohibition rolled on. By late 1914, five more states had gone dry. Fifty percent of the American people lived under total prohibition, and another seventy breweries had closed their doors.

The ASL picked that moment to test its strength. On December 22, 1914, Representative Hobson introduced the prohibition amendment on the House floor. An enormous banner adorned the south gallery: a petition containing the names of twelve thousand organizations representing six million Americans who wanted a dry nation. A set of easels in front of the Speaker's rostrum held posters emblazoned with type large enough to be seen from the back of the hall: "Crime is caused by drink," one read. "Liquor fills the asylum," announced another. Floral arrangements decorated Richmond Hobson's desk, tokens of favor from women in the galleries. Pages scurried back and forth delivering stacks of telegrams to members, pleas from constituents for votes for and against.

The result stunned supporters and opponents alike. A majority of the House—197 to 190—voted aye on Hobson's measure, an "exceedingly gratifying" result. Though well short of the two-thirds needed, it was far more than anyone had expected. More than enough to hearten the crusade's soldiers.

ITS MEMBERSHIP distracted and dwindling, the leadership of the United States Brewers' Association finally got serious about the enemy. In the spring of 1913, just a few weeks after Congress approved the Webb-Kenyon Act, the group's executive officers voted to fund an organization specifically aimed at fighting the ASL on its own turf. To lead it, they hired Percy Andreae, an Ohio brewery executive who had mounted a successful counter-offensive on the ASL in its birth state.

The result was the National Association of Commerce and Labor (NACL), an alliance of brewers, glass and bottle-cap manufacturers, corn and rice processors, wholesalers and retailers, and saloonkeepers and hotel workers. Andreae used members' dues to hire a full-time staff of researchers and writers who studied congressional and state legislative contests and analyzed candidates and issues. He also contracted with writers who planted articles in rural and foreign-language newspapers and national magazines. These essays lambasted the coercive nature of the proposed amendment, reminded readers of beer's virtue as a "temperance" drink of moderation, and touted its value as a nutritious foodstuff. A stable of sympathetic experts toured a lecture circuit that included trade and professional conventions, men's and women's clubs, and any church group willing to give them a listen. The group published two "wet" magazines and funded an acting troupe that produced "The Passing of Hans Dippel," the tale of a respectable German-American saloonkeeper brought to destruction by the drys.

Andreae knew, however, that no matter what he did or how fast he moved, the brewers lagged far behind their opponents. In order to catch up, he needed to move men, raise money, and implement his ideas quickly and efficiently. Scouting about for a mechanism to help him compete with the ASL behemoth, he latched onto the National German-American Alliance.

The GAA had been founded in 1899 by Charles Hexamer, a Philadelphia civil engineer born in the United States to German emigré parents, as a way to celebrate and preserve German heritage, history, and culture in the United States. The Alliance lobbied against immigration restriction and for German-language instruction in public schools; supported German-language newspapers; and funded historical studies. But as the ASL's tentacles burrowed into the fabric of national life, the GAA's leadership had diverted its energy and funds to defending drink.

On its own, the GAA could not match the League's organizational superiority. More to the point, the Alliance's cultural arrogance hobbled its effectiveness as an opponent: The educated middle-class men who made up the group's ranks regarded German culture as superior to American and themselves as the spokesmen for a unified and homogeneous German-America. That eventually proved to be a fatal mistake, and it also explains the GAA's relatively limited membership. Most German-Americans, who numbered 8.2 million in 1910, longed to assimilate and regarded themselves as Americans first and only incidentally as Americans of German descent. Many of them supported prohibition and thousands more disdained the GAA's crusade to celebrate all things German. And non-German Americans who opposed prohibition could see no reason to ally themselves with an ethnic-based organization.

Still, as far as Andreae was concerned, the GAA boasted an impressive array of gears and cogs: a membership devoted to the wet cause, a printing press, and access to thousands of German-American social, political, religious, and labor organizations as well as connections to the nation's foreign-language press. In the late summer of 1913, Andreae offered Hexamer a cut of the NACL's brewery money in exchange for access to the GAA's network.

Hexamer needed the funds, but he resisted the idea of mixing beer's unsavory reputation and tainted money with the Alliance's good name. Andreae assuaged Hexamer's fears by devising a way to pay the GAA under the table. Joseph Keller, another GAA officer, distributed Andreae's laundered money to GAA field agents and placed anti-prohibition articles in national magazines and newspapers. Everyone benefited: The German-American Alliance received a steady supply of cash, and the brewers enjoyed access to a well-organized political action group with no apparent connection to the liquor industry.

But no matter what Andreae did, his efforts were a sponge swabbing an ocean of superior Anti-Saloon League organization and propaganda. In January 1915, Andreae strolled into the Chicago Athletic Club for a meeting of the NACL and the USBA, now led by Gustav Pabst, whose influence had mushroomed since the death of Adolphus Busch. By the time Andreae left a few hours later, he had been stripped of his authority. He couldn't have been entirely surprised. He had spent over a half million dollars of the USBA's money, and yet the House of Representatives had edged perilously close to approving a prohibition amendment. Meanwhile, every town and county that voted dry led more brewers to close their doors. Since 1904, nearly five hundred had gone out of business.

The extent to which Andreae and the brewers had failed to make their case became clear when, in April 1917, the United

States entered the world war that had been raging for almost three years. Congress banned alcohol from a five-mile "dry zone" around military installations and imposed abstinence on the armed services. No alcohol for troops or officers in uniform. Not on base, not on leave, not even in private homes. As spring turned to summer, senators and representatives turned to the task of rationing food and supplies. The ASL seized the opportunity and turned the debate over bread into a prohibition revival.

"Just think," mused Mississippi senator James Vardaman, "of the absurdity" of rationing bread to the "laboring man" and "starving babe" while permitting the liquor interests the privilege of using those grains to make "a beverage that kills the body and damns the soul." Close the distilleries and breweries, urged William Thompson of Kansas, and save the equivalent of eleven million loaves of bread a day. There is "no patriotism among the liquor interests of the country," he warned, arguing that brewers and distillers would just as soon "sell liquor under the Government of the Kaiser as under that of the President, and the chances are they would prefer to do so."

The great flock of the sober flooded the House and Senate with petitions, from the Christians of Senatobia, Mississippi, and the Woman's Missionary Society of the Methodist Episcopal Church South to the faculty and students at the Wooster Summer School, the students of Bates College, and the Drexel Biddle Bible Class of Portland, Maine. All were "praying" for "the prohibition of the manufacture and sale of all intoxicating beverages during the period of war . . ."

Hallelujah and amen. The congregation ended the service in a chorus of "ayes." Congress banned the sale of grain to distillers for the duration of the war, a move that effectively closed that industry's doors.

The USBA still had enough clout to succeed in keeping beer out of the bill, but as a compromise, Congress empowered the president to ration brewers' supplies whenever he deemed it necessary. Wilson did just that in early December 1917, when he ordered the alcohol level in beer reduced to 2.75 percent and slashed the industry's grain allotment by 30 percent.

August Busch came out swinging: "We cannot tell just how the public will take the change in taste," he told reporters. "It may be that it will be readily accepted, but a falling off in consumption is a possibility . . ." But, he pointed out, the new rules would free up 999,000 bushels of corn, rice, and barley in St. Louis alone, and some 20 million nationwide. Otto Stifel, who presided over the city's Union Brewery, offered a less optimistic assessment of the situation. "I do not think the expected saving of food products will be brought about," he groused, "but the food value of beer will be decreased." As far as he, a diehard of the old school, was concerned, beer was food, and one that provided as much nutritional value as milk.

Alas, poor Stifel, the worst was yet to come. The Senate had already approved the prohibition amendment resolution. The House wrangled over the wording for several months, but on December 18, four years after the amendment's first appearance in Congress, the House voted 282 to 128 to send it to the state legislatures.

The ASL's leadership believed that it had lined up sufficient support in statehouses around the country to ensure ratification. But nothing is certain in war, so the League marshaled its forces for one last barrage of firepower, this one aimed at rallying the public's support for the momentous step of amending the Constitution. The task? Discrediting what was left of the brewing industry. The weapon of choice? Wayne Wheeler.

WAYNE WHEELER had begun his anti-drink career in 1893, when Howard Hyde Russell had hired him to help launch the anti-saloon crusade. He had managed League affairs in Ohio but spent nearly as much time in Washington, D.C., where he strong-armed recalcitrant lawmakers and helped plan the League's political strategy. In 1915, he had moved to the nation's capital to work as the ASL's general counsel, chief lobbyist, and manager of legislative affairs.

To a casual observer, Wheeler appeared to be the soul of middle-class respectability: Tidy pince-nez straddled an acceptably straight nose perched above a meticulous mustache. A stiff, snowy white collar, a perfectly knotted tie, and immaculate lapels completed the uniform of the proper man. Only his lips—curled in a prissy sneer or, more often, curved into a self-satisfied smirk—belied the zealot lurking within, for Wheeler was a natural crusader, one of those high-energy, single-minded souls who are prepared to labor day and night for their chosen cause. The reform-mad 1890s offered a host of crusades for people of his ilk—civil rights, woman suffrage, child labor, the eradication of prostitution. It was unfortunate for the nation's brewers that Wheeler chose booze.

Admirers and enemies alike described him as "indefatigable and shrewd," a man who combined "the zeal of a Savonarola and the craft of a Machiavelli." Wheeler regarded morality as a flexible concept and believed that the end determined the means. Convinced of the sanctity of both himself and his cause, and incapable of compromise, he bullied the recalcitrant and steam-rollered the undecided. One critic complained that the man would "cohabit with the devil himself to win."

During his years as superintendent of the Ohio League, Wheeler routinely weaseled his way into meetings of brewers, distillers, and liquor retailers. On one occasion he boarded a train for Youngstown, where he hoped to gain entry to a liquor convention being held there. Luck smiled on the teetotaling Savonarola, who discovered that he'd taken a seat next to a convention delegate. Wheeler struck up a conversation and the unsuspecting dupe confided that he was scheduled to make a speech, a terrifying prospect because he had no experience writing or delivering public talks. Wheeler offered to write the speech in exchange for the man's convention badge.

Wheeler boasted later to a friend that he had put pen to paper and written "a red-hot Personal Liberty tirade" denouncing "prohibition and its fanaticism." At Youngstown, he traded the speech for the liquor man's badge and strolled into the convention hall. All went well until a convention official announced that spies from the Anti-Saloon League had infiltrated the gathering. Wheeler froze in his seat—and sighed a prayer of relief as convention marshals escorted two other men from the hall. Wheeler, a performer to the core, joined the rest of the audience in the applause that accompanied the men's departure.

And now, in early 1918, he had the brewers cornered. Two years earlier, a Pennsylvania grand jury had indicted most of that state's brewers and the officers of the United States Brewers' Association on charges of violating corporate tax law and the federal corrupt practices act, a case that had been pushed to fruition by a Democratic U.S. district attorney and by A. Mitchell Palmer, the state's Democratic party boss. The defendants had pleaded nolo contendere before the case could go to trial, but the biggest payoff had been the confiscation by the district attorney of two trunks and one suitcase full of brewers' records.

Wheeler was friendly with the men who pressed the case, and so gained access to the records. There he had found evidence of Percy Andreae's payments to the GAA. Wheeler persuaded William King, a senator from Utah, to introduce a bill to repeal the GAA's congressional charter—on the grounds that the organization had violated said charter when it lobbied against prohibition, an issue with no direct connection to German heritage, and therefore an activity outside the bounds of the GAA's stated aims. Wheeler also persuaded King to hold hearings on the matter.

King agreed, but charged Wheeler with the task of providing witnesses who would make the effort worthwhile.

No problem. On February 23, 1918, the senator opened a hearing into the GAA's activities. For two days, a handful of witnesses dissected and maligned the Alliance. "We could not have secured for $25,000 the publicity against the German Alliance which we got through the Sunday papers," Wheeler bragged.

The best was yet to come. On day six, Percy Andreae showed up. "Was the National Association of Commerce and Labor organized in reality by the United States Brewers' Association?" one senator asked. "Yes," Andreae replied. And the GAA's money came from the USBA as well? "Oh, yes," said Andreae. How much money did the NACL have on hand? Andreae guessed perhaps as much as a half million dollars. "It may have been a million?" queried another senator. "No; I do not think it was a million," said Andreae, adding that he was sorry it had not been.

So was Wayne Wheeler. Still, Wheeler had gotten what he'd come for: a public dissection of the GAA and the link between German treachery and American brewers. He picked the right tactic at the right moment. The war had sparked outbursts of inflammatory rhetoric and violence toward German-Americans. A mob in Collinsville, Illinois, had lynched a German-American believed—wrongly—to be a spy. In Milwaukee, a gang of patriots positioned a machine gun in front of a theater, a way of warning patrons to stay away from a performance of *Wilhelm Tell*. A Lutheran minister in Texas received a public whipping for preaching in German. All over the country, mobs tarred and feathered suspicious persons, dragged them through the streets, and forced them to kiss flags. Doused houses and churches of German-Americans with yellow paint. Flogged anyone foolish enough to speak German. Burned German books and changed the German names of newspapers, streets, and food.

John Strange, a former lieutenant governor of Wisconsin,

had given a speech in which he warned against "German enemies across the water." But, he added, "We have German enemies in this country, too. And the worst of all our German enemies, the most treacherous, the most menacing, are Pabst, Schlitz, Blatz and Miller. They are the worst Germans who ever afflicted themselves on a long-suffering people. No Germans in the war are conspiring against the peace and happiness of the United States more than Pabst, Schlitz, Blatz, Miller and others of their kind."

A former governor of Indiana joined Strange in his denunciation, writing in a national magazine that the nation had never faced an "organization of power so brutal, so domineering, so corrupt . . . as the brewers of America." He urged state legislators to dispatch "firing squads" to destroy the enemy. A writer for *American Issue* accused the "German breweries in America" of abetting the enemy. "Every bushel of grain that is destroyed" in the Busch or Pabst or Ruppert brewhouse "serves the Kaiser just as well as a bushel sunk by a submarine at sea." A Methodist bishop denounced beer as "the most brutalizing" drink available. "The unthinkable barbarism of the German armies in this present war," he wrote, "is, in all reasonableness, to be accounted for largely by their centuries of beer-drinking, which has deadened their moral sense and coarsened their moral fiber."

A congenial atmosphere indeed for the prohibitionists, and one particularly suited for the work of A. Mitchell Palmer. Palmer had been appointed Custodian of Alien Property, a position created in late 1917 when Congress passed the Trading With the Enemy Act, legislation which, among other things, forbid Americans from conducting business with enemies during time of war. The Custodian was charged with seizing and administering properties in the United States that were owned by enemy nationals. In World War I, that consisted of a collection of forty thousand holdings worth millions of dollars.

Palmer had no particular qualifications for the job other than party loyalty. He'd served in the House of Representatives some years earlier, but had lost a bid for the Senate in 1914. Since then he'd occupied his time practicing law, serving on the Democratic National Committee, and helping Woodrow Wilson get re-elected in 1916. Wilson offered Palmer the post of Secretary of War, but the Pennsylvanian declined because of his Quaker upbringing. He was happy, however, to take the Custodian's post. The original legislation authorized the Custodian to hold enemy-owned property for the duration of the war, but Palmer, no stranger to wheeling and dealing, convinced Congress to allow him to sell it, too. Alien property and investments, he explained, were "part of the deliberate plan of Germany to conquer the world by trade."

In Palmer's mind, it was but a short step from enemy-owned property to property owned by Americans of German descent. In early December 1917, he had launched an investigation into the financial affairs of Clara Busch von Gontard and Wilhelmina Busch Scharrer, the German-wed daughters of Adolphus Busch. Thanks to the war and their marriage and residence in Germany, they were classified as enemies of the United States. Palmer wanted to know if, when, and how brother August was funneling money to them. Busch sent Charles Nagel to Washington to explain that, since April and the declaration of war, the family had been investing the sisters' portion of the estate in United States liberty bonds.

Next Palmer had turned to the affairs of Lilly Busch. Mrs. Busch and son August and his family were vacationing in Germany when war broke out in 1914. August and his brood returned to the United States; Lilly, who turned seventy a few weeks before the conflict began, stayed on. "Believing with many others that the war would not last long," she explained later, "feeling a deep concern for my daughters married in Germany, and being a wretched traveler at sea, I concluded not to return at that time," hoping and believing that the fighting would end soon and that she would be able to make the trip "under more favorable conditions."

The favorable conditions never developed, and in late 1917 she was still in Europe, working for the Red Cross far from the front lines but in enemy territory nonetheless—evidence of disloyalty as far as Palmer was concerned. He informed the Busch family that he planned to commandeer her entire estate—stocks, bonds, bank accounts, houses, real estate, and all—on the grounds that her residence in Germany made her an alien. Never mind that she had lived in the United States for all but six months of her seventy-four years, the daughter of naturalized parents. Nagel managed to prevent Palmer from seizing the estate outright, but only because Palmer conceded that Lilly Busch's precise legal status was not clear. As a compromise, Nagel gave all of Lilly's titles and deeds to the Union Trust Company of St. Louis, which agreed to hold them until the matter could be settled.

In early May, Palmer helped himself to George Ehret's forty-million-dollar estate, claiming ownership of his brewery, his real estate, his mansion at Ninety-fourth and Park Avenue, and the art collection inside. Ehret had been an American citizen for forty years, but he, too, had been in Germany when the war broke out and, at age eighty-three, had found it difficult to leave. That was good enough for Palmer. "If Mr. Ehret, Sr., should return to America and thus lose his enemy character," Palmer told reporters, "the Department of Justice would entertain any claim which he might make . . . to have his property returned."

Wayne Wheeler recognized opportunity when he saw it. With news of war filling the daily papers, and with everything German discredited and vilified, this was an auspicious moment in which to move in for the kill. He dispatched a polite letter to Palmer. "I am informed," he wrote, "that there are a number of

breweries in this country which are owned in part by alien enemies. It is reported to me that the Annhauser [sic] Busch Company
and some of the Milwaukee Companies are largely controlled by
alien Germans . . . Have you made any investigation? If not would
you be willing to do so if we could give you any clue that would
justify your taking such action?"

Whether by coincidence or intention, Wheeler queried Palmer
at the same moment that another piece of news had arrived in the
United States: Lilly Busch was on her way home. Son August, desperate to remove his mother from harm's way, had persuaded
Harry Hawes, his attorney and a trusted family friend, to venture
across the Atlantic and help Mrs. Busch travel home. Lilly made her
way out of Germany to neutral Switzerland, where she met Hawes
in mid-January. He explained that she could stay there, but the old
woman, now seventy-four years old, announced that she preferred
to undertake the six-thousand-mile trek to the United States. In
preparation, she rested for two months, tended by a physician,
Hawes, and two traveling companions: her maid and Ruby Baumann, a St. Louis woman who recently had divorced her German
army officer husband. The doctor declared her fit to travel and in
March 1918, the party set off for Spain and passage home.

That news inspired a flurry of activity, rumor, and advice back
in the United States. A New York newspaper eager to discredit
anything Busch described her—falsely—as "prominent in German court circles"; claimed—falsely—that the Kaiser and
Crown Prince paid regular visits to her "castle on the Rhine"; and
reported—falsely—that she had given a million dollars to a German hospital. A concerned St. Louis citizen wrote to Attorney
General Thomas Gregory urging him to search Mrs. Busch and
the rest of her party when they landed in the States. "Mrs Bush
[sic] has relatives and son-in-laws in the German army," explained
the patriot, and "its [sic] best to be sure than sorry, and see that

they dont [sic] slip one over on us by sending some secret code or other information to agents here."

It was just as well that Lilly Busch knew nothing of the roiling clouds back home; she needed all of her strength to negotiate the ravaged European landscape, which confronted the travelers with closed borders and railroad strikes, an air raid in Paris, canceled sailings, and submarine scares. Finally, on June 17, 1918, the party reached Key West and American soil.

There began the brief but well-publicized nightmare of Lilly Busch, suspected German sympathizer and spy. Four days earlier, unbeknownst to her or anyone else in the family, the director of Naval Intelligence had ordered Lieutenant J. Vining Harris to "Question, Search, and report Destination" of the Busch party. Harris turned the task over to A. E. Gregory, an employee of the Justice Department. Gregory boarded the travelers' steamer and took custody of Lilly Busch, Harry Hawes, Mrs. Baumann, Busch's maid, and all of their luggage and papers.

Out on the dock stood August Busch, Mrs. Hawes, and a small swarm of other Busches and friends, all of them expecting the party to appear. Journalists hovered nearby, pencils at ready. Two hours later, a reporter trotted up from town with breaking news: Mitchell Palmer had just seized Lilly Busch's property. The "entire estate [had] reverted to the Government" and was now "subject to such disposition" as Palmer saw fit.

No sooner had August Busch heard that news than his mother appeared at the gangway with a U.S. marshal guarding her party. Lilly Busch burst into tears and tottered toward her son. A marine darted forward and restrained her. "August," she sobbed, "they won't let me see you tonight." Mother and son were allowed an embrace before the marshal led her into the nearby Customs House. Eventually the entire party, minus their baggage, boarded cars and cabs and motored through downtown Key

West—speaking only English, as instructed by Gregory—to the Oversea Hotel on Fleming Street. The marines positioned themselves outside Lilly Busch's room; the marshal's wife deposited herself inside; and the distraught Mrs. Busch collapsed in a heap of fear and exhaustion.

The next morning Gregory permitted August and Mrs. Hawes to visit Lilly—in the company of Justice Department agents, and speaking English only. Just after lunch, however, Gregory and Lieutenant Harris returned to the hotel, closeted themselves with Mrs. Busch, and interrogated her for two hours. What she and they said is not known, but it failed to satisfy the apparently insatiable Gregory, who informed Harris that he intended to search "the person and effects" of Mrs. Busch, Mrs. Baumann, and the maid. A doctor and the marshal's wife escorted Mrs. Busch into her room, where he "laid the old lady on a bed and examined her private parts, making a very thorough examination of her vagina and womb." When he had finished with Mrs. Busch, he set to work on Mrs. Baumann and the maid. Lilly Busch spent the rest of what was surely one of the worst days of her life in the company of a federal agent and the marshal's wife, speaking to her son in English only.

At least the affair was nearly over. The next morning, Lieutenant Harris returned to the hotel and quizzed Mrs. Busch one more time. "No person in the world could doubt that woman's sincerity," he announced an hour later, and promised August Busch that he would recommend a public statement that "absolutely vindicated" her of any crime or improper activity. The guards left. Lilly Busch was finally free to go.

BUT PALMER had not finished with the brewers. Just days after Lilly Busch's arrival in Key West, he found evidence that a group of prominent beermakers, including Gustav Pabst, Jacob Ruppert, Joseph Uihlein, and George Ehret, had loaned Arthur Brisbane the money to buy the *Washington [D.C.] Times.* (Brisbane, one of the nation's most respected newspaper editors, was an outspoken critic of prohibition.) At the time, Palmer was also arranging for the arrest of Edward A. Rumely, the owner of the *New York Evening Mail,* because Rumely had bought that newspaper with money from German sources. A month later, Justice Department agents arrested Rumely for perjury. A. Mitchell Palmer told reporters that German cash paid for the purchase of the *Mail*; that Kurt Reisinger, a grandson of Adolphus Busch, had invested in the newspaper; and that Lilly Busch had been questioned in Key West in part because federal officials believed she had supplied Rumely with money (she had not).

In the time it took to say "German brewers," Palmer and Wayne Wheeler strung together these otherwise unconnected facts—the brewers' loan to Brisbane and Rumely's use of German money to purchase an American newspaper—and concluded that American brewers were financing and organizing enemy propaganda in a nation at war. By September 1918, Palmer and Wheeler had engineered Senate hearings to investigate charges that German-American brewers were using newspapers and illegal campaign contributions to control the outcome of elections and spread pro-German propaganda.

The hearings began on September 27. Over the next few weeks, five senators quizzed Brisbane, USBA director Hugh Fox, and three officers of the USBA. They wasted their time. Arthur Brisbane sliced the accusations against him into tiny bits, undermining Palmer's credibility and the entire purpose of the hearings. "From the day I owned the Times," he told the senators, "I wrote as vigorously, as savagely and as earnestly . . . against the German side and in favor of America as I have ever done on any subject in my life." As to the brewers' alleged "German" connection? "The only brewers I know," said Brisbane, "are men who were born in America . . ."

The senators got even less from Hugh Fox, whom they questioned for two days. He denied having organized a boycott against men or companies that supported prohibition. He denied that the USBA owned any newspapers, and denied that he or the USBA had received money from the German government or promoted German propaganda.

And so it went. Mostly the senators made fools of themselves. It was clear that they could not—or would not—distinguish the USBA from the NACL, or the GAA from either one. But the only way the average American could know that was by sitting in the hearing room itself, because the nation's press tried the brewers and found them guilty. *"Enemy Propaganda Backed By Brewers,"* read a headline in the nation's newspaper of record. Only someone willing to read past the incendiary headline and the article's first few inaccurate sentences would learn that the evidence linked nobody to anything; that the "evidence" consisted of a speech that Charles Hexamer wrote in 1915, two years before the United States entered the war; that Hexamer protested the sale of munitions to the Allies, as did millions of other Americans; and that Hexamer's text urged German-Americans to remain loyal to the United States.

Outside the hearing room, war alone had become sufficient reason to shut the brewers' doors. On September 6, President Wilson announced that in order to preserve precious supplies of grain and fuel, breweries would close at midnight, December first. A few days later, the Food Administration cut brewers off from corn, rice, or barley. They could use their stock on hand; they could purchase any malt they could find. But when those supplies were depleted, well . . . that was that.

New York beermakers huddled in emergency session to discuss the bomb. "Nobody at the meeting had any suggestion to make as to what can be done with our properties," Jacob Ruppert said afterward. "I haven't the remotest idea as to what we can do with ours."

Ruppert could always fall back on the income from his stud farm or from his New York Yankees, which he had purchased three years earlier. August Busch was less blasé. He had already converted his Busch-Sulzer Diesel Engine Company into a submarine engine manufactory for the navy. Now he offered the brewery to the United States government for use as a munitions factory and set off for Washington to seal the deal. "Give me a chance," he promised, "and I'll make the cartridge manufacturers look like pikers." As for prohibition? asked a reporter. "I am not now interested in the prohibition question," Busch replied. "I am only concerned now in doing what I can to help the Government, and, secondly, to take care of my employes [sic] in St. Louis."

His New York colleagues scoffed at the idea. It was unlikely, said one of them, that the federal government wanted or needed yet another munitions factory. And, he added, "our men, brewers and malsters [sic] and the like, who have done nothing but the work they are engaged in all their lives, would make a poor fist at learning the munition-making trade or any other. None of them is young and it is difficult to teach old dogs new tricks." His attitude may explain why August Busch survived Prohibition and many of the New York brewers did not.

Busch forged ahead, determined to save his family's investment and his reputation. He ran a full-page advertisement in St. Louis newspapers announcing that he would hand over the entire seventy-five city blocks and $60 million worth of Anheuser-Busch facilities to federal officials if they wanted it, announcing, "We consider it a privilege to co-operate with the Government in making its war program effective."

Busch devoted most of the ad to refuting the "false reports and statements" being "circulated with reckless disregard for truth." Anheuser-Busch was "an American institution, founded by Americans more than 60 years ago, and continuously owned and operated by Americans" since then. (That, by the way, is true: Eberhard Anheuser became a citizen in 1848; Adolphus Busch in 1867.) He reminded readers that the company paid more than $3 million in taxes every year and employed nearly seven thousand men and women. The Busch family had contributed a half million dollars to the Red Cross and purchased $3 million worth of Liberty bonds. It was true that he and his mother had bought German bonds, but they'd done so eighteen months before the United States entered the war. "Anheuser-Busch was founded upon the solid rock of Americanism," Busch concluded, "and grew to be a great institution under the protection of American democracy." Now the company stood "*ready to sacrifice everything except loyalty to country, and its own honor, to serve the Government in bringing this war to a victorious conclusion.*"

Government officials decided against converting the brewery to munitions production, but leased a large chunk of one Anheuser-Busch building for the storage of weapons and ammunition. The lease proved to be short-term: The war ended on November 11. On December 1, the nation's breweries turned out their lights, as per President Wilson's order of the previous September.

None of it mattered. While Wayne Wheeler and A. Mitchell Palmer hatched their plots; while August Busch struggled to save his name and his livelihood; while the Senate subcommittee muddled through an embarrassing waste of taxpayer money; while a generation's finest—American and German, English and French—fought and died in the trenches of Europe, one state legislature after another had ratified the prohibition amendment. On January 16, 1919, Nebraska legislators voted aye. Theirs was the necessary thirty-sixth nod of approval. Prohibition had become the law of the land.

Best Brewing Company in its early days. This undated photograph likely was taken in the mid-1860s, not long after Phillip Best expanded the brewery and about the time that Pabst and Schandein joined the firm.

Photo courtesy of the Milwaukee County Historical Society

Frederick Pabst and his wife, Maria, c. 1865, not long after he joined Best Brewing. A rare early image of the young man who twenty-five years later would own the largest brewery in the world.

Photo courtesy of the Captain Frederick Pabst Mansion Archives

Adolphus Busch, c. 1890, when he ruled over one of the two largest breweries in the world. "I am an eternal optimist," he once said.

Photo from Western Brewer

Best Brewing teamsters, c. 1875. The drivers are hauling their cargo to the rail yard for shipping to distant markets, but nineteenth-century brewers also paraded their drivers and wagons through the streets as a way of advertising their firms' size and brewing prowess.

Photo courtesy of the Milwaukee County Historical Society

The Uihlein brothers, c. 1900. From left: August, William, and Alfred.
Photo courtesy of the Milwaukee County Historical Society

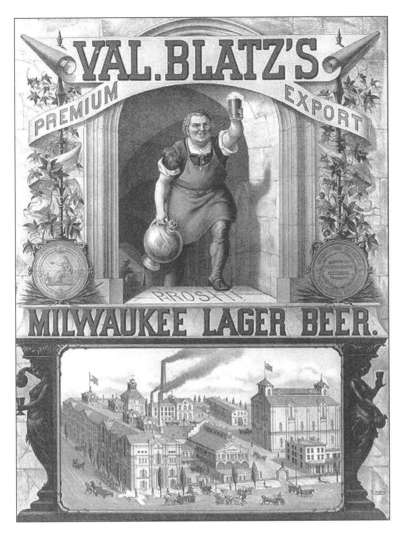

Brewers provided their "tied" houses with plenty of advertising material. Posters like this one often alluded to both the brewers' old-world heritage and their American success—notice the image of Blatz's imposing factory complex.

Photo courtesy of the Library of Congress, Prints & Photographs Division
(LC-USZ62-17080)

(LEFT) This poster from an unknown brewer emphasizes beer as a "healthy" drink respectable enough to be drunk at home. As the forces of temperance gathered strength after the Civil War, beermakers touted lager as the national drink and the beverage of moderation.

Photo courtesy of the Library of Congress, Prints & Photographs Division
(LC-USZC4-4439)

The World's Columbian Exposition of 1893 marked the last great face-to-face confrontation between Frederick Pabst and Adolphus Busch. Both men's exhibits featured detailed models of their breweries. Even in miniature, this replica of Anheuser-Busch is imposing.

Photo from Western Brewer, *courtesy of the Anheuser-Busch Corporation*

The temperance movement regained strength in the years just after the Civil War. This magazine image from 1874 shows members of the "Women's Crusade" on the march, stopping at saloons to pray that the owners would abandon their evil trade. More often than not, they were met by ridicule or worse; in some cases, tavern patrons pelted the women with fruit or threw buckets of water on them.

Photo courtesy of the Library of Congress,
Prints & Photographs Division (LC-USZ62-90543)

Beer was never as popular as liquor during Prohibition because it cost more to make and ship. That didn't stop racketeers from making "alley brew" or federal agents from seizing bootleg beer when they could find it. But the man managing a two-fisted dump of illegal brew (RIGHT) was a civilian, part of a vigilante group in Zion, Illinois, that waylaid a truck carrying beer out of Chicago and staged a public demolition of the entire load.

*Photos courtesy of the Library of Congress, Prints & Photographs Division
(LC-USZ62-96024 and LC-USZ62-95873)*

A Prohibition raid in Detroit. There's no way to know if the seized
bootleg beer came from the breweries named on the wooden cases, or
if racketeers had loaded their illicit brew into whatever packing boxes
they could find. But many legitimate brewers who once vowed to obey
the law found it hard to resist the temptation of illegal brewing.

Photo courtesy of the Walter P. Reuther Library, Wayne State University

On May 14, 1932, these residents of Detroit heeded the call of New
York City's mayor, Jimmie Walker, and joined tens of thousands of
Americans in "beer parades," demanding "Beer for Taxation."

Photo courtesy of the Walter P. Reuther Library, Wayne State University

On February 16, 1934, an enormous crowd at Grant's
Farm, the palatial estate of August A. Busch, Sr., watched
as pallbearers loaded the casket of Busch's body into a
hearse. He had committed suicide three days earlier.

Photo courtesy of the St. Louis Post-Dispatch

Fritz Maytag and his San Francisco brewery, c. 1970. The equipment Maytag inherited had more in common with Phillip Best's 1844 brewhouse than with ultramodern beer factories. But perseverance paid off: By the mid-1970s, he and his employees had put Anchor Brewing on the nation's zyomtechnic map. The tie-wearing Maytag looks out of place among his long-haired employees, but they respected him. Some of the people in this photograph were still working at Anchor thirty years later.

Photos courtesy of Fritz Maytag and Anchor Brewing Company

Jack McAuliffe, founder of the nation's first microbrewery, in 1978. McAuliffe designed and built much of New Albion's equipment, but he also relied on material that he salvaged from scrap yards, including this antique barrel washer.
Photo courtesy of Michael E. Miller and Jack McAuliffe

Ken Grossman in 1981, with one of his brewery's original vats, which he and partner Paul Camusi fabricated from pieces and parts gathered from dairies and salvage yards.
Photo courtesy of Ken Grossman and Sierra Nevada Brewing Co.

Even the labels of craft brewers heralded a new era. These examples from New Albion, Mendocino, and Sierra Nevada reflect the personalities and passions of the men who made the beer.

New Albion label courtesy of Dave Gauspohl. Mendocino Brewing label courtesy of Michael Laybour. Sierra Nevada label courtesy of Daniel Bradford.

Jim Koch at the White House. Koch launched Samuel Adams in 1985.
In 1987 the White House called and Koch paid a visit, beer in tow.
Koch's salesmanship won him both friends and new customers. Since
1987 Samuel Adams has been served at the president's residence,
at Camp David, and on Air Force One.

Photo courtesy of Jim Koch and The Boston Beer Company

CHAPTER FIVE

Happy Days?

S UMMER OF 1932. For the first time in many years, August Busch had reason to believe that his family's company might survive. Since the onset of Prohibition, the maverick, now sixty-six, and his two sons, Adolphus III and August Junior (known around the plant as Adolph and Junior, although Adolph also answered to "Third" and most people called August "Gus"), had struggled to hang on to Adolphus's creation. Father and sons had pinned their hopes for profit on Bevo, the brewery's "near beer." With characteristic foresight, August had put the brewery's chemists to work developing a "soft" grain-based beverage in 1906, and, after ten years of near-misses, messes, and mishaps, had finally concocted one that met his approval. In May 1916, the brewery released Bevo, a nonalcoholic drink made from malt and hops, which Busch hoped would revive his company's bottom line.

Their hopes were misplaced. Since January 1920, Americans had turned a decisive thumbs-down on near beer, whether from Anheuser-Busch or one of the hundred-odd breweries still in business. In 1921 the nation consumed 300 million gallons of Bevo, Pivo, Famo, Lux-O, Quizz, Hoppy, and other fake beers, but in 1932 they choked down a mere 85.7 million gallons. In the intervening years, Americans had discovered the obvious: It was more fun to drink "alley brew," the sludgy and sour but punchy concoction cranked out by racketeers in filthy brewhouses tucked into big-city alleys, and more pleasant still to Charleston the night away under the influence of hard liquor, its mostly foul and sometimes fatal wallop masked by juice and ginger ale. And when all else failed, they could indulge in what Gus Busch called the "great indoor sport" of the 1920s: making and drinking homebrew.

Still, August, Sr. and his sons were not about to concede defeat. Busch baking yeast, sold in grocery stores, had paid most of the bills, but they had also produced ginger ale and root beer. They'd built refrigerated trucks and ice-cream cabinets and manufactured ice cream, too, including a frozen eggnog and a chocolate-coated bar called "Smack." None paid particularly well, especially after the bottom fell out of the economy in the crash of 1929. They'd sold off large chunks of their real-estate holdings and rented out sections of the brewery to other concerns. But they'd kept the doors open.

So had Fred Pabst, Jr. Back in 1905, he had resigned as company vice-president, leaving the brewhouse in brother Gustav's hands and retreating to his farm at Lake Oconomowoc. But in the early days of dryness, he returned to Milwaukee and demonstrated a surprising fearlessness, a gambler's willingness to discard the past and embrace the unknown. Pabst put some of the company's equipment to work manufacturing malt syrup and scraped together enough cash to buy the Sheboygan Beverage Company, which enabled him to diversify into soft drinks and soft drink syrup. He converted his passion for Holsteins into making cheese products, though he struggled to compete against giant cheese manufacturer Kraft, whose network of distributors had already cornered the grocery-store shelf space needed to make the venture profitable.

Pabst understood that he didn't have time to build a comparable distribution system of his own if he wanted to keep his company afloat. In 1932, he approached Premier Malt Products of Peoria Heights, Illinois, one of the nation's largest manufacturers of malt syrup. Fred Pabst and Premier's Harris Perlstein each had what the other wanted or needed: Perlstein wanted to invest in beer if it returned, but owned no brewing plants and had no brewing experience; Pabst owned a brewery but lacked the expertise to distribute cheese (and beer if the amendment was repealed) on a national scale. In late 1932, Pabst and Premier merged and adopted the name Pabst-Premier Corporation.

Across town at the Schlitz plant, the Uihleins fared better than most. They'd handed over management of the brewery—now devoted to making soft drinks and near beer, and renamed Joseph Schlitz Beverage Company—to outsiders more familiar with the grocery trade and instead devoted the 1920s to banking and to managing, in some cases selling off, their two thousand properties. The earnings funded the quixotic construction of a sprawling new factory with a marble-paved lobby and an elaborate garage modeled after an orangery on an English noble family's estate, built to produce E-line chocolates and cocoa, the idea being that superior Wisconsin milk provided a superior base for superior confections. The rest of the world did not agree. After just ten years the family closed the plant, perhaps relieved to be free of their one rare failure.

But the Uihleins, Pabsts, and Busches shouldered their burdens without complaint. After all, their companies were alive. On life support, perhaps, but still breathing. There were so many who'd gone under during the 1920s. In 1918, a thousand brewers had been in business; by 1920, only half still had their doors open. Things worsened as the decade wore on. "Business is very, very poor," warned the president of Golden Grain Company, the non-alcoholic wing of Minneapolis Brewing Company, in a letter to a stockholder in late 1926. "The people are all making 'Home Brew', and as long as this keeps on the non-alcoholic beverage consumption will grow less, and the outlooks are very discouraging." Golden Grain limped along with a program of diversification that included using denatured alcohol as the base for Koonz Vigoton, a body rub ("Wonderful Body Stimulants For Use After Golf, A Swim, A Bath, Any Exercise"). The operation never turned a profit.

The story was the same around the country. Most brewers gambled their futures on one of three things, all of them in some way related to the original business of brewing: soft drinks, yeast, or near beer. But Americans already had plenty of soft drinks to choose from, and giant Fleischmann owned the yeast market. Nor, as the statistics showed, were Americans particularly interested in near beer. All of which meant that the surviving brewers were competing against each other or, in the case of soft drinks and yeast, with established companies with popular brand names.

Survival came down, in the end, to one thing: a cushion of cash provided by pre-Prohibition diversification. Take the Yuengling family in Pottsville, Pennsylvania. The brewery, founded in 1829, is today the nation's oldest, a crown the Yuenglings treasure and that they wear only because Frank Yuengling kept the doors open during Prohibition. Like many brewers, he had invested in saloon real estate, and leases and sales from those properties paid some of the bills, as did income from shares in gold mines, railroads, and a local bank. But the family stayed alive in large part thanks to ice cream. There were hundreds of dairy farms in the surrounding area, and Yuengling gambled that he could make and sell a high-quality dairy product to the same people who'd remained loyal to the family's beer. He was right; the Yuengling Creamery was so successful that it stayed in business until 1985.

But not every brewer enjoyed the comfort of diversification, and not every brewer had cultivated a loyal customer base. Nor was every brewer willing, as Fred Pabst had been, to admit his weaknesses and adjust his operations accordingly. And even the smartest, strongest, and shrewdest found it hard to cope with the stomach punch of 1929, when the stock market collapsed and the economy fell off a cliff. From 1929 to 1932, 100,000 businesses entered bankruptcy and more than four thousand banks shut their doors. By late 1932, eleven million adults had lost their jobs. The effects insinuated themselves into the very fiber of the nation: Workers first lost their jobs, then their homes. The destitute and desperate crowded into city parks and under railroad bridges, living in shacks cobbled from tarpaper and wood scraps. Hoovervilles, they called their new neighborhoods.

The economic havoc pummeled what little stability the brewers still clung to. For twelve years, Alvin Griesedieck and his father, Joe, had kept their family's company, Griesedieck Brothers Brewing, afloat on a raft cobbled out of "sheer nerve" and dogged determination. They'd sold near beer and ginger ale, lemon soda and bacon. They'd begged money from banks and friends and family and niggled each dime to death. But by early 1932, they'd run out of ideas and the company hovered on the brink of collapse. The ledger book boasted nearly a half million dollars of debt, about $5,000 in cash, and another $50,000 or so in real estate and equipment that could be converted to cash. The only other valuable asset on hand was the trademark, "Falstaff," purchased from William Lemp, Jr., in 1921. One more shove, and Alvin and his father and their fortunes would tumble into the same oblivion that had claimed tens of thousands of other American businesses in the three years since the market crash.

By the summer of 1932, they and 185 other brewers were gasping for air, staggering under the weight of debt and despair. If they could hang on just a few months more! Lately a drumbeat of glad tidings and small mercies had rumbled across the land. Lately it felt as if the dark days were nearing an end. Lately August Busch and the Griesediecks and Yuenglings and their fellow brewers had begun to believe that beer might return. Not tomorrow. Not even next month. But soon.

THE BEGINNING of the end had come in January 1931, when President Herbert Hoover released the results of his campaign promise to analyze the impact of Prohibition. The National Commission on Law Observance and Enforcement, more commonly known as the Wickersham Commission, declared the Great Experiment a failure and portrayed a nation adrift in an ocean of crime, drunkenness, and flagrant disregard for the law. The eleven members of the study panel refused to recommend outright repeal, but the report's exhaustive detailing of organized law-breaking confirmed what many had argued back in 1919: Prohibition had not and never would prohibit.

It was not hard to see why. As soon as the enforcement legislation, known popularly as the Volstead Act, had gone into effect, an underground economy bloomed, devoted to the manufacture, transportation, and sale of alcohol. Liquor came into the country along the borders, in rickety boats that bounced from the Bahamas or Cuba to Key West or the coast of the Florida panhandle, and hidden under car seats or stashed in trucks filled with crates marked "bananas." The busiest spot was the Detroit River, which separated Detroit from Windsor, Ontario. Even the harsh winters could not stop the flow: Drivers loaded their cars and drove across the ice.

The business of making and moving illegal alcohol was as organized and efficient as that of any major corporation in the country, thanks to the mostly Italian gangs who, by the mid-1920s, had grabbed the lion's share of the black market's profits. Most of their contraband was spirits, which, ounce for ounce, were cheaper to make and far cheaper to transport than beer. A case of spirits sold for as much as $100, while a case of beer, which weighed as much and took up as much space in a truck, fetched perhaps $25. Still, there was beer for those who wanted it: The only way to make "near" beer was by first making beer itself. Many brewers, both large and small, began the dry years intending to obey the law, but once they realized that they were not likely to get caught, they began bottling and selling the real thing. But as with rumrunning, gangs controlled the brewing industry, too: They snapped up defunct breweries, of which there were plenty to be had, and filled the vats with mash.

Almost everyone who wanted to found a way to make crime pay. Swanky speakeasies that featured uniformed doormen, linen tablecloths, orchestras, and entertainers could be found in all the major cities, comfortable hideaways where the well-to-do could sip the finest spirits, wines, and beers. For every posh nightclub, there were hundreds of holes-in-the-wall where drinkers crowded into a single room—often inside a private home—to drink whatever swill happened to be on hand. Ingredients for making gin, wine, and beer could be found in any drug or grocery store, and millions of families turned a basement corner or their bathtub into a small alcohol factory. In the backwoods and hills of the Appalachians, Americans continued to do what they'd been doing for two centuries: making small batches of whiskey in homemade stills.

Most bootleggers broke the law because the immense profits made it worthwhile, but everyone else embraced a life of crime because they resented the law and the chances of being caught breaking it were slim to none. The Volstead Act established the Prohibition Bureau (originally called the Prohibition Unit) as an agency of the Treasury Department. But the Bureau's agents never numbered more than three thousand, not enough to patrol the 18,000-mile border, let alone thousands of cities and counties. Nor were they particularly qualified for or enthusiastic about their mission. Thanks to Wayne Wheeler, who wrote most of Volstead, the Unit's thousands of jobs were patronage positions, rather than merit posts dispensed by the Civil Service. Wheeler's reasoning was simple: Control the patronage jobs and you also control the patrons, in this case the senators and representatives who used the posts to reward loyal constituents. As a result, while some Unit agents were honest, most supplemented their meager salaries with bribes or by selling confiscated booze. In theory, local police departments and the Coast Guard assisted the effort; in reality, in most cases they, too, turned a blind eye, paid off by deep-pocketed booze mobs.

But to focus on the colorful, albeit often tragic, excesses— machine guns jutting out of Model Ts rattling through Chicago's streets; flappers swilling cheap gin in smoky nightclubs; hobos blinded or paralyzed by "Jamaican Ginger" or moonshine—is to miss the reality: The majority of Americans honored the Eighteenth Amendment and obeyed the law, and alcohol consumption plummeted during Prohibition. That is not surprising: By 1920, millions of Americans had grown up under some form of prohibition, or embraced with fervor the notion of an alcohol-free society. Gallup polls taken in the 1930s showed that 40 percent of adults had never consumed any alcohol. Government statistics confirmed it: In 1915, Americans consumed about 2.5 gallons of spirits and thirty gallons of beer per capita; in 1934, the first full calendar year after repeal, they drank 0.64 gallons of spirits and about fourteen of beer. Per capita consumption of beer did not reach its pre-Prohibition highs again until 1970, while the population grew at record rates. Prohibition did not prohibit, but it certainly curtailed Americans' fondness for drink.

Yet at the time, reports of bootleggers and speakeasies, highjackings and gangland murders, convinced most Americans that their society had gone mad. Then, as now, the *image* of Prohibition belied the reality. And because headlines of gang murders trumped rarely reported tales of obedience to law, the Wickersham Report fueled an anti-Prohibition movement that had been gaining strength since the mid-1920s.

Organizations like the Association Against the Prohibition Amendment and the Women's Organization for National Prohibition Reform garnered their support in part from the apparent crime wave, but they also got a boost from the ASL itself. The League had drifted through the first few dry years as its leadership dithered over the group's future. One faction favored a focus on continued education about the evils of alcohol and the benefits of Prohibition; another, headed by Wayne Wheeler, favored an emphasis on enforcement. Wheeler won out, but his victory backfired: In the public's mind, the ASL became the quasi-official, extralegal body responsible for the corruption and incompetence of the federal agents who raided speakeasies and demolished illegal stills. In 1927, the year that Wheeler died, Congress reorganized the Prohibition Bureau and placed its many employees under the Civil Service Act and beyond the reach of the ASL.

The Association Against the Prohibition Amendment capitalized on that moment. The group, which incorporated in late 1920, limped through its first few years, crippled by a shortage of funds and most Americans' belief that a constitutional amendment was impossible to repeal. But as reports of alcohol-related crime filled newspaper front pages and the ASL's influence dwindled, the AAPA regrouped under new leadership. Among the organization's members were Marshall Field, the department store owner; the president of a major railroad; publisher Charles Scribner; several senators and federal judges; and a former mayor of New York City. Many of them had originally supported the Anti-Saloon League and Prohibition.

Among them was Henry Bourne Joy, the retired president of Packard Motor. Joy had donated to the ASL and favored the Eighteenth Amendment. But in the mid-1920s, horrified by the lawlessness rampant in the region near his home in northern Michigan, he threw his weight, and his money, behind the AAPA. So did the three Du Pont brothers, Pierre, Irénée, and Lammot. Irénée was particularly vocal about the evils associated with Prohibition: He was shocked by the amount of money earned by bootleggers, money that was not taxed and so did not contribute to the national treasury or the nation's well-being. He was appalled, too, by the extent to which a taste for hard liquor had taken hold among young people. Pierre supported the AAPA for different reasons: He was outraged that private property in the form of breweries and distilleries had been shut down, and through no fault of the owners. He also abhorred the intrusion of federal power into private lives, a clear violation, he believed, of the treasured American concept of states' rights. All of it— the amendment itself, the shoddy and usually corrupt enforcement, and the increase in crime and invasions of privacy—constituted "an outrage to American institutions."

These ideas resonated with a nation weary of arguing, weary of crime, and by the time the Wickersham Report appeared, already weary of an economic disaster that had barely begun. As the depression deepened, more critics called for repeal in the name of taxation. They reminded Americans that for decades, brewers, distillers, and vintners had paid heavy taxes, monies that had dried up when the Eighteenth became law. Bring alcohol back, and jobs, paychecks, and tax revenues would return, too.

A vast throng of people made that point in May 1932, on a sunny spring Saturday morning, when the mayor of New York, James John Walker—known affectionately as "Jimmie"—hosted a beer parade in his fair city. He led tens of thousands of New Yorkers in a march to tell Congress and the president that they wanted "Beer for Taxation." One police officer estimated that the marchers passed by at the rate of two thousand souls per hour: former Olympic champions, German-Americans dressed in cos-

tume, and a "Negro" contingent from Harlem; Tammany politicians who tipped shiny top hats and unemployed stockbrokers
from Wall Street. The Lambs Club and the Friars marched, and
so did the National Vaudeville Artists. Thousands lined the sidewalks or sat picnicking and watching on the lawn of Central Park.

Nor were New Yorkers alone. Walker, who originated the
idea of the Beer Parade, had urged Americans in other cities to
join New Yorkers in marching that day. They did—from Boston
to Detroit, from Scranton, Pennsylvania, to Daytona Beach,
Florida. East and west, north and south, Americans marched for
beer and for the tax dollars it would bring to an impoverished,
frightened nation.

It was not clear—yet—if Congress got the message, but the
Democratic Party did: Its 1932 platform called for repeal of the
Eighteenth and for modification of Volstead to allow for legal beer
while the states voted on a repeal amendment. Senator Gilbert
Hitchcock's reading of the plank at the party convention unleashed a cacophony of cheers, whistles, and applause that lasted
for twenty-five minutes. Nominee Franklin Roosevelt swept away
any doubts as to his party's sincerity: Prohibition, he told a New
Jersey audience in late August, had provided the "enemies of society" with money that would otherwise flow into the people's
treasury. It was time, he announced, for Americans to reclaim
those "unaccounted millions." Time to correct the "stupendous
blunder" that was Prohibition.

So the summer of 1932 drowsed to a close. One out of every
four adults was out of work. Nearly fourteen hundred banks
closed that year, hundreds during the summer alone. Farm foreclosures and bankruptcies numbered in the tens of thousands.
And there seemed no end in sight, unless Washington came up
with a plan, something Hoover had proved unwilling or unable to
do. August Busch, Frank Yuengling, Alvin Griesedieck and dozens

of other brewers, many of them lifelong Republicans, prayed for a Democratic victory, willing voters to send Hoover back to Iowa.

On the evening of November 8, Roosevelt carried just over 57 percent of the popular vote. Beer was on the way. "Beer," Walter Lippman told the readers of his nationally syndicated column, "would be a great help in fighting off the mental depression" inflicted upon the "great multitudes" by winter weather, bank failures, and unemployment. "Beer is nourishing, consoling, and warming, and it should be made available as soon as possible." August Busch weighed in, too. "I want it," he told a Kansas City reporter, "so a man can go into a decent place again, open and aboveboard, and get a 5-cent glass of beer." Every family, he insisted, ought to be "able to order bottled beer from the grocer, the same as they do milk and bread," and not be forced to buy the "poisonous stuff from an alley rat."

Babe Ruth wanted beer, too, although for less noble reasons. "Ho, ho," the Yankee star shouted to reporters after a workout. "Just give Colonel Jake Ruppert the right to make good beer again and I'll have no trouble signing any contract with the Yankees for 1933." Boss Ruppert, the team's owner, would be "so tickled" by the return of beer, explained The Babe, that he'd "be a real soft touch . . ."

The lame-duck Congress was not about to let anyone down, and certainly not Babe Ruth. Ratification of a Twenty-first Amendment would take some months—there was no way around that—but modification of the Volstead Act would provide immediate revenue from sales of legal beer. Volstead defined as "non-intoxicating" any beverage that contained less than half a percent alcohol. All Congress had to do was increase that percentage and legal beer would flow out of the breweries, and tax dollars into the treasury. Simple enough—once the House and Senate had arrived at a new definition of "non-intoxicating."

The brewers knew the answer: 3.2 percent. At congressional hearings convened to discuss the issue, Alfred Schedler, a chemist employed by Pabst Brewing, explained the science behind the superiority of this number. In simple language, the more alcohol the better the beer, because the chemical reactions that generated alcohol also produced acids and esters that contributed to the beer's "character" and "palatability." There "can not be any doubt," he argued, that "preference must be given to the [beer] with the higher alcoholic content."

But was 3.2 percent beer intoxicating? The Honorable William E. Hull, a congressman from Illinois and a man devoted to amending Volstead, shouldered the burden of proof. He had traveled to Sweden to investigate that nation's "Bratt system," by which the Swedish government classified beer and wine as nonintoxicating. To test this claim, Hull skipped breakfast one morning and traveled directly to a brewery laboratory. As a company chemist monitored the event, Hull downed four bottles of beer (he stopped at four, he explained to the committee, because his stomach "would not hold any more"). "I am a man who does not drink," Hull explained, "and therefore would be susceptible to intoxication probably equal to any adult." The chemist then tested the congressman's faculties and prepared an affidavit affirming that the beer "had not affected [Hull] mentally or physically and that every symptom showed that four pints of beer on an empty stomach had not in any way intoxicated" him. "You can laugh," Hull added, "but there is no better way of testing out a problem . . . than to test it out on yourself . . ." Committee member Allen Treadway asked an obvious question: "Do you think the Supreme Court would be likely to hear that kind of evidence?" "I don't see why the Supreme Court wouldn't take my word for it as well as that of any chemist," Hull replied. "I certainly have a reputation for telling only the truth, as you know." "Absolutely," Treadway assured him.

R. A. Huber, vice-president of both Anheuser-Busch and the USBA, devoted most of his testimony to sketching the economic benefits of legal but nonintoxicating lager. He told the committee that USBA members expected to spend $360 million to modernize and renovate their plants. "In addition to that," he added, "there would be a vast amount of money spent in the retail distribution, for equipment, ice boxes, glassware, and the Lord knows whatever else goes into that." All told, the government could expect brewers, distributors, and retailers to hire some 300,000 men. "That does not include," Huber added, "the vast number of men that would be employed in cooperage works and the bottle manufacturing plants," on farms and in coal mines, on railroads and in factories making the new equipment for the breweries. The record does not indicate whether the congressmen salivated during Huber's testimony, but they surely recognized that the legalization of beer would provide the kind of pump-priming for which Franklin Roosevelt and the New Deal were about to become famous.

The drys showed up at the hearing, too, in order to denounce the "parasitic" brewers and their lies. But they would not win this time. On Wednesday, March 22, just before two P.M. Eastern time, FDR hoisted himself from his chair in the Oval Office and walked down the hall to the cabinet room, already crowded with journalists and cameramen. (Or so reporters said; it's not clear how the partially paralyzed and image-conscious president negotiated the few feet from his office to the signing room.) There a staff member handed him the precious six pages of text that legalized 3.2 percent beer. Roosevelt picked up one of the four pens lying in wait, flipped to the last page, and began signing. He laid the last flourish to the last "t" at 2:02 P.M. At midnight on April 7, beer would flow once more.

———

THE NEWS ZIPPED through telegraph and telephone wires to cities around the country. Impromptu celebrations erupted everywhere, but most especially in Milwaukee, St. Louis, New York, Philadelphia, and other beer cities. In Milwaukee, tugboat captains opened their sirens, and employees at factories and fire departments responded with every whistle, siren, and bell they could find. A snarled maze of people, cars, and horses filled downtown streets as motorists braked to a halt and laid on their horns. Workers streamed out of offices and shops and onto the sidewalks and streets, cheering, singing, and clapping. Some stayed put and tossed a blizzard of confetti on the celebration below. The unemployed standing in line at a relief station on the city's northwest side applauded and cheered. Local radio stations interrupted their regular programming to carry impromptu speeches and songs. The 250 women playing cards at the Eagles club abandoned their tables to clap and sing.

Most of the city's brewers had 3.2 percent lager on hand, laid in weeks or months earlier as the basis for near beer. But they expected to ship all or most of it out in the first minutes after midnight on April 7, so they needed to brew more—and fast. "We have a large volume of orders from all over the country," said Sol Abrams, the treasurer at Schlitz, "and every one seems to want the first car." The day after President Roosevelt signed the bill, Abrams's clerks spent eight hours opening and processing new orders. Inside the plant, employees bottled existing stock and others mixed new batches of malt and water. Outside the main office, thousands of men lined up to apply for hundreds of positions.

The economic tonic extended beyond the breweries. The president of a Milwaukee bottling-equipment company scrambled to keep up with $1.2 million in new orders, and to hire three hundred new workers. The manager at Cream City Bottle Company could spare little time to answer questions. "[O]rders are piling up, all hands are busy, smiles are too numerous to count, and we are viewing the future with the rosiest of expectations," he told reporters. Froedtert Malt and Grain Company, one of the nation's largest malt suppliers, operated twenty-four hours a day, and had been for several weeks in anticipation of the beer bill. Every day, fifteen rail cars of barley arrived at the plant, and ten to twelve carloads of malt rolled out.

In New York, Jake Ruppert hauled one of his old beer wagons out of storage, loaded it up with (presumably empty) barrels, decorated it with banners bearing his name, rounded up two horses, and trotted the advertisement around town. Over in Brooklyn, the vice-president of Piel Brothers Brewing told reporters that his plant was booked beyond its capacity. "It is quite possible," he warned, "that there may be a shortage of beer at first." But he hastened to reassure his regular customers, those who'd purchased his soft drinks and near beer during the dry years, that they would get first dibs on the available lager. Nearby Trommers Brothers was making no such promises. "We have been swamped," said a spokesman. "We are going to have to serve every customer . . . on a ration basis."

And so it went from East Coast to West. On March 30, the Commerce Department reported that the beer bill had already generated millions of dollars in ancillary sales. Brewers expected to order thousands of new delivery trucks and $3.5 million worth of tires. A bottle maker reported that one brewer had placed a boggling request for thirty million bottles. Workers at a Massachusetts box factory chipped away at a request for 125,000 wooden beer crates.

The leadership of the Women's Christian Temperance Union reminded Americans that "no nation ever drank itself out of a depression." But the brewers and their employees were too busy to listen, and Americans weary of racketeering, hijackings, bad booze, and bankruptcy were beyond caring.

By the evening of April 6, the cavalcade of trucks and cars lined up outside Anheuser-Busch stretched for a full mile down Arsenal Street. A special police detail monitored a crowd that swelled to twenty-five thousand. Up in Milwaukee, ten thousand people milled about streets surrounding the Schlitz plant, forcing the drivers of hundreds of delivery trucks to approach the loading docks at a pace that made snails look like racing roadsters. Three thousand souls braved a light snow and trudged up the hill to the Pabst plant, where every employee and every member of the Pabst family was busy sorting through orders and trying to answer telephones that refused to stop ringing. On State Street, a smaller throng monitored the proceedings at the Miller plant. That company's train of vehicles included forty with Indiana license plates and one from Montana.

At one minute past midnight, horns and sirens blared, factory whistles howled, and the thirsty masses hooted, hollered, danced, and sang. In St. Louis, six hundred people jammed the dining room at the Hotel Jefferson to enjoy food and drink. When a photographer asked to take a shot, one woman hopped up on a table and hoisted her mug high, as did the two dozen men and women who surrounded her.

Alvin Griesedieck was too busy to celebrate what he later described as one of the most important, and happiest, days of his life. His loading dock was nearly obscured by a honking, gassy maze of trucks, a special security detail, police, and the curious hoping for free samples. The brothers Busch were just as busy. Their ailing father celebrated at home, where he listened as August Junior commemorated the moment on the air, thanks to the Columbia Broadcasting System, which provided listeners at its seventy-five affiliates with live coverage from Chicago, St. Louis, and Milwaukee. At twelve precisely, Gussie took the microphone and urged Americans to honor "personal liberty" by repealing the Eighteenth as quickly as possible and promising that brewing would never again become entangled in politics. "Happy days," he announced in closing, "are here again."

Indeed. In rainy Washington, D.C., a brand-new beer truck bearing a sign announcing "Mr. President, the first real beer is yours!" rolled to a halt on a street between the White House and the State Department at 12:04 A.M. Eight hundred delighted souls cheered as a squad of motorcycle police escorted the vehicle the rest of the way to 1600 Pennsylvania Avenue. Cheering erupted, too, in restaurants and bars in downtown Baltimore as delivery trucks rolled to various front doors and waiters and bartenders distributed the precious nectar. In San Francisco, where three breweries were up and running, cars, trucks, and tens of thousands of celebrants jammed streets in every direction, impeding the progress of delivery wagons headed to the airport, to Los Angeles, and to a host of smaller, brewerless burgs.

Down in Hollywood, Gary Cooper and Mae West settled a bet: She wagered that when the great moment came, she could outdrink Mr. Cooper. He produced two oversized steins, and the pair began guzzling. Their appointed judge declared the match a draw. Miss West took a moment to catch her breath and then turned to the reporters who recorded the event. "Now that beer is really back and we will all be drinking it why not wage a campaign for the return of the woman's natural figure?" she asked. "We haven't had any perfectly natural figures since the war took beer away from us."

At City Hall in Milwaukee, a mob cheered as a man from Blatz Brewing hopped out of a limousine clutching a carton of Old Heidelberg beer, which he deposited in one of two birchwood crates situated nearby. He told a reporter that he'd made the short run from the brewery in thirty seconds. A minute later, another car pulled up: the Schlitz man this time. At 12:04, a third car arrived from Independent Milwaukee Brewery. "You jumped the gun," one by-stander shouted, certain that the Independent representative and his prize could not have made the trip from South Thirteenth Street in three minutes. "No, no," gasped the courier, still trying to catch his breath from what had obviously been a harrowing trip. "I had a police escort and we came the back way." The traffic jam in downtown Milwaukee slowed the arrival of Pabst Blue Ribbon, which arrived at 12:10; Cream City Pilsner (12:20); Miller High Life (12:22); and finally, at 12:29, Fred Gettelman and seven bottles of Gettelman's $1,000 Beer.

A city official nailed both crates shut, loaded them into a waiting vehicle, and the entire convoy—limo, coupe, taxi, and all—headed for the Milwaukee County airport. There waited a special Midwest Airways plane, the "Spirit of 3.2." The city's delivery man climbed into the cabin as workers hoisted the crates onto the plane. Each box carried a simple message: "To President Franklin D. Roosevelt. Beer 3.2 per cent. From—The Nation's Beer Capital, Milwaukee. In Gratitude."

Poor New Yorkers. Jacob Ruppert, USBA president, had insisted that the city's brewers refrain from making midnight deliveries in order to avoid a "carnival" atmosphere. As a result, the city that never sleeps drowsed through the celebration that brightened the night elsewhere. Things picked up at daylight, when drivers began delivering the real thing. Crowds lined up ten or twelve deep at bars, waiting for a stein of foamy. Restaurants posted "standing room only" signs on the sidewalks out front. Thousands braved the chilly weather and descended upon Coney Island to pretend it was summer and that Prohibition had never happened.

At mid-afternoon, an unusual sight greeted shoppers and revelers on Thirty-fourth Street: six Clydesdales, their manes dressed in red and white roses and tails braided with red, white, and green ribbons. They pulled a shiny red Anheuser-Busch wagon loaded with three hundred wooden cases stamped "Budweiser." Only one case actually contained any beer, but who cared about details when the Clydesdales came to town?

A cheering and cheerful mass of New Yorkers followed the animals to their destination: the Empire State Building. The wagon driver, one Billy Wales, formerly of the Buffalo Bill Show, clucked his team to a stop and handed down the one real case to its new owner, former New York governor Al Smith, he adorned with his trademark black derby and cigar. As onlookers bellowed their approval, Smith faced a bank of waiting cameras. "I have seen many amusing, interesting and imposing sights on the corner of Fifth Avenue and Thirty-fourth Street," he said, "but nothing has thrilled me as much as the sight of these six big horses . . . My only regret is that the wagonload is not all mine."

And nothing thrilled American brewers as much as beer mania during the spring and summer of 1933. Forty-eight hours into legality, brewers had deposited $10 million worth of taxes into federal, state, and municipal treasuries. Brewers in Los Angeles had already run out of beer and those in Chicago and Louisville operated twenty-four-hour shifts trying to keep up with demand. "We are begging people to hold back their orders," August Junior told a St. Louis reporter. In two days, he and brother Adolphus had sold 75,000 cases and seven thousand half barrels of beer, and his staff was wading through orders for another five million cases. When the brothers hosted a celebratory party at the company's offices on Saturday, April 8, they served near beer because there wasn't any 3.2 percent on hand.

By August, federal beer receipts had risen to a whopping $54.1 million and beer had become Washington's third-largest revenue producer. Only income taxes and cigarettes generated more money. In December, the same month that Utah became the magic thirty-sixth state to embrace the Twenty-first Amendment, the nation's brewers (who, thanks to newcomers, now numbered more than five hundred) tallied their efforts and announced that since April 7, they'd rolled out twenty-one million barrels of beer. That was a far cry from the sixty million they'd made during the peak pre-Volstead year of 1914, but it was a good start.

Gus Busch had been right: Happy days had arrived at last.

THE EFFECTS of more than a decade of Prohibition did not evaporate overnight. Racketeers and mobsters who had invested—and earned—millions in beer during Prohibition dug in their heels and refused to exit the scene. Why should they? The brewing equipment was in place. All they had to do was find outlets for their beer, and that was easy enough: Just hire a few "distributors" to visit neighborhood taverns and "suggest" that the owners serve a particular beer. When a Brooklyn woman refused one such hint, a man named Bugsie and his pals smashed her tavern's furniture and fixtures. They finally left, but phoned an hour later to warn her that if she called the police she'd end up in a funeral home.

Then there were the "Wall Street" brewers, as critics called them by way of distinguishing these opportunists from more experienced beermakers. They were perhaps the worst of the lot, because they *looked* respectable. The combination of a devastating economic depression, a thirteen-year thirst, and a low entry fee in the form of hundreds of empty breweries for sale at near-theft prices proved irresistible to anyone with a pocketful of change and a smooth line. They dived nose-first into a beer vat and found plenty of investors willing to join them. The New York Stock Exchange warned people to avoid the get-rich-quick brewery schemes outlined in glossy prospectuses touted by men of often dubious reputation. But a desperate public handed over its money anyway. Who could blame them? At a time when soup kitchens and tarpaper shacks were more plentiful than jobs, brewing shone like a beacon of salvation. Was not beer the national drink? Had not beer made the brewers of yore rich beyond measure?

The result was a parade of disastrous publicity and even worse beer. Many of the brewers-come-lately ignored—or knew nothing about—such necessities as pasteurization and sterile conditions. When some Los Angeles residents became ill after drinking bottled beer, the county Health Department seized and quarantined the suspect products. Tests revealed that much of the brew had been bottled right out of the keg, without being pasteurized or treated with preservatives. The same thing happened in Dallas, where a city health inspector traced an outbreak of food poisoning to tainted brew. He confiscated 26,000 cases of beer that had been siphoned into filthy bottles. A mixture of disgust and self-preservation drove many Americans back to homebrew.

Comfort lay in the fact that dodgy dealers eventually fell by the wayside. At the end of the day, an unscrupulous racketeer or a Wall Streeter was an inexperienced brewer who never learned rule number one of brewing: Fine beer sells, while bad beer does not. By late 1934, most had vanished.

But the troubles that plagued brewing ranged beyond shoddy brew and mobsters. On the first anniversary of repeal, the nation's brewing capacity stood at 80 million barrels, but consumption at less than half of that. An industry analyst calculated that 85 percent of all breweries had run aground on the shoals of financial problems. Ten percent were in receivership, and dozens had already gone bankrupt. It was "a foregone conclusion," he added, in case anyone had missed the point, "that a great number of the present breweries will disappear from the roster before very long."

Part of the problem, of course, was the overall economy, whose problems ran so deep that beer alone could not begin to fix them. People standing in line at soup kitchens or living under bridges had no change to spare for beer. But even those lucky few with incomes and jobs were not returning to beer in pre-

Prohibition numbers, and brewers were learning a hard truth: The world had changed. Beermakers could not own or lease taverns; could not hold mortgages on properties where alcohol was sold; could not loan tavern owners or other retailers money or provide them with fixtures, glassware, or furniture. The old beer gardens were gone and they would never come back. Nor would the "tied" houses and ten saloons per block. Both were part of an older, slower time when most people used their legs as transportation and the beer joint as an escape from a cramped apartment. Years of Anti-Saloon League rants had persuaded millions of Americans that saloons were dens of iniquity into which no respectable person would venture. Even the word "saloon" had fallen out of fashion and been replaced by the less threatening "tavern."

On the flip side of restrictions stood opportunities: The legislators who constructed repeal encouraged citizens to scorn saloon and tavern in favor of convivial drinking 'round the family hearth. They passed a spate of laws that legalized the sale of beer in grocery and department stores. Brewing's future lay not in barrels of beer rolled behind mahogany bars, but in the cool, well-lighted interiors of the nation's refrigerators. If brewers could learn how to market, distribute, and advertise beer to the "home market," as it was known, they could regain lost ground.

But even assuming brewers figured out how to negotiate this new landscape, would Americans still want what they had to offer? While brewers slumbered, factories had unleashed an unprecedented quantity and variety of consumer goods: automobiles and radios, lipstick and rouge, mouthwashes and shampoos, cloche hats and silk stockings. Advertising dollars ballooned as Madison Avenue blanketed the nation with slogans, jingles, and images designed to persuade the citizenry to buy things they didn't know they needed—to spend money on something other than beer.

One of those things was the automobile. When the Volstead Act went into effect in 1920, there were some nine million cars and trucks in the United States; by the end of the decade, nearly twenty-seven million vehicles clogged the roads. Back in the old days, one observer lamented, "boys and girls stayed at home evenings." No more. Now young folks stepped out every night to "dance halls [and] cabarets," where they indulged in "[g]in parties and other 'wild doings'"—habits cultivated, of course, during the dry years.

Or they necked in the dark comfort of a movie house. Movies were already popular when the 1920s began, and by decade's end, 75 percent of the population visited the movies at least once a week. The tavern's smoky gloom paled in comparison to the allure of a shimmering screen populated by charming mustachioed men and impossibly thin women in chic frocks, all of whom held a cigarette in one hand and a martini in the other.

Balanced against these competitors for time and money spent on beer was the home itself. Where Americans had once gravitated toward saloons for comfort and company, now they could enjoy both at home. The first commercial radio broadcast aired in 1920 and by 1929 nearly half the nation's households owned at least one radio, a percentage that had risen to 60 by the time beer came back. They enjoyed the new entertainment in unprecedented comfort thanks to coal- or gas-burning furnaces, which Americans had purchased in record numbers during the 1920s. Forty-seven percent of urban houses were wired for electricity in 1920; by 1933, more than 80 percent enjoyed that convenience. Twenty-five percent of homes contained a mechanical refrigerator (up from less than one percent in 1920).

Unfortunately for the brewers, those refrigerators were more likely to contain Coca-Cola than Budweiser. Just because Americans had voted for repeal, it did not follow that they planned to drink; an entire generation of men and women had not tasted alcohol for decades—or ever—and had no plans to do so. They'd spent the dry years quaffing oceans of soft drinks, and as one advertising expert told brewers, "[v]ery few people are going to drop a fifteen year old liking for a favorite beverage merely because they can now get beer . . ." Especially not if the soft-drink manufacturers had anything to say about it. They'd started cashing in on dry mania as local option laws had eradicated saloon and drink. Between 1911 and 1934, sales of Coca-Cola, ginger ale, root beer, and other soft drinks had tripled. For thirteen years the makers of soft drinks had bombarded consumers with billboards, radio ads, window and counter displays, and glossy magazine images designed to persuade a beer-bereft citizenry how much better their lives would be if they drank Coca-Cola or Vernor's ginger ale. Battle-hardened soft-drink makers were not about to cede ground to beer.

Women were particularly resistant to beer's charms, and not just because they regarded the martini as a more attractive accessory. During the 1920s, they abandoned their mother's serge skirts and high-neck blouses in favor of clingy rayon stitched into mere slips of gowns. The clothing left nothing to the imagination and led women down the merry path of weight obsession. Dieting became a national pastime. Women's fear of fat spawned a loathing for beer, especially given brew's stodgy reputation and the old stereotype of the female beer drinker as a "Munich matron with double chins running all the way to her ankles."

So the old days when beer was king and a man's saloon his empire were dead and gone. Americans were drinking less than half the brewing industry's capacity, and demand would stagnate for decades. Until and unless Americans returned to beer, it was impossible for them to keep two or three thousand breweries in business, as an earlier generation had during the golden age of the saloon and beer garden.

But in post-repeal America, it would be easier for fewer breweries to fulfill more of the demand, thanks to roads and cars. To accommodate the growing flotilla of automobiles, Americans had begun building a network of paved highways. It was nothing like the sprawling interstate system that would exist later, but nonetheless a giant leap forward from the handful of (mostly un-paved) roads that had existed during the railroad era of the nine-teenth century. The new highways linked town with country, state with state, East with West, and so offered the potential for long-distance shipping that dwarfed anything envisioned by even Frederick Pabst or Adolphus Busch, who had been at the mercy of north–south, east–west rail lines.

OVER THE NEXT few decades, these new realities would reshape the brewing industry. The dearth of breweries created an oppor-tunity for those smart enough—and wealthy enough—to grab it. Brewers who would thrive in the middle and late twentieth century were those who used highways and wholesalers as well as modern advertising methods to move their beer into lager vacuums. The shift from saloons to the home market, and from local sales to long distance shipping, also turned the old pre-Prohibition ratio of bottled beer to tap—about 90 percent tap—upside down. By 1935, about one-third of beer sold was already in a package. By 1940 it was half, and by 1960, 80 percent of beer would leave its brewery in a bottle or can. Successful brewers would learn how to capitalize on this shift.

In those first few years after repeal, none of this was yet ob-vious. But if we turn to the company whose owners visualized the new dynamic faster and more clearly than any other brewers, we understand the scope of the Busch family's achievement. If any one factor explains the dramatic growth of Anheuser-Busch after repeal, it is that August A. Busch and his two sons accepted the challenge that Prohibition and repeal forced upon them: to learn how to do business—how to *make* business—beyond the insular world of nineteenth-century brewing.

For eighty-odd years, the Busch men had sold just one product—beer—and sold almost all of it in one place—saloons. They had long ago mastered the art of selling beer to bartenders, and of manipulating mortgages and leases in order to build a network of tied houses; they knew how to hand out beer trays and penknives stamped with the company name. But after January 1920, none of those skills mattered. "We had to forget that we were brewers, bred in the bone and trained that way for years," August A. Busch told a reporter, a painful process that he likened to "tearing trees up by the roots." The keys to not just survival but success, Busch understood, lay in diversification, distribution, and marketing.

Through trial-and-error, and more than a few failures, he and his employees gained an understanding of how to create a diverse line of products and introduce them into new territories. To sell ice cream, for example, Busch organized a marketing department—itself an innovation of the 1920s—and targeted four markets in four different regions of the country. Into each, his employees dispatched the new ice cream; $10,000 per week for advertising, which went "a long way in one place;" and a product-specific sales crew. If "demand persist[ed] after the nine-days'-wonder of the first promotion," and the staff had amassed the necessary "experience on which to proceed, and the certainty" that it would "get [its] money back, and something more," only then was it time for Anheuser-Busch to "undertake a *national* campaign."

Looking back, the Busch strategy sounds absurdly basic, almost stupidly obvious, because it's become the basis of the twentieth-century way of doing business. But to a brewer in the 1920s, it was all new, and after April 7, 1933, it became the key to the company's success. In that respect, August A. Busch, like his father before him, stands as one of brewing's greatest innovators. Like his father, he led rather than followed. Because he had been willing to first rip out and then replant the company's roots, and had sworn to protect and preserve his father's legacy, he did more than just endure Prohibition. He used the noble experiment as a school in which to learn a new way of doing business. That, along with a dedication to making a superior beer, enabled Anheuser-Busch to break away from its lesser competitors and thrive in the harsh terrain of post-repeal brewing—to become, and remain, the world's largest brewing company.

Anheuser-Busch survived; August Busch did not. The nearly Sisyphean struggles of his life—first against his imperious and domineering father, then against Prohibition—had worn him down. On the morning of February 13, 1934, exhaustion and the ravages of ill health—heart problems, gout, and asthma—finally won out. He picked up a pearl-handled revolver and ended his life.

At the funeral, his friend Daniel Kirby remembered the "sweetness of nature" of a man who "never did a mean thing." Kirby might have added that August Busch was one of the heroes of the industry. Busch would have shrugged off such praise, but the description is apt. Few brewers had worked harder to survive Prohibition. No one paid a greater price. And no brewery reaped greater rewards.

CHAPTER SIX

"You Have to Think About Growth"

T
HEIR BREWERY on State Street—Plank Road, once upon a
time—was a dilapidated shadow of its former self, but
their bank accounts were fat, and so the Millers of Milwaukee—Frederick A., Clara, and Elise (brother Ernest, who had
"stolen" Budweiser, had died in 1925)—made the only logical
choice: Spend money to make money. In the summer of 1933, the
siblings began overhauling the aged plant built by their father.

The place needed it. During the 1920s, the Millers had kept
the doors open by making near beer, soft drinks, and malt syrup.
But none of those ventures paid well enough to justify refurbish-
ing their nineteenth-century brewhouse. Instead, the family had
focused on their other investments, which were many and profitable. Their real-estate holdings stretched from storefronts—
former saloons, for the most part—in downtown Milwaukee to
apartment buildings in Chicago to hotels in Miami, with gas stations, shops, and offices scattered hither and yon in between.
They'd invested heavily in municipal bonds, a good choice during
the 1920s when most cities were redesigning their landscapes to
accommodate automobiles, with a major holding in Canadian
bonds "so that if the US should go Bolsheviki, like Russia," Ernest

Miller once explained, they would not lose their entire fortune. But for reasons best known to themselves, they skirted one category of investment: stocks. As a result, they also avoided the bloodbath of 1929, and sailed into repeal with cash in hand.

But their father, company founder Frederick J. Miller, had taught his children to put the brewery first. That in turn nurtured in all of them an uncanny ability to measure their actions and decisions in terms of whether those injured or aided the enterprise that lay at the center of the family's life. In many nineteenth-century brewing families, fathers and sons regarded daughters and sisters as accessories rather than partners. Not so the Millers, who cultivated in both Elise and Clara a ferocious devotion to the brick buildings on State Street. When beer returned, the siblings knew where both their duty and their self-interest lay.

Over a period of three years, they dumped more than $1.5 million into the plant. They modernized the cooler room, adding giant suction fans, an air-filtering system, glazed tile floors and walls, and stainless steel catwalks. They rebuilt the cellar, as brewers still called them, although this one stood five stories above ground. They bought new keg washers and upgraded the generators in the powerhouse. A newly hired chemist presided over a state-of-the-art laboratory.

But where the heart of the original facility had been the brewhouse, in the 1930s it was the plant's bottling line and, after 1936, its canning equipment, which filled two hundred cans with beer each minute. Here, the Millers recognized, lay the future. Fred A. Miller said as much in 1930, when, recognizing that beer was likely to return, he warned Clara that they needed to start thinking about their aging bottling line. Employees had repaired and refurbished the equipment, which dated to the 1890s, but if "beer should come back . . . the present machinery could not stand the strain, because [their sales] would be mostly bottled beer."

He was right. If the home market and long-distance shipping represented the path to brewing's future, containers, or "packages" as the industry called them, served as the bricks that paved the way. Bottled beer had been around for years, of course, but a bottle was relatively fragile and heavy, and expensive to ship. Customers paid a deposit on each one, and brewers spent small fortunes recovering their empties, shipping them back to the brewery, sorting them, hunting for those that were chipped or cracked, and sterilizing those that could be reused. That system worked well when a brewery bottled only a small fraction of its beer. But in post-repeal America, no brewer could bottle, say, 75 percent, or even just 50 percent, of his output and expect to earn a profit if he had to pay freight to ship the empties back home.

What the new industry needed were lightweight, inexpensive containers that held up under the stress of shipping, fit into a refrigerator, and could be thrown away when empty. A sturdy, disposable can would eliminate most of the bottle's shortcomings. But it presented two stumbling blocks: The container had to withstand the high temperatures required for pasteurization, and, more problematic, it couldn't foul the beer, which is highly sensitive to metal.

Researchers at the American Can Company had begun working on a suitable metal container in 1909, a project they shelved when Volstead became law. But in the late 1920s, company executives dragged their files out of storage and began a new search for the perfect can. Fred Pabst and August Busch, attuned to market changes thanks to their Prohibition experience, also tackled the matter. Pabst was particularly interested in metal packaging. In the months leading up to repeal, he worked closely with a Milwaukee manufacturer to develop a metal replacement for the wooden barrel. He regarded his staff's research into the can as an extension of that task, since, after all, a can was nothing more than a miniature barrel.

Sometime in 1931 or 1932, American's researchers found the answer: Vinylite, a moldable plastic developed by Union Carbide that the can manufacturer used to line the container's interior. Initial tests by Pabst-Premier were positive, but Perlstein and Pabst refused to commit until American had tried the new package in real-market conditions. William Krueger, president of Krueger Brewing of Newark, volunteered his company as a guinea pig. He, like most brewers, understood that the realities of post-repeal brewing dictate that he ship his beer well beyond his hometown. He had already waded into urban markets along the eastern seaboard as far south as Richmond, Virginia. He would test canned beer there.

Richmond provided an ideal laboratory. First, about 75 percent of the city's beer was sold in bottles, the reverse of what was true nationally but the ratio predicted to become the norm in another decade or so. Second, Krueger already owned a chunk of the Richmond market. Third, it shared the city with a handful of local and East Coast brewers as well as the three major shipping brewers, Anheuser-Busch, Pabst, and Schlitz, which meant that the Krueger cans would face limited but varied competition: national brewers supported by hefty advertising and regionals and locals backed by hometown loyalty and name recognition.

In June 1934, a crew of messengers hand-delivered four cans of eer and a questionnaire to one thousand households, chosen be-
se they'd been identified as Krueger customers. The question-
e cut to the chase: Did you like the beer? Would you drink it
? Is the no-deposit, no-return package worth the extra money?
e results surprised even Krueger: Eighty-nine percent liked
enough to drink it again. That was more than good enough
ad. Krueger and American created an advertising cam-
plete with streamers, signs, window cards, and plenty
er ads ("KRUEGER'S . . . in the amazing new KEG-

LINED CAN." "HAVEN'T TRIED IT YET?...you're missing something"), and on January 24, 1935, the beer went on sale city-wide. Within a month, more than 80 percent of Richmond's beer distributors were handling Krueger's brew—and canceling orders for beer from Pabst, Schlitz, and Anheuser-Busch.

By late 1935, brewers could choose from two kinds of cans—the flat-top still familiar today and a short-lived version shaped like a bottle—as well as several sizes and shapes of thick-walled, lightweight disposable bottles. The new packages accelerated the trend toward shipping. Prior to Prohibition, the vast majority of brewers shipped no beer at all or limited their reach to perhaps fifty miles from their home base. By the late 1930s, three-quarters of brewers were transporting at least part of their brew over state lines. True, much of the interstate beer ended up in adjoining markets: a Brooklyn beermaker sending trucks of beer across the Hudson to Newark, a Milwaukee brewer shipping to Chicago, Philadelphia beer being sold in Baltimore. But every day more and more beer traveled farther and farther, and brewers who could afford to began thinking of their markets in national, rather than regional or local, terms.

The Miller siblings, who introduced their canned beer in March 1936, recognized that brewing's future lay far from home. Pre-Prohibition, the brewery's beer rarely traveled beyond Wisconsin and a half dozen other northern midwestern states. But in 1936 and 1937, the family made its first strike to push Miller Brewing into the industry's top ranks, spending a half million dollars on radio and newspaper advertising. In 1937, Fred and Clara both retired, a move that injected new energy into the company in the form of Clara's son, thirty-one-year-old Frederick C. Miller, who joined the board of directors and replaced his mother as vice-president. In 1938, Elise, now company president, and her young nephew accelerated their campaign, advertising Miller High Life in forty states. The following year they made a run for the other eight when they purchased advertising, much of it full-page and in color, in a host of national magazines. By that time, they'd moved out of the crowded bottom tier of small, local brewers and into the top twenty nationwide. The Millers had grasped the essential dynamic of beer-selling in post-repeal America: The race would be won by he and she who moved quickly and decisively.

Building a shipping market required money most of all, and not every brewer could afford to make the same choice as the Millers. Nor did every brewer try to do so. A handful of small, family-owned breweries survived the rambunctious post-repeal period by sticking to their pre-Prohibition game plan: cultivate local markets and local loyalty. Small beermakers like Yuengling in Pennsylvania, Leinenkugel in western Wisconsin, and the Matt family's West End Brewing in upstate New York endured in part because of hard work, careful management, and fine beer. But they were also protected by their location in rural areas characterized by sparse population and limited highway access. For many years, the largest brewers—Anheuser-Busch, Schlitz, and Pabst—simply ignored these isolated pockets in favor of the swelling urban centers that proliferated alongside increasingly congested highways. The Matts, Yuenglings, and Leinenkugels took advantage of that fact, and, rather than gamble on risky expansion and shipping, chose instead to pour all their resources into building customer loyalty in their own backyards.

As a result, it was small urban brewers who bore the brunt of the assault from shipping brewers and were the most likely to crumple when the Millers, or an even bigger gun like Anheuser-Busch, already experienced in the complexities of retailing and distribution, released a barrage of advertising. Nor could the urban locals rely on low price to keep their customers. Thanks to Prohibition's alley beer and the Wall Streeters' tainted brew, shoppers shied away from bargains, fearing that low price indicated low quality. One grocery owner explained to a brewing trade journal that the women who frequented his store preferred quality over price, which was another way of saying that they preferred the consistently high-quality brews from old-line nationals like Schlitz and Pabst. This was more than one man's anecdote. A survey in the spring of 1935 showed that, nationwide, half of all beers sold were in the medium price range ($1.60 to $2.00 a case), while the cheap brews (priced at less than $1.60 a case) captured only about 17 percent of the market. Premium beers like those from Pabst, Schlitz, and Anheuser-Busch snagged a full third. And those were only national averages. In Columbus, Ohio, for example, the lowest-priced beers accounted for only about 3 percent of sales, while the most expensive brands hogged a whopping 68 percent of the market.

The nature of post-repeal distribution exacerbated small brewers' woes and inadvertently fueled the dynamic that favored giant breweries. Prior to Prohibition brewers sold their beer directly to saloon owners, but after repeal they handed it over to a middleman, the distributor, who resold the beer to grocery stores and taverns. In a perfect world, a distributor's trucks left the warehouse loaded with cans, bottles, and kegs from a half dozen or more breweries. The more cases of Brand X that the driver unloaded at Sam's Corner Grocery, the more money the distributor earned. If Sam's Corner Grocery closed, or if Sam stopped carrying Brand X, or, worse, if Brand X Brewing closed its doors, the distributor's income dropped and his employees drove half-empty trucks.

From the brewer's point of view, the distributor owned the key that unlocked the door to Sam's Grocery. If Brewer A wanted to break into the market in, say, El Paso, he had to find a distributor who was willing to carry his brand and place it on grocery store shelves.

But the biggest brewers' command of larger and larger shares of the market enabled them to exercise an informal but lethal power over wholesalers. A giant could pressure his distributors to truck his beer and only his beer; to drop competing brands; or to drop soft drinks, liquor, and wine. If the wholesaler refused, a brewery representative would show up at the warehouse and threaten to cancel the carrier's contract.

Most distributors caved to the pressure. How could they refuse? Not with fleets of trucks and warehouses to pay for. And so the wholesaler informed his weaker, smaller customer—usually a local brewer—that he could no longer carry that brand of beer, leaving the beermaker with a brewhouse of woes in the form of unsold kegs, bottles, and cans.

Those who played the distribution card wisely created a buffer that sheltered them from hard times and other competitors. But no one could control the weather or the economy, and drought in 1936 and a recession in 1937 put even more pressure on the smaller players. When the drought began in the summer of 1936, there were 739 brewers in operation; by late 1938, that number had plunged to 625.

World War II proved another matter. Early in the conflict, federal officials ordered distillers to convert their plants to military production of industrial alcohol, but protected brewing as a vital component of the war effort. With spirits in short supply, beer consumption soared—or at least as much as rationing would allow.

Tin was rationed, so beer cans were banned except for sales to the military. Schlitz transformed shortages of glass and bottle caps into an advertising campaign. "When you share a quart of Schlitz and make one cap do the work of three it isn't a question of patriotism," the company's advertisements announced. "You are just helping the other fellow get his share of the beer that made Milwaukee famous. That's the friendly, American way." When gasoline and tires ran short, Rudolph Schaefer bought one hundred draft horses and rented dozens more; it was the only way he could deliver his beer. Rainier Brewing of San Francisco hired teams of Clydesdales to haul wagons of lager through the city's hilly streets.

In 1943, the Food Distribution Administration ordered brewers to hand over 15 percent of their production to the troops, a seemingly innocuous mandate that inadvertently exacerbated small beermakers' woes. Fifteen percent of production from Anheuser-Busch, Pabst, and Schlitz was almost enough to meet demand, which meant that many small beermakers missed the opportunity to introduce their lagers to the people most likely to drink it: young men. Cut off from the front lines, the small fry focused on selling their beer to civilians at home, but they often ran short of bottles or kegs, or the gas needed to make deliveries.

Pinned down by rationing and ambitious national shippers on one side and a fusillade of federal regulations on the other, small beermakers joined forces in a Small Brewers Committee (later the Brewers Association of America). The twenty-five men who gathered in Detroit in the spring of 1942 appointed as secretary William O'Shea, a hot-tempered, loose-tongued wheeler-dealer whose Chicago printing company made labels for a number of breweries. He lobbied Congress for a graduated tax system based on barrelage and devoted the war years to railing against big brewers, whom he accused of ignoring the small guy's plight. His members, he warned in what would not be the last of his hyperbolic pronouncements, would rather be put out of business by what was left of the enfeebled Anti-Saloon League than by rapacious cutthroats like the Busch brothers. "The big brewers are going to destroy the opportunity of young men who someplace, this very day, are giving their lives for one purpose; preserving the American way of life." He demanded that the "paternal government . . . protect the weak like the police protect us from thugs."

Others begged to differ. A man who had directed a brewing trade group during the dry years argued that too many small brewers clung to outdated business methods, content to coast along trolling for tavern trade and equating salesmanship with throwing a few bucks on the bar and buying a round for the house. Where were the small brewers during the push to conquer the home market? he asked. Nowhere to be found, and so the largest brewers had commandeered new territory around the country, filling grocery shelves from coast to coast with their beer, while the small boys whined about their poor sales and low profits. Another critic blamed the small beermakers' woes on carelessness and ineptitude. Too often they hired an inexperienced friend or relative to manage the plant, and then exacerbated that mistake by refusing to pay good wages for a trained brewmaster. The beer went bad, sales plunged, and the brewery landed in bankruptcy.

Harsh words, but in many cases accurate ones. As one beermaker pointed out, anyone who failed during the war surely only had himself to blame. With distilling off-limits for the duration, most brewers were selling as much beer as they could make. Sales rose 10 percent in 1941, 12 percent in 1942, and another 12 in 1943.

Still, the shortages of brewing materials forced every brewer, large or small, to make a difficult choice: brew as much beer as possible using inferior substitute grains, or stick to high-quality but scarce barley, corn, and rice and reduce output accordingly. Many brewers took the path of least resistance and experimented with rye, oats, or potatoes. But rye produced a doughy wort, and oats resulted in a tongue-curling swill. One brewing chemist pleaded with brewers to avoid the potato, which produced beer that tasted as foul as it smelled. In the end, the brewers who created rationing-inspired recipes stuck with either yellow corn (oilier than the white corn that brewers typically employed) or unmalted barley. It was mostly marginal beermakers who tampered with their recipes; those with long histories and solid reputations didn't dare.

Among them were the Millers. Back in 1937 when drought and recession had sent materials costs into the stratosphere, Elise, Clara, and Frederick had ordered their brewmaster to keep paying top dollar for the same fine materials that the family had been using for eighty years. In 1944, when the brewery turned out a record 730,000 barrels of beer, Elise made the same decision, but this time it forced her to curtail production. She slashed the advertising budget, pulled Miller beer out of seventeen states, and eliminated every label except the company's flagship brand, Miller High Life, most of which was sold in slender bottles adorned with a gold-foil neck wrapper and Miller's famous "Girl in the Moon" logo. The results were not as disastrous as they might have been: Because the family had positioned it as a national beer, Americans, back at work now and with hefty paychecks, passed up ten-cent bottles of lesser-known brews in favor of the fifteen-cent Girl in the Moon. The brewery earned a profit of $2.2 million in 1945, more than twice the amount of 1940, while selling in far fewer markets.

The war ended in 1945, but rationing did not. President Truman told Americans that Europe needed their help. Brutal weather there was killing both people and livestock. There was flooding in Italy and food shortages in Holland. Worse yet, the specter of communism lurked in every bleak street and dark alley of every European city. Better to endure Meatless Mondays and Wheatless Tuesdays here at home, Truman told the nation, than to allow the red menace to wrap its loathsome arms around the starving millions of Belgium or France.

No one knew when rationing would end, but Elise and her nephew Fred C. decided that, scarcities be damned, it was time to get busy. Job one: Replace the brewery's nearly prehistoric 700,000-barrel capacity. In March 1946, company officers broke ground on a new stockhouse, phase one of a grand plan to rebuild the plant from the ground up.

Having launched that effort, Elise stepped down as president. She was in her late sixties and in poor health. Her side of the family held the majority interest and she insisted on passing the post to her untrained, uninterested, unkempt son Harry John, Jr., known to all as Buddy.

Her reasons had less to do with the brewery than with Buddy himself. Like all of the Millers, a devoutly religious family, he practiced Catholicism. But during his years as a student at the University of Notre Dame, he had fallen under the spell of a priest who promoted an extreme, mystical version of the religion. By the time he graduated in 1941, Buddy had become convinced that his wealth, which was considerable, stood between him and salvation. He moved to a farm outside Milwaukee, but continued to visit his mystical mentor at Notre Dame. In the mid-1940s, he began a lifelong campaign to hand over his fortune, which then amounted to $2.5 million (about $20 million in today's dollars), to Catholic charities, monasteries, and convents. Elise was none too pleased about the plan, but became nearly apoplectic when she realized that he intended to scatter his Miller stock, too, which amounted to a quarter share of the brewery.

Work, she decided, would set him free of what she regarded as an irresponsible-bordering-on-insane project. She installed Buddy in the president's post. But Elise Miller John was no fool: She gave her son exactly one year to prove himself. If he failed, she warned, the job would go to his cousin, Fred C. Miller.

Buddy showed up at the office and attended board meetings, but he spent most of his time trying to separate himself from his assets. He emerged from that project on occasion in order to join his father, Harry Senior, Elise's estranged husband, in an attempt to sell the brewery. Father and son kept their intentions secret until Harry Senior was discovered escorting executives from other breweries on guided tours through the plant.

Fred C. chastised his uncle and scrambled to assure his employees that the company was not for sale. And sighed with relief when, in May 1947, his aunt Elise kept her word. Buddy was out. Fred C. was in.

The second time, Elise made a wise choice. Her nephew was born to lead. He'd played three seasons of football under Knute Rockne at Notre Dame, serving as team captain and being named All-American (tackle) not once but twice. Fred had graduated cum laude in 1929, and returned to Milwaukee to run his parents' sprawling lumber and real-estate interests. He was a big man— six feet tall—with big shoulders and an even bigger personality. He thrived on risk, danger, and Notre Dame football. Every week during football season in the 1940s and 1950s, he traveled to South Bend to serve as an assistant line coach to head coach Frank Leahy. Usually he flew, sometimes piloting the plane himself (by the early 1950s he'd survived three plane crashes).

One weekend he and a few friends headed for Philadelphia, where Notre Dame was to play Penn. Bad weather forced the plane down in Pittsburgh, so the group piled into a car, Fred navigating, another man driving. When the travelers discovered that the highway patrol had closed the road to Philadelphia, Fred hopped out of the car and shoved the barricade aside. The reluctant driver forged onward, but soon wearied of maneuvering around the stalled and snow-bound cars that clogged the road. He called it quits. "What do you mean we can't get through," Fred demanded. "Get out of there, I'll drive." He seized the wheel and plowed on, steering and veering his way through the maze of snow-covered mounds, rolling down the windows when fog clouded the windshield. His passengers froze and no doubt aged several years during the drive, but Miller got what he wanted: He arrived in time for mass and breakfast with the team.

As far as Miller was concerned, his appointment as president of Miller Brewing came not a minute too soon. His competitors were busy expanding into multiple breweries around the country—the next logical move in an industry where national markets had become the great prize each brewer sought. Multiple plants increased a brewer's vat capacity, of course, but, more important, a second or third plant mitigated the costs associated with long-distance shipping. The Busch brothers, for example, had purchased fifty acres in Newark, where they planned to spend $20 million building a new, state-of-the-art brewery. Nothing said more about brewing's future than this announcement; nothing did more to enable the industry's largest beermaker to grow still larger.

Not surprisingly, those who could do so matched the maneuver. Perlstein and Pabst parried with the purchase of Hoffman Beverage in Newark. In June 1946, the first Pabst beer rolled off that line and onto grocery store shelves in the New York metropolitan area. The New Yorkers fought back: Rudy Schaefer spent $2 million enlarging his Brooklyn plant, and the Liebmann family, makers of Rheingold, purchased a local competitor's 500,000-barrel facility.

Erwin Uihlein pondered the scene. Since war's end, he had managed to push Schlitz Brewing into the number-one spot, a rare blow to Anheuser-Busch. He'd done so by expanding the brewery and spending millions on advertising. But if he wanted to stay on top, he had to keep moving, keep buying. In early 1949, Uihlein bought the old Ehret brewery in Brooklyn and spent $6 million modernizing the plant.

Fred Miller would not be left behind. Bulldozers and wrecking balls demolished large chunks of his grandfather's nineteenth-century plant. Construction workers swarmed the newly cleared land and raised a brewhouse outfitted with three five-hundred-barrel vats, as well as a new bottling facility that could handle two million containers a day.

By the time the Miller family hosted Milwaukee dignitaries

and press at the official dedication in July 1949, Fred had added a new warehouse, a second brewhouse, and a grain storage building. Gone were the dark brick, the turrets and castellation of his grandfather's day. Gone the statue of Gambrinus, the Gothic windows and arched entryways. The new buildings loomed over the city's western edge, a hulking, monolithic, anonymous mass of pale brick and blank facades, softened by rounded corners but not much else. Sleek. Streamlined. Modern.

The brewery exemplified the dynamic future that Miller and other beermakers saw before them. The top four—Schlitz, Anheuser-Busch, Ballantine (an old Newark brewery reopened after repeal by two engineers), and Pabst—and those angling for a spot to dislodge them had expanded into a country flush with full employment, more than $100 billion Americans had socked away in savings during rationing, and a belief that war and depression were behind them. In 1948, Americans drank 86.9 million barrels of beer and their per capita consumption hit 18.5 gallons, the highest numbers since repeal. Surely a blissful era of nonstop growth and profits had arrived.

IN ONE WAY IT HAD: Between 1950 and 1960, the volume of American industry as a whole increased 54 percent. In the fifteen years after the war's end, the gross national product rose 250 percent and per capita income a whopping 35 percent. Beer, however, would not keep pace. In 1949, beer sales dropped by more than a million barrels. In 1950 they plummeted another two million, and they slid again in 1951. Per capita consumption dropped to 16.8 gallons. For the rest of the decade, sales barely budged from the 84-million-barrel mark and per capita consumption drifted downward, falling below fifteen gallons in 1961. As the rest of New America roared into the future, brewing's engine sputtered and stalled right out of the gate.

Thus began the era that many people now see as the age of

corporate beer, during which, they argue, a handful of giants, Anheuser-Busch chief among them, elbowed their way into domination of the industry. A time when those same giants diluted their beer with cheap corn and rice, reducing once fine lagers to little more than yellow water. A time when, coupling that low-cost beer with millions spent on advertising to promote the swill, they systematically destroyed smaller beermakers who clung to honest traditions and pure barley malts.

The truth is more complex, and the era itself both short-lived and anomalous. The dynamics created by post-repeal laws and the switch to the home market favored brewers with deep pockets. Only they could afford the investment in multiple plants, the high-speed bottling and canning equipment, and the advertising campaigns in magazines and on television that allowed them to fully exploit a national market. But even the largest, healthiest beermakers struggled to make sense of a nation that had turned its back on beer.

One factor that haunted brewhouses large and small was demographics. The birth rate had plunged from twenty-eight births per thousand people in the 1920s to twenty-one in 1930 and a mere eighteen in 1936. In the 1950s, that demographic chicken came home to roost, as the number of Americans between the ages of twenty and forty—the prime beer-drinking ages—slid to historic lows.

Worse yet, those few adults turned their noses up at beer. They might have been willing to drink it during the war, when liquor was in short supply, but not any longer. Many drinkers celebrated the post-war return of spirits with martinis or the syrupy sweetness of Manhattans, Rob Roys, and Singapore Slings. Others had never given up their Prohibition-ingrained preference for sugary soft drinks. By 1960, consumption of spirits had risen by nearly a quarter of a gallon per capita, even as that of beer declined by nearly two gallons. Over the next decade, spirits consumption doubled but beer inched up a modest two gallons, thanks mostly to the first wave of baby boomers hitting the drinking age. But that jump in sales was too late for smaller, marginal players. During the 1950s, the environment for brewing was, in a word, brutal. If it is true that only the strongest survived, make no mistake: They earned their victories.

Beer suffered another blow as the diet craze of the 1920s and 1930s blossomed into full-blown mania in the fifties. Magazine editors stuffed their pages with weight-loss plans and publishers grew rich on mountains of diet books. The food industry crammed grocery shelves with low-calorie jams and peanut butters, frozen dinners and salad dressings. The easy-pour artificial sweetener Sucaryl adorned kitchen tables from coast to coast. Dieters dumped money and time into programs like Slenderella and TOPS ("Take Off Pounds Sensibly"). Beer had never lost its reputation as a fattening beverage favored by beefy men; the contest between dieting and beer was no contest at all.

But beer also fell victim to a national palate that, since the 1920s, had gravitated toward the sugary and the bland, both of which can be seen as hallmarks of a modernizing society. Historians mark the decade of the 1920s as the true beginning of the twentieth century. It was then that Americans shrugged off the values and ideas that had characterized the nineteenth century in favor of those that can be regarded as "modern." Americans embraced a more casual attitude toward sex, to name one example. Thanks in part to the automobile, they expanded once small boundaries of sociability—islands, one historian has called them—and abandoned a local outlook in favor of a more national view. Advertising became more ubiquitous, and its content changed. Nineteenth-century advertising focused on the object itself and its qualities: This is fine soap. This is a well-made chair. But in the early twentieth century, advertising targeted not the object but the person buying it: This soap will make you beautiful. This mouthwash will make you popular. This car will enhance your virility.

One of the most important changes of the first half of the twentieth century was the way in which Americans associated modernity with convenience, most especially in food. Adults living in the 1920s remembered watching mothers and grand-mothers spending hours preparing food—and they rejected that hard labor, which had devoured women's energy, in favor of con-venience: soups, vegetables, and fruits from cans; factory-made bread; store-bought mayonnaise. Washing machines. Detergents in boxes. These modern conveniences evoked a new age a uni-verse away from the old days when women had worn skirts to their ankles and had hands scuffed by harsh soaps.

But the more processing that food endures, the more flavor it loses, so the generations born in the 1920s and 1930s grew up eating a blander diet than their parents had and a more limited one as well. It was also a sweeter diet, as processed foods tend to contain more added sugar than unprocessed. In the 1970s, Amer-icans would rebel against soft, tasteless breads, "instant" coffee, and even corporate beer, but in the early and mid-twentieth cen-tury, the American palate favored the light, the bland, and the fla-vorless. Consider cigarettes: Between the 1920s and the 1950s, the percentage of rich, full-flavored Turkish leaf tobacco in ciga-rettes dropped from about 20 percent to less than 6 percent. Dis-tillers diluted their liquors with neutral spirits in an effort to please customers on the hunt for a light liquor. Vodka, virtually unknown in the United States before the 1950s, became one of importer Heublein's best sellers, thanks to the spirit's lack of color and flavor.

But nothing exemplified Bland America like TV dinners and canned soups, instant coffee and packaged pudding, dehydrated potatoes and instant rice—all flew off grocery store shelves and into the nation's kitchens. Americans liked it that way. They scorned homemade breads in favor of light-as-air, textureless Wonder Bread. When the kitchen at a posh Boston restaurant switched from fresh beans to frozen, customers raved about their flavor.

Beer? Too bitter. Too hoppy. Too flavorful.

Brewers struggled to adjust to these unexpected and confusing developments. Some gambled on new recipes. They had to if they wanted to please a bland-happy public. Back in the 1870s, Americans had demanded a less malty, less hoppy version of European lager, and brewmasters had accommodated their new countrymen's tastes by developing a unique American version of Bohemian-style lagers. Now a new generation asked for—and received—an even less demanding version of American lager: a sexy, vibrant beer that went down as easily as instant mashed potatoes or pudding and never asked much of its recipient. The president of the Master Brewers Association of America urged his membership to brew "streamlined," "modernized" beers with a pale color, "an agreeable, mild hop flavor," and no "bitter aftertaste." The president of the Wahl-Henius Institute, one of the nation's leading beer schools, warned brewmasters to pay heed: They might prefer full-bodied, hoppy brews, but they weren't the ones buying the beer. The public preferred "blandness," and so blandness it must have.

Some critics denounced what a business reporter in 1952 described as "the dethronement of the old-time brewmaster," but they missed the point: For nearly a century, American brewers had been accommodating the demands of the public's palate. They'd done so in the 1860s and 1870s. Now a new generation of brewmasters heeded the insights gleaned from sophisticated consumer research that showed that the average American beer drinker disliked overtly malty or hoppy beers. The importance of the style of American beer at mid-century is that it was a response to demand.

Consider events that unfolded at Renner Brewing in Youngstown, Ohio, where sales had drifted downward from the moment of repeal. The company survived its first post-repeal decade largely because of the demand induced by war. But when peace returned, red ink again nudged black out of the company's ledgers. In 1949, the board of directors hired new management and created a new beer, but to no avail. Renner's executives turned to a market research firm for help. Its surveys revealed that people rejected Renner lager because it was "too bitter and strong." Out went the old and in came a light brew, along with a new sales pitch and slogan. Renner's sales soared.

Much the same thing happened at Fort Pitt Brewing in suburban Pittsburgh. In early 1952, that company responded to the demand for light lagers by introducing Fort Pitt Pilsener, a "pale, dry, less filling" beer. So, too, at Red Top Brewing in Cincinnati, where executives ordered their brewmaster to dump his old recipe in favor of an "extra-dry" light lager. The new beer went on the market in 1951 and sales rose 100,000 barrels over the previous year.

Lighter beer saved Ruppert Brewing. The company had drifted aimlessly since the death of Jake Ruppert in 1939. George Ruppert, Jake's brother, stuck with dark, heavy beer sold mostly in barrels for the draft market. Sales plunged. When George died in 1948, the new management dumped the old brew and the emphasis on tap beer in favor of a light lager sold in bottles and cans. "The full flavor remains but the bulk is gone," announced the company's advertisements. Knickerbocker, "sparkling-clear" and "**extra** light," was a "modern, low-calorie beer that's far less 'filling' than beer of the past." Ruppert would never regain its place at the top of the heap: During its years of drift, it had suffered fatal wounds at the hands of Anheuser-Busch and Pabst. Still, the decision to alter the beer in order to accommodate changing tastes staved off the inevitable and kept the company alive for another fifteen years.

Fred Miller was ahead of the game: He didn't need to tinker with his recipe. Grandfather Frederick J. Miller had brewed a modern beer before Americans knew that they wanted one. Miller High Life, the "Champagne of Bottle Beer," was light, pale, and dry. Very light. Very pale. Very dry. A beer best suited, sneered one competitor, for "women and beginners." Fred C. knew better. High Life, he reckoned, was the perfect beer for a new, modern America, just as his sleek brewery and its high-speed, high-tech equipment was the right design for the times. Together the beer and the brewery would propel his company into the industry's top rank.

So would the exquisitely fine-tuned business acumen that seemed to be imprinted in Miller's DNA. Consider the way he averted what might have been a disaster of bad timing: The new brewery with its capacity of three million barrels had gone online in late 1948, the worst possible time of year in an industry where the average brewer sold about 80 percent of his beer during warm-weather months. Miller knew he had to sell beer and sell it now, not later, so he did what few of his competitors had ever tried: He unleashed a new sales campaign in the dead of winter. It paid off, and Miller Brewing could boast that it sold half its beer in what had been the "off season." One reason was advertising, about $7 million worth a year (a breathtaking $54 million today), far more than most brewers spent. But the way he advertised the beer made more difference than the money he spent doing it. Yes, he geared some of his ads toward men, sponsoring sporting events on radio and television. But the family had long touted Miller High Life as the "Champagne of Bottle Beer," so Miller carried that idea directly to a group of people most brewers overlooked: women. He ran full-page color ads in women's magazines like *McCall's* and *Vogue*. He hired Brooks Stevens, one of the most important industrial designers in the country, to create in-store displays aimed specifically at the women who spent their family's food dollars. Miller even sold his beer in six-ounce splits, a dainty package aimed at women's appetites.

Everything Miller touched turned to profit. In the space of just five years, the brewery's sales soared 275 percent in an industry whose overall increase amounted to 2 percent in a good year. By 1951, he'd spent $25 million on his new brewery; he was selling High Life in all forty-eight states and Hawaii; and he'd pushed Miller Brewing into the number-eight spot. In late 1952, his employees bunged their three-millionth barrel of the year, a new company record and enough to push it from sixth place to fifth nationwide behind Schlitz, A-B, Pabst, Ballantine, and Schaefer.

But that was not enough for Fred Miller. Barrel three million had no sooner been packed off for sale than he announced another $20 million worth of expansion. "Our goal," he told reporters, "is to be the largest producer of the best beer."

He faced a steep climb. Impressive as those three million barrels were, they amounted to only half the annual output across town at Schlitz or down in St. Louis at Anheuser-Busch. Still, for a guy who'd been number twenty just a few years back, he was doing fine. And no, he told reporters and employees who asked, he did not plan to buy or build outside of Milwaukee. That likely struck many observers as an odd decision. After all, Milwaukee almost seemed too small for a man of such oversized ambition and energy. But Miller insisted: One plant had been good enough for his grandfather, and it was good enough for him. He would stay right where he was.

Among the major players, he was alone in that decision. In the early 1950s, it had become clear to ambitious brewers that a stronghold in the eastern United States was not enough to guarantee brewing supremacy. The future of New America lay in the other direction, in the golden West in general and in California in particular.

In the fifteen years after the war, a combination of Cold War politics and warm sunshine enriched California to the tune of millions of people—five million new residents between 1950 and 1960—and billions of dollars. Gigantic aircraft factories sprawled out into the desert, along with thousands of new housing and shopping developments, all of it embroidered with ribbons of interstate and freeway. Magazines and newspapers raved about the California lifestyle with its backyard swimming pools (40 percent of the nation's total), lush lawns, and year-round sunshine. The Dodgers and Giants exchanged creaky, bleak New York for youthful California, and in the space of a year, *The Mickey Mouse Club,* a California production populated by wholesome California kids, forced the New York–based *Howdy Doody Show* out of its Monday-through-Friday slot. A reporter for *Life* magazine was not far off the mark when he predicted that California would "radically influence the pattern of life" in post-war America.

Twenty years later, California would "radically influence" American beer culture, but in those first years after the war, Big Brewing knew only that the Golden State was the place to be. In 1948, just three years after his Newark purchase, Harris Perlstein negotiated to buy the 600,000-barrel Los Angeles Brewing Company. A few months later Tivoli Brewing of Detroit bought Aztec of San Diego, a purchase that promised to push tiny Tivoli, ranked thirty-fourth, up into the top fifteen. In the summer of 1952, Erwin Uihlein announced a California acquisition of his own: thirty-five acres in the rapidly growing Van Nuys section of the San Fernando Valley not far from Los Angeles.

Uihlein's news release came just days after a similar bulletin out of Anheuser-Busch headquarters in St. Louis: Gus Busch had purchased sixty-five acres in Van Nuys; there he would spend $15 million to build a 750,000-barrel brewery.

It was the shrewd move of a man with Busch blood in his veins. For the last five years, he and Anheuser-Busch had suffered the ignominy of sitting in second place, having been ousted from first by the Uihleins. Busch was determined to regain the throne. No one doubted that he would succeed. "Being second," he once said, "isn't worth anything."

August A. Busch, Jr., began working at the brewery in 1922 and was promoted to general superintendent in 1924, when he was just twenty-five years old. After his father's suicide in 1934, he became second vice-president and the brewery's general manager. He'd been the number-one man since the death of older brother Adolphus III in August 1946.

Gus was every bit as flamboyant as his grandfather Adolphus, perhaps even more so. Like Adolphus, he oozed self-confidence. He was any situation's center of attention, just as Adolphus had been, and exuded the same irresistible charisma. There, perhaps, the comparisons peter out. Gus, an "almost defiantly uninhibited" man, was a bit more crude, a bit more blunt than Adolphus. He was less educated than his multilingual grandfather, but he compensated for a lack of book learning with a universe-worth of street smarts that were unexpected in a man born into unbridled wealth.

"He rarely talks in a normal voice," a reporter once observed. He "sounds more like a hoarse lion" and "lopes in a half-walk, half-trot, arms pumping like a sprinter," all the while shouting orders to the flunkies racing to keep up with their full-speed-ahead boss. He indulged in frequent fits of rage, especially when encountering fools, a species he did not suffer gladly—or, for that matter, at all. In short, Gus was the right Busch for the moment. If he couldn't bring Anheuser-Busch out of its slump, no one could.

In 1953, Gus regained the number-one slot during a lengthy brewery strike that shut down his Milwaukee competitors. For decades, brewing had been one of the most unionized of American industries, and prior to World War II, relations between employers and employees had been friendlier than most, perhaps because labor and management shared the same burden of persecution by a dark force that was always trying to put the brewer out of business and the worker out of his job. But in the decade after the end of the war, union workers nationwide, sniffing the opportunities of a go-go economy, embraced a new militancy that resulted in tens of thousands of strikes and affected nearly every industry. Brewery workers and owners squared off repeatedly in contests over working conditions and pay scales.

Most walkouts ended within a week or two, but the Milwaukee strike that began in the spring of 1953 dragged on for seventy-six days. All told, the city's residents lost $100 million in income and the breweries three million barrels of beer during the peak selling season. Pabst and Schlitz both owned other plants and could keep making beer. Fred Miller could not, and for the first time, brewing's Golden Boy conceded that his one-brewery, one-city strategy might be a mistake. He put plans for another $20 million expansion at State Street on hold and told reporters that he was thinking of spending the money on a new facility elsewhere.

When the picketers returned to work, Miller and Milwaukee's other major brewers, Schlitz and Pabst, raised their prices in an attempt to recapture lost profits. Down in St. Louis, Gus Busch had escaped the labor bloodbath, but he joined them in raising prices anyway, presumably because he thought he could get away with it.

Customers balked. No one knew why. Perhaps it was because brewers had done such a good job of accommodating the nation's taste buds. One pale, light lager tasted much like another, so why pay more? Whatever the reason, for the first time since repeal, consumers deserted the premiums for cheaper regional brands like Falstaff and Hamm's. Gus Busch missed the point and raised his prices again in 1954. Disaster ensued: Anheuser-Busch sales plunged 15 percent, and A-B handed the number-one slot back to Schlitz. Gus apologized to stockholders, calling it the "worst mistake" he'd ever made. Then he took off on a cross-country tour, visiting every wholesaler who handled Anheuser-Busch products, explaining his error and urging them to fight the good fight. Back home, he invited eleven thousand wholesalers, retailers, and tavern owners to his home, a thousand each night, greeting each one at the door with a welcoming handshake. "When midnight came," he said later, "my hand would be so swollen I couldn't move my fingers."

All told, 1954 was not a particularly good year for Gus Busch, and not just because of his pricing blunder. He had acquired the St. Louis Cardinals a year earlier, and winced at the attacks the purchase earned him. A Colorado senator who was also president of a minor-league baseball association introduced a resolution that would have banned A-B from owning the team and added insult to injury by holding hearings on the matter. Gus showed up and defended himself, but the assault was humiliating. He shrugged off criticism that he'd bought the team only for its sales-pitch potential, but he and everyone else knew that it wouldn't hurt to have Anheuser-Busch signs plastered all over the infield and scoreboard. Nor did it hurt that baseball fans were choosing to stay home and watch on television rather than take themselves out to the ballpark; Gus's advertising would reach them there, too. The new owner knew little about baseball, but he dived into this new adventure with the same gusto with which he grabbed everything else in life. "We hope to make the Cardinals one of the greatest baseball teams of all time," he announced.

A few weeks later he traveled to Milwaukee, where Fred Miller had just persuaded the Boston Braves to move to Wisconsin. A bemused Gus posed for pictures at a celebratory luncheon, standing behind the seated Fred with his hands on Miller's shoulders, as if to say "Down, boy, down!" In the center of the table sat a cake decorated with small figures of two baseball players, one in a Cards' uniform, another dressed as a Brave, foreheads touching, leaning into an imaginary shouting match as a tiny plastic umpire stood nearby.

BUT IF MILLER BREWING and Anheuser-Busch represented one face of the brewing industry in the 1950s, Pabst exemplified another—one that was, although few recognized it at the time, more emblematic of Big Brewing's coming fate. Pabst Brewing had ridden high and fast into the post-war era under the leadership of president Perlstein and board chairman Fred Pabst Junior. The brewery, ranked number three in the nation, owned a plant in Newark, and in 1953 opened a high-efficiency, ultramodern brewery in Los Angeles months before Gus Busch and Erwin Uihlein.

But in 1954, Fred Junior retired, an event that marked the first time since 1864 that no company officer bore the name "Pabst." With him went the Pabst magic that had once made Chestnut Street in Milwaukee home of the world's leading brewery. He had given up a role in daily management some years earlier, but his place on the board had rooted the company in its past. After all, Fred had joined the company back in the 1880s, and learned the business under his father's tutelage. No one else could or would replace that connection to the past, and it's not likely anyone cared. Since repeal, most of the company's officers had been chosen from the ranks of superior salesmen, or from the cadres of college-educated young men interested in making a career in booming corporate America. Now a parade of presidents, vice-presidents, and marketing directors could not reverse the flow of red ink; they could not figure out how to market a beer in a world where beer drinkers proved few and fickle. By 1956 the company had slid to seventh place in the brewers' ranks, and the stock had plunged from its post-repeal high of $32 to a mere $6. In 1957, the board of directors replaced Perlstein with a marketing executive from

Colgate-Palmolive, who stanched the wounds with a combination of lower prices and gimmicks like coupons redeemable for salt shakers and barbecue tools.

It was too little, too late. Frederick Pabst's beloved brewery, with its turrets, Gothic windows, and lanterns emblazoned with "P," lay near death. A proxy fight erupted in early 1958, when one group of stockholders tried to sell the brewery to Pepsi-Cola and another group resisted, determined to resuscitate what was left of the company. In the end, the combatants reached a weird compromise: Pabst bought Blatz Brewing from its owner, spirits maker Schenley, not because it needed more brewing capacity—it most assuredly did not—but because it needed Blatz's president, a whiz-kid accountant who had doubled Blatz's sales and prodded the company from its position at number twenty-four up to number eighteen. Whether he could save Pabst remained to be seen.

If Pabst hoped to survive, someone needed to get cracking. A pack of aggressive mid-sized regional brewers were grabbing bankrupt breweries and using those and space on wholesalers' trucks to bully their way up the ranks. They got a boost from consumers' disenchantment with high-priced brews. No one worked this game better than the men at Hamm Brewing in St. Paul, Minnesota. They modernized the company's one plant, then purchased Rainier's San Francisco facility, which opened doors to wholesalers in coveted California. They dumped their old ad campaign and replaced it with one built around the phrase "the land of sky blue waters." It was not particularly fresh, but it was transformed into sheer genius when paired with an irresistible animated bear and a jingle inspired by "voodoo rhythm" and pounded out on an empty Star-Kist tuna carton. Sales climbed 36 percent in 1955. The company rose to seventh place that year and to number five in 1956. After that, nothing seemed impossible. Over the next few years, Hamm continued to snap up bankrupt breweries and to hold its place in the top five. Hamm was joined there by Falstaff of St. Louis and Carling of Cleveland, regional breweries that elbowed their way up using similar strategies, although neither ever employed as seductive a jingle or as adorable a mascot as Hamm.

But even the Hamm bear could not catch up with Gus Busch and Erwin Uihlein, who resembled bulls on a rampage, building or buying breweries as fast as they could sign the checks, apparently oblivious to the stagnant demand that was killing others, banking on some far-off day when Americans would perform an about-face and fall in love with beer again. In 1956, Erwin Uihlein bought an empty brewery in Kansas City, Missouri. A year later, he broke ground on a new plant in Tampa, Florida, the company's first foray into the rapidly growing Southeast. In July, Busch informed the world that he had purchased 160 acres about a half mile from the Schlitz site; there he planned to build a $20 million plant. Anheuser-Busch added to its Florida holdings in early 1958 when it bought a Miami brewery. The purchase didn't last long—the Federal Trade Commission ordered A-B to shed the acquisition on grounds that it violated federal antitrust laws—but it's not likely Gus Busch lost much sleep over it, especially when he ended the year 1.1 million barrels ahead of the Uihleins.

Other brewers questioned his sanity. Gus Busch wasn't brewing at 100 percent capacity now. No one was. Why did he want another plant? Busch had an answer, of course. "You have to think about growth," he said. "You have to plan for it."

That was what it took to stay on top in the near-fatal 1950s: Aggression. Planning. Risk. But in such precarious times, risk sometimes proved fatal. Consider the case of the Liebmanns, Julius and Alfred, both in their eighties but still active, and Alfred's son Philip, brewery president. The family had never sold its Rheingold anywhere except the urban Northeast, where the annual "Miss Rheingold" contests attracted millions of voters and generated as much excitement and anticipation as the Oscars did

in California. The company's two New York City breweries provided a capacity of 2.5 million barrels a year. During the early
1950s, that, plus the Liebmanns' fine beer, business smarts, and
the various but always beautiful Miss Rheingolds, enabled the
company to power its way into brewing's top five.

But in early 1954, the family paid $6 million for Acme Brew-
ing's Los Angeles and San Francisco plants. The decision to sell
its beer on what might as well have been another planet led to
disaster. The family opened its newly refurbished California
plants in 1954, brewing Rheingold at the Los Angeles facility and
Acme's Gold Label in San Francisco. A year later, Philip Liebmann shut the Gold Label plant and pondered the dismal scene
in Los Angeles, where sales of Rheingold had fallen 48 percent
since opening day. Two years later, he sold the facility to Hamm
Brewing.

To his credit, Liebmann owned up to his mistakes, most of
which boiled down to his failure to understand the complexities
of the modern market. First was the beer: It had been brewed for
New Yorkers, and Californians turned thumbs down on its (relatively) heavy, (relatively) bitter flavor. Second was distribution: In
New York, Liebmann relied on his own drivers and trucks. That
didn't work in California, where brewers had long since learned
to coexist with union teamsters and powerful wholesalers.

Last, the company's advertising and marketing missed its mark.
Back east, Liebmann told a reporter, the family targeted its lager
and its ads at neurotic, hard-driving New Yorkers and "a sophisticated market, where [people] work like hell so they can live in
Scarsdale, and then drop dead in an elevator." That message
bombed with Californians, who, Liebmann recognized too late,
prized "leisure and casualness. At 5 o'clock there is a rush to the
barbecues, and at home they live in their backyards." Liebmann
had missed the point of the pun in the slogan attached to the
state's bestselling Lucky Lager: "It's Lucky when you live in Cali-

fornia." Even the Miss Rheingold contest, which drew millions of voters in New York, flopped in the land of beauty queens and starlets. Lesson learned, Liebmann told a reporter. "You don't sell soapsuds and beer the same way."

The Liebmanns' tale of California woe was symptomatic of a deeper problem. Many brewers were following the mid-twentieth-century equivalent of a saloon-era game plan: sports-oriented sales pitches aimed at the "worker," a mythological creature believed to be (a) lower income; and (b) addicted to watching or listening to sporting events.

On the face of it, that seemed like a logical move. After all, sixty years earlier brewers had gotten rich selling beer to the workingmen who thronged saloons. Nor could anyone blame brewers for assuming the continued existence of a sizable and powerful working class, given their ongoing, head-to-head confrontations with union labor. But union membership peaked in 1955, and in New America, the "workingman" was almost as likely to be female as male, to wear a white collar rather than a blue one, and to favor three-martini lunches over bologna sandwiches out of a metal lunchbucket. Moreover, the new working class enjoyed more disposable income than previous generations. They tended to buy according to reverse pricing: Higher-priced brews conveyed status and signified, in their own minds if no one else's, that they were just as able to enjoy life's finer things as their suit-clad bosses.

Perhaps this workplace fluidity explains an unintentionally goofy mid-1950s magazine ad for Ballantine ale. "Enjoy the game with light refreshing Ballantine! THAT'S ALE, BROTHER!" read the headline. The accompanying photograph featured two men sitting in a posh den outfitted with a bookcase stuffed with rows of matching moroccan-bound volumes. The pair held glasses of foaming beer, wore suits and ties, and sat in front of a television tuned to a baseball game. Pictures of athletes in action hung on the wall. Whom, exactly, was this ad supposed to woo? Blue-collar workers who devoted their weekends to yearning for the high life? Corporate executives getting in touch with their hidden "Joe Regular"?

FRED MILLER would never know. Just days before Christmas in 1954, he and his son headed for a holiday hunting trip in Canada. Minutes after taking off from General Mitchell Field on the city's south side, the plane crashed. The Millers and their two pilots died. In one moment, Miller Brewing lost not just its dynamic president, but Fred Junior, twenty-one, a senior at Notre Dame, a high-school All-American quarterback, and, by all accounts, a near-clone of his father, so surely headed for brewing leadership, too.

Norman Klug, Fred C.'s able vice-president, carried on in his boss's place. The company expanded, added more equipment, created the Miller High Life Open golf tournament, and aired its commercials during such TV blockbusters as Steve Allen's *The Tonight Show* and the *Mitch Miller* sing-along program.

But the Champagne of Bottle Beer had lost its fizz and the Girl in the Moon her glow. The devotion to family and business that had sustained and inspired Elise, Clara, and the two Freds had run dry. This time there were no relatives eager to take charge. That included Buddy John, who was more devoted than ever to his Catholic charities and cared what happened in the brewhouse only insofar as it affected the stock dividends that fueled de Rancé, the foundation he had created to manage his philanthropic work.

From 1947 to 1953, Miller sales had risen 379 percent. From 1954 to 1960, they climbed a mere 13 percent. In-fighting and power struggles among various factions of the Miller family stymied Klug's efforts to push the company forward. In the late 1950s, he investigated the possibility of several acquisitions, but followed through on none. Falstaff, sniffing disarray, tried to buy the brewery, but family members blocked the move. In 1960, Klug bid for Burgermeister, but family quarrels slowed the process and the California brewery slipped out of his hands and into the Uihleins'. The next year he succeeded in purchasing nearby Gettelman, but its 132,000 barrels hardly constituted a serious power play.

Where Miller Brewing might have wandered had it stayed in family hands is an unanswerable question. In July 1966, Lorraine Mulberger, the daughter of Elise Miller John and sister of Buddy John, startled Milwaukee and the brewing industry with the announcement that she was selling her company stock—by that time she held the controlling shares—to W. R. Grace, a billion-dollar conglomerate whose holdings included shipping, chemicals, and chocolate.

The outside world may have been shocked, but insiders were not. J. Peter Grace, the company's president, was no stranger to the Millers or their brewery. He was an old family friend and, as a fellow Catholic and philanthropist of the first order, had mentored Buddy John in the art of giving money away. Buddy had chosen Grace to serve as treasurer of de Rancé and, more important, as one of his two representatives on the brewery's board of directors. Grace, in turn, wanted the brewery, a fact he never tried to hide. Once on the board, he hounded both Buddy and Lorraine to sell him their shares of the company, which he regarded as an attractive addition to his already diverse holdings. Brother and sister had wrestled with the idea of selling, but neither was willing to make the first move. Only God, it seemed, was going to push one of them off center.

Like the rest of the Miller family, Mulberger had been raised Catholic, but in the early 1960s she had left the family faith to join a Protestant fundamentalist church. And in July 1966, she told a handful of reporters that God wanted her to remove the evil of alcohol from her life. Price? Thirty-six million dollars, not a bad return on God's will. Brewery president Norman Klug died not long after, perhaps of a broken heart, and Peter Grace installed his own man at the top.

The ramifications of the Miller–Grace merger would ripple through brewing for years to come: A few years later Peter Grace would in his turn sell the company to another, much larger corporate conglomerate that would rewrite the rules of engagement among brewing competitors. But in 1966 it was just another of thousands of corporate marriages. Between 1951 and 1968, nearly fifteen thousand American firms surrendered their independence, twelve hundred of them giants holding assets of $10 million or more. Seventy percent of the deals were "conglomerate" mergers like the Miller–Grace marriage, wherein a company that manufactured, say, copper wire, acquired one that produced nylon stockings.

Many small and regional breweries that had survived both stagnant demand and the national giants' power seized on merger as a way to gain strength through diversity. Many had no choice: Every year it became harder to compete against the giants, and every year Americans, who had become accustomed to the still new but powerful sway of television advertising, turned their backs on "local" products in favor of ones with national name recognition. The biggest manufacturers, aware of that fact and that more Americans were changing residences more and more often than ever before, advertised regularly in national media, and it was their names—Hunt's, Heinz, Colgate, Schlitz—that won out over names recognizable only to locals born-and-bred. Family-owned businesses with mostly local markets found it hard to compete.

Thus they turned to mergers. National Brewing bought an olive oil company and Heileman purchased Machine Products, which fabricated airplane parts. Iroquois Brewing of Buffalo acquired an investment firm, a maker of natural food supplements, and a company that manufactured parts for computers and spacecraft.

More than one ailing brewery surrendered its independence to outsiders. The Liebmann family, which never recovered from its California fiasco, sold Rheingold to Pepsi-Cola United Bottlers, Inc (PUB). Jake Ruppert's brewery suffered a similar ignominious fate. In 1963 Marvin Kratter, a New York real-estate developer, bought the brewery and then leveraged it two years later to buy the Boston Celtics basketball team. Kratter's heart wasn't in beer; it was in wheeling and dealing. Soon after the Celtics deal he sold the Ruppert brand to PUB/Rheingold, thus closing the hundred-year-old brewery on Manhattan's Upper East Side. (He held on to the Celtics for three years, and then sold them to Ballantine Brewing. The reason? A computer manufacturer had absorbed Kratter's company and the new management had no use for a basketball team.)

But most brewery mergers consisted of like joining like, as strong players gobbled weaker ones. Narragansett Brewing of Rhode Island bought Heffenreffer and 103-year-old Krueger, the canned beer pioneer, then was itself acquired by Falstaff. Drewry's bought Piel Brothers of Brooklyn; Pfeiffer of Detroit bought E. & B. Brewing; and Rochester Standard absorbed Haberle Congress in Syracuse, New York. Peter Hand of Chicago merged with Buckeye of Toledo, Ohio. Ortlieb Brewing of Philadelphia took over Fuhrman and Schmidt of Shamokin, Pennsylvania; Sunshine Brewing in Reading, Pennsylvania, snatched Columbia Brewing in Shenandoah. Blitz-Weinhard of Portland, Oregon, grabbed Great Falls Breweries of Great Falls, Montana, and Oshkosh Brewing in Wisconsin picked up Rahr Green Bay Brewing. Carling bought Arizona Brewing in 1964, but sold it two years later to National Brewing of Baltimore (which staged a successful takeover of Carling in 1975).

The mergers reduced the number of breweries—and the array of beer brands found in grocery stores. It's easy to blame mid-century brewing's shrinking numbers on corporate giants, but as the roll call above reveals, small and medium-sized brewers were hardly innocent victims; they played their own part in downsizing the industry. Mergers provided marginal players with additional brewing capacity and so a chance to make a run for glory, but in the 1950s and 1960s, vat capacity mattered less than that most valuable of all assets: space on a distributor's truck. When Blitz-Weinhard of Oregon, for example, bought Great Falls Brewing of Montana, Blitz bought not just a brewery, but access to its distributors and so to another market.

As the brewers' ranks dwindled, the competition between them intensified, and the wholesaler himself became vulnerable. An Illinois wholesaler for Falstaff learned that truth in a particularly brutal manner. First the brewery sold him lager contaminated with phenol; many of his customers dumped him and his bad beer. Then Falstaff's sales manager showed up at the warehouse and demanded that the wholesaler capture 98 percent of the territory for Falstaff, and do so using "chiseling" tactics, such as offering lower prices to favored customers, or providing free kegs to tavern owners who would switch to Falstaff. The wholesaler struggled, torn between the need to protect his investment in trucks and warehouses and his desire to preserve his integrity. When he refused Falstaff's demands, the brewery terminated his contract. The wholesaler lost everything, and sold his trucks, warehouses, and other assets for a few cents on the dollar.

Wholesaling functioned, in other words, as the old tied-house system had worked before Prohibition. And as in the days of the tied house, one man's disaster was another man's opportunity. No one understood this dynamic better than Roy Kumm, the president of Heileman Brewing in La Crosse, Wisconsin. In the early 1960s, Kumm bought five failing breweries in order to gain access to their distributors. Kingsbury Brewing gave him an entrée into Minneapolis, northeastern Wisconsin, and parts of California and Washington. Brewmaster provided accounts in Ohio and Michigan. Foxhead opened doors in New York and New Jersey.

California, which had become one of the largest beer markets in the country, proved a harder lock to pick. Those brewers who had invaded the state back in the early 1950s controlled distribution and thus retail outlets. The only way in was by purchasing an existing California beermaker, which Kumm tried to do in 1966, when he bid on, but failed to win, Lucky Lager. "There is," he groused, "no other way to do it. You cannot get in with any of the wholesalers out there. It is an absolute impossibility. It is a locked door."

As it had back in the 1880s, the merger movement of the 1960s kept some small players alive for a few more years. But in the end, it also inadvertently fostered the giants' ambitions and placed the smaller players in an even tighter squeeze. In 1966, the Supreme Court upheld a lower court decision that found Schlitz guilty of violating antitrust statutes when it had acquired another brewery. That decision haunted—and shaped—the industry for years.

Barred from acquiring competitors' plants and equipment, Schlitz and Anheuser-Busch simply dug into their pockets and built more plants. They'd started doing so back in the 1940s, but their pace of construction accelerated significantly in the 1960s, and the new factories were far more efficient than any of the tiny, aging breweries available through merger. With these behemoth brewhouses, the Big Two could produce more beer at a much lower cost than anyone else and slash their distribution expenses as well. By the early 1970s, A-B and Schlitz owned fourteen breweries between them, produced eight or ten million barrels apiece each year, and measured their annual growth in double digits. No one could catch them. That was unfortunate, because the two giants built those plants at a moment when seismic shifts rattled the industry. In the 1960s, the decade and a half of stagnant demand ended and beer consumption shifted upward. The moment Gus Busch had planned for had arrived.

ROBERT A. UIHLEIN, JR., grandson of August, did not intend to let Gus run away with his lead. He had joined Schlitz Brewing in 1942, starting in sales and working his way up to a vice-presidency in 1951—just in time to watch A-B knock Schlitz out of the number-one slot. Bob Uihlein longed to fight back, but his uncle Erwin, the company president, wasn't interested. Nor was Sol Abrams, general manager and a Schlitz employee for some sixty years. The two older men settled into second place. For much of the 1950s, one employee said later, Schlitz Brewing resembled a "big lion dozing in the sun."

That worried Bob Uihlein and the four hundred or so other Uihleins whose comfortable lifestyles depended on stock dividends. In 1961, the family-dominated board of directors replaced Erwin Uihlein with his nephew. Eighty-seven-year-old Sol Abrams retired.

Bob Uihlein was a tall hulk of a man with a passion for tennis, polo, and big-game hunting. He was decisive, smart, and ready to tackle a job for which he'd been training his entire life. He purchased an IBM computer and hired a slew of "genius-I.Q. types," including Fred R. Haviland, Jr., who came to Schlitz via advertising and a stint at Anheuser-Busch. Sales rose 19 percent in Uihlein's first year on the job, thanks in part to a new advertising campaign ("Real gusto in a great light beer"). He plowed some of the profits into acquisitions, on the theory that a diversified company was a healthy company. His new vice-president for finance spent $100 million on Chilean fishing fleets, a Pakistani glass factory, and breweries in Puerto Rico, Spain, Belgium, and Turkey. None of the investments returned a profit, but by the time Uihlein figured that out, it didn't matter, thanks to Haviland and the whiz boys in marketing.

Indeed, the new gusto in Schlitz stock was due less to Uihlein than to Fred Haviland. When you drink, he explained to a reporter, "you imbibe the image along with the brew." He and his computer analyzed consumer behavior, trying to figure out "what makes the beer drinker tick and how to get to him . . . Beer to us is a product to be marketed—like soap, corn flakes, or facial tissues." "It's the Procter & Gamble way," he added, in case anyone had missed the point. "We're Procter & Gamblizing the beer business."

Procter & Gamblizing meant determining how, why, when, and where people drank beer; why they chose one brand over another; and how and why the color of the label, its wording, or even the shape of the bottle affected their decision. Haviland and his staff determined that people regarded beer as an extension of themselves, and most wanted their chosen brand to convey a sense of "premiumness": If the beer appeared to be refined and high class, so, by extension, was the person drinking it. Never mind that the brew in question probably looked, tasted, and cost the same as any other; advertising and image created the "premiumness" that drinkers desired.

Haviland's efforts inspired the campaign built around the word "gusto" and new labels for Old Milwaukee, the company's lower-priced beer, that featured "lots of white to suggest lightness." Clearly, Bob Uihlein had seen the light.

He wasn't the only one. Other brewers hunted for what marketing mavens called "segments" of potential profitability. That explains "Lite" beer, introduced in 1967 by Meister Brau of Chicago, an agglomeration of small midwestern breweries. Back in the 1950s, some brewers had tried to promote ordinary beer as diet friendly and no more fattening than grapefruit or crackers—without changing their lager's recipe. Lite beer was a whole different animal: Unlike its predecessors, it contained fewer calories than regular beer. The company supported the new brew with television ads that featured a lithe blonde dressed in a sleeveless black-and-white striped cat suit who performed exercises and urged viewers to "Meet the beer you needn't hold back on . . ." A few months later, Forrest Brewing, a division of Rheingold, trotted into the segment with Gablinger's, which contained sixty fewer carbohydrate calories than a regular bottle of beer, or about the same number as a slice of bread. Drink Gablinger's, suggested the advertising campaign, and "save the bread for a sandwich."

The diet beer segment was just one of many fragments into which the brewing industry was splintering. Demand was back—but Americans seemed suddenly, almost inexplicably, to want something other than basic American lager. Consider imported beer: In the 1960s, it comprised less than 1 percent of the total beer market, but that slice grew at the rate of 9 percent a year, a gallop compared to domestic sales' 2 percent trot. Choosing an imported beer over a domestic one, opined an advertising manager for Heineken, was like buying a Cadillac instead of a Ford. The decision bespoke sophistication, worldliness, and appreciation for "the finer things." "It's fun when you have guests in to ask, 'Would you rather have German or Mexican beer?'" said a man interviewed for a report in *Newsweek* magazine. He stocked up at Tony's Liquors in suburban Los Angeles, where thirty-two different imports lined the shelves.

Fun? Not as far as American brewers were concerned. "It is particularly irritating," groused a vice-president at Carling, "to see someone pay 75¢ for a bottle of Heinekens." Even more irritating to see visitors at the 1965 World's Fair in New York drink three million glasses of Löwenbräu. And positively maddening to watch Americans flock to the British-style pubs that, along with the Beatles and Mary Quant clothes, were all the rage in the mid- to late 1960s. Dozens of pubs, complete with darts, fish and chips, and British beers and ales (served cold to accommodate Yankee palates), opened in New York (thirty opened in the space of about a year), Chicago, St. Louis, Los Angeles, and even Atlanta.

The Carling executive ought to have paid closer attention, because the sudden popularity of imports marked the onset of a transformative moment in the American palate. Had the Carling man but known it, the era of bland food was grinding to a halt, and the next twenty years would see what amounted to a revolution in American food and drink. The cause of these tectonic shifts in cultural markers are always hard to pinpoint with precision, but post-war affluence was surely one factor. So was travel abroad and a generation of kids determined to reject whatever the establishment had to offer.

Whatever the reason, in late 1966, *Time* magazine analyzed the trend. A shop owner in San Diego reported that he stocked three thousand different "fancy foods, from kippered sturgeon and kangaroo tails to pickled rooster combs." A grocery store manager in Washington, D.C., remarked that just ten years earlier, an average chain store carried perhaps a half dozen kinds of cheese. Now, he said, any self-respecting grocer stocked "at least 50 assorted, high-powered imported cheeses." An array of photographs illustrated the report, most of them showing notable Americans at work in their kitchens. It's a measure of the times (and their difference from our own) that the "celebrities" included Vice President Hubert Humphrey, an MIT provost, the wife of an architect, and historian Barbara Tuchman. Augie Busch, Gus's son, was there, too, preparing doves broiled with butter and served rare.

If Americans wanted something exotic, then smart brewers were going to give it to them. Gus Busch put Michelob, a beer developed by his grandfather sixty years earlier, into a sleek new bottle, slipped an importlike foil wrapper around its neck, slapped on an eye-opening price (an astonishing $7.30 a case, more than twice the price of Bud), and sent it to market. Meister Brau introduced Meister Brau Bock and bought the North American distribution rights to a German beer. Others followed suit, signing franchise agreements and brewing pseudo-imports, dark beers, bocks, and anything else that might tempt the palates of the "discriminating drinker" segment.

But in the 1960s, the most important segment was "youth." Brewers understood that their future success rested on the ability to capture and keep the millions of "war babies," as Americans called them, tumbling into adulthood. Easier said than done. The kids of the 1960s, at that time the most well-educated, affluent young adults in American history, were not behaving quite like anyone had expected them to. In the spring of 1962, several dozen students gathered at a camp on the shore of Lake Huron in eastern Michigan and drafted a political statement that condemned American foreign policy, racism, capitalism, colonialism, and the military-industrial complex, and inspired dozens of antiwar, antinuclear marches.

From Greenwich Village to Hibbing, Minnesota, from Chicago to Denver and beyond, kids flocked to coffee shops to hear guitar-strumming folk singers. On the radio, shoo-bop and doo-wop gave way to youthful angst in the form of "The Sound of Silence" and "Eve of Destruction." At Drop City in southern Colorado, one of hundreds of experiments in communal living, the inhabitants built geodesic domes out of scrap material and new lives out of their imaginations, and believed that "anything was possible . . ."

Brewers tried to make sense of this potentially lucrative segment. The editors of *Brewers Digest* bombarded beermakers with articles that explored drugs, young people's sense of alienation, and the sociology of pot smoking. One series examined teenagers' passions for fads and tattoos and the relationship between existentialism and drugs. But a Chicago advertising executive spoke for many when he admitted that the new crop of young people "are a puzzle to us and we are a puzzle to them." They have "their own ideas" and "won't accept as fact the values and symbols of their elders." Surveys showed that they were also none too keen on beer. A full 40 percent of young people quizzed in one market analysis described beer as "unpleasant or bitter," and most females preferred hard liquor to beer.

And some of them simply preferred pot. The manager of a discothèque in Miami told a reporter for the *New York Times* that marijuana "spell[ed] disaster to the liquor trade. If they ever legalize it, the liquor business is dead." Parts of the business, anyway. A store owner in Boston said that he'd "been selling a lot more wine since the drug thing started." "It used to always be beer that the kids wanted," he mused. No more. "Beer drinking is very bourgeois," explained one student, "but wine is ideal for sipping while you smoke pot." Out in Colorado, a beer distributor reported that beer consumption had plunged at bars near the university campus in Boulder.

At West End Brewing, the Matt family fought back. Since the end of the war, the Matts had stayed low to the ground, sticking with their Utica Club brand and the familiar environs of upstate New York and northern Pennsylvania. During the 1950s, they lured consumers with a series of captivating television commercials based on talking beer steins Schultz and Dooley and their friends Farmer Mugee and the lovely Bubbles La Brew. The decision to keep it simple enabled the Matts to sell about 600,000 barrels a year, about one-tenth of what poured out of Anheuser-Busch or Schlitz, but enough to pay the bills and keep the doors open.

But in the spring of 1968, as long-haired kids wearing flowers in their hair marched against the war, the Matts launched a new advertising campaign centered on an imaginary discothèque called the Utica Club ("where it really swings"). The series of TV commercials served up a screwball mixture of the hip and hilarious and allowed the Matts to poke fun at themselves and at brewing's stodgy reputation.

The campaign's centerpiece opened with flashing lights and a go-go girl dancing to "The Utica Club Natural Carbonation Beer Drinking Song," played by the Natural Carbonation Band. The camera panned to the club's entrance, where a gorilla showed his membership card to a doorman and slid down a chute to the dance floor. Over the next forty-five seconds, the gorilla chased and captured a hunter; Rip Van Winkle and Ichabod Crane showed up; brewery salesmen showed off their dance moves; and boxer Rocky Graziano stumbled into the scene in his role as a baffled representative from the older side of the generation gap. "Utica Club is where it really swings," announced the voice-over. "You never know what might happen or who might show up at the Utica Club."

Inventive, funny, and surprisingly hip for an otherwise old-line, establishment brewery, the ads spoke directly to the same young adults who, as children, reveled in the antics of Schultz and Dooley, and pushed company sales to new heights. But the Matts weren't taking any chances. They wooed the next generation down the line with another venture, a Victorian-theme tour center, complete with a Gay '90s bar, a collection of nineteenth-century mechanical music machines, and a Utica Club trolley that hauled visitors around the grounds. The brewery sat in the foothills of the Adirondack Mountains, prime resort territory, and the Matts' free tour focused on families and fun in a manner that echoed the delights of beer gardens of a century earlier. Kids loved the music machines, the root beer, and the going-away gift, an easy-to-assemble cardboard replica of the brewery and trolley.

A similar scenario played out a thousand miles west at Jacob Leinenkugel Brewing in Chippewa Falls, Wisconsin. Like West End, Leinenkugel sat in the heart of a forested lake district that offered vacationers plenty of fishing and swimming, canoeing and camping. The region drew people from Wisconsin, northern Illinois and Chicago, and Minneapolis-St. Paul. The family capitalized on that seasonal influx by offering brewery tours twice a day, conducted by young women dressed in Indian maiden outfits complete with a headband out of which sprouted a ten-inch feather. (Bill Leinenkugel's daughter agreed to the costume but drew the line at the feather, which she deemed too ridiculous to bear, an example, apparently, of a young person refusing the symbols of her elders.) Every visitor who signed the guestbook received a Christmas card from Bill Casper, the company's president and grandson of founder Jacob Leinenkugel.

This was building for the future, small-brewery-style, and a smart move for a tiny operation surrounded by hungry predators. It helped that rural Wisconsinites remained loyal to local brewers, and that the area was so isolated and relatively unpopulated that the big brewers ignored it. The brewery always made a profit, but the pressure to do so was, as Bill Leinenkugel later recalled, "horrible"; neither he nor any of the other Leinenkugels enjoyed much more than a modest lifestyle. They invested most of their profits in two areas: first, modern machinery, because too many small brewers stuck with outdated or poorly maintained equipment from which, inevitably, flowed bad beer; and second, a well-trained brewmaster, who, as per an unwritten Leinenkugel law, came from outside the family. (If the brewmaster was an uncle or brother, Bill Leinenkugel explained, no one would want to tell him his beer had gone bad.)

THE MATT AND Leinenkugel families were safe for the time being, protected by their small size and rural locations relatively distant from the kingdoms of the giants. Not so the mid-sized beermakers who wrestled each other for a spot in the top tier, or tiny outfits whose only crime was proximity to a kingpin. Fred Haviland made short work of much of Schlitz's Wisconsin competition when he unleashed the revamped version of Old Milwaukee. He spent $2 million on advertising in just five counties, which worked out to between $200 and $300 a barrel, and then deployed the dreaded "price promotion," slashing the price per case from $2.59 to $1.85. Dealers who bought thousand-case lots got an even better deal. "Now no brewery can match that," complained Roy Kumm of Heileman. "It was absolutely unmerciful." He and twenty other Wisconsin beermakers convened in emergency session, but they could not stop the juggernaut. "I think," he said in 1966, "there are only three of them left that were in that room." The rest had gone bust. Kumm helped himself to a few of the fallen, closing the breweries and keeping the distributors' contracts. The giants left him no choice. It was the only way he could gain access to wholesalers' trucks.

In 1958, 211 beermakers operated 252 plants and the four largest owned only 18 percent of the market. By 1967, 124 brewing companies operated 153 plants and the top four accounted for about one-third of all sales. Anheuser-Busch reigned as the undisputed leader, selling eighteen million barrels of beer in 1968. Number-two Schlitz lagged by a full two million, and number three Pabst, with just under eleven million, was no longer in the race. Nor for that matter were the rest of the top ten. Falstaff might boast that it was the fourth-largest brewer in the United States, but its six million barrels placed it firmly in the category of also-ran.

As for Miller Brewing? Fewer than five million barrels and the number-eight spot. Not good enough for J. Peter Grace, who was fed up with beer. His investment in Miller Brewing had not paid off. Financial frustration was complicated by the constant irritation of thorn-in-the-side Buddy John, who held 46 percent of the company's stock and meddled in Miller affairs every chance he could. On a Sunday evening in June 1969, Grace sat in the bar at the Ritz Hotel in Paris and phoned Joseph Cullman III, chairman and chief executive officer of Philip Morris, a multibillion-dollar conglomerate with one fist clenched around cigarettes and the remaining hand rummaging through adhesives, packaging, chewing gum, and razor blades. Two days later, Philip Morris owned Miller Brewing.

Any sensible person might be excused for assuming that here lay brewing's future: beer as a cog in the wheel of a giant corporate conglomerate. But a few months later, a young man from Iowa bought a brewery in California. The acquisition went unnoticed by anyone in brewing, but he, not the Philip Morris purchase, signified the industry's future.

CHAPTER SEVEN

Make Mine Small, Pure, Real, and Lite

THE INTRICACIES of brewing circa 1969—IBM computers and market segments, vanishing breweries and predatory pricing—were lost on Fritz Maytag. He was too preoccupied with trying to save his own brewery, a two-bit, ramshackle affair in downtown San Francisco where he was making Anchor beer.

Frederick Louis Maytag III—Fritz to family and friends—ended up in California via Iowa, where he was born in 1938, and Massachusetts, where he attended prep school at Deerfield Academy. Maytag enjoyed the challenge of Deerfield, but he disliked the East Coast's narrow roads and even narrower people. He preferred California, where his sister attended Stanford. The kids there "wore Levis to class and there were girls everywhere," just what he wanted and needed after the all-male confines of Deerfield. In 1955, he enrolled at Stanford.

Tall, lanky Maytag fell in love with northern California and especially San Francisco's North Beach neighborhood, as yet untainted by tourists and commercialism. He also fell in love with all things Japanese, and in the fall of 1960 he entered Stanford's graduate program in Japanese language.

Most of his classroom colleagues had grown up speaking and reading Japanese or came to graduate work armed with years of study, and Maytag's effort to catch up resembled a hike through quicksand. For the better part of three years he waged a herculean effort to learn the language and culture. But weeks and months of the day-in, day-out assault finally collided with exhaustion and the sense that he was trudging along the wrong road. One morning in February 1964, he drove to the campus but could not get out of the car. He turned the wheel and headed away from town. He drove for hours. Then he dropped out of graduate school and moved to San Francisco.

The city's bohemian/hippie scene—the drugs, the dances, the music—had intensified while Maytag had been occupied with Japanese. In June of 1964, Ken Kesey and the Merry Pranksters piled into their painted bus and set off on a cross-country acid trip. Maytag watched, amused but uninterested. "I would no more have gotten on an acid bus," he said later, voice dripping with derision, "than the man in the moon."

He pondered, instead, the notion of investing his considerable wealth (courtesy of the washing machine company founded by his great-grandfather) in social missions in underdeveloped countries. Maytag needed to do something—that much he knew, because Iowa Maytags were not the kind of people who frittered their time in loafing and daydreaming. One day while riding the cable car, he noticed a passenger wearing a jacket and tie and carrying a rolled blueprint under his arm. Maytag later recalled staring at the man's bundle and thinking, "I wish I had a blueprint." A blueprint or a plan or something.

The "something" landed in his lap a few months later, in August 1965. Days before he was due to depart on a trip to Mexico, Maytag strolled into the Old Spaghetti Factory, a North Beach institution and one of his regular haunts. Fred Kuh, the café's owner, told him that the Steam Beer Brewing Company, a dilapidated shop a few blocks away on Eighth Street, was about to shut its doors.

Most San Franciscans would have been surprised to learn that Steam Beer, maker of Anchor, was about to close—but only because they assumed the place had gone under years earlier. The brewery, which dated to 1896, had closed briefly in the summer of 1959 before it was rescued by an unlikely duo—Lawrence Steese, a laid-back, pipe-smoking dreamer, and Bill Buck, a member of a wealthy Marin County family—who, between them, knew next to nothing about brewing. They hobbled along, making inconsistent and often foul beer that almost no one but Kuh wanted to buy. In 1964, Buck threw in his brewer's apron (figuratively speaking; it's unlikely he owned one or had even been near the brewvat) and sold his 51 percent share to two advertising men who believed that Steam Beer Brewing and Anchor needed only a walloping good ad campaign to point the company toward profit. Experience soon persuaded them otherwise. By the summer of 1965 they'd had enough of the brewery, its antediluvian equipment, and the headaches of trying to sell a truly terrible beer.

This was bad news for Fred Kuh. Anchor beer was the beacon that had lured him to San Francisco. On a visit to California in the early 1950s, Kuh had fallen in love with the city, with North Beach, and with Anchor and the notion of local beer. By the late 1960s, Kuh was one of the few tavern proprietors willing to foist it on a mostly reluctant citizenry.

Now the brewery was in danger of closing. Kuh tagged Maytag as a possible savior. He'd gotten to know Maytag over the years; he knew he had an independent income and that he was a bit of a romantic. Perhaps—who knows—Kuh sensed that Maytag longed for direction and purpose and that Anchor might light the way.

In any case, the next day Maytag, who rarely drank Anchor

and recognized it for the sour brew that it was, trekked the mile and a half from his apartment to the brewery. He walked around, talked to Steese, and confirmed that, indeed, the admen wanted out. He visited his lawyer, and then, one hundred years after another young man bought a share of a brewery in St. Louis (and about the same time that thirty-four people died in the Watts riots in Los Angeles and the Jefferson Airplane debuted at a San Francisco nightclub), Fritz Maytag purchased 51 percent of Steam Beer Brewing.

What he'd gotten himself was a dilapidated operation that turned out about six hundred barrels of beer a year—a brewery about the size, in other words, of Phillip Best's 1844 brewhouse in Milwaukee. The equipment was crude, to say the least, and mostly hammered together by a sheet-metal worker. Refrigeration was nonexistent; the tanks were steel and lined, as near as the new owner could tell, with varnish; and the whole place was, to put it charitably, less than clean. That's what Fritz Maytag had bought—that and a pile of debts.

Steese manned the brewvat, so Maytag appointed himself head salesman. Over the next few months he trudged the streets of San Francisco, trying to persuade restaurant, shop, and tavern owners to carry the beer, a task as uphill as the city's terrain. Many people refused to believe it existed, explaining, as if to the village idiot, that Anchor had long ago shut its doors. No, Maytag would counter, Steam Beer Brewing and Anchor were very much alive and he was the owner. "No, no," people would say. "That brewery's gone, they closed years ago." "They thought," an amused Maytag recollected, "I was some kind of weirdo, a psychopath or something, pretending I owned a brewery."

That was not as bad as what happened when people remembered Anchor. One day Maytag stopped by Schroeder's, a decades-old German restaurant located on Front Street, and launched into his spiel. A bellow emanating from overhead interrupted him. It belonged to the restaurant's owner, who leaned over a balcony railing and announced, in a voice that oozed its German origins, "Ja, I know your beer. It is horrible. It is sour. It is terrible beer. I will never serve that beer here." Maytag retreated, "tail between [his] legs."

The rebuff marked a pivotal moment. There was no point in tromping from one bar to another trying to sell the unsalable. It was time to get serious about the beer or get out of the business. Maytag had long been fascinated with science; he'd owned a microscope since boyhood. This was a challenge he understood. He cleared a small area on the brewing floor, hung a shower curtain around a desk to keep out the malt dust, installed his microscope, hunted down some books, and set to work educating himself in the mystery and science of brewing.

Night after night, Maytag stayed up reading, turning his copy of Jean de Clerc's brewing text, his "bible," he called it, into a tattered, dog-eared rag. He got help from a guardian angel in the form of John Borger, a retired brewing-supplies salesman who showered Maytag with advice and encouragement. He joined the Brewers Association of America. Bill Leinenkugel, a long-time BAA member, remembered him as "very, very quiet" at those first few meetings, due in large part to the fact that Maytag "listened like mad" to the goings-on, anxious to soak up any wisdom that flowed his way.

Some BAA members dismissed the newcomer as a rich kid with a new plaything but all of them tasted his beer, which, per BAA tradition, Maytag shipped to the meeting so the conventioneers could drink it. In the case of Anchor, the other brewers sipped—and then stashed the bottles out of sight, unable to finish the contents because Anchor was so bad. Still, Leinenkugel understood that Maytag was sincerely trying to learn, and was working as hard as, if not harder than, any man in the industry. Maytag, in turn, admired the other members' family histories, in which he found echoes of his own family's entrepreneurial past. After a few meetings, he even felt a bit sorry for them. None tended their own vats—they left that to hired brewmasters—and their modern equipment tied them to one or two types of beer. Maytag realized that his tiny, beat-up shop bestowed a kind of freedom on his work. He could make any beer that he wanted to.

But first he had to learn how. In late 1966, he flew to the east coast to attend a two-week seminar sponsored by the United States Brewers' Academy, where he and two dozen other young men learned "everything from enzymes to how to drive a fork-lift." Maytag sat next to Dick Yuengling, Jr., there to learn the business so he could take his place at his family's brewery. Yuengling told Maytag that his family was struggling. Times were tough for a small brewer, he lamented. How small? asked Maytag. Fifty thousand barrels a year, Yuengling replied. Maytag gazed at the other man a few seconds, and then said: "Well, try five thousand barrels."

On the way back to California, Maytag stopped in Chicago at Sieben's Brewery Company, which was about to close its doors. Just a few years earlier, president Joseph Sieben had told a reporter that, yes, lacking the "cash surpluses and advertising" of the big brewers, he was having a "rough time." Still, he insisted, he could "hold his own" as long as Chicagoans kept coming to his beer garden for lager and "3-inch-thick ham-and-cheese sand-wiches." Sieben's optimism was misplaced. The good people of Chicago didn't need Sieben's quaint beer garden located in a deteriorating neighborhood on Chicago's near north side, not when they could head to the chic Old Town neighborhood and sip a nationally advertised beer at the Bratskeller, a "mock-Bavarian" restaurant complete with "black-bread sandwiches 'mit kraut,' and candlelight." By late 1966, Sieben was ready to call it quits.

Sieben's loss was Anchor's gain. Maytag bought the brewery's bottling line and hauled it to San Francisco.

It's not clear if either man recognized the irony of the transaction: Sieben, unable to compete against the relentless onslaught of Anheuser-Busch and Schlitz, closing his doors, and Maytag, fired by near-obsessive determination and oblivious to industry bankruptcies and bloodshed, opening his.

Back home, Maytag realized that he and Steese were a poor match for the enterprise. Steese was happy to "smoke a pipe, let nature take its course." Maytag was more ambitious: he wanted "to make the best beer in the world." By 1968 the business was sliding toward bankruptcy, and it might have failed completely had Steese not decided, in the waning weeks of that year, to sell his 49 percent to Maytag.

In early 1969, Fritz Maytag became sole owner, president, and brewmaster of the tiny shop on Eighth Street. His assets consisted of truly awful beer with an even worse reputation; a collection of nearly unusable equipment; an outmoded bottling line; a hardworking helper in the person of Gordon McDermott; and a guy who drove the delivery truck. Another man might have given up, but Maytag possessed ambition, stamina, a nose for gustatory trends, and shrewd entrepreneurial instincts. He set to his task, more determined than ever to make if not his fortune, at least a product that would bring honor to the Maytag name, as cheese and washing machines had in years gone by.

That vow to succeed opened his eyes to possibility. Looking around San Francisco, watching his friends order drinks during evenings out, Maytag noticed that many people were drinking expensive imported beers that cost even more than the highest-priced domestics. Maytag coupled that observation with another fact: He was not and never could compete with, say, Anheuser-Busch. He would never be able to brew more than a few thousand barrels of beer each year. The economies of scale that drove the giants would forever elude him. If he hoped to turn a profit, he would have to aim for that thin but discriminating slice of the market now owned by the pricey imports.

The rest of his strategy followed from those two facts. He would brew with high-quality, two-row barley imported from Europe, and he would use whole hops rather than hop extracts. He opted for flash pasteurization, which subjected the beer to fifteen seconds of heat rather than the fifteen minutes demanded by conventional heat sterilization. As for marketing, there was none except an idea: Anchor was an old-fashioned beer, pure of heart and grain. Maytag reinforced that image on the beer's label, with its hand-lettered look and a neckband that affirmed the brewery's "exceptional respect for the ancient art of brewing."

Put another way, Maytag grasped what was lost on mainstream brewing: Out there was an audience eager for authenticity. Out there, the same people glued to Julia Child's cooking show, which aired on more than one hundred television stations, and buying European cheeses, were ready for a new kind of beer. More important, his willingness to act on that belief signaled a transformative moment in American brewing. He would inspire a new generation of brewmasters, but his example also served as a beacon for his fellow BAA members, many of whom had despaired at being able to reverse a tide that once seemed inexorable.

In later years, some of the microbrewers who followed in Maytag's path argued that he succeeded only because his personal wealth erased the red ink that otherwise would have drowned his venture. And even Maytag admitted that, denied conventional financing, he sometimes drew on his own resources to pay the bills. But a focus on Maytag's name and inheritance obscures the brewer's prescience. The signs were everywhere for those who took the time to look.

———

CONSIDER THE WORDS of Mike Royko, a Chicagoan whose syndicated column appeared in hundreds of newspapers and was read
by millions of people. In May 1973, Royko informed his readers
that he hated big beer. "I have tried them all," he wrote. "I've
grabbed for all the gusto I can get. I've said it all when I've said
Bud." But "regardless of what label or slogan you choose," he complained, "it all tastes as if the secret brewing process involved running it through a horse."

The column hit a large, sensitive nerve. Some readers casti-
gated Royko for criticizing the national drink. In a beery version
of "Love it or leave it," one writer instructed him to "Go to hell,
if you don't like this country's beer. Maybe you'll like what you
are served there." But others, sensing a kindred spirit, bombarded
Royko with names of excellent but lesser-known local beers and
of imported brews that put the Big Brands to shame.

Royko weighed the mixed responses and decided that, indeed, perhaps his opinion carried little weight. He would solicit
others. In July, he organized a panel of eleven men and women for
a blind taste test of twenty-two beers, including imports, the
major American names, and lesser-known brands from tiny breweries such as Stevens Point, Huber, and Pickett.

The results surprised even Royko. The top three beers, in
order from first to third, were Würzberger, a German brew; English Bass Ale; and Point Special from Stevens Point, Wisconsin,
brewed by a tiny outfit whose owners sold their annual output—
a mere thirty thousand barrels—within a seventy-five-mile radius
of home. The bottom three? Old Milwaukee, made by Schlitz, as
well as that company's flagship brand Schlitz, and, dead last with
only thirteen points out of a possible fifty-five, Budweiser.

Royko fired another salvo six months later when he used his
column to broadcast the contents of a pamphlet titled *The Chemical Additives in Booze,* a mishmash of pseudo-science, innuendo, and
half-truths penned by Michael Jacobson, a microbiologist who had

spent the 1960s working for Ralph Nader, the gadfly lawyer who fashioned a career as a consumer advocate. In 1971, Jacobson left Nader to launch the Center for Science in the Public Interest, a group devoted to informing consumers and harassing purveyors of food and drink. The CSPI, he would say later, "is proud about finding something wrong with practically everything."

Jacobson charged big brewers with conducting "slick, multimillion dollar advertising campaigns" that promoted an "image of near holiness and purity." Beware, he warned. In reality, their beers were life-threatening thanks to the brewers' practice of lacing their "booze," as Jacobson called it, with additives. These included gum arabic, seaweed extract, caramel, enzymes, and asorbic acid (vitamin C). Beermakers, he explained, were not required to list said additives on their labels, so consumers placed their lives in danger every time they sipped one of these toxin-laced poisons.

Jacobson was correct that most brewers employed some or many additives. Most also had no choice: Competition demanded lower prices, and the only way to cut price was by reducing production costs, shortening lagering time, or using hop extract instead of whole hops. Long-distance shipping demanded that a beer's shelf life be lengthened with stabilizers that prevented haze from forming. Last, consumers' preference for ultra-pale, ultra-bland beer resulted in brews that could not generate, let alone hold, a foamy head the way an all-malt beer could. Seaweed extract—propylene glycol alginate—to the rescue.

None of these additives was dangerous; most had been in use for decades, in many cases even before Prohibition. But only the most careful reader would glean that fact, or notice that Jacobson merely *suggested* that brewers employed such additives rather than offering proof that they did so. Nor did he provide evidence that these ingredients were or could be toxic. He also failed to support his most outrageous assertion: that brewers filtered their beers through asbestos.

"At least with a horse, we'd know what we're getting," Royko wrote after reading Jacobson's pamphlet. "When you pop the top of your favorite brew, for all you know there might be any of 59 chemicals or other additives that are permitted by law." Even if the additives were safe, he added, "it just doesn't seem right for a man to belly up to a bar and ask for a beer without knowing he is also getting some alginate. If I want a belt of alginate, I'll ask for it."

In another time, Royko might have ignored Jacobson's crack-pot science. But in the early 1970s, the chemicals-are-bad message cruised straight into the hearts and minds of consumers rattled by other bad news about the environment and their food. Jacobson's pamphlet appeared just as the newly created Environmental Protection Agency banned the domestic use of DDT, a long-controversial pesticide, and as the Food and Drug Administration warned consumers about the dangers of mercury in tuna, violet food coloring, kepone in fish, and diethylstilbestrol in cattle feed. A former staff scientist at the FDA published *Eating May Be Hazardous to Your Health: How Your Government Fails to Protect You From the Dangers in Your Food,* with chapter titles like "Poisoned by Accident: Incidental Additives" and "Cancer in Hot Dogs, Ham, Bacon . . ." It was all too easy for a public already unnerved by toxic food, oil slicks, killer canals, and other environmental dangers to take Jacobson's rant at face value. Moreover, his pamphlet revived an old headline: Back in 1965, more than three dozen people died after drinking beer brewed with a cobalt-based foam stabilizer. All of them were heavy drinkers, a factor that contributed to their deaths. Most were Canadian, but a handful of Americans died, too, after downing beer from a small brewery in Omaha. The news made headlines around the country and cast a bad light on all brewers even though scarcely any American beer-makers used that particular stabilizer.

But in the early 1970s, Americans were rejecting more than corporate food and drink. Disaffection with the establishment, once the province of long-haired hippies, had filtered out into the general population, thanks to the Vietnam war, crushing recession, and Watergate. Back in the late 1950s, nearly 80 percent of Americans said they trusted government; by the mid-1970s, only one-third would say the same. Many Americans believed that corporate executives lined their pockets with profits made from fleecing consumers with overpriced, poorly made products, that they perpetuated racism and sexism, and that they polluted the air, water, and food supply. The mistrust fertilized a rejection of anything large, corporate, and impersonal.

That explains the popularity of economist E. F. Schumacher's claim that small is beautiful. It explains as well the phenomenal success of Stewart Brand's *Whole Earth Catalog,* the bestseller filled with advice about how to buy, build, and use geodesic domes, tents, kayaks, maps, plows, axes, and bees that exemplified the moment. A "realm of intimate, personal power is developing," Brand argued, including the "power of the individual to conduct his own education, find his own inspiration, shape his own environment, share his adventure with whoever is interested."

As a result, the sea change in the American diet first visible in the 1960s swelled to ocean-sized proportions. Inspired by Schumacher's ideas, dismayed by corporate greed, and shocked by environmental damage, many shoppers rejected mass marketing and celebrated the small, the local, and the pure; they flocked to health food stores and food cooperatives stocked with additive- and chemical-free produce. Frances Moore Lappé's *Diet for a Small Planet* appeared in 1971 and has never gone out of print. Robert Rodale, publisher of *Organic Farming & Gardening,* watched as his readership rose by 40 percent in 1971 alone. Bennett Cerf at Random House, about as mainstream a man and company as was possible to find, paid alicia bay laurel [*sic*], a member of a Sonoma County commune, a hefty sum for distribution rights to her ostentatiously hippie/alt-lifestyle guidebook, *Living on the Earth.*

In Berkeley, California, Alice Waters opened Chez Panisse in 1971 and urged gastronomes to cook locally: The farm stand down the road, she argued, offered food of higher quality than the stuff in the grocery store and money spent there supported a family rather than a corporation. She also inspired a generation of professional chefs who carried her ideas far from Berkeley. Bakers invested in hearth ovens and produced chewy, dense breads of a kind not seen since their great-grandmothers' day.

Where food went, drink followed. Seattle resident Gordon Bowker launched his entrepreneurial career in 1971 with a coffeehouse called Starbucks. Within a decade, nearly every city of any size boasted at least one "new" coffee shop whose owners tutored their customers in the differences between Sumatra and Estate Kenyan, latte and cappuccino. So, too, Americans' attitudes toward wine also changed. Since the end of Prohibition, the nation's wine had consisted of cheap, generic jug drinks that leaned toward the sweet. That changed during the 1960s, in part because of people like Robert Mondavi, a member of a long-established California winemaking family. Mondavi first visited Europe in 1962 and there discovered wine's complexity and flavor. In early 1966, he opened his own winery with the goal of creating excellent but affordable wines and teaching Americans that wine could and should be part of a quality life. In the late 1960s and early 1970s, dozens more wineries opened, mostly along the Pacific Coast.

A similar trend was occurring with beer. In the space of a few years in the early 1970s, small family-owned breweries that had struggled for years to hang on to what was left of their market became exemplars of all that was pure, good, decent, and delicious. Like Royko, other writers for national newspapers and magazines stumbled over each other in a race to find, taste, test, and rank the nation's smallest, realest beers. Articles in the *Washington Post* and *U.S. News and World Report* introduced readers to Peter Hand and Ortleib. An essay in the *New York Times Magazine* praised Iron

City of Pittsburgh and its Pennsylvania brothers: Yuengling of Pottsville, Koehler's of Erie, and Stoney's of Smithton. A writer for *Esquire* conducted that magazine's "first-ever American regional beer survey," and praised Pickett's Premium from Dubuque, Iowa; Royal Amber from George Wiedemann of Kentucky; and Fyfe & Drum from Genesee Brewing of Rochester, New York.

The Leinenkugels in Chippewa Falls, Wisconsin, reaped their own rewards, and just when they needed it. In the early 1970s, students at nearby colleges in Wisconsin and Minnesota developed a passion for Leinie and Bill Leinenkugel became a bit of a celebrity with the collegians, who invited him to speak on campus. That, he decided, was his target audience. He bought cases of T-shirts and had them printed with the company logo. The board of directors scratched its collective head over that move. "Bill," said one board member, "we're in the beer business. Why are you making shirts for fifty cents and selling them for a dollar?" The answer was obvious: He wanted the "young people" to wear them. Walking advertisements, thousands of them.

In 1974, a Los Angeles newspaper touted the virtues of Leinenkugel and the beer finished second in a taste test sponsored by *Oui* magazine. Tom Paulus, a Skokie, Illinois, beer distributor, pleaded with Leinenkugel to let him sell the beer in the Chicago area. Leinenkugel resisted, arguing that Chicago was too far away and the risk was too great. Paulus disagreed. Leiney, he reminded the brewer, outsold anything else on campus at the University of Wisconsin. Leinenkugel yielded and Paulus loaded a semi and drove back to Chicago. The beer was gone in three days. "Some people," a Chicago tavern owner told a reporter, "get hysterical when they find out I have it."

Small also paid off for Harry Jersig, the owner of Lone Star Brewing in San Antonio, Texas. Jersig was doing okay; Texans drank about one million barrels of his beer each year. But Jersig was no fool. He knew that if Anheuser-Busch or Miller ever decided to get serious about Texas, he'd end up looking like an armadillo after its last trip across a highway. How to save himself? Enter Barry Sullivan, the vice-president for marketing that Jersig hired in the fall of 1973. Sullivan had learned the beer business working for the Narragansett brand owned by Falstaff, and had cut his marketing chops staging rock concerts throughout Narragansett's New England territory, downplaying the beer, which was not even sold at the venues, and focusing on the music: Santana. Crosby, Stills, Nash, and Young. Led Zeppelin.

He applied the same formula to Lone Star in Texas, a state with an aggressive music scene—not old-fashioned Bob Wills–type stuff, but a new kind of country steeped in rock and roll and rhythm and blues. Sullivan gave free beer to the groups playing the Armadillo World Headquarters, a cavernous club—it could accommodate fifteen hundred people—that opened in August 1970. He hired those same players to record a one-minute Lone Star radio jingle, "Harina Tortilla." When producers from public television began filming sets at the Armadillo and broadcasting them as the program *Austin City Limits,* Lone Star underwrote the project.

Outside the Armadillo, Sullivan focused on print and TV. His art director was about as far off Madison Avenue as it was possible to get: a skinny, bearded kid who dressed in shorts, T-shirts, and sandals and who fancied armadillos—he painted the Armadillo's murals and designed its posters. One of his first Lone Star ads pictured a desolate landscape, where "everything was laid to waste and the only things that were left were [Lone Star] longnecks sticking out of the ground and armadillos running around." The television commercials were just as goofy: A camera crew filmed real Texans as they engaged in "bizarre cultural rituals," Texas style: seed-spitting and buffalo-chip-tossing competitions, an armadillo beauty contest, a "Cuero turkey trot." Funny, irreverent, off the wall, they were perfectly suited to baby boomers who'd long since departed from their parents' paths. Sales rose by one million cases in 1974. Lone Star, small regional beer *par excellence,* was hip.

But no brewery benefited more from the pure–real confluence than Coors Brewing of Golden, Colorado. For years the Coors brothers, Joseph and William, grandsons of Adolph Coors, who founded the brewery just west of Denver in the 1870s, had stuck to the family game plan: one beer, limited distribution, and minimal, almost simplistic marketing. Since repeal, the company had sponsored a few radio programs, but mostly it hung its sales, profits, and future on advertising that touted the "pure Rocky Mountain spring water" used to make the beer. In the early 1970s, the brothers spent about seventy cents per barrel on their ads as compared to the $2.50 or $3 spent by giant beermakers. They employed no brewmaster, preferring to trust science and their engineering talents, a passion for precision and machinery having been imprinted in the Coors DNA at conception. They used a strain of barley grown specifically for them and designed (and probably knew the precise dimensions of) much of the equipment in their plant. They manufactured their own cans and even some of their own trucks.

The beer itself was eccentric: The brothers eschewed pasteurization in favor of a filtering method, the success of which depended on keeping the beer at near-freezing temperatures. That explained their decision to limit sales to the western United States: It was the only way to make sure that distributors kept the beer properly chilled from warehouse to delivery truck to store and tavern.

For decades, the family had sold their lager in eleven states to folks who regarded it as nothing special, an ordinary beer that tasted particularly good in hot weather. That all changed in the early 1970s. Suddenly, or so it seemed, the family's name was on everyone's lips, and the beer in everyone's mouths. Actor Paul Newman told *Esquire* magazine that Coors was the best beer in America. President Gerald Ford had cases flown into Washington and drank it every Thursday (Mexican food night at the White House). Ethel Kennedy drank Coors, as did members of the Miami Dolphins and Boston Red Sox. Consumers in Washington, D.C., and environs, where it was available only because some of Coors's western distributors violated company policy and smuggled it east, paid $13 a case for the stuff (a mind-boggling $50 in 2006 currency).

The author of a 1975 book about beer praised Coors for its lack of additives. The beer was so pure, so clean, he told readers, that it "must be handled almost like milk." "For many connoisseurs," gushed a correspondent for *Time* magazine, "Coors is the Château Haut-Brion of American beers."

Not surprisingly, Coors became the darling of young drinkers, and especially college students. Many had discovered Colorado's mountains and rugged, earthy lifestyle, and they latched on to Coors, with its unpasteurized pure mountain water and its company president who wore jeans and boots and insisted on being called "Bill." Members of a University of Florida fraternity collected $3,000 and dispatched a brother to Colorado to buy a truckload. Lots of kids were doing the same thing, but this particular kid and his cargo made the news when he got caught at a weigh station in Tennessee, where, because the load had entered the state untaxed, the attendant confiscated all four hundred cases. (No word on where the beer finally ended up.) The kids' passion for Coors was evidence that the beer's near mythic qualities had little to do with politics and everything to do with an image imposed on it from the outside: If only those kids, longhairs of left-leaning politics for the most part, knew that the brothers Coors, and especially Joe, embraced politics so far to the right that even conservatives shook their heads in wonder. ("Pleasure-loving parasites" is how Joe Coors described hippies.)

In 1965, Coors ranked just twelfth among brewers; by the early 1970s, it had climbed to fourth. At twelve million barrels, less than half the annual output at Anheuser-Busch, they had a long road to travel to catch up to the top three. The only way to do so was by going national, a route the family had resisted. But in 1975, company policy collided with the Supreme Court, which upheld a Federal Trade Commission ruling that found the company's distribution policy amounted to price-fixing and restraint of trade. With Coors middlemen free to sell the beer anyplace they wanted, Joe and Bill took the company public. They still owned the controlling shares of stock, but the additional funds enabled them to build new breweries and play hardball with Busch and Uihlein.

It would not be easy. The Coors mystique stemmed largely from its lack of availability. Coors on a grocery shelf in, say, Nashville, lacked the panache and glamour of Coors smuggled out of Colorado in the trunk of a car. Nor did the Coors family politics sit well with others. Union organizers complained about being forced to take lie-detector tests, and teamsters in California, Coors's most prized market, organized a successful boycott over a labor dispute. Latinos and gays boycotted, too, claiming the company practiced discrimination, an accusation that the Equal Opportunity Commission backed with formal charges. The company's stock plunged as Joe and Bill Coors struggled to find their footing in this strange new terrain.

But if "local" beers like Coors were suddenly hip, imports were even hipper. American sales of German, French, Belgian, Mexican, and other foreign beers rose 88 percent in the first half of the 1970s. Import mania wasn't hard to understand. As they had in the 1960s, adventurous baby boomers and the affluent middle-aged traveled abroad in record numbers, and they returned home with a taste for European-style beers. Never mind that much of the imported beer was skunky from too much travel and not enough care; never mind that much of it was watery lager no better, and often worse, than the beers made by the American

Big Brewers. All that mattered in the early 1970s was that imported beer, like homemade bread and organic gardening, allowed its drinkers to thumb their noses at the establishment, to assert their sophistication and worldliness. In that respect, there was not much difference between the import drinkers and those who, during the 1960s, drank Schlitz because the company's advertising persuaded them that the beer bestowed an aura of prestige on those who consumed it. If beer had once been the province of the workingman and the saloon, it was now a badge signifying education and affluence.

A New England man, Larry McCavitt, acknowledged the shift in tastes when he launched a short-lived crusade to promote "real" beer with a Committee for Real Ale, modeled after the Campaign for Real Ale (CAMRA), a grassroots British movement to save English beer from corporate takeover. At its peak, the CRA numbered but two hundred members, most in the New England area, but a California wing alerted the northeasterners to the existence of Fritz Maytag's small brewery.

Beer lovers like McCavitt, import madness, the demand for the authenticity of the local—all of these things kept Fritz Maytag going during his first difficult decade. He invested in new brewing equipment and began selling the beer in six- rather than four-packs. But otherwise he stuck to his original game plan: to make a quality beer from four ingredients. The customers, he believed, would come. In 1975, a decade after he wrote the check that had made him a partner in the brewery, he finally turned a profit. Two years later, California-based *New West* magazine ranked thirty beers, foreign and domestic. Anchor Steam came out on top.

TOGETHER, THESE cultural trends—food scares, environmental concerns, and disaffection with big corporations—transformed Americans' attitudes toward beer. But the times also boosted the popularity of homebrewing, and that hobby in turn inspired millions of Americans to rethink their ideas about beer and, equally important, provided a training ground for some of the finest brewmasters of the late twentieth century.

Homebrewing had fallen from favor since its glory days during Prohibition, in part because it was illegal, thanks to an accidental bit of poor wording written into repeal laws in the 1930s. But in the 1960s it had staged a comeback, for many of the same reasons that Fritz Maytag was succeeding. Michael Lewis had first-hand knowledge of homebrewing's resurgence. Lewis, a biochemist in the Department of Food Science and Technology at the University of California, Davis, specialized in brewing yeasts and processes. He'd joined the faculty in 1964 and immediately suffered an inundation of homebrewing enthusiasts who bombarded him with phone calls and letters, each one wanting to know why his or her beer had gone bad or what kind of yeast to use. In 1965, Lewis began teaching the craft through the university's extension program, cautioning his students not to sell their wares and to avoid discussing their illegal hobby *too* openly, just in case.

But in the early 1970s, a new breed of enthusiasts grabbed hold of homebrewing. "[N]ow that growing your own (food, dope, hair, younameit) is hip," wrote the author of an essay widely reprinted in alternative newspapers, "it's time to resurrect the Dope of the Depression—Homebrew." Homemade beer inspired "good vibrations" and a "pleasant high." Unlike the rest of the "plastic, mass-produced shit" of modern America, homebrew represented "an exercise of craft" and empowered the "politically oriented" to retaliate against "Augustus [*sic*] Busch and the other fascist pigs who [were] ripping off the Common Man." "If you're looking for a cheap drunk," added the beer adviser, "go back to Gussie Busch. But if you dig the good vibes from using something you make yourself, plus an improvement in quality over the commercial shit," brew on, brothers and sisters, brew on.

There is no way to measure the number of Americans who embraced homebrewing in the early and mid-1970s, but by the summer of 1973 there were enough that the Treasury Department issued a formal warning advising Americans to "leave the beer-making to the brewers." Treasury's warning was a bit bizarre, even laughable, given that Senator Sam Ervin was a few blocks away conducting the Watergate hearings into gross illegalities on the part of the Nixon administration.

Peter Brehm, who owned Wine and the People, a wine-making and homebrewing supply store in Berkeley, knew something was going on. His sales had soared. But Brehm and his employee Byron Burch wearied of answering the same questions over and over—many of them prompted by errors written into the few available how-to books. Both men were also troubled by the facts of homebrewing circa 1974: First, most customers aimed at quantity rather than quality; and second, most home-brewers knew nothing about hops and how to use them.

Burch decided to write his own book. But he wanted to provide more than the standard "buy a can of Blue Ribbon malt and a packet of yeast," so he felt a visit to an actual brewery might be useful. He phoned Anchor Brewing in hopes that someone there would agree to answer questions. To his surprise, Fritz Maytag answered the phone. Of course!, the brewer responded; come for a visit. Maytag had good reason to assist Burch and other serious homebrewers. What the nation, or at least the Bay Area, needed were serious, well-educated beer enthusiasts who could appreciate what Maytag had to offer. Homebrewers fit the bill. Burch spent three hours exploring the brewery with Maytag, who answered questions and offered advice. The brewer attached but one caveat to the aid: Please, he said, don't credit me in the book, explaining that federal agents had been around warning professional brewers not to consort with the lawbreaking amateurs.

Burch borrowed $5,000 to print *Quality Brewing: A Guidebook for the Home Production of Fine Beers*. It was the first American homebrewing book to focus on accuracy, technical detail, and quality ingredients; the first to provide substantive information about yeasts; and the first to include a detailed discussion of hop varieties and the way in which hops could enliven the home-brewer's art. It also included the usual sop to the law: According to the Internal Revenue Service, Burch reminded readers, home-brewing was illegal, but "this interpretation is somewhat dubious, and enforcement is nonexistent." Besides, he might have added, we've got a president and various higher-ups who've been break-ing the law right and left. Times are tough; homebrew is cheap. Have fun.

The Maltose Falcons were having fun. It is a measure of home-brewing's appeal that the first American brewing club sprouted in the most unlikely of places: suburban Los Angeles. Organized in 1974, the club was the brainchild of Merlin Elhardt, who developed a passion for German beer while stationed in Europe during and after World War II. Elhardt was a homebrewer's brewer: He ground his own malt and pitched a yeast smuggled out of the Tuborg brewery in Denmark. The Falcons' member-ship reflected homebrewing's widespread popularity: A utility lineman and a college student, a church deacon and a Ph.D. can-didate at UCLA, a teacher and an artist. They tasted each other's wares, discussed techniques, and swapped yeasts and recipes. "Most of us," said one member, "are into the taste of beer, not the 'buzz.'"

Patrick Baker, who owned a Connecticut homebrewing sup-ply shop that catered to both wine- and beer-makers, also turned to beer in the early 1970s. He started hosting Saturday-morning "Beer Doctor" sessions at his store, but in 1975 he and others sup-plemented them with a monthly meeting at night, which, in a nod to the Treasury and Justice departments, they dubbed the "Underground Brewers' Club." Dozens of other clubs followed. By 1978, homebrewing had become so mainstream that the Carter administration finally legalized it.

That was the same year that the hobby gained its own national organization, thanks to Charlie Papazian. Papazian had discovered homebrewing in the early 1970s during his college days at the University of Virginia and continued to brew after graduation, when he moved to Boulder, Colorado. There he developed a minor reputation around town as a guy who served up good times and good beer, and the staff at the Community Free School asked him to share his skill one night a week. Papazian jumped at the chance. He loved to teach and relished the fellowship and community that homebrew inspired.

But Papazian was an entrepreneur at heart. He wrote and self-published a homebrewing pamphlet, a short, breezy affair that touted homebrewing as an easy, fun-filled venture. He sold copies to students enrolled in his brewing classes, but he wanted to find a larger audience for it and fashion a career out of his passion for beer. He found plenty of role models and inspiration close at hand in Boulder, a city that, in the 1970s, oozed entrepreneurial passion. Mo Siegel had created a profitable empire out of herbal teas; by the late 1970s, his Celestial Seasonings company boasted $9 million in sales. Green Mountain Grainery, which sold health foods like granola and trail mix, operated in a smaller local market, but each year it pulled in well over $1 million. The Naropa Institute sold ideas and religion, and owned entire blocks of Boulder real estate. Creating odd businesses was itself a kind of religion in Boulder, a town where "everybody," mused one observer who visited in the late 1970s, "believes like crazy in something or somebody."

Two events set Papazian's ship on course. In January 1978, he read Michael Jackson's *World Guide to Beer,* a glossy book on beer styles written by an English journalist. In the space of a few hours, Papazian's knowledge about brewing and beer and their possibilities "expanded by leaps and bounds." But Jackson's work also empowered Papazian to perceive "community" as a larger, more complex entity than he had found in his homebrewing classes at the Free School. Then there was Jackson himself: an otherwise ordinary guy making a living from beer. The second event presented itself in October 1978, when President Carter signed the legislation that legalized homebrewing.

That was enough for Papazian. Out there, he sensed rather than knew, were beer lovers like himself, men and women who enjoyed not just the flavor of homebrew, but the pleasure and fellowship it inspired. In December, he and a friend, Charlie Matzen, founded the American Homebrewers Association and mailed off about a thousand copies of a homebrewing newsletter they'd written called *Zymurgy*.

Against all odds, the group thrived. Each issue of *Zymurgy* was fatter than the last, thickened by an array of advertisements, mostly for homebrew supply shops, new magazines like *Home Fermenter's Digest* and *All About Beer,* and instruction manuals like Patrick Baker's 1979 publication, *New Brewer's Handbook.* News about homebrewing clubs filled several pages of each issue.

Homebrewing would ultimately serve as a breeding ground for microbrewing, nurturing the skills and ambitions of many of the people who later laid the foundation of that new brewing industry. But in the 1970s, that consequence was not yet obvious. Homebrewing was but one manifestation of a profound transformation in American beer culture. A line had been drawn: small, pure, and foreign versus big, toxic, and domestic. Beautiful Davids versus Grotesque Goliaths.

THAT SUCH A LINE existed was lost on corporate brewing. In the 1970s, the industry's giants were concerned not at all about homebrewing, Fritz Maytag, or "real" beer; they were too busy dreaming up new "segments" and providing more of the same bland lager they'd been making for thirty years.

Certainly the suits-and-ties at Philip Morris were oblivious, caught up as they were in their own vat of woe. The tobacco giant had gained complete control of Miller Brewing in 1970 when it bought Harry John's 47 percent share for an astonishing $96 million. But the company was performing badly and they longed to see a return, preferably in profit rather than headache, on their gamble.

John Murphy to the rescue. By his own admission, Murphy, who had trained as an accountant and lawyer and risen through Philip Morris's ranks to the office of executive vice-president, knew nothing about beer—except how to consume it, he being, also by his own admission, "an Olympic-class beer drinker." But PM's leadership was less interested in Murphy's beer gut than in his gut instinct, and as far as he was concerned, beer was first cousin to cigarettes: Both were agricultural products—barley and tobacco—processed within an inch of their lives in automated factories and sold in highly competitive markets. Selling beer, Murphy concluded, was about the same as selling smokes: Give customers what they want, do it efficiently and cheaply, and break the other guy's knees while you're at it.

Murphy, a gregarious guy with a hulking build and a cool self-confidence, arrived in Milwaukee in 1971 and began weeding Miller's genteel but stodgy management. Next, he reduced the hops and barley in Miller High Life as a way of wooing the otherwise uncommitted, and started selling it in seven-ounce containers, an enticement for women. He dumped the "country club" tone of the company's ads and bombarded the nation's eyes and ears with a new campaign based on "Miller Time": "If you've got the time, we've got the beer." The ads needed a few months to soak in, but in 1973, sales lurched forward—29 percent that year, another 31 percent the next. Miller Brewing moved from seventh place to fifth.

Having grabbed his competitors' throats, Murphy delivered his knockout punch: Miller Lite. Murphy purchased the Lite brand in 1972 from Meister Brau, the Chicago conglomerate that introduced the beer in 1967, and pondered its possibilities. Sure, diet beers had failed before. Who remembered Gablinger's except as a total flop? But that was then and this was now and John Murphy was John Murphy, and "[a]fter all," he said, "we're not in the brain-surgery business." In the hands of a skilled marketer and wedded to the right advertising campaign, low-calorie could be the next new segment, and if Miller created the segment, it would also control it.

Miller Lite made its national debut in February 1975 escorted by a passel of "convincing beer-drinking personalities" like Mickey Spillane, the tough-guy novelist; Rodney Dangerfield, the not-so-tough comic; and an assortment of former baseball, basketball, and football players. One series of TV spots featured two "teams" chanting their respective mantras: "Tastes great," roared one side; "Less filling," responded the other. In another ad, football player Bubba Smith demonstrated Lite's "easy-opening" cans by ripping the top off one. In another, Dangerfield hung out in a tavern "so tough that the hatcheck girl is named Dominick."

Was Miller Lite a success because of its humorous ads, or its contribution to good health at a moment when organic produce and jogging had become popular? It didn't much matter. Murphy unloaded five million barrels of Lite during its second year on the market. Company sales rose 43 percent in 1976, pushing Miller from fourth place to third. And in 1977, a year in which Miller Brewing sold 25 million barrels of all its brands, Miller knocked Schlitz out of second place. "I've been in this business 20 years," marveled an Atlanta wholesaler, "and I've never seen anything like this acceptance."

Humbug, replied Robert S. Weinberg, one of the industry's most respected analysts, in a rare misjudgment: "The whole light beer thing is a fraud. It's people rationalizing. The beer tastes awful." Joe Ortlieb wasn't buying it either—except as a way to sell his own lager. Ortlieb, who owned Henry F. Ortlieb Brewing, a tiny outfit in Philadelphia, ran a TV campaign called "Drink Joe's Beer." The shots featured Joe, a bottle of Ortlieb, a half-full glass of beer, and a pitcher of water. "This is how we make light beer," he announced, and then poured water into the glass. "Now that's why we don't make it."

August Busch III, recently named president of Anheuser-Busch, was not convinced either. Augie, as some called him, was, at thirty-six, already seasoned in the ways of both brewing and war. He was an odd mixture of the Busch trio who preceded him: He possessed great-grandfather Adolphus's attention to detail but none of his flamboyance. From grandfather August A., he inherited a steely resistance to an overbearing father. And he shared his father's impatience with incompetence, but whereas Gus laughed off his explosive fits of temper, Augie froze his victims with an icy glare, reserving his warmth for those who earned it.

Augie studied brewing at the Siebel Institute in Chicago, the first Busch since his great-grandfather to earn a reputation as a fine brewmaster. By the early 1970s he was vice-president and general manager of the largest brewery in the world, but one that was struggling to maintain its footing at a time of economic upheaval. The OPEC oil embargo fueled inflation that ran as high as 10 percent. In 1973, corn prices rose 40 percent and barley 30. Can prices went up 35 percent. Federally imposed price ceilings exacerbated the misery. Many brewers switched to cheaper extracts and syrups—anything to cut costs.

Gus Busch, still in control and loath to compromise method or recipe, stayed with rice even as the price rose 78 percent in 1973, stuck with a forty-day brewing cycle, and dumped real hops rather than cheaper extracts into the brewvats. "I could cut production costs by 50%, but where quality is concerned, the subject is *verboten*," sighed Russell Ackoff, a Wharton professor who conducted A-B's computer-based research, planning, and forecasting.

Earnings and profits tumbled, and the company's stock performed a rare nosedive. Richard Meyer, the company's president (the first non-Busch to hold the position), resigned over what he regarded as inept and inappropriate management. Augie succeeded him and turned his cold gaze to the fray. In five years, he told a reporter, "You can be sure that we will still be No. 1." To another he said, "Tell Miller to come right along, but tell them to bring lots of money."

No worries on that last point. Philip Morris inhaled and exhaled money. Buckets and barrels and vats of money; more than anyone had ever seen in brewing. Pre–Philip Morris, brewers spent, on average, about one dollar a barrel for advertising. PM spent four. Between 1969 and late 1977, the company poured $600 million into plant expansion, more than tripling Miller's capacity.

Other brewers could not match PM's bottomless pockets, but they could see the lite. By mid-1977, Americans could choose from at least twenty light beers. Piel's, Pearl, or Peter Hand. Gibbon's, Gablinger's, or Goebel. Joe Pickett, owner of tiny Joseph S. Pickett and Sons Brewing in Dubuque, Iowa, scoffed at the idea. "This light stuff is strictly Madison Avenue," he grumbled. "It's the pizza you eat with it that makes you fat." But when a fellow brewer went bankrupt, Pickett snapped up the man's light brand and reintroduced it as his own.

Eventually even Augie Busch jumped on board. Light beer "has exceeded our expectations," he announced in June 1977 in a masterpiece of understatement. An Anheuser-Busch version would be available soon. An anonymous brewery official was a bit more blunt. "We didn't really want to make it," he told a St. Louis reporter, "but were forced into it. The light beers, especially Miller's, were taking away some of our business. We are just trying to get it back."

But this was Anheuser-Busch, and so this was no ordinary light beer, but "Natural Light." "It's an entirely organic product," enthused one distributor. "In fact, it's the only beer that truly could be sold in a health store." A-B light, said Augie, "exemplifies the company's dedication to completely natural ingredients. In view of customer concern about artificial ingredients and additives in food products, we think this will be an increasing asset for all of our products."

Perhaps, but more to the point, Natural Light represented Round One in an Anheuser-Busch campaign to demolish Murphy and Miller. Round Two began a few months later, when A-B filed a complaint with the Federal Trade Commission against Miller's advertising for its ersatz import, Löwenbräu. Like most brewing executives, the suits at Miller wanted a slice of the expanding import segment. They had purchased the American rights to the German Löwenbräu name and label, then brewed their own version of the beer itself, packaging it in a green bottle whose label and foil-wrapped neck mimicked its German counterpart. Only the fine print revealed its Milwaukee birthplace.

Anheuser-Busch charged that Miller was duping consumers by passing off a domestic beer as an import. Real German lagers, the complaint explained, consisted of water, hops, yeast, and malt, but Miller Löwenbräu contained corn grits and two "non-natural additives."

"We find it incredulous [sic]," responded Miller, "that the world's largest brewer would ask the FTC to protect them." Not so incredulous, mind you, that Miller minded filing its own complaint, accusing its foe of running its own misleading advertising. Natural Light, argued Miller, contained a mishmash of its own brew of chemical additives and other unnatural ingredients.

Natural. Unnatural. In the end, all that mattered was the money. F. X. Matt from West End Brewing calculated that five years after Lite's debut, Miller's perpetual money machine had cost brewing and related industries ten thousand jobs; owners and stockholders of failed breweries had lost $250 million. Shielded by armor fashioned from Philip Morris money, he argued, "Miller people . . . believe they are so big, so powerful . . . that no one can stop them." Only Anheuser-Busch could afford to keep pace with Miller and its deep-pocketed parent.

No one lost more than the Uihleins and Schlitz. The company began the decade in good condition because Bob Uihlein unloaded the bad investments of the 1960s—the fishing fleets and most of the foreign breweries. But he still fretted over the company's dependence on its aging flagship brand, Schlitz, which provided 80 percent of sales. Uihlein, an accountant at heart, told Fred Haviland to develop a new plan for diversification. Haviland dispatched a flock of newly hired MBAs on scouting expeditions for solid but related investments: wine perhaps, or an import with a solid base. The Schlitz troops pursued Löwenbräu, but Miller beat them to the punch. They negotiated with the French wine distributor Nicolas, and with Paul Masson, but those deals fell through when Uihlein saw the price tag.

He turned to the Boston Consulting Group for advice. BCG's people persuaded Uihlein and his vice-presidents that the path to profit lay in cost-cutting. But how to do that? New breweries, Uihlein decided. But not just any breweries—breweries that were four times larger than any that had ever been built. Ultra-mechanized, ultra-efficient, and ultra-expensive: about $150 million apiece. The aging Milwaukee plant required twenty-four men per shift; the new ones would need but two. Sure, there would be expenses up-front, but the new facilities would slash operating costs by as much as $2 a barrel. Lower costs. Higher profits. "We are the company with the momentum now," Uihlein announced in early 1973.

There was just one catch, or rather, 460 of them: the rest of the Uihleins. They refused to sacrifice shares or dividends for future profit. "[T]hat board," a company executive said later, "wanted nothing less than an immediate return . . . It's not a small matter to cut the dividend of a guy who has 6,000,000 shares and counts on that money for his entire income." If Bob Uihlein wanted new plants, he would have to go into debt to get them. Lots of debt. More than the company had ever shouldered. A dangerous move when 80 percent of the company's portfolio rested on one brand of beer.

It was too dangerous for Roy Satchell, who was named company president in February 1973 and resigned six weeks later. For reasons no one understood, but for which many would pay dearly, Bob Uihlein chose not to replace Satchell. Nor did he resume the post. Over the next eighteen months, his great-great-uncle's brewery resembled a captainless ship adrift in a vast ocean of inflation and recession.

And so began the fall. Like company founder August Krug in 1855, Schlitz Brewing tumbled and never recovered. The production department proceeded with the next phase of the great cost-cutting scheme: "accelerated-batch fermentation"—adding air to stimulate the yeast's growth, a process that reduced fermentation from twelve days to less than four and allowed the brewmaster to cut the brewing cycle from twenty-five days to two weeks. Corn syrup replaced corn grits; hop extract replaced hop pellets. The finance department, unaware of the "new" beer coming out of the brewhouse, raised prices, a misguided attempt to reposition Schlitz as a premium beer at a moment when inflation was wreaking havoc with consumer spending.

Sales slipped and so did the stock price, but Fred Haviland and his marketing people forged on, determined to give wholesalers and retailers encouragement in the form of good advertising. The wholesalers, who loved Haviland, gave him a rousing ovation when he spoke at a sales meeting in early 1974. Bob Uihlein was there, too, but won only polite bordering on tepid applause from an audience less interested in a Harvard-schooled polo player than in Fred Haviland, the man with the plan.

Several weeks later at a company cocktail party, Bob Uihlein's wife Lorraine marched up to Haviland, jabbed him in the chest with her finger—its nail perhaps painted red and trimmed to a sharp point?—and said, "When we want you to become president, we'll let you know." In August, the board of directors named the vice-president of finance, an accountant to the core, as the new general manager. Marketing and sales, wholesaling and distribution were foreign territories that the new guy had no desire to explore. Ten days later, Haviland cleaned out his office, the victim of a forced "early retirement."

Then the Food and Drug Administration announced that it was considering mandatory ingredient labels for beer, and Schlitz executives ordered company brewmasters to replace silica gel with Chill-garde. Both additives stabilized the beer and improved shelf life, but Chill-garde dissipated during the brewing process, so could not be considered an ingredient and need not appear on labels. Unbeknownst to the powers-that-be, however, Chill-garde interfered with the beer's foam stabilizer. The chemical reaction spawned a flake-laden haze—nothing dangerous but ugly to look at, and unnerving to anyone drinking the beer.

One vigilant plant manager noticed the problem right away

and alerted Milwaukee headquarters. The response was to ignore
the matter in the hope that it would go away. Six months passed
before the honchos ordered brewmasters to stop using the stabilizer. Another mistake: Thanks to years of cost-cutting measures,
Schlitz beer contained little barley. Tip a can's unstabilized contents into a glass and the brew looked "flat as apple cider."

Customers fled. Stock drifted downward. Two grand juries and
the Securities and Exchange Commission opened investigations
into illegal marketing practices. The Internal Revenue Service accused Schlitz of tax fraud. That was in the summer of 1976. In
late October, Bob Uihlein was diagnosed with leukemia. He died
a few weeks later. The board of directors replaced him with a tri-
umvirate, none of whom had any sales or marketing experience.
"Here were three guys running the second largest beer company
in the world," sighed an employee, "and not one of them had ever
sold a case of beer in their lives. It was amateur night at the zoo."

In early 1977, the SEC charged Schlitz with making more than
$3 million in illegal payments to vendors and retailers. Grand ju-
ries in Milwaukee and Hawaii indicted the company on seven
hundred charges of violating the Federal Alcohol Administration
Act. Schlitz faced the possibility of losing its license to operate in
more than a dozen states. The company's stock, once the darling
of Wall Street at a share price of $60 or more, sold for as little as
$12. The board of directors—Uihleins trying to protect their in-
come—began looking for a buyer.

Across town, Pabst's management—marketing men and accountants—floundered, too. None of them could figure out what
kind of image would make their beer sell. The recession of the
early 1970s hit hard, and a decision was made to "position," as the
marketers called it, Pabst Blue Ribbon as a low-price bargain beer
for the blue-collar set. It was too late. For decades, old Frederick's pride had been sold only as what it once was: a high-quality,

high-priced premium brew. Beer bargain hunters had long since settled on other brands; they weren't interested in what Pabst had to offer. The stock price dropped. The parade of rotating executives continued. The company would never recover.

As BIG BREWING fumbled, stumbled, and rumbled, John A. "Jack" McAuliffe looked toward a different brewing future. In October 1976, the same month that Larry McCavitt incorporated the Committee for Real Ale, McAuliffe and his business partners, Suzy Stern and Jane Zimmerman, filed papers for their venture, New Albion Brewing Company. The following July, they heated the water in their forty-five-gallon vat and brewed the inaugural batch of ale at what was the most important failed brewery in the industry's history.

McAuliffe's road to that time and place stretched back more than a decade. He'd joined the navy in 1964 at age eighteen. After a stint in electronics school, he shipped out to the submarine base at Holy Loch in southwestern Scotland and his assignment with the USS *Simon Lake,* whose crew provided maintenance for Polaris submarines. McAuliffe rented a small house in Dunoon and settled in to his post at the ship's antenna repair shop.

McAuliffe savored the local ales, porters, and stouts, which were unlike anything he'd tasted before and a universe away from the pale lagers he knew in America. The only drawback in this otherwise blissful revelation was that the ale he most enjoyed was a local brew firmly attached to a town far from Holy Loch. Jack knew nothing about brewing but he was mechanically adept, in possession of more than ordinary common sense and intelligence, and open to new ideas. If he could repair nuclear submarines, he could figure out how to make ale.

Homebrewing catapulted McAuliffe's understanding of beer's complexities and potential into a new universe. Over the next two years he brewed regularly and read everything he could find on beer and beermaking. He bought a motorcycle and spent a month's leave touring western and northern Europe, expanding his zymotechnic horizons.

When McAuliffe's tour of duty ended in 1968, he headed back to the United States and college. He graduated in 1971 and took a job as an optical engineer with a firm in Sunnyvale in California's South Bay. But he spent his free time devouring the knowledge needed to build and operate a brewery. He visited Wine and the People in Berkeley and Michael Lewis at Davis. McAuliffe told the professor he planned to start a brewery. Lewis was, understandably, skeptical—but not for long. He recognized that McAuliffe was "very smart" and had presented a "complete story" about why he wanted to found a brewery and how he planned to do it. The university owns an extensive collection of brewing books and magazines, Lewis told McAuliffe, advising him to study them and let him know what else he could do to help.

McAuliffe pored over the materials in the Davis library, especially the nineteenth-century texts and read Pasteur and works on microbiology. He taught himself basic accounting. He found copies of *Brewers Digest* and studied the ads, hunting for suppliers and equipment, although when he called them for information, they "acted like he was from Mars." Never mind. McAuliffe had served a two-year apprenticeship at a welding shop during high school. He would build what he needed, using the beer books for ideas and inspiration.

He nosed about his San Francisco friends and acquaintances, hunting for adventurers willing to invest in what he proposed to call the Barbary Coast Brewing Company. There were no takers, and San Francisco real estate was too expensive for McAuliffe to act on his own. Sonoma, forty miles north, was another story. Rents were cheaper there, and the town offered something more. In the 1970s, Sonoma inspired offbeat ventures and gustatory passion. The area's burgeoning wine industry pulsated with the energy of its own renaissance. A new generation of chefs had converged on the area, influenced by Alice Waters and anxious to employ local wines as a springboard for a new kind of American cuisine. The town contained an artisanal bakery and shops selling superb local cheese. A man who had studied sausage-making in Germany introduced locals to charcuterie elevated many notches above American hot dogs. This, McAuliffe decided, was the kind of place and these were the kinds of people who would support quality beer.

In 1975, McAuliffe quit his job and rented a piece of property three miles southeast of Sonoma. Eucalyptus trees shaded a corrugated steel warehouse and small shed. There was no potable water at the site, so McAuliffe trucked what he needed from a well in the nearby hills. The brewer's funds were limited to about five thousand dollars, which meant that he had to rely on ingenuity and elbow grease. He removed the structure's existing floor and poured a new one that sloped toward a drain. He built a malt bin and fashioned fermenters from fifty-five-gallon barrels. He fabricated a malt mill based on a design in a nineteenth-century brewing book and salvaged a vintage 1910 labeling machine, a goofy contraption whose glue pot and treadle-operated mechanism attached labels to bottles "with the approximate velocity and cadence of a horse swatting a fly with its tail."

He christened the place "New Albion." Seventy years earlier, San Francisco had been home to the Albion Brewing Company, and McAuliffe wanted to revive its name. The appellation allowed the twentieth-century sailor and explorer-of-beer to honor another sailor-explorer: Sir Francis Drake, the sixteenth-century Englishman who sailed San Francisco Bay in the *Golden Hind* and dubbed the land of hills and fog "New Albion." McAuliffe hired a local artist to design the brewery's logo and labels. The result was one of the most graceful labels to adorn a bottle of American beer: In the center was an image of the *Hind* framed by the hills of the San Francisco Bay, the ship's sails billowed in full wind. Two sheaves of barley stood on either side, and across the top a simple furled banner read "new albion brewing company SONOMA CALIFORNIA."

Word spread through the tight-knit northern California homebrewing community. A crowd showed up for the grand opening that summer of 1977—showed up and proceeded to get drunk on beer that delivered more of a punch than most people were used to. Byron Burch and his soon-to-be wife Nancy Vineyard made the pilgrimage to Sonoma that day. Nancy promptly decided that Jack was crazy. He looked for all the world like a "sea captain . . . listing to one side," a "squint and a cock to his head."

Vineyard wasn't the only one who questioned McAuliffe's state of mind. Making beer when the only potable water lay miles away? Using equipment straight out of Dickens? Crazy perhaps, but . . . successful, at least when measured by his goal, which was to make and sell beer. McAuliffe and Suzy Stern (Jane Zimmerman jumped ship early on) brewed a barrel and a half five times a week—making ale, porter, and stout—and bottled it on Wednesday. They promptly sold every drop, and with no advertising. "If you make good beer," McAuliffe told a reporter from the *Washington Post* who visited in the summer of 1978, "you don't have to pay for advertising." The beer's selling point was its purity: McAuliffe used nothing but malt, hops, water, and yeast. No enzymes or corn grits; no stabilizers. Not even any pasteurization, New Albion products being bottle-fermented for five weeks in a cool cellar. This was a risky road to travel, but McAuliffe managed because he understood the importance of sanitation and monitored his yeast and beers with religious devotion in his inner sanctum, the laboratory.

New Albion's reputation spread thanks to a stout that rattled beer connoisseurs' senses and a porter that sang with flavor. The Maltose Falcons visited, as did other homebrewers. Frank Prial, who covered wines for the *New York Times*, paid a visit. The editor of *Brewers Digest* toured the tiny brewery and paid the compliment of treating Jack as a peer rather than as the nut-case crank that many brewers no doubt thought he was.

Don Barkley showed up, too. Barkley had begun homebrewing in 1971, the same year he graduated from high school. He heard about McAuliffe when he visited Michael Lewis to discuss enrolling in the Davis brewing program. A few weeks later, Barkley and his wife-to-be headed to New Albion, where he planned to offer his services—free—for the summer. The couple found the proprietor in the brewery office. Barkley introduced himself and explained that he wanted to intern for the summer. McAuliffe, known less for his smooth business manner than for eccentricity and a bluntness that often bloomed into rudeness, responded in form. "Get out," he commanded.

Barkley left, but returned a few weeks later. This time he found Suzy Stern. He repeated his offer: free labor for the summer. Sure! said Stern. In June 1978, Barkley pitched a tent on property owned by a nearby homeowner, donned rubber boots, and started work. He earned a case of beer a week and all he could drink on the job.

New Albion, he soon learned, had been built with meticulous care, the handiwork of a professional at heart. It was also no place for the indolent, the lazy, or the indifferent. "You have to be totally committed," McAuliffe said. "The only thing you think about is beer and brewing." The job involved working ten or twelve hours a day, six or seven days a week. Fighting with suppliers who were not used to penny-ante orders of malt and hops. Hauling carloads of beer to San Francisco and driving back for the empty bottles. Landing a distributor and then hoping he would keep the beer refrigerated until it was delivered to the retailers. Driving to

San Francisco to retrieve a shipment that exploded on the shelf because it had gone bad or, more often, because the retailer had stored it improperly. This was not Schlitz or Miller, something designed to withstand nuclear attack. New Albion products were living creatures that demanded care and respect.

The boss was not the easiest guy to work alongside, but his respect for the past and his optimism about a new brewing future permeated New Albion. "We knew we were doing something completely bizarre in terms of the brewing industry," Barkley said later, "but also that there was this unique history that nearly commanded that this happen, that we do this."

Outside New Albion's small yard, beyond Sonoma's utopian confines, lay inspiration in reverse. Barkley's classmates in the Davis program planned to grab their degrees and head for an executive position at one or another of the big beer factories where they would wear suits and ties and tell union workers "what button to push." Neither they nor their future employers grasped that a new chapter in brewing had begun—that Americans had changed, and that brewing must change with them. The same was true at meetings of the Master Brewers Association that McAuliffe and Barkley attended. Most members were corporate brewers—suit-and-tie-wearing button-pushers—and they didn't think that McAuliffe and Barkley belonged in their group. Michael Lewis, who sat on the Association's board of governors, defended the two brewers, the one bearded, the other with hair hanging down to his waist. McAuliffe and Barkley, he pointed out, met membership criteria: They operated a commercial brewery, and a successful one at that; and they possessed considerable experience, and in Don's case, formal education.

The irritation of the MBA's arrogance evaporated once the two brewers returned to New Albion, where beer's new era unfolded on a daily basis. So did the brewery's woes. Several years of experience had taught McAuliffe that the sticking point of his operation lay at the retail end of the equation. He sold bottles of New Albion to tavern owners for about sixty-seven cents and they passed them on to consumers for as much as two dollars. There, McAuliffe realized, was where the money lay. There and in large-scale production, more than he could manage in his current location.

On, then, to Phase Two: First, move to a larger location and expand production beyond the current forty-five barrels. Second, switch from returnable bottles to one-way packages, an expensive but necessary proposition. McAuliffe knew that although most people supported ecologically correct reusable bottles in theory, in reality consumers, retailers, and distributors hated having to pay the deposit and then lug the bottles back to the store. Third, and most important, open a pub where McAuliffe could sell his wares and collect that hefty markup currently landing in others' pockets.

The plan required the pioneers to hurdle two obstacles. First, they had to eliminate the state law that forbid brewers from selling their products at retail, and second, find money to pay for the projects.

They vaulted the legal hurdle with comparative ease. McAuliffe and Fritz Maytag contacted Tom Bates, a California assemblyman, and the trio constructed a bill that would eliminate the half-century-old ban on "tied" houses and allow brewers to sell beer in an attached outlet that also offered food. The wine industry supported the bill, for many vintners recognized that wineries attached to tasting rooms and sales shops could become profitable components of California tourism. The bill passed and would go into effect in January 1983.

Alas, the new law did nothing in the short term to counteract the impact of the Catch-22 of small brewing: The path to solvency and profit lay in large-scale production. Getting to large production required a larger operation. But McAuliffe could expand only if he earned money by selling more beer, and he couldn't sell more beer until he could expand. And so on.

As for conventional funding, well, bankers were not accustomed to dealing with brewers, who, by virtue of the product they sold—alcohol—operated in a different risk pool than someone who, say, wanted to open a restaurant or a clothing store. Besides, who ever heard of someone starting a brewery? Did this guy think he was going to compete with Augie Busch? Besides which, Don slept in a tent and bathed in spring water, and Jack "lived like a spider" in a cubbyhole above the brewery that he reached by climbing a ladder. Hardly the face and place to inspire bankers and other deep-pocketed members of the community.

McAuliffe was determined to break into mainstream finance or go down trying. He wrote a detailed business plan and designed new packaging that demonstrated New Albion's willingness to accommodate consumers and retailers. He designed new labels, too, which, while less stunning than the originals, looked more conventional. He obtained an option on a piece of property in Sonoma, a lot with an old Victorian house and a second structure large enough to accommodate a thousand-gallon brewery.

The preparations lured McAuliffe and Barkley straight into the brewer's Catch-22. The prospectus and the paper on which to print it, the property option, and the labels—all of it cost more money than New Albion was bringing in. Barkley added $5,000 of his own money, but it was not enough.

The end came in November 1982. Barkley emptied the brewvats for the last time. Over the course of a few days, the crew jackhammered Jack's graceful sloping floor into oblivion and dismantled every piece of equipment. Even then, Barkley's optimism overruled his regrets. "We knew," he said later, that small brewing "could work, knew it was the right idea. We knew the whole concept was good."

HE WAS RIGHT. Jack McAuliffe forged a seminal moment in American brewing, his importance rooted in the very failure that ordinarily relegates fallen pioneers to history's dustbin. He demonstrated that it was possible to build a brewery from scratch using scrap metal and salvaged equipment. Most of the first generation of new brewers followed his lead. Many avoided the small brewer's Catch-22, but only because McAuliffe's tumble into that merciless trap illuminated the snare.

Together, McAuliffe and Fritz Maytag represented two sides of the new brewing coin. Maytag had demonstrated that there was a viable market for a new kind of beer—or, more accurately, a new market for an older style of full-bodied beer made from barley and hops, a kind of beer that had not been made in the United States for well over a century. McAuliffe provided penniless entrepreneurs and ambitious homebrewers with a model of how to build a small, functional, affordable brewhouse. Together, these two men and their breweries, and the sea change in attitudes toward beer, provided the building blocks for a new era in American brewing.

CHAPTER EIGHT

Something Old, Something New

IN 1978, THE NUMBER of breweries in the United States plunged to its all-time low: eighty-nine plants owned by a mere forty-one companies. Beers made by the top five brewers—Anheuser-Busch, Miller, Schlitz, Pabst, and Coors—dominated coolers at grocery stores and gas stations. By the year 2000, those forty-one companies would balloon to nearly fifteen hundred, and two of the breweries in the top ten would be companies that had not existed back in 1978. Grocery store beer shelves would groan under a cornucopia of new beers, including ales, stouts, and porters, beer styles that had not been seen in the United States for a century, except as imports. Americans would drink freshly made beer at brewpubs, or tour one of the thousand-plus breweries, where the owners, who were often the brewmasters too, greeted guests with a smile and a beer. Americans would enjoy more varied and higher-quality beers than at any time in the nation's history.

THEY DID SO BECAUSE of people like Ken Grossman, who founded Sierra Nevada Brewing Co., and was perhaps the most talented brewmaster of his generation. In 1964, ten-year-old Ken's focus of interest in his otherwise ordinary suburban Los Angeles neighborhood was a house a few doors down from his own. His best friend, Greg Moeller, lived there, and Greg's dad, Calvin, a metallurgist, ruled over that great Shangri-La of boys everywhere: a basement laboratory. But this was no ordinary lab. Moeller devoted his to the alchemy of liquor, mixing up batches of wine, sake, and beer. The basement brewery's marvelous aromas and the science and magic of homebrewing lured the boy into a life-long passion. Grossman was surely the nation's youngest and shortest assistant brewer, working alongside the neighborhood master, absorbing wisdom as only a child can do.

In junior high, Grossman converted his own basement into a brewhouse. He befriended the owner of a local homebrewing supply shop and joined the Maltose Falcons. A high-school teacher with the wisdom to see the hobby as a strange but useful path to science encouraged the teenager to subject his beers to laboratory analysis. Ken's parents indulged their son's interest. By his own admission, he was a bit of a wild child, and, things being what they were in the late 1960s, Mr. and Mrs. Grossman no doubt concluded better a brewhouse than a bong in the basement.

Besides, their son enjoyed other interests, although some of them were just as strange. He built a house in the backyard—no "isn't that cute" weekend project but a functioning miniature house, complete with code-approved plumbing and electricity. He developed an enthusiasm for bicycling and, Ken Grossman being Ken Grossman, taught himself everything there was to know about bicycle mechanics and maintenance. He joined his older brother and his friends on biking trips, usually camping expeditions along the coast or up into the Sierras. One trek landed them in San Francisco, where they stopped by Anchor Brewing. Ken was impressed that there was an American beer out there with as much complexity and depth as those he was making on his own.

In the spring of 1972, Grossman picked up his high school diploma, packed his brewing equipment and bicycle tools into a VW microbus, and headed north with a vague plan to attend college and the more immediate goal of escaping Southern California's freeways. Destination: Chico, a small town nestled between two national forests, Plumas to the east and Mendocino to the west. He settled in, taking classes at a nearby community college and at California State University, Chico, working at area bicycle shops, and a few years later opening a homebrew supply shop. There were plenty of customers, including students and professors from the university and local doctors and lawyers. Hippies "came down out of the hills" in search of cheap ingredients for making cheap booze. He taught classes to the hobbyists who were more interested in quality than price.

And pondered the notion of starting his own brewery. The obstacles loomed large for a young man with no money and a weird idea. Sure, Fritz Maytag had done it, but the older man enjoyed the pleasure of a fat bank account, and besides, there weren't any other Anchor-sized outfits standing around empty, waiting to be bought.

But in 1978, Grossman visited New Albion. Later, he could not remember much about the beer except that it was "hoppy." He only had eyes for the brewery. New Albion, with its Rube Goldbergian labeler and its three-barrels-lashed-together fermenter, was a dream come true. Here, he knew, was the shining brewery on a hill, the model for high-quality, small-scale brewing. If McAuliffe could do this, so could he. McAuliffe had little money and neither did Grossman. McAuliffe knew how to weld, hammer, saw, cut, and fit. So did Grossman. McAuliffe cobbled together salvage and scrap; Grossman could do that, too. In short, there was nothing about McAuliffe's accomplishment that lay beyond his own grasp or skill.

Why not seize the moment? He told his friend Paul Camusi, also a homebrewer, about his vision. Count me in, said Camusi.

Grossman sketched a design for a ten-barrel brewery, a manageable size but large enough to turn a profit—and to avoid the brewer's Catch-22. The wife of a friend helped the pair write a business plan. But the bankers laughed, so Grossman and Camusi borrowed from family and friends, $50,000 all told. Grossman had befriended the faculty in the chemistry department at a nearby community college and they granted him access to laboratory facilities. He enrolled in vocational courses that provided entrée to forklifts, drill presses, and the like. The pair made numerous trips to Davis to consult with Michael Lewis, who was no longer surprised when young men showed up announcing their intention to build a brewery.

In 1979, they rented a three-thousand-square-foot metal building outside Chico. Grossman and Camusi gutted the structure, installed drains and wiring, poured floors, and put up new interior walls, phoning McAuliffe when they needed advice. Grossman drove his 1957 Chevy all over northern California and into Oregon and Washington, stopping at every scrap yard, dairy, and farm to pick through piles of discarded pumps, pipes, and tanks. They scrounged bottles from defunct breweries in Southern California. Maytag was building a new brewery and no longer needed the old pressure filler that he'd bought from Sieben Brewing back in 1966. He sold it to Grossman, in whom he recognized a kindred spirit.

The first $50,000 ran out and Camusi and Grossman borrowed that amount again. Now they had to succeed: Everyone they knew and loved was on the line with them. Deep into the project, they realized their building was too small. Grossman's uncle, an architect, drew plans for an addition, and the partners took them to city hall. Their addition was five hundred square feet, the clerk told them, and any project that size or larger required payment of a fee. Grossman drew a line across the back end of the plan. "We'll build it to here," he said, "499 square feet." No fee necessary.

A friend designed the labels: a furled banner reminiscent of New Albion's and sheaves of barley framing a central image of fir trees, a winding river, and in the background, the Sierra Nevadas, the brewery's namesake. Grossman drove to Oakland to tell Byron Burch about his plans and to show the local homebrewing "guru" the artwork. Burch and Nancy Vineyard marveled at the labels, whose colors and images "jump[ed] off the page." Vineyard admitted to feeling "a little bit jealous." Here was a friend making the leap into every homebrewer's dream: commercial brewing.

Mostly the dream consisted of endless hours of work and worry, which ramped up several notches when, in November 1980, Grossman and Camusi finally inaugurated their brewvats. Like most of that first generation of new brewers, they decided to make ale rather than lager, and, like Maytag and McAuliffe, to use but four ingredients: malt, hops, yeast, and water. But even with this road map in front of them, the pair soon realized that commercial brewing presented potholes, pitfalls, and detours for which homebrewing had not prepared them. Brewing five gallons at a time was one thing; trying to achieve that same quality in ten barrels was another matter. Their first batches failed. Eleven of them, to be precise.

While they struggled to tame their yeast, they tackled the last step: determining where to sell the beer and how to get it from brewery to retailer. They knew, thanks to Maytag and McAuliffe, that distribution would be their biggest challenge and their greatest danger. They talked to local distributors, but the middlemen wanted an impossibly large piece of the pie, too much for two young men already neck-deep in debt. Grossman and Camusi would deliver their own beer. Which meant they also had to line up their own retail accounts. In between brewing beer, scorning regular sleep and meals as only the young can, they visited every restaurant and tavern in Chico, trying to persuade other small entrepreneurs to take a chance on their beer.

Finally, glorious day, a perfect brew emerged from their vat, one they could duplicate. In March 1981, the first bottles of Sierra Nevada landed in stores and taverns in and around Chico. The pair sold 950 barrels of beer that first year, and twice that the next.

GROSSMAN AND Camusi were leaders of a larger wave of small breweries that opened at about the same time, most of them in northern California and other parts of the western United States, nearly all of them following the McAuliffe–Grossman model. Tom DeBakker, a Marin County firefighter and devoted home-brewer, opened DeBakker Brewery in 1979; his best year was 1980, when he sold eighty barrels. Charles and Shirley Courey opened the doors of Cartwright Brewery in Portland, Oregon, in early 1980; two years later, a sheriff's deputy padlocked the door. Jim Schleuter, who studied at UC Davis under Michael Lewis, quit his job at Schlitz and founded River City Brewing in Sacramento in the summer of 1981. He rolled out one thousand barrels of beer in 1983, but that was not enough to offset his losses. The brewery entered bankruptcy in early 1984. Charles Rixford, a Berkeley homebrewer, operated Thousand Oaks Brewing out of his basement; he, too, lasted but a few years.

Of the early starters, only three enjoyed any longevity. In 1979, two University of Colorado professors founded Boulder Brewing in a goat shed outside the namesake city; their creation would survive the century. Bert Grant started selling his eponymously named ales, stouts, and porters in Yakima, Washington, in early 1982. In August of that year, Paul Shipman and his partner, Starbucks founder Gordon Bowker, poured the first Redhook at Jake O'Shaughnessey's restaurant in Seattle.

Why did so few succeed and so many fail? Camusi and Grossman believed that too many would-be beer magnates failed to understand the basics of commercial brewing: Quality beer comes from quality equipment, and sanitation must reign supreme. Failed to understand, too, that, as Grossman put it, "[h]ome-brewing and brewing at this scale are pretty much unrelated." More often than not, he complained, homebrewers tried to go commercial "on a shoestring, and with such low technology and understanding of producing a high quality beer" that they produced foul swill. "It's the few that put out a marginal product that discourage us and may give the whole small brewing industry a bad image," he said. "I don't want to knock homebrewers," Grossman added, "some homebrewers make excellent beer, but the technology of operating a bottling line and dealing with such large volumes make it a different process."

Another pair of homebrewers heeded the warning and in so doing pioneered another component of new brewing, combining craft brewing with an American-style pub to create the brewpub. Michael Laybourn and Norman Franks had met in the early 1970s in Mendocino, which was fast becoming a refuge for hippies, dropouts, and escapees from the growing congestion and high rents of the Bay Area. There they taught at an alternative school, cooking up batches of wine and beer in science class so that the kids could understand the fermentation process. In the mid-1970s, the pair left teaching to start a construction company specializing in solar systems and remodeling. But homebrewing had become a passion, and that plus their entrepreneurial bent led them to think seriously about transforming their hobby into a commercial venture.

They visited New Albion and talked to McAuliffe. They listened when he warned them of the Catch-22 and understood that the retail side of brewing posed more dangers than anything that might infect the brewvat's contents. But they were also inspired by the new state law that allowed brewers to retail their beer on site. They envisioned a brewery with an attached tavern and garden where people could drink quality beer and enjoy life: a new generation's version of the pleasure gardens owned by the German émigrés of yesteryear.

The location—Hopland, about sixty miles north of Sonoma in Mendocino County—proved an inspired choice. Mendocino County was populated by a mix of ranching families who raised cattle and horses, winemakers, and a growing population of hippies and organic gardeners, courtesy of what Don Barkley described as a "tremendous migration of back-to-the-landers." The hops fields that once dominated the region were gone, replaced by vineyards. Fetzer Winery had established operations in the county, including a wine tasting room in the old high school in Hopland. The town itself was tiny—just a few hundred people— but it sat on Highway 101, the ribbon of road that runs from Los Angeles north to the Oregon border. Every day, twelve to thirteen thousand cars zoomed past.

The partners, a trio once John Scahill joined the venture, leased a hundred-year-old structure that fronted the highway and built the brewery out back. By that time, New Albion had failed, and the Mendocino partners, who had no illusions about their brewing skills, bought McAuliffe's equipment and hired McAuliffe and Barkley to operate the brewery.

Mendocino Brewing's beer traced its ancestry to McAuliffe's hearty ale and to the "Thunder Beer" that Laybourn and Franks used to brew for their friends. As for the name, the owners wanted something that paid homage to the time and place. They settled on Red Tail Ale, in part because of the beer's color. But the main inspiration came from a song much loved by northern Californians, "The Redtail Hawk," a simple hymn to the "golden rolling hills" of California, where the redtail hawk "writes songs across the sky." The peregrine falcon served as namesake for their second beer, a lighter, more delicate ale. An image of a black hawk adorned bottles of the brewery's stout, and Blue Heron honored a nearby preserve for that bird. The labels, vivid ovals of color and life, depicted their respective creatures with wings spread in triumphant salute.

An enthusiastic and appreciative crowd packed the place when it opened to the public on August 14, 1983. California's first brewpub was in business: a beer garden and brewhouse that would warm the hearts of Phillip and Jacob Best.

ON THE OTHER SIDE of the country, a sixth-generation descendant of German brewers chose a different approach to reinventing the industry. The family of Charles James Koch—"Jim" to one and all—spanned the history of beer in America. Jim's great-great-great-grandfather, a brewer by trade, emigrated from Germany in the mid-nineteenth century and settled in the Soulard district of St. Louis, where son Louis founded the Louis Koch Brewery. The next three generations of Kochs (pronounced "Cook") worked in beer as well, including Jim's father, Charles Joseph Koch, Jr., who settled near Cincinnati.

The elder Koch graduated from brewing school in 1948— just in time to see one Ohio brewery after another close its doors. As the 1950s wore on and breweries vanished, Charles Koch traveled farther from home to find work as a brewmaster. To hold his last job in the industry, Koch left home on Sunday and drove back Wednesday, arriving late to spend a few hours with his three children. On Thursday he left the house before daybreak and returned again Friday for an abbreviated weekend. Jim, born in 1949, realized early on that he, the oldest son of the sixth generation, would not make a life in beer.

But Charles Koch taught his children to appreciate what was left of the fine Cincinnati beers, and to distinguish good brew from bad. This is green, he'd say; not lagered long enough. This is infected. This was overpasteurized. He taught them how to enjoy beer as well: You may drink as much as you want, he told them, but you must drink it with me. One day he brewed beer at home with his three children, so they would understand what he did all day long.

Jim graduated from high school in 1967. Many of his peers joined communes or departed for Haight-Ashbury, but Koch headed east, into the heart of the nation's establishment: Harvard. Cambridge socked him in the gut with a culture punch. There'd been no sex, drugs, and rock and roll back in Cincinnati, at least not any that he'd noticed. Harvard Square was awash with all three. Awash, too, with East Coast, oxford-shirt, loafers-and-no-socks, prep-school culture that bore no resemblance to the world he'd known back in Ohio. He rose each morning at 5:30 and, while his trust-fund dorm mates snoozed, Koch delivered newspapers, "schlepping bags of papers up and down stairs at apartment buildings." Then he returned to the dorm, donned a jacket and tie—required attire—and ate breakfast.

After graduation, he applied to the four-year Harvard law/business program. Koch figured that the joint degrees would get him somewhere, and, at the very least, law school would provide more of the liberal arts–based education he'd enjoyed for the past four years. It did not. Law school, he discovered, was nothing more than "vocational school" for the ambitious. Two years into the program he sensed that he was careening toward a place he was not ready to go. Once you launch your career, his dad reminded him, you don't get summers off.

It was time to slow down. Koch took a leave and spent the next three years working odd jobs in between stints with Outward Bound, teaching people how to climb mountains and camp in winter conditions. He returned to Harvard, married in 1976, graduated in 1978, and accepted a position at Boston Consulting Group.

BCG pulsated with intellectual excitement thanks to founder Bruce Henderson, who devoted his career to challenging the paradigms of basic economics. He expected his troops—talented, smart, imaginative people like Jim Koch—to rethink basic business models, and to employ creative thinking to solve even the smallest problems. Koch was good at the work, and making more money than any of the five generations of firstborn Koch sons had dreamed possible. He was also dissatisfied. His clients, big names like General Electric and International Paper, were located outside Boston, so he spent most weeks on the road. His wife hated that he was not home at 5:30 every night. He knew that in another year or two, he might make partner. But did he want that? Did he want to wake up someday at fifty-five and regret this choice?

Jim Koch's life became, in short, a nearly perfect example of the way the 1960s zeitgeist had settled into Americans' bones. A man of his father's generation would have celebrated that kind of success and tucked his discontent, assuming he even noticed it, away in a dark, hidden corner. A woman of his mother's generation would have accepted her husband's long hours and travel. But that was back before life tumbled down a rabbit hole and several generations of Americans chased after it. Koch decided he had to get out while he could.

But what to do next? He didn't want to work for a corporate behemoth. "When you think of the values that are associated with the survival and prosperity of the human spirit," he said later, "they are not found in big corporations."

The answer was all around him. By the early 1980s, microbreweries, as their proprietors were starting to call them, had become regular fodder for newspaper features. The story of New Albion, of Sierra Nevada, of the fifty-odd breweries and brewpubs that made up the craft beer industry, had been reported in the pages of the *New York Times,* the *Washington Post,* and *Newsweek.* Fritz Maytag's beer was available on both coasts. "Yuppies," as the press was fond of calling baby boomers with big incomes and a penchant for the expensive and exotic, were sitting in fern bars sipping $3 bottles of imported beer.

This beckoned a guy like Jim Koch, steeped as he had been since birth with a love and knowledge of brewing. Gradually the strands of his life merged: His years at Harvard and with Outward Bound and BCG had shaped his entrepreneurial vision. The industry that had fed his family for decades was reinventing itself on a daily basis. All of it, he decided, added up to "destiny." Jim Koch, oldest son in his family, would continue the tradition. He would make beer.

Koch's investigative and business instincts kicked in. He had to learn about this new wing of brewing and find some niche that he could call his own. He contacted Bill Newman, an Albany, New York, craft brewer, who generated income for his ailing business by offering a one-week course for people interested in commercial brewing. Koch paid his money and headed to Albany. He was not impressed. Newman's beer had a shelf life of about a week; worse, it was inconsistent, which Koch knew doomed any brewer. Newman also sold only draft beer, a bad move in a nation where 80 to 90 percent of beer was packaged. Add in mediocre equipment and Koch could see the writing on that brewery wall.

Koch probed deeper. He discovered what Camusi and Grossman had learned a few years earlier: Most of the new brewers, many of them coming from homebrewing, were making bad beer, or, worse, inconsistent beer, and palming it off on a gullible public that could not tell the difference between fine beer and slop. Part of the problem was their equipment: Brilliant mechanics like Grossman and McAuliffe could get away with using homemade equipment fabricated from salvaged material, but for most brewers it spelled certain contamination and spoiled the beer.

Koch concluded that, Sierra Nevada and Anchor aside, microbrewing consisted of mostly bad beer and even more "marketing smoke and mirrors, marketing baloney." The same was true, he discovered, of the import beer craze: People were paying big bucks for beer gone skunky and stale after thousands of miles of travel under poor conditions.

The McAuliffe–Grossman model of microbrewing became even less attractive once Koch had refined his vision: He wanted to brew from superior ingredients; he wanted to provide Americans with an alternative to skunky imports, bland corporate beer, and sour amateur microbrews; and he wanted it to be lager. In that he was nearly alone. Most craft brewers made ale, either because they shunned corporate lager's reputation or because ale required less fermenting time. Lager brewing also demanded an investment in storage space and expensive cooling equipment.

Those two goals—to brew lager rather than ale and to produce a high-quality, fresh beer—led Koch to another conclusion. The means mattered less than the end, and if that were the case, he "didn't feel the need," he said later, to own an actual brewery. All he needed was access to professional-grade equipment and a professional brewmaster. A bit of research revealed that many old-line small and regional breweries were operating under capacity. Surely he could rent vat space and a brewmaster's services from one of them.

In one swoop, Koch reduced his start-up costs by hundreds of thousands of dollars and eliminated the two bugaboos that felled so many microbrewers: bad equipment and undercapitalization. This was the BCG mind at work: Apply creative thinking to worn-out problems. Think so far outside the box that you end up back at go, reinventing the wheel, but making it better than anyone else.

The rest involved number-crunching and details: How much for bottles? How much for cartons? How much for malt and hops? How many barrels must he brew and sell to earn a profit? How many employees did he need to make and sell those barrels? His father found recipes in the attic of his family's house in Ohio, a precious inheritance from great-great-grandfather Louis Koch.

Recipe and statistics in hand, Koch wrote a business summary for Boston Beer Company. "Sales of 5,000 barrels per year are required for attractive profitability based on the Boston market alone," he informed potential investors. "I believe this will take 3–5 years, but appears to be achievable." The sales pitch drew in about $140,000 from family and friends; he added another $100,000 of his own. That was enough to produce a sample batch, which he brewed on contract at Pittsburgh Brewing, a struggling small brewery with plenty of vat space for rent.

By early 1985, he was ready for phase two: rounding up some retailers. Koch believed the beer's quality would sell itself: Based on his family's nineteenth-century recipe, it was made only of the four basic ingredients—no adjuncts. Of himself, he was not so sure. Up to that moment, he said later, he'd "never sold anything in [his] life." He packed his briefcase with six bottles of beer and some ice and set forth to launch his sales career at a bar not far from the BCG office. Koch unrolled his sales pitch and offered to pour a glass for the manager. The manager looked at the guy in the pinstriped suit, tasted the beer—and ordered twenty-five cases.

The rest, as the saying goes, was history. Koch and his sole employee, Rhonda Kallman (his secretary at BCG), traveled from one Boston tavern and restaurant to another, carrying beer samples and wooing owners and managers. Distributors refused to touch the stuff, so the pair rented a truck and delivered the beer, too.

That projection of five thousand barrels in five years? It took Koch and Kallman all of five months to hit the mark. A decade later, Koch was selling 700,000 barrels of lager a year and Boston Beer Company was the nation's tenth-largest purveyor of beer.

Koch's success was not hard to understand. His father had taught him the cardinal rules of brewing: consistency and quality. Koch was able to achieve both because he hired the services of a professional brewmaster who employed state-of-the-art brewing equipment. In that sense, he had more in common with, say, the

Leinenkugel family than with most craft brewers. The Leinen-kugels invested their slender profits in the services of a trained brewmaster and in replacing and repairing outmoded or damaged equipment because they understood that just one batch of bad beer would destroy their reputation and their livelihood.

But Koch's decision to rent brewery space also provided him with a flexibility denied the owners of microbreweries. Because he had not invested in an actual plant, he could free some of his funds for marketing and promotion. Too, as his sales grew, he could in-crease production by renting more vat space. More conventional craft brewers were stuck with the equipment they had started with, and had to raise money before they could build new plants.

In the early days, Koch's methods and success fueled animos-ity. As far as many craft beermakers were concerned, he was not a "real" brewer because his beer came out of a rented brewery, just as Carl Conrad's Budweiser had back in 1876. "I think contract brewers should represent themselves as just what they are . . . ," Ken Grossman argued, "brokers who are having their beers man-ufactured by another brewer. I don't think they should put them-selves over as brewers." Kurt Widmer of Widmer Brewing in Portland, Oregon, accused contract brewers of being "more in-terested in making a buck than in actually brewing quality beer." "I'm not sitting here in a three-piece suit telling you I'm a serious brewer," Maine craft brewer David Geary, owner of D. L. Geary Brewing, told a reporter. "I'm dripping wet [with beer], wearing torn shirts and rubber boots up to my knees."

Even Matthew Reich joined the chorus of outrage—ironic given that he had been the first of the new contract brewers, pay-ing the Matt family in Utica, New York, to brew New Amsterdam Amber for him in 1982. He sold 44,000 cases in 1983, and doubled his sales the following year. That gave him enough money to open a brewery of his own in Manhattan's Chelsea district—and dis-avow his own past. When questioned about contract brewing in

1986, Reich replied, "If a contract brewer wants to sell beer he has to lie . . . Basically, he has to perpetrate fraud." That comment came back to haunt him in 1987, when his "real" brewery failed. Reich returned to Utica and contract brewing—returned, it would seem, to perpetrating fraud.

The conflict contained more than a hint of the puritanical and condescending—real brewers wear rubber boots; fake ones wear suits—to say nothing of ignorance of history. Consider Vince Cottone's 1986 *Good Beer Guide,* an introduction to the "new" beers and breweries of the Pacific Northwest, and one of the first published surveys of craft beer. Cottone advised readers that he would focus only on what he called "True Beer," which he defined as "ideal, uncompromised beer . . . hand-made locally in small batches using quality natural ingredients, served on draft fresh and unpasteurized." True beer was pure beer; the brewer added nothing "to cheapen the beer," including such disgusting adjuncts as corn or rice. "It's not a new kind of beer . . . ," he explained. "Before prohibition, it was served in nearly every tavern in town, until corporate mergers and osmosis rationalized it into the bland and boring Industrial Brew."

Cottone was wrong, of course. Before Prohibition, beermakers created rich, hearty lagers brewed with corn and rice. Historical inaccuracy aside, though, there is much to ponder in Cottone's words. By his definition, the beer made at Anchor was not "true" because it was pasteurized and bottled. The stuff from Mendocino was out of the running (bottled), as, of course, was Sam Adams (bottled, pasteurized, and, its worst sin, not "local"). Aside from that, what was "handmade" beer? Did "true" brewers stand over their vats, à la Jacob Best and sons, stirring the wort with huge paddles? And then there's the "ideal, uncompromised" segment of Cottone's equation. Who knew what that meant?

But the most curious aspect of Cottone's ideal is the emphasis on "small batches." How small was small? The new brewers faced the same bottom line as any other entrepreneur: They were in business to make money. In order to stay in business, they had to be large enough to earn a profit so they could grow even larger. But once they achieved a level of success that enabled them to increase production, were they still making "true beer"? Grossman and Camusi, to name one example, aimed at national, not local, distribution, a goal they could achieve only by expanding. In 1988, they built a larger brewery that was more efficient, because more mechanized, than the original shop. Did Sierra Nevada Pale Ale still count as a "handcrafted" beer? Not according to Carol Stoudt, owner of Stoudt Brewing in Pennsylvania. "True micros," she sniffed, "should stay in their own area."

What about Redhook? Paul Shipman and Gordon Bowker also opened a new brewery in 1988. Like Grossman and Camusi, the Seattle entrepreneurs abandoned their cobbled-together start-up gear in favor of new, state-of-the-art equipment that allowed them to double production, from about ten thousand barrels a year to twenty thousand. Shipman boasted that the computer-controlled, automated plant was one of the most "technologically advanced" outfits in the country. A reporter who attended the company's grand opening asked him if the focus on technology meant that Redhook had given up on "handcrafted" beer. Of course not, Shipman replied. "You don't taste the automation. You taste the brewing."

Therein lay the point that Jim Koch—and the Busch family and Frederick Pabst and other great brewers—had understood all along: What mattered most was not a brewery's size or location but the integrity, consistency, and quality of its beer. As it turned out, the contractors had the last laugh. By the early 1990s, contract breweries numbered forty-seven—only half the number of microbreweries (and far fewer than the 165 brewpubs), but enough to indicate that plenty of consumers and brewers alike measured quality by ingredients and process rather than by place or size.

Nor did the controversy affect craft brewing's upward trajectory. By the late 1980s, microbrewing had matured from a screwball idea into a viable industry. Sales were climbing at an average rate of 40 percent a year. National press coverage fueled interest in the phenomenon, which in turn inspired still more breweries and brewpubs. Jim Koch's early success and the money he spent on marketing and touting the virtues of fresh, full-bodied American beer also boosted the industry. Homebrewer Fred Eckhardt, who had launched a career as a brewing journalist, admitted as much, stating the case with his usual bluntness. "We need contract brewers," he wrote. "Without them, the craft brewing industry would still be small time." Koch and other contract brewers, he told readers, had "done more for craft beer and craft brewing than almost anyone else," by running "educational" advertising and by producing high-quality "gateway beers" by which an otherwise uninformed public learned about "the delights of taste in beer" and then went on to sample and enjoy other craft brews.

Craft brewing benefited as well from the influence and vision of Charlie Papazian, the man who had co-founded the American Homebrewers Association. As microbrewers opened their doors, homebrewers reported the news in letters to *Zymurgy*, the AHA newsletter, so that by accident rather than design, the AHA became a clearinghouse of information about the brewing renaissance.

In the spring of 1981, Papazian sponsored a brewing conference, the centerpiece of which was a ninety-minute session titled "The Small Commercial Micro-Brewery in America—Its Revival." Panelists from Boulder Brewing and Cartwright Brewing of Portland, Oregon, showed slides, discussed their journey from home to commercial brewing, and answered questions from an audience that was less interested in the history of the revival than in how to get in on it themselves.

With that conference—the first of many—Papazian provided a home base for the people who were forging a new era in American brewing. But in that same year, Papazian also persuaded Fred Eckhardt and Michael Jackson to join the *Zymurgy* staff as advising editors, and so provided a platform for new brewing's two most important chroniclers.

In 1969, Eckhardt, who lived in Portland, Oregon, had published a short homebrewing pamphlet. "A Treatise on Lager Beer" was less important for its instructional content—even Eckhardt conceded it contained errors—than for its manifesto-like call to arms. American brewers, he charged, had transformed traditional lager into "pasteurized carbonated malt 'pop'" designed for "the female palate." "Even the German beers imported into this country are being made to so-called American taste. Pablum and pap for babies." Thanks to his strong voice and forceful opinions, and his proximity to the microbreweries opening along the Pacific coast, Eckhardt emerged as one of the most important voices for "new" brewing.

So, too, Michael Jackson. The Englishman's 1978 *World Guide to Beer* had introduced Americans to the complexity and range of beer styles, but his columns in *Zymurgy* provided insight into and information about the craft-brewing revolution. Over the next thirty years, both men would broaden their reach, as each published hundreds of articles and columns in magazines and newspapers, Eckhardt offering cogent commentary on new brewing and Jackson providing beer drinkers and journalists alike with a vocabulary for thinking about and analyzing beer.

Papazian followed the 1981 conference with the Great American Beer Festival in May 1982. The first event proved modest, consisting as it did of a handful of craft brewers and about a thousand gallons of various lagers, ales, porters, and stouts. Papazian sandwiched the four-hour fair in between a homebrewing competition and the small brewers' conference, which had grown into a two-

day affair and included panels on packaging, bacteria control, marketing, and legal issues.

The projects required every penny Papazian could lay hands
on and then some, but whatever doubts he had about the wisdom
of his actions vanished in November 1982, when he traveled to
Fort Lauderdale for the annual gathering of the Brewers Association of America. Most of those present came from mainstream
small breweries—West End, Hudepohl, Spoetzl, Stevens Point—
and they'd never heard of Papazian or his venture. Though some
of the old-timers welcomed him, Papazian felt "uncomfortable"
and "out of place." Still, he was nothing if not a genius when it
came to seeing opportunity, and he returned to Boulder convinced that the needs of regional and small beermakers like
Yuengling and Leinenkugel were not the same as those of microbrewers, and that his plan to provide microbrewers with an alternative made more sense than ever.

Papazian's assessment of the BAA was only partially correct.
It was true that the BAA's membership had shrunk in recent
years, along with its budget, but Bill O'Shea, in his late seventies
and in poor health, still provided small commercial brewers with
essential services: lobbying, good relations and constant communication with the USBA and with behemoths like Anheuser-
Busch, and information about tax laws and regulations that
applied to every brewer regardless of size. That explains why the
two most successful microbrewers, Ken Grossman and Fritz Maytag, had already joined the BAA. They regarded themselves as
part of a larger brewing industry, not as homebrewers grown
large. Charlie Papazian didn't agree, at least not in the early
1980s. As far as he was concerned, microbrewing was an "extension of homebrewing" and therefore an extension of the AHA.
Tax issues? Labeling laws? Relax and have a homebrew.

On the other hand, Papazian's naiveté proved to be a powerful
and liberating tool. His lack of knowledge about the complexities

of the larger brewing industry allowed him to shape the infra-
structure for what amounted to a new branch of an established industry. In that regard, he proved a direct descendant of Frederick
Pabst and Adolphus Busch, both of whom entered brewing unencumbered by ideas about how things ought to be done. Papazian
recognized, for example, what Bill O'Shea did not: Microbrewers
faced a unique set of problems, such as locating equipment sized
for a small operation, or persuading maltsters to sell product in
small lots. Had O'Shea understood that (or had the association
replaced O'Shea with someone less rooted in the past), the BAA
might have become "home" for craft brewers.

But O'Shea did not, and so Papazian seized the day. In early
1983, he launched the Institute for Fermentation and Brewing
Studies (later the Association of Brewers). The IFBS sponsored
an annual conference devoted entirely to microbrewing and published *New Brewer,* a magazine for microbrewers—defined as
breweries and brewpubs that produced fifteen thousand barrels a
year or less—that contained articles on everything from marketing, label design, and trademark law to water treatment, hop varieties, and yeast.

Microbrewing now had a home of its own. Papazian's confer-
ences and *New Brewer* provided forums where people who were
passionate about beer could share their energy and ideas, where
novices learned from professionals, and where everyone learned
how to create a brewery in an industry otherwise oriented toward
plants that made five million, rather than five hundred, barrels of
beer.

All of it fueled brewing's newest wing. Nearly two hundred
new breweries opened between May 1993 and October 1994,
and the volume of craft beer produced in the United States
doubled between 1990 and 1994.

Not everyone was prepared for the difficulties they faced, but
the second wave of brewers enjoyed one advantage over the pio-

neers: easier access to funding. Bankers that once laughed at the likes of Ken Grossman and Jim Koch lined up to loan money in the early 1990s. When Gregory Kelly decided to open a micro-brewery in Atlanta in 1994, he started with $150,000 of his own funds, but a group of professional investment managers anted up another $1.2 million. The money allowed Kelly to hire a professional brewmaster and buy brewing equipment imported from England. Nor did Kelly, who chucked an executive post at Guinness to open his own shop, conceal his motives. "I didn't do this to get free beer," he told a reporter. "I'm in a business."

This summarized the attitude of that second wave of new brewers, who were less starry-eyed homebrewers than hard-headed entrepreneurs elbowing their way into a booming industry. Certainly that explains the continued growth of the Association of Brewers' programs and services for craft brewers. By the early 1990s, Papazian had replaced his cadre of volunteers with a professional paid staff and expanded the conference to include a trade show. He moved the annual event from city to city, but wherever it landed, thousands of people showed up to prowl cavernous convention centers filled with industry-related booths and exhibits—malt dealers, sign makers, and purveyors of glassware, hop pellets, and yeast.

THE INVESTORS kept coming—followed closely by Big Beer, which had finally noticed the revolution in its midst. Not, of course, because anyone at Anheuser-Busch, Miller, or Coors regarded the new brewers as a viable threat. In 1982, A-B and Miller together controlled an astonishing 56 percent of the market for beer, 32 percent of which belonged to A-B. But that share, enormous as it was, was also stagnant, growing at single-digit rates if at all. In the last two decades of the century, Americans' consumption of alcohol in any form plunged to historic lows. In 1975, for example, Americans drank 1.1 gallons of alcohol in the form of spirits; in 1985 they consumed 0.90 gallons, and that amount tumbled by another third by the early 1990s. Per capita beer consumption hit its post-repeal peak in 1981 at 23.8 gallons. By century's end, that would fall to fewer than twenty gallons.

The explanation for the drop was twofold. First, the wave of baby boomers who boosted beer sales in the 1960s and 1970s had aged past the "peak" drinking years of young adulthood. To brewers' dismay, they were not being replaced by an equally large cohort of young drinkers. Second, and more important, temperance had reared its head again. A century earlier, reformers had defined drinking at any level as a social evil and a moral issue. But the failure of Prohibition forced Americans to adopt a more subtly calibrated stance on alcohol: Drinking itself was not bad; the problem was lack of moderation.

The medical establishment took over from there. The word "alcoholism" appeared in the psychiatric literature as early as 1915, but in the 1930s and 1940s, medical and mental health professions began defining the inability to moderate consumption as a disease. They adopted the word to label people who could or would not practice restraint. From this new paradigm came Alcoholics Anonymous and a view of immoderate drinking as a medical rather than a moral issue. In 1970, the nation's legislators caught up with this cultural shift when Congress passed the Comprehensive Alcohol Abuse and Alcoholism Prevention, Treatment and Rehabilitation Act, the first major federally funded effort to manage alcohol use since the Eighteenth Amendment.

One result was the National Institute on Alcohol Abuse and Alcoholism (NIAAA), which sponsored studies of drinking as well as programs designed to educate the public about alcohol's dangers and develop treatment for those who abused it. Under its first director, NIAAA programs provided general information about alcohol and spread the gospel of "responsible drinking."

That changed in the late 1970s, when the agency's second director announced his intention to "stabilize per capita consumption" and to treat alcohol as a "dangerous drug."

That message reached receptive ears. In the late 1970s and early 1980s, millions of baby boomers hit their thirties. Waistlines expanded. Wrinkles appeared. Many now had children to protect and care for. Add to that bad news about the environment and deteriorating global politics, and the result was a near manic desire for control, which, in turn, sparked an outburst of moral rectitude and self-righteousness. A consumer analyst observed: "It's not easy to get up at five-thirty every morning to go running. People who do it become very prudish about it, and very judgmental about people who don't." Another observer offered a somewhat more charitable view of the scene. "The sixties generation is no longer engaged in political activity," he explained. "People feel profoundly guilty and are directing that guilt against themselves." Jogging, dieting, denial, and abstinence allowed aging boomers to "feel whole and pure and clean again."

Whatever the motivator, the result was the same: A broad swath of Americans affiliated with an array of organizations launched a full-bore assault on drinking. The coalition included such groups as Mothers Against Drunk Driving (MADD, founded in 1980); Remove Intoxicated Drivers (RID, 1979); Students Against Driving Drunk (SADD, 1981); the National Parent–Teacher Association; and the Seventh-Day Adventist, Methodist, Mormon, and Baptist churches. They were joined by Michael Jacobson of the Center for Science in the Public Interest, who stuck with his original modus operandi—inflammatory rhetoric interspersed with half-truths—in his ongoing campaign against the manufacture, sale, and consumption of alcohol. Together this coalition lobbied for higher taxes on alcohol, warning labels on alcohol containers, and a ban on alcohol advertising.

It is a measure of the times that they got almost everything they went after, only failing to restrict advertising. Congress attached federal highway funds to a stipulation requiring that states raise the drinking age to twenty-one; by the late 1980s, every state had complied. Stadiums and arenas banned seat-side beer sales. Many venues created alcohol-free "family" seating, limited customers to two beers, or stopped selling altogether after the seventh inning or third quarter. Spectators at the 1987 Orange Bowl game between Miami and Oklahoma watched the game sober after Bowl sponsors banned all alcohol at the stadium. "Happy hour," that two- or three-hour period at the end of the workday when many bars offered customers special prices on drinks, came under attack. Some states outlawed the practice and others placed restricted hours on such promotions. Bar owners appeased the zealots by removing happy-hour signs, but retaliated by discounting the tabs of regular customers or by handing out free food.

The press generally played along, printing as fact Michael Jacobson's assertion that advertising caused people to drink excessively and ignoring a more substantive series of studies that indicated that advertising merely sealed brand loyalty by making consumers feel good about the brand they already drank. When his Project SMART (Stop Marketing Alcohol on Radio and Television) failed in its original goal—derailed by alcohol industry lobbyists who bombarded congressional hearings with evidence from the fact-based studies—Jacobson threw children into the mix. Kids, he argued, were being led down the path of ruin by beermakers who designed humorous commercials specifically for child audiences.

The press picked up the story and ran with it, despite the lack of evidence that children favored beer commercials over others or that advertising of any sort caused them to drink. Moreover, study after study showed that the rise in teenage drinking had little to do with alcohol advertising and everything to do with the neo-temperance crusade itself and the social upheaval that rippled through American society in the wake of the economic turmoil of the 1970s. Nothing could have been better designed to promote youthful drinking than the non-stop message, taught as early as grade school, that alcohol was a drug and therefore evil and forbidden. Teenagers being hormonally programmed to do precisely what their elders warn them not to, underage drinking ballooned, and then escalated further after the national drinking age rose to twenty-one, as eighteen-, nineteen-, and twenty-year-olds who had assumed they'd be allowed to drink imbibed anyway, laws be damned. Other studies showed that kids turned to drink to manage the stress of a soaring divorce rate, parents working longer hours at fewer jobs, and overburdened school systems and teachers.

The anti-alcohol campaign forced beermakers to rethink their spring-break and campus promotions, which even the most pro-drink fanatic was forced to admit had spiraled out of control. Consider *Beachin' Times,* a glossy, sixteen-page insert that Miller Brewing distributed on campuses just prior to spring break. Filled with pictures of buxom young women in beach attire, the text tutored male readers on ways to "turn spring break into your own personal trout farm." An article about beach volleyball asked readers to "[n]ame something you can dink, bump, and poke. Hint—it's not a Babe." Anheuser-Busch's contribution to spring break that year—a two-foot-tall inflated beer bottle—seemed positively Victorian by comparison.

Pressed by the threat of restrictive legislation on one side and angry parents on the other, brewers toned down their beachside presence. Representatives offered kids free phone calls home and doughnuts and coffee at rest stops en route to and from spring break destinations, and replaced the inflatable bottles and free T-shirts with banners and buttons that urged partiers to "Think When You Drink" and "Know When to Say When." The popular Anheuser-Busch "party animal" of the mid-1980s, Spuds McKenzie, and the animated frogs of the early 1990s went by the wayside, and A-B and Miller pulled their advertising from MTV.

Alcohol consumption rates plunged. But what might have been a disaster for fledgling craft brewers turned out to be a blessing, because this variation on temperance fostered both self-indulgence and snobbery. Perhaps a jogger decided that ice cream, for example, was bad for her. Having decided to limit her intake to a single dish of the forbidden once a month, she also determined to maximize her pleasure. Why eat the cheap stuff packed with artificial flavors and fillers when she could savor pricier confections made with real milk and eggs?

The same held true for beer. Drinking just one beer? Make it a rich, satisfying, expensive bottle of microbrew. You could enjoy your beer and be both healthy (just one bottle!) and in the know (factory beer is passé; hip people drink microbrews).

As a result, sales of microbrewed lager and ales soared. And that turned out to be a good thing for old-line small local and regional brewers as well. They had thrived in the early 1970s thanks to the mania for "real" and local beers. But as that decade had wound to a close, the tide and times had turned against them. The late 1970s battle between Anheuser-Busch and Miller resulted in a series of price wars that hurt the group of brewers ranked just below the two giants—regionals like Heileman and Stroh, who, damaged by the cheap beer coming from the giants, turned on the still smaller local brewers ranked below them.

The Matt family experienced the brunt of this chain reaction in the early and mid-1980s when Stroh, desperate to grow its market, unleashed a barrage of price promotions in largely rural upstate New York, territory it had previously ignored in favor of more populated urban markets. Sales at F. X. Matt Brewing, as the company was called after 1980, dropped by 200,000 barrels in the space of a few years, a devastating loss for a company barely able to hang on in the best of times. The family pinned its hopes for survival on contract brewing, making beer for Matthew Reich and microbrewers Dock Street, Brooklyn, and Harpoon.

F. X. Matt, the grandson of the brewery's founder, recognized that brewing was undergoing a profound transformation, one that might change his family's fortunes. After consulting with Joseph Owades, the brewing chemist who developed "diet" beer, Matt introduced full-flavored Saranac 1888, a malt-rich lager that recalled the brewery's nineteenth-century heritage. This was a risk for a company that had survived for more than a century on local loyalty: Would upstate New Yorkers, their wallets already battered by a badly depressed local economy, be willing to spend a few more cents on a new beer?

The initial answer was a resounding no. Saranac 1888 limped along until 1989, when F. X., his brother Nick, and other Matts bought the brewery outright from the family trust that had owned it since their grandfather's death in 1956. The new owners expanded the Saranac line and dumped all their sales and advertising resources into it. In 1991, they took a Saranac beer to the Great American Beer Festival. It won the gold medal in its category, American Premium Lagers. The award granted the beer, and the brewery, a new cachet, linking both in the public's mind with the new microbreweries. Over the next few years, company sales doubled as a new generation of northeastern beer drinkers fell in love with Utica—and its baby brother, Saranac—all over again.

So, too, down in Pottsville. Dick Yuengling had left his family's brewery in the 1970s, a victim of the generation gap that caused father and son to spend more time shouting at each other than working together. Dick Junior wanted to modernize and revamp for efficiency. His father, concerned about the impact on his employees and the layoffs that would result, refused. Frustrated by his father's resistance, the younger Yuengling bought a beer distributorship and struck out on his own.

But in the early 1980s, Dick Senior became ill. The son returned to Pottsville and bought the brewery, determined to save it and his family's heritage. He and his brewmaster developed their own hoppy, malt-rich special brew, Yuengling Traditional Amber Lager, and introduced Black & Tan, a mix of porter and lager. But Yuengling recognized that he needed help negotiating the terrain beyond Pottsville and the brewery's traditional market. In 1990, he hired a marketing director who revamped the company's labels with a modern design that emphasized its heritage. Sales jumped upward in double-digit increments and rose 400 percent during the 1990s. Students from nearby colleges trekked to Pottsville to tour the plant and have their picture taken with local hero Dick Yuengling, who was, by the late 1990s, the nation's fifth-largest brewer.

The Leinenkugel family followed a different path to new brewing. In 1982, Jake Leinenkugel left the Marine Corps and returned to Chippewa Falls at the request of his father Bill, who wanted to retire. The younger Leinenkugel dived into a crash course in the ways and means of making and selling beer. Minneapolis and Chicago represented two important markets for the company and it was there that he first noted the new craft beers. He also watched as sales of Leinenkugel Bock, a decidedly old-fashioned brew, soared as much as 30 percent in a year. "Something," Jake realized, "was going on."

The "something" became more clear in 1987, when he met Jim Koch and some of the other craft brewers. Later that year, Jake took his beer to Denver and the Great American Beer Festival. As it happened, 1987 marked the first year of the professional blind judging. Leinenkugel won a gold medal and, Jake being his father's son, he returned home convinced not just of the advertising potential but the possibilities that this new breed of brewers and beer had for his own company.

But he also recognized that in beer, as in life, there were no guarantees. Rural Wisconsin was still rural Wisconsin, and younger drinkers, especially college students, were handing their money over to his new competitors, microbreweries in Milwaukee and Madison. Jake was not sure the company and its minuscule 120,000-barrel output would survive.

That explains the shocking announcement he made in 1988: He had sold the company to Miller Brewing. The news stunned Leinie-heads, who feared the worst, but the deal enabled the Leinenkugels to keep the company's doors open and its workers in paychecks, an important consideration to a family that had provided their neighbors with employment for over a century. The partnership provided Leinenkugel with funds, world class technical assistance and, most important, access to the Miller distribution network. And, to nearly everyone's surprise, Miller executives kept the promise they made not to meddle in Leinenkugel affairs.

PERHAPS THAT WAS because Miller Brewing needed Leinenkugel as much as Leinenkugel needed Miller. Executives at A-B, Miller, and Coors had watched, frustrated, as microbrewing grew in double digits. The question was what to do about it.

People "are bored with mainstream beers," groused the president of Heineken USA. "With a micro, they're not drinking a brand at all, but an idea." And a scary one for marketers who lived and died by brand and image. A Heileman executive complained that the "meddlesome thing" was not the small brewers, but the "consumer's willingness to spend more—lots more—to leave their traditional brands for wholesomeness, variety and novelty."

If that's what customers wanted, that's what Miller Brewing would give them. Miller followed its Leinenkugel acquisition with the purchase of tiny Celis Brewing of Austin, Texas, and

Shipyard Brewing, a micro located in Portland, Maine. The trio made up the core of American Specialty Craft Beer Company, a Miller subset where company employees explored the mysteries of making and marketing "small" beers. "We have people in here helping us train our palates and our noses, working with our sensory development," explained the manager of American Specialty. "We listen to guys tell us how they built their microbrewing businesses, about investment, capital. We talk to entrepreneurs. We are immersing ourselves in this world."

In the mid-1990s, the Big Three struck back with their own "craft" beers, an odd assortment with names like Elk Mountain Amber Ale, Red Wolf, Blue Moon, and Eisbock. Red Dog came from the "Plank Road Brewery," located in the bowels of Miller Brewing on State Street, formerly called Plank Road, in Milwaukee. Coors left its name off its specialty beers—a bock, a wheat, an Oktoberfest, and a Winterfest. "They will not say Coors," announced a Coors official. "We want them to be disassociated from the Coors family. If people see a major brewer's name on a micro, it loses some of the cachet that makes the beer interesting to begin with."

It didn't help. For the most part, the small Big Beers flopped. As one brewing executive marveled, "A big name on a small label carries no weight in the world of micros."

Anheuser-Busch tried another tack in the form of "American Originals." Company researchers scoured the archives and came up with three names and recipes that dated back to the days of Adolphus Busch: Black & Tan; Faust lager; and the "Munich-style" beer that Adolphus had taken to the 1893 Columbian Exposition. History proved worthless to microbrew drinkers, who were not impressed.

Then, in a move that echoed Mr. Potter offering George Bailey a cigar and a cut of the action in *It's a Wonderful Life,* August Busch flew to Seattle, toured Redhook, and dangled an irresistible carrot in front of its owners and board of directors: space on A-B delivery trucks and access to the giant's distribution system. In exchange, A-B acquired 25 percent of the company. The agreement, which the parties announced in June 1994, enabled Redhook to build a new plant outside Seattle and another brewery in New Hampshire.

What felt to some beer fans like treason was simply business. Like hundreds of other small beermakers before and after, the crew at Redhook had struggled with distribution. Unless they could gain access to warehouses and delivery trucks, they could not grow, and the owners of Redhook wanted to grow. Deals like the one with Anheuser-Busch provided the opportunity and allowed A-B to gain a share of craft brewing's shelf space at the grocery store.

That was the sunnier side of Big Beer's efforts to cope with this intruder in its midst. Things got much uglier once Redhook and several other microbrewers, including Koch's Boston Beer Company, issued stock offerings in 1995. The shares roared out of their gate.

Time, Big Brewing decided, to take off the gloves. Less than two months into the new year, Anheuser-Busch added its name to a petition filed with the Bureau of Alcohol, Tobacco and Firearms by the Oregon Craft Brewers Guild. The complaint targeted Oregon Ale and Beer Company, a subsidiary of Jim Koch's Boston Beer Company. Oregon Ale's products were contract beers, the draft coming from a micro in Lake Oswego and the bottles from the Blitz-Weinhard plant in Portland. But Koch marketed the products as Oregon beers rather than Boston Beer Company beers and in doing so, the state's brewers complained, tried to capitalize on the state's reputation as a font of fine beers. The petitioners urged the BATF to require brewers to include their name on all of their beer labels and to ban the use of "fictitious" brewery names. In the end, thirty brewers from around the nation added their names to the plea.

What might have been an industry-only conflict went national when a prime-time television news program aired a report on the squabble. Koch appeared on the segment, and the program's content devolved into an attack on Koch's "factory" beer, which the reporter compared unfavorably to the "traditional" brewing methods employed by Anheuser-Busch. Anheuser-Busch tightened the noose by running ads accusing Koch of "tricking" consumers into believing that his beer was microbrewed.

Other giants entered the fray by offering $200 "tap bounties" to retailers who agreed to dump their microbrews in favor of small beers brewed or distributed by the giants. A-B imposed a policy of "100-percent mind share"—translated into plain English, distributors had to rid their trucks of everything but Anheuser-Busch products. When A-B distributors in California abandoned four of that state's microbrewers, the craft beermakers filed suit. But the damage had been done, as the micros scrambled to find new distributors.

Then came the June 1996 issue of *Consumer Reports,* which confirmed what experienced craft brewers already knew and what Koch had discovered a decade earlier: Many "expensive microbrews and imports were flawed and stale-tasting." No surprise, contract brewers and Sierra Nevada landed at the top of the rankings. Nor was it a surprise that so many expensive craft beers ranked low: As in the late 1930s, there were too many new brewers turning out too many beers with annoyingly cute names—Moose Drool, Whistle Pig Red, Dog's Breath Brown Ale, Big Nose Blond—and forgettable flavors.

In October 1996, Koch announced that company sales were off 5 percent over the previous year. Boston Beer's share price plunged 20 percent, and stocks of the other publicly owned micros dropped, too. "Boston Beer: The Sad Fall of An I.P.O. Open to All," read one newspaper headline.

The turmoil rattled the infant industry. And it was about to get worse. In 1997, Kurt Widmer of Portland, Oregon, sold part of his Widmer Brothers Brewing to Anheuser-Busch in exchange for space on delivery trucks. (A few years later, Widmer, once one of Jim Koch's most severe and vocal critics, began brewing some of his beer under contract at Heileman.) Michael Laybourn and the other founders of Mendocino Brewing also faced facts: Their beer was winning one award after another, but their stock offerings had not raised the money they needed to expand. Without help, they would fall prey to the brewer's Catch-22. In 1997, the Mendocino partners sold a minority share of stock and a majority share of the company's board to United Breweries Group, the largest maker and distributor of beer and spirits in India. Before the year was over, UBG had purchased shares of two more craft breweries.

As it turned out, these were growing pains, not death throes, and they were good for the industry. The encounters with the Big Boys toughened the survivors, who either fashioned new, and better, strategies for growth or reeled in their ambitions and stayed close to home. Customers came back. The number of breweries and brewpubs soared, reaching well over one thousand by century's end. By the late 1990s, Ken Grossman's annual output inched toward a half million barrels and he was outproducing Leinenkugel and F. X. Matt. Jim Koch shot past the million mark.

The late-twentieth-century reinvention of American brewing laid bare the industry's bone structure and revealed a fundamental truth about brewing: Almost alone among commercial enterprises, it is one in which, regardless of the brewery's size, success depends less on number-crunching, share value, and MBA management than on basic entrepreneurship and a personal passion for the product.

Consider the sad story at Schlitz, which, already bleeding from the carnage of the 1970s, did not survive the century. In June 1981, striking brewery workers walked out of the Milwaukee plant. Company officials, most of them accountants rather than men with beer in their veins, announced that they planned to shut the brewery for good in September, even as Pabst and Heileman battled for ownership of the tattered remnants of what had been one of Milwaukee's finest. Schlitz's board of directors approved a sale to Heileman, but the Justice Department nixed the deal as a violation of antitrust laws. In the spring of 1982, Schlitz finally found a home, with Stroh of Detroit.

Stroh was one of the family-owned survivors, having been in business for 149 years under five generations of Strohs. But the family made its bid for grandeur at the wrong moment, demonstrating that brewing heritage and passion alone do not make great breweries. Had they maintained their "small" mystique and cachet, they might have survived. But in an industry hobbled by fragmentation, fickle consumers, and dwindling demand, no one wanted beer from an ordinary Big Brewer wannabe, and it was impossible for Stroh to catch up with giants A-B and Miller. Add the new burden of debt and stagnant demand, and the pressure proved fatal. In 1998, the company's board sold its Tampa plant to Dick Yuengling; a year later they disposed of the rest of the assets, including the cornucopia of brand names Stroh had acquired over the years: Schlitz, Old Milwaukee, Old Style, Schmidt's, Lone Star, and Special Export.

In 2000, the nation's tenth-ranked brewer was Minnesota Brewing Co. of St. Paul, but the company was nearing the end of its short-lived run for glory. Management would file for bankruptcy in 2002, selling its Grain Belt label to August Schell Brewing in nearby New Ulm, Minnesota (the second-oldest family-owned brewery in the country).

The number-nine spot belonged to Ken Grossman, now sole owner of Sierra Nevada Brewing Co. and as passionate about his beer and his future as he had been back in 1978.

At number eight sat the nation's oldest beermaker: D. G. Yuengling & Son. Dick Yuengling, Jr., had devoted the 1990s to making the kinds of careful business decisions that only a hands-on entrepreneur could: He used secondhand equipment when possible and saved on stamps by having his drivers deliver necessary mail to the brewery's wholesalers. But when Yuengling did spend money, he did so dramatically and effectively: In 1998 he announced plans to build a new brewery from the ground up in Pottsville; a year later, he bought Stroh's Tampa plant. In 2001, Yuengling would break the one-million-barrel mark.

Number seven, Latrobe, was an oddity: The Pennsylvania maker of Rolling Rock, which had become the favorite of collegians in the 1980s, was owned by Labatt, which was itself owned by Belgian giant Interbev.

Jim Koch's Boston Beer Company claimed the number-six spot. He still brewed some beer on contract, but in 1996 he'd bought the old Hudepohl-Schoenling brewery in Cincinnati, the town where he'd grown up. Few brewers had been as personally battered by the late-century beer wars as Koch; but few proved more tenacious and passionate than he when it came to making fine beer.

Genesee of Rochester, New York, in the number-five spot, had been around western New York for more than a century, owned and run by the Wehle family since repeal. But in 2000, the Wehle at the top, dying of cancer, decided to sell what had become an ailing company. A group of investors, nearly all of them Rochester locals, bought it, intent on saving some local history and the brewery's five hundred jobs. The owners immediately aligned themselves with the microbrewing end of the industry, hiring a brewmaster with a craft brewing background and launching a new line of full-bodied brews.

At number four was an entity named Pabst, but which had nothing to do with the Pabst Brewing that had once been the world's largest beermaker. Pabst officials, uncertain how to navigate a stagnant market and changing tastes, spent the early 1980s leaning into a whirlwind of mostly hostile takeover bids. In the end, Paul Kalmanovitz, a California investor, won. He acquired Pabst in 1985 and proceeded to strip its management, its advertising, its employees, and its sales. When Kalmanovitz died in early 1987, his successor vowed to save the brewery.

It was too late. In 1996, Phillip Best and Frederick Pabst's proud factory—the acres of soft red brick, the wrought-iron lamps with their ornate "P," the once-bustling shipping yard—fell silent, locked behind an ugly chain-link, barbed-wire-topped fence, its only companions a growing community of weeds, rats, and birds. Captain Pabst's beloved Blue Ribbon brand survived—in name only and as one of an array of beer labels owned by the Kalmanovitz Charitable Foundation, a San Antonio, Texas, holding company. Blue Ribbon became the darling of the bike messenger and retro-chic crowd in the early 2000s—but it was brewed at the Miller plant out on State Street.

In 2000, the Coors family still clung to their number-three spot, but Pete Coors's plans to topple the two leaders had never panned out. Indeed, the brewery's share of the market slipped in the 1990s, perhaps because for the first time in company history, the family turned the wheel over to an outsider, a man who had once run Frito-Lay.

As for the top two, they were the same pair who had held the spots since the late 1970s. But in 2000, Miller produced less than half of A-B's 96 million barrels, and its market share dwindled slightly each year. In 2002, Philip Morris conceded defeat and sold Miller to a South African outfit. Would things have turned out differently if Fred C. Miller had not boarded that plane in December 1955? Perhaps.

And then there was the leader: Anheuser-Busch. At the beginning of the new century, half the beer consumed by Americans sported the Anheuser-Busch eagle, and just one of those brands, Budweiser, accounted for a staggering 18 percent of all the beer sold in the United States—proof that microbreweries notwithstanding, many Americans still favored a light-bodied, effervescent beer of the kind created by Carl Conrad and Adolphus Busch more than a century earlier. In 2002, August Busch IV, the great-great-grandson of Adolphus Busch, took over as president of Anheuser-Busch, the fifth Busch to serve in that post.

That as much as anything else explains why Anheuser-Busch is the world's largest brewery: For more than 150 years, the family has nurtured and built and fought, trusting almost no one but themselves to care as much about the company's name and its beer as they did. The craft brewers, the brewpub owners, the contract brewers, and everyone in between could take a lesson from the Busch family: Stick to the basics, in this case uncompromised quality and consistency. And if anyone needed proof beyond the sales figures, they need only visit the St. Louis brewery. There, in its immaculate grounds, in Adolphus's still-pristine stables, in the perfectly maintained 1893 brewhouse, stands evidence of the family's constant vigilance and its justifiable pride in its history, products, image, and reputation. Evidence, in short, of the entrepreneurial passion—and ambition—that had served the company for a century and a half.

Adolphus would be proud—but then again, he would have expected nothing less.

Epilogue

IN LATE 2005, Sam Calagione, the founder of Dogfish Head Craft Brewery in Delaware, traveled to New York City to participate in an odd but instructive competition: He and a sommelier served their respective specialties during a five-course dinner, a different wine and beer with each course. Calagione brought along Fort, a fruit-based ale concocted from more than a ton of Oregon and Delaware raspberries and with an alcohol content of 18 percent. He also poured Pangea, only 7 percent alcohol but flavored with an ingredient from every continent (including ginger and basmati rice); India Brown Ale (7.2 percent), with its notes of coffee, ginger, and chocolate; Raison d'Extra (18.5 percent), brewed from brown sugar and raisins; and World Wide Stout (18+ percent alcohol), a desert beer that the brewer compared to port. Calagione left behind at the brewery his Chateau Jiahu, a concoction brewed from honey, grapes, hawthorn fruit, and chrysanthemum flowers; his Immort Ale, made from peat-smoked barley, organic juniper, and maple syrup, and aged in oak casks; and his Burton Baton, an oak-aged ale with hints of citrus and vanilla. At the end of the evening, the guests voted on which they preferred with each course—beer or wine. Calagione won three of the five courses (and might have won a fourth had his staff not inadvertently packed the wrong beer for one of the courses).

On the other side of the country, the folks at Russian River Brewing in Santa Rosa, California, age their Temptation in oak wine barrels for a year. Supplication also sits in oak barrels— Pinot Noir casks, to be precise—for a year before the brewmaster declares it ready. Little White Lie, a wheat beer, contains coriander, cumin, and orange peel. None of those sound good? Then try some of the brewery's other offerings: Pliny the Elder, Dr. Zues, or Parking Violation. Deification, Beatification, or Sanctification. Redemption, Perdition, or Damnation. Erudition, Salvation, or Rejection.

And back on the East Coast, Jim Koch, still sitting comfortably in the ranks of brewing's top ten, reigns as current king of what he calls "extreme beers." The 2003 vintage of his Utopias rippled with the flavors of vanilla, oak, and citrus and possessed an alcohol content of 25.6 percent, high enough to land it a place in the Guinness Book of World Records. Too much, you say? Try a bottle of Samuel Adams Millennium, with a (somewhat) lower alcohol content and hints of cinnamon, butterscotch, and pear. Or for something a tad more mundane (relatively), how about a bottle of Koch's seasonal Cranberry Lambic?

Welcome to American brewing in the twenty-first century, where anything goes; where brewmasters are not just pushing the boundaries of beer, but redefining this ancient beverage. Where, in 2005, fifty breweries and brewpubs went under, but forty-nine new ones appeared to take their place. It is this kind of creativity that has defined the industry for decades. Like beer itself, the business of brewing seems a living creature—often buffeted by forces beyond its control, but constantly adapting, changing, shifting shapes and direction in order to survive. How many industries can claim to have been reinvented not by government bodies or huge corporations, but by individuals? How many industries can claim an entry bar so flexible that a guy with welding skills and a few thousand bucks can shake it up and fashion something new?

And therein lies the mystery, the wonder, and the excitement of American brewing and its history: At its core are passionate men and women. In that sense, today's industry—some fifteen hundred breweries and brewpubs, ranging from giant Anheuser-Busch making 100 million barrels a year to individually owned brewpubs dispensing a few thousand barrels a year at bars located fifty feet from the brewvats—has not changed much from its inception in the 1840s, except that there are more fine beers and a greater variety of them than at any time in American history.

At present, craft beers command less than 5 percent of the beer market. That's not much, and it probably explains why the number of breweries and brewpubs has remained flat over the past decade: There are only so many consumer dollars that can be siphoned away from Anheuser-Busch, a behemoth that is determined to grow, not shrink, its own already gargantuan market share.

Per capita consumption of beer has continued its downward slide, and while A-B continues to post gains, the few remaining mainstream brewers are fighting a losing battle to stay in the game. Most analysts think Pabst Brewing, to name one battered example, is terminally ill, a claim that's easy to believe given how hard it is to find Pabst Blue Ribbon in an ordinary grocery store.

To a certain extent, Big Beer has only itself to blame for its sagging fortune: It keeps playing the same old song, over and over and over. Remember the Anheuser-Busch ads during the 2005 Super Bowl? A snowy scene, an old-fashioned sleigh, two lovers snuggling—and the Clydesdales passing gas. Or the company's anti-Miller ads in which A-B touted its beers as "American," in contrast to foreign-owned Miller? (When Coors merged with Canadian Molson, A-B immediately did the same to the Colorado brewery.) Miller retaliated with, among other things, TV commercials that featured taste tests in which bar patrons are shocked—shocked!—to discover they've chosen Miller Lite over Bud Light, or Miller Genuine Draft over Budweiser. Set advertising like that next to the beers being made by Koch and Calagione, and the ads seem not just stodgy, but hopelessly out of synch with today's consumers.

Still, there's no denying that American beer drinkers today live in a barley-based paradise. How long will this current golden age last? Impossible to say. Already there are corporate-owned chain brewpubs that serve mediocre beers. But that was true back in the nineteenth century as well, when more than one brewer served up indifferent beer simply because he could find an equally indifferent saloon to carry it. More troubling to beermakers of all stripes are the wines and spirits gnawing at their share of the alcoholic drink market.

On the other hand, craft brewers continue to do what they've done, and done well, for a quarter of a century—treat beer as a sophisticated, sensual, flavorful delight—and so their small market grows each year, even as beer consumption slides. Perhaps that explains a move on the part of Anheuser-Busch in early 2006, when the company suggested that brewers join forces to improve beer's image. The idea was to borrow a tactic employed in recent years by producers of milk, eggs, and pork: Mount an *industry*-based campaign that would tout the virtues of beer, regardless of brand. In this case, the ads would focus on the art and craft of brewing and suggest ways to pair beer with food. As an Anheuser-Busch spokesman put it, "Craft beers have pushed hard on selling the romance of the product, but we [mainstream brewers] have not," choosing instead to dump money into TV spots centered on babes, sports, or "brown bottles in icy water." It's an idea long overdue, but only time will tell if any of A-B's competitors will join in the project (as of this writing, May 2006, none had).

Of one thing I am certain: the heart of brewing will always be its people. In the course of writing this book, I met some of the most intelligent, passionate, and energetic people that I've ever had the pleasure to know. They gravitate toward brewing, I think, in part because beer is itself an exciting, lively creature capable of almost infinite complexity and nuance. So I am optimistic: American beer will continue to attract the brightest and the best, and those people will, in turn, continue to reinvent the beer and the industry. Indeed, perhaps American beer's best days are yet to come.

Prosit!

ACKNOWLEDGMENTS

Iᴛ's ʙᴇᴄᴏᴍᴇ fashionable of late for some to scoff at lengthy acknowledgments. To those ignorant souls, I return the scoff:
Anyone who so indulges either has (a) never written a book,
or (b) written only fiction concocted entirely of imagination. Because if they'd slogged through a project like this one, they'd know
just how much the writer of nonfiction depends on the input, assistance, and kindness of other human beings.

One of the first people I met when I began working on this
book was John C. Eastberg, the director of development at the
Captain Frederick Pabst Mansion in Milwaukee. John, a man of
great warmth and charm, is also the soul of generosity; he never
hesitated to share whatever Pabst-related goodies he found. I am
certain that he and the Captain would have been great friends.

I thank the people of Milwaukee for having the good taste and
wisdom to spend money on their magnificent main library, where
I conducted much of my initial research. I also thank the men and
women, who, as employees of the Works Progress Administration
during the 1930s, compiled a superb index of the *Milwaukee Sentinel*; the American taxpayers for funding the work; and President
Franklin Roosevelt and his staff for conceiving of such projects in
the first place. (Yes, okay, maybe it's possible to get carried away
with acknowledgments, but trust me: The thanks in this case are
well deserved.)

The New York Times Company deserves some sort of congressional or presidential medal for its index, which is an indispensable tool for historians studying the United States. If it happened or mattered, the *Times* covered it and the indexers included it, and some sections of this book could not have been written without that newspaper's index. I am sincerely grateful, and I wish everyone at the *Times* many years of good health, good writing, and happy indexing.

This is the third book I've written at the Parks Library at Iowa State University. It's still the finest library I've had the pleasure to work in. The microfilm equipment and the staff are second to none (and there are a good many libraries, whose names I shall not mention, that could take a tip or two from the staff at Parks).

At the library, the people in the Interlibrary Loan Department once again provided me with superb service. I am grateful for their efforts on my behalf. I especially thank Kathy Thorson, who ran interference on more than one book-request-gone-haywire.

I thank the staffs at the Central Library of the Milwaukee Public Library system, the Wisconsin Historical Society, the Missouri State Archives, the Missouri Historical Society, the National Archives—Great Lakes Region (Chicago), and Fred Romanski and Shannon Hickey of the National Archives at College Park, Maryland.

I conducted a large chunk of research at the Anheuser-Busch Corporate Library. I thank the Busch family for allowing me access (although I wish they had let me into the archives) and for having the good sense to maintain this great collection. At the library, Ann Lauenstein and Mary Butler provided efficient assistance. I am especially grateful to Ann for the time and care she took to supply me with materials and one of the photographs used in the book.

Richard Hamm at SUNY-Albany unraveled a perplexing legal question about Prohibition. Tom Tate of anheuser-buschbottles.com and Robert Klein both heeded my cry for help and supplied me with images of early Budweiser labels. Christopher Eck of the Broward County Historical Commission supplied me with a copy of his thesis. Drew Beechum and the crew from Maltose Falcons answered questions and offered much-needed information. Lew Bryson kindly provided a copy of his interview with Fritz Maytag. Renee De Luca provided contact information for Jack McAuliffe.

John Gurda and Tim John provided me with manuscript copies of their works-in-progress and I thank them for their generosity. Tim also took time from his own work to answer questions about his family, the Millers of Milwaukee.

Early on in this project, Philip Van Munching gave me a copy of his book and words of encouragement. Jen Robinson devoted most of a precious week's vacation to reading and critiquing the manuscript. As soon as she heard about the project, Julie Johnson Bradford of *All About Beer* magazine stuck out a hand (electronically speaking), said howdy-do, and offered to help. I never managed to persuade Brad Davis at WanderWear that the Franklin beer quotation was bogus, but I thank him anyway for a truly hilarious twenty-minute phone conversation.

I thank Matt Braun, formerly of Jacob Leinenkugel Brewing Company; Michelle Sullivan of Boston Beer Company; and Laura Harter at Sierra Nevada Brewing Co. for their help in setting up interviews. Michelle and Laura also tracked down photographs, as did Kelli Gomez of the Brewers Association and Fritz Maytag at Anchor Brewing. Dave Gauspohl, breweriana collector extraordinaire, provided images of beer labels. Mary Wallace of the Walter Reuther Library at Wayne State University also assisted with photographs. I thank Michael E. Miller for giving me permission to use the image of Jack McAuliffe, and Bill Ristow of the *Seattle Times* for helping me to find Mike.

A sincere thanks and a big smooch to the generous, dishy, and talented Gilbert King, who spent a morning tromping around

Manhattan with me, taking publicity photos, and a wonderful afternoon eating and drinking at Gramercy Tavern.

Mike Cormican, owner of the Dublin House in Manhattan, kindly allowed me to use his lovely bar as a setting for some of those photographs. The name may say "Irish," but the spirit of this establishment on West Seventy-Ninth Street, open since 1921 and the oldest bar on the city's Upper West Side, is very much American. It's a place I frequented back in my youth during the time I lived in the city, and it's still dear to my heart. I am grateful to Mike and to Catherine Nicholson (as beautiful as she is kind) for their help. (And I urge one and all to visit this marvelous tavern. Look for the neon harp hanging above the door.)

One of the nearly sublime pleasures of writing this book was the opportunity to explore and write the history of living people. Beer folk, I discovered, are smart, funny, lively, and fully engaged with the world around them. I enjoyed every minute of the many I expended in interviewing them. I am grateful to all those who took time out to help make this a better book: Patrick Baker, Don Barkley, Larry Bell, Scott Birdwell, Daniel Bradford, Byron Burch, Fred Eckhardt, Charles Finkel, Ken Grossman, Jim Koch, Michael Laybourn, Mr. Bill Leinenkugel, Jake Leinenkugel, Michael Lewis, Nick Matt, Charlie Matzen, Fritz Maytag, Jack McAuliffe, Larry McCavitt, Bill Owens, Charlie Papazian, Nancy Vineyard, and Dick Yuengling.

I must give extra thanks to Jim Koch, Charlie Papazian, and Fritz Maytag. Jim read part of the manuscript and then took the time (when he could have been sitting on the beach!) to phone me and provide a cogent and thoughtful critique. Charlie Papazian answered what surely felt like five million questions and did so with good humor. He made sure his staff provided the photographs that I needed, and has proved unfailingly generous in ensuring that people both in and out of the industry know about the book. Fritz Maytag, arguably one of the busiest people on the planet, made time for me and the book. He invited me to dinner (and he no doubt agrees it was one of the weirdest meals ever), found the time for a long interview, tracked down photographs, and offered up the brewery for a book signing event.

None of the interviews would have happened without the extraordinary generosity of Daniel Bradford. From the first moment he learned of this project, he threw himself into it with passion and enthusiasm that rivaled my own. He introduced me to brewers; leaned on them when they ignored my emails, phone calls, and letters; answered enough questions to last a lifetime, and did all of this with humor, wit, and intelligence. In the process we became friends—and for that I am even more thankful. Daniel, you may not be able to see it, but this paragraph is engraved, embossed, and framed in gold leaf.

I likely would not have written this book or any others had it not been for Phil Metzidakis, who prodded me to envision a life centered on writing and ideas. My agent, Anna Ghosh, sold the proposal from which this book came. She has more character and dignity in her little finger than most humans can even imagine having during a lifetime. My armor gleams brighter for having her by my side.

I am incredibly lucky that she sold it to Harcourt, where everyone I met greeted me with respect and enthusiasm. I thank Patty A. Berg, Mike Harrigan, Jennifer Gilmore, and Paul Von Drasek for taking the time to sit down with me and for marshalling their troops to support this project. My publicist Jodie Hockensmith came to her task with genuine excitement for my work. David Hough shepherded the manuscript through production with kind words and care. I thank publisher André Bernard for taking on this book and for having the good sense to hire such terrific people.

Janine Kozanda appointed herself as my personal cheering squad. Her determination and dedication to her own work inspire me daily; her friendship brings me great joy.

The Trollops provided the kind of sustenance and support that words cannot describe. Without them, I long since would have descended into the slough of despair: Karen Abbott, Maggie Dana, Elizabeth Graham, Sara Gruen, Colleen Holt, Carrie Kabak, Jill Morrow, Yvonne Oots, Marina Richards, Kristina Ringstrom, and Danielle Schaaf.

Karen Abbott read and commented on key portions of the manuscript, cheered me on, made me laugh, and deepened my understanding of the word "friend." I thank her, the lovely Chuck, and, of course, Poe and Dex.

Maggie Dana was always there with a big shoulder, lots of Kleenex, and an ocean of love and understanding.

Sara Gruen is a friend tried and true—always ready to lend support and encouragement and, more importantly, never too busy with her own writing to join me in a grouse-fest, of which there were many. Now if only I can figure out how to stop losing bets to her.

I thank Carrie Kabak and the inimitable Mark Kabak for the fabulous food, warm hearts, and loving support.

My family is small but their love is large: my mother, Carmen Ogle; my step-daughters Alys Robinson and Jen Robinson; and my son-in-law, Trevor Barnes, all encouraged and supported this venture.

If this book has any merit, it is thanks to my editor at Harcourt, Andrea Schulz, a woman of tenacity, generosity, patience, and immense talent. She found a story amid the clutter of a disjointed proposal and taught me how to make a book. I am grateful for that—and honored to call her "friend."

Finally, the most important thanks of all: to my husband, Bill Robinson. I am humbled by his loyalty and friendship, his devotion and love.

ENDNOTES

CHAPTER ONE
German Beer, American Dreams

PAGE

1–2 "I [am] familiar": Quoted in Thomas C. Cochran, *The Pabst Brewing Company: The History of an American Business* (New York: New York University Press, 1948), 20.

2 "music of riveting": Quoted in ibid., 20.

3 "love for dramatic speech": Ibid., 19.

3 "was filled with great joy": Quoted in ibid., 21.

8 "[O]ne cannot describe": Nicholas Frest to Marhoffer, Chicago, August 30, 1841; Letter 70, Box 1; Germans in the United States Collection, Archives, State Historical Society of Wisconsin.

9 "We sing": Hermes to his brother, Milwaukee, January 1846; Letter 325, Box 2; Germans in the United States Collection, Archives, State Historical Society of Wisconsin.

9 "A fellow": Quoted in Earl S. Pomeroy, ed., "Wisconsin in 1847: Notes of John Q. Roods," *Wisconsin Magazine of History* 33 (1949): 217.

10 "The public houses and streets": Quoted in John Gurda, *The Making of Milwaukee* (Milwaukee, WI: Milwaukee County Historical Society, 1999), 68.

11 "One hundred persons": Quoted in Bayrd Still, *Milwaukee: The History of a City* (Madison: State Historical Society of Wisconsin, 1965), 73.

13 "Best & Company, Beer Brewery": Quoted in Cochran, *Pabst Brewing Company*, 33.

14 "then and there with divers": Quoted in Harry H. Anderson, "The Women Who Helped Make Milwaukee Breweries Famous," *Milwaukee History* 4 (1981): 68.

18 "the most delicious lager": Memoir of C. T. Wettstein; quoted in Albert Schnabel, "History of Milwaukee Breweries," History of Brewing in Milwaukee Folder, Milwaukee County Historical Society.

18 "Something must be done": "Lager Bier," *Milwaukee Sentinel,* September 12, 1854, p. 2.

19 "I could never have imagined": Quoted in Cochran, *Pabst Brewing Company,* 25.

19 "In Germany": Quoted in ibid., 24.

19 "[N]obody has any idea": Fredrika Bremer, *The Homes of the New World; Impressions of America,* trans. Mary Howitt (1853; reprint New York: Johnson Reprint Corp., 1968), 616.

19 "like an animal": Quoted in Frederic Trautmann, "Missouri Through a German's Eyes: Franz von Löher on St. Louis and Hermann," *Missouri Historical Review* 77 (July 1983): 375.

20 "neither bench nor chair": Quoted in Kathleen Neils Conzen, *Immigrant Milwaukee 1836–1860: Accommodation and Community in a Frontier City* (Cambridge, MA: Harvard University Press, 1976), 157.

20 "bubbles as fresh and clear": Quoted in Cochran, *Pabst Brewing Company,* 34.

22 "a good creature of God": Quoted in Ian R. Tyrrell, *Sobering Up: From Temperance to Prohibition in Antebellum America, 1800–1860* (Westport, CT: Greenwood Press, 1979), 16.

23 "I am sure": Quoted in Allan M. Winkler, "Drinking on the American Frontier," *Quarterly Journal of Studies on Alcohol* 29 (June 1968): 419.

23 "[I]f I did not drink": Quoted in ibid., 421.

25 "Intemperance": Quoted in Thomas R. Pegram, *Battling Demon Rum: The Struggle for a Dry America, 1800–1933* (Chicago: Ivan R. Dee, 1998), 18.

25 "gangerous excrescence": Quoted in W. J. Rorabaugh, *The Alcoholic Republic: An American Tradition* (New York: Oxford University Press, 1979), 198.

25 "Capital,—Enterprise": Quoted in Tyrrell, *Sobering Up,* 130.

26 "liquor power": Quoted in Jed Dannenbaum, *Drink and Disorder: Temperance Reform in Cincinnati from the Washingtonian Revival to the WCTU* (Urbana: University of Illinois Press, 1984), 84.

26 "they [would] earn": Quoted in Tyrrell, *Sobering Up,* 274.

26 "pestilent": Quoted in Thomas P. Baldwin, "The Public Image of Germans in Louisville and in Jefferson County, Kentucky, 1840–72," *Yearbook of German-American Studies* 29 (1994): 86.

29 "[N]early all the Germans": *Milwaukee Sentinel,* August 11, 1854, p. 2.

29 "veto pen": "A Barleycorn Edict," *Milwaukee Sentinel,* March 30, 1855, p. 2.

30 "And yet": "Beer Business at St. Louis," *Milwaukee Sentinel,* September 25, 1854, p. 2.

31 "liver-eating gin": Quoted in David A. Gerber, "'The Germans Take Care of Our Celebrations': Middle-class Americans Appropriate German Ethnic Culture in Buffalo in the 1850s," in *Hard at Play: Leisure in America, 1840–1940,* ed. Kathryn Grover (Amherst: University of Massachusetts Press for the Strong Museum, 1992), 53.

31 "if it takes a pail-full": "Lager Bier Is Decided to be Not Intoxicating," *New York Times,* February 6, 1858, p. 8.

32 "he was in the habit": "Is Lager Bier an Intoxicating Beverage?," *New York Herald,* May 21, 1858, p. 2.

32 "Good lager beer": "Lager Beer," *Harper's Weekly* 3 (July 9, 1859): 434.

32 "There is no denying": "Beer Drinking," *Milwaukee Sentinel,* March 3, 1860, p. 2.

32 "a good deal too fashionable": "Total Abstinence," *New York Times,* October 15, 1856, p. 3.

33 "in the habit of drinking": "Lager Bier—Change in the Beverages of the City," *New York Times,* September 17, 1855, p. 4.

33 "A German festival": Quoted in Gerber, "'The Germans Take Care,'" 52.

33 "forms refreshment": Charles Cist, *Sketches and Statistics of Cincinnati in 1859* (Cincinnati, OH: n.p., 1859), 246.

33 "Lager has gone ahead": Samuel Mordecai, *Richmond in By-Gone Days* (1860; reprint Richmond: The Dietz Press, 1946), 246.

33 "A dozen years ago": D. W. Mitchell, *Ten Years in the United States: Being an Englishman's Views of Men and Things in the North and South* (London: Smith, Elder and Co., 1862), 86, 87.

38 "'set 'em up'": "Milwaukee's Ancient Saloon," *Milwaukee Sentinel,* August 13, 1890, p. 1.

39 "apostles of Temperance": "The Carnival in Milwaukee," *Milwaukee Sentinel,* February 25, 1857, p. 3.

CHAPTER TWO
"I Must Have Nothing But the Very Best"

PAGE

40 "inundated with breweries": "Local Matters—Beer," *St. Louis Republican,* June 21, 1857, p. 3.

43 "I see nothing but ruin": James W. Goodrich, ed., "The Civil War Letters of Bethiah Pyatt McKown, Part I," *Missouri Historical Review* 47, no. 2 (January 1973): 237.

43 "I never saw a city": Peter Josyph, ed., *The Civil War Letters of John Vance Lauderdale, M. D.* (East Lansing: Michigan State University Press, 1993), 85.

44 "regulates the bowels": "Sanitary Commission. No. 17. Report of a Preliminary Survey of the Camps of a Portion of the Volunteer Forces Near Washington," *Documents of the U.S. Sanitary Commission,* vol. 1 (New York: n.p., 1866), 12, 23.

46 "I spent my early life": "Spends Youth on Rafts; Breaks Jam Years Later," *St. Louis Post-Dispatch,* October 12, 1913, p. 3:4.

46 "assertiveness and good-natured": "Body of Adolphus Busch Will Lie in State in St. Louis," *St. Louis Post-Dispatch,* October 12, 1913, p. 3:3.

47 "He wills and does": "Adolphus Busch, Esq., St. Louis," *Western Brewer* 7 (1882): 1575.

47 "I love my work": Adolphus Busch to Charles Nagel, December 8, 1909; Charles Nagel Papers, Box 2/Folder 25; Manuscripts and Archives, Yale University. Hereafter Nagel Papers.

47 "I an an eternal optimist": Adolphus Busch to Charles Nagel, February 1, 1912; Nagel Papers, Box 7/Folder 98.

47 "the ultimate good of man": Charles Nagel, "Adolphus Busch: A Great Life Understood," *Western Brewer* 41 (1913): 231.

47 "more ambitious and industrious": "'Work Double Time You Are Paid for,' Busch's Advice to Young Men," *St. Louis Post-Dispatch,* October 11, 1913, p. 2. This interview with Busch first appeared in the

Post-Dispatch in 1911 and then in Walter B. Stevens, *Eleven Roads to Success—Charted by St. Louisans Who Have Traveled Them* (St. Louis, MO: n.p., 1914).

48 "delightful companion": "August Uihlein Dies in Germany," *Milwaukee Sentinel,* October 12, 1911, p. 4.

49 "deep seated . . . modesty": Ibid., p. 4.

50 "open hearted, congenial man": "Death Spreads Sorrow in City," *Milwaukee Sentinel,* January 2, 1904, p. 1.

50 "a hale fellow": "Capt. Pabst Was Always Liberal," *Milwaukee Sentinel,* January 2, 1904, p. 4.

50 "one of nature's noblemen": "Death Spreads Sorrow in City," p. 3.

50 "remarkable genius": "Death of Frederick Pabst," *Western Brewer* 19 (January 1904): 16.

53 "tremendous iron heart": Quoted in David E. Nye, *American Technological Sublime* (Cambridge, MA: The MIT Press, 1994), 121.

54 "athlete of steel and iron": Quoted in Ibid., 121.

57 "Dear father": Frederick Pabst to My dear Parents-in-Law & Heinrich, July 16, 1867; Pabst Family Archives, Captain Frederick Pabst Mansion; Milwaukee, Wisconsin.

61 "Schlitz has loomed": *Milwaukee Sentinel,* May 9, 1874, p. 8.

65 "humiliating nature": Charles Best to Frederick Pabst, February 19, 1884; Charles Best, Jr. Papers, 1874–1917, Folder 2; Archives, State Historical Society of Wisconsin. Hereafter cited as Best Papers.

65 "an extraordinary interest": Charles Best to Frederick Pabst, May 30, 1884; Best Papers, Folder 2.

65 "the dark side": Frederick Pabst to Charles Best, March 2, 1891; Best Papers, Folder 4.

66 "Don't worry, Charles": Frederick Pabst to Charles Best, August 12, 1890; Best Papers, Folder 4.

66 "My dear Sir!": Frederick Pabst to Charles Best, February 19, 1884; Best Papers, Folder 2.

66 "What I desire to say": Charles Best to Frederick Pabst, May 30, 1884; Best Papers, Folder 2.

66 "investing and accumulating": Ibid.

67 "We have a large overgrown": Ibid.

69 "knew more about the details": "Knew Every Minor Detail," *Milwaukee Sentinel,* January 2, 1904, p. 4.

69 "He knew the different": "Employes [sic] Pay Their Tributes," *Milwaukee Sentinel,* January 2, 1904, p. 1.

69 "practical brewer": *Charles Conrad v Joseph Uhrig Brewing Company*; testimony of Adolphus Busch; St. Louis Court of Appeals, Case No. 1377; Missouri State Archives. Hereafter cited as *Conrad v Uhrig.*

69 "I am the maltster": *Anheuser-Busch Brewing Ass'n v Fred Miller Brewing Co.,* Deposition of Adolphus Busch, April 26, 1894; Chancery Case Files, 1862–1911, Chancery Case F190; United States Circuit Court, Eastern District, Wisconsin; National Archives and Record Administration, Great Lakes Region (Chicago). Hereafter cited as *Anheuser-Busch v. Miller.*

70 "mouldy": Quoted in William J. Vollmar, "Hops—Brewer's Gold," in *An Oral History of Anheuser-Busch,* Myron Holtzman as told by William J. Vollmar; typescript at Anheuser-Busch Corporate Library, III: 4, 5.

72 "nourishing qualities": J. E. Siebel, "The Use of Unmalted Grain," *Western Brewer* 3 (October 1878): 671.

75 "highly esteemed": *Anheuser-Busch v Miller,* Final Record Books in Chancery, 1862–1911, vol. Q, p. 619.

76 "very pale, fine beer": *Conrad v Uhrig,* testimony of Adolphus Busch.

76 "exquisite aroma": *Anheuser-Busch v Miller,* Deposition of Adolphus Busch, May 6, 1897.

77 "we take the malt": *Conrad v Uhrig,* testimony of Adolphus Busch.

77 "a peculiar, fine flavor": *Anheuser-Busch v Miller,* Deposition of Adolphus Busch, May 6, 1897.

77 "is . . . very fine": *Conrad v Uhrig,* testimony of Charles Conrad.

78 "Can't you give us": Cochran, *Pabst Brewing Company,* 116.

78 "There is no doubt": Ibid., 117.

79 "Now Charley": Frederick Pabst to Charles W. Henning, March 31, 1882; Pabst Family Archives, Captain Frederick Pabst Mansion, Milwaukee, Wisconsin.

80 "I never found a business": *Conrad v Uhrig,* testimony of Herman Kramer.

81 "to put up a similar label": Ibid., testimony of George King.

82 "We stopped": Ibid., testimony of Charles Conrad.

82 "indignantly": Ibid., testimony of Otto Lademan.

82 "would have to stand": Ibid., testimony of Charles Conrad.

82 "go ahead": Ibid., testimony of Otto Lademan.

82 "pirating": Ibid., Petition.

82 "according to the Budweiser process": Ibid., testimony of Charles Conrad.

83 "I don't know anything about": Ibid., testimony of Lawrence Lampel.

83 "I know the process": Ibid., testimony of Otto Lademan.

84 "immense sensation": "American Beer the Best," *New York Times,* September 7, 1878, p. 5.

84–85 "We use bi-carbonate": "Answers to Correspondents," *Western Brewer* 6 (June 15, 1881): 703.

85 "'sour' and 'bitter'": "The Million's Beverage," *New York Times,* May 20, 1877, p. 10.

85 "tried the experiment": Ibid.

85 "so accustomed": "The Coloring of Beer by Yeast," *Western Brewer* 4 (1879): 43.

CHAPTER THREE
"Masters of the Situation"

PAGE

87 "all the leading brewers": "The Schlitz Park," *Milwaukee Sentinel,* May 24, 1880, p. 8.

87 "best citizens": Ibid.

90 "nausea and exhaustion": Dorothy Richardson, "The Long Day: The Story of a New York Working Girl," in *Women at Work,* ed. William L. O'Neill (Chicago: Quadrangle Books, 1972), 257.

91 "Six beers": Ibid., 258, 259.

92 "wailing and gnashing": "The Impending Calamity," *Milwaukee Sentinel,* February 14, 1874, p. 8.

92 "Papa Best": "The Tapsters," *Milwaukee Sentinel,* February 26, 1874, p. 8.

92 "business worth $23,000": "Beerschaum," *Milwaukee Sentinel,* February 23, 1874, p. 1.

93 "[i]t strikes me": Frederick Pabst to Charles W. Henning, March 31, 1882; Pabst Family Archives, Captain Frederick Pabst Mansion, Milwaukee, Wisconsin.

93 "was away from home": Erwin Uihlein quoted in Robert W. Wells, "The Uihleins of Milwaukee," *Milwaukee Journal, Insight* Sunday supplement, April 23, 1972, p. 19.

93 "In this manner": Edward G. Uihlein, "Memoir," trans. Rosina L. Lippi and Jill D. Carlisle; Edward G. Uihlein Reminiscences, Chicago Historical Society.

94 "Presto!": "Abolish Brewery 'Agents,'" *Western Brewer* 5 (January 1880): 58.

94 "I laughed at him": Quoted in Thomas Cochran, *The Pabst Brewing Company: The History of an American Business* (New York: New York University Press, 1948), 143.

95 "[Y]ou will notice": Charles Nagel to Adolphus Busch, February 13, 1894; Charles Nagel Papers, microfilm set; Manuscripts and Archives, Yale University. Hereafter cited as Nagel Papers.

96 "[Brewers] were so anxious": Quoted in Ronald Jan Plavchan, "A History of Anheuser-Busch, 1852–1933," (Ph.D. dissertation, Saint Louis University, 1969), 123.

97 "Mr. Blatz": "Mr. Blatz's 'Clubhouse' Again," *Milwaukee Sentinel,* June 1, 1884, p. 8.

99 "not as good": Quoted in Cochran, *Pabst Brewing Company,* p. 167.

99 "[S]ecure such men": Frederick Pabst to Charles C. Henning, June 1, 1882; Pabst Family Archives, Captain Frederick Pabst Mansion, Milwaukee, Wisconsin.

100 "a good warm overcoat": July 1880, Pabst Brewing Company Ledger 1880–1890, MSS 0780; Milwaukee County Historical Society.

100 "Danzinger uses money": Quoted in Cochran, *Pabst Brewing Company,* 166.

100 "Concerning a suitable agent": Quoted in Ibid., 167–68.

102 "[K]eep on the lookout": Fred Pabst, Jr., to Branch Managers, April 17, 1903; Pabst Brewing Company, Box 2, Clippings, Milwaukee County Historical Society.

103 "control the price": Quoted in Peter Hernon and Terry Ganey, *Under the Influence: The Unauthorized Story of the Anheuser-Busch Dynasty* (New York: Simon & Schuster, 1991), 41.

103 "The men we have": Quoted in Cochran, *Pabst Brewing Company,* 151.

104 "behind": Quoted in ibid.

104 "Now a perfect understanding": Quoted in ibid.

105 "wordy altercation": "War Among Brewers," *Chicago Daily Tribune,* October 25, 1893, p. 1.

106 "very much annoyed": "Capt. Pabst Indignant," *Milwaukee Sentinel,* January 14, 1890, p. 3.

106 "There is no Piece": Frederick Pabst to Charles Best, May 2, 1891; Charles Best, Jr., Papers, 1874–1917, Folder 5, Archives, State Historical Society of Wisconsin. Hereafter cited as Best Papers.

107 "enough to make": "Capt. Fred Pabst Dies at His Home," *Milwaukee Sentinel,* January 2, 1904, p. 3.

107 "I'm very glad": Frederick Pabst to Charles Best, August 12, 1890; Best Papers, Folder 4.

108 "I am very often greeted": *Anheuser-Busch Brewing Association v Fred Miller Brewing Company,* Deposition of Adolphus Busch, April 26, 1894; United States Circuit Court, Eastern District Wisconsin; National Archives and Records Administration, Great Lakes Region (Chicago). Hereafter cited as *Anheuser-Busch v Miller.*

110 "exceptionally expensive": *Anheuser-Busch v Miller,* Final Record Books in Chancery, 1862–1911, vol. Q, p. 619.

110 "ordinary": Ibid., 622.

110 "deepest, shrewdest": Quoted in John Gurda, *Miller Time: A History of Miller Brewing Company 1855–2005* ([Milwaukee, WI]: Miller Brewing Company, 2005), 56.

110 "the best Bohemian barley": *Anheuser-Busch v. Miller,* Deposition of Ernst J. Miller, May 31, 1894. All remaining testimony quotations from Miller deposition.

112 "Miller Bros.": Charles Nagel to Rowland Cox, November 11, 1896; Nagel Papers, microfilm set.

112 "As to the question": Charles Nagel to Rowland Cox, January 16, 1897; Nagel Papers, microfilm set.

113 "We have done": Frederick Pabst to Charles Best, May 2, 1891; Best Papers, Folder 5.

113 "We will not quite reach": Frederick Pabst to Charles Best, December 5, 1891; Best Papers, Folder 6.

117 "I often think": Quoted in John C. Eastberg, "The Paramour and the Press: Society, Scandal and the Schandeins" (Master's essay, Marquette University, 2000), 8.

118 "Now my dear Boy": Frederick Pabst to Gustav Pabst, December

24, 1888; Pabst Family Archives, Captain Frederick Pabst Mansion, Milwaukee, Wisconsin.

118 "I made up my mind": Frederick Pabst to Charles Best, August 12, 1890; Best Papers, Folder 4.

119 "Everything is lovely": Frederick Pabst to Charles Best, March 2, 1891; Best Papers, Folder 4.

119 "Gustav is out": Frederick Pabst to Charles Best, December 5, 1891; Best Papers, Folder 6.

120 "Your father": Charles Nagel to Peter Busch, July 11, 1898; Nagel Papers, microfilm set.

121 "I must repeat": Quoted in Carlota Busch Giersch, *Gussie* (Los Angeles: Petersen Publishing, 1985), 24, 25.

121 "Be moderate": Quoted in Ibid., 26.

122 "It is grand out there": Frederick Pabst to Charles Best, May 2, 1891; Best Papers, Folder 5.

122 "the most aristocratic": Quoted in Giersch, *Gussie,* 30, 31.

123 "Come in": Alice Busch Tilton, *Remembering* (privately printed, 1941), 62.

125 "It is a working model": "The World's Fair," *Western Brewer* 18 (July 1893): 1540.

125 "the standard bearer": Ibid., 1284.

125 "correct to the minutest detail": Ibid., 1539.

126 "every outline": Ibid., 1780.

127 "specific points of excellence": "Capt. Pabst Satisfied," *Milwaukee Sentinel,* December 22, 1893, p. 1.

127 "We exhibitors": "Absurd Score of the Beer Jury," *American Brewers' Review* 7 (October 12, 1893): 240.

128 "'march[ed] at the head'": Ibid., 240, 241.

129 "the hottest": "Beer Prizes in Doubt," *Milwaukee Sentinel,* October 28, 1893, p. 1.

129 "suppers, banquets": "Milwaukee Beer First," *Milwaukee Sentinel,* November 17, 1893, p. 5.

129 "self-puffing": Editorial from *Illinois Staats Zeitung* reprinted in English translation as "Much Ado About Nothing," in *Milwaukee Sentinel,* October 30, 1893, p. 3.

129 "King of Brewers": "The King of Brewers," *Chicago Daily Tribune,* October 27, 1893, p. 9.

129 "[B]y using": "The Anheuser-Busch Victorious," *Chicago Daily Tribune,* October 27, 1893, p. 8.

130 "The stuff published": "Milwaukee in the Race," *Milwaukee Sentinel,* October 29, 1893, p. 3.

130 "by what authority": "Brewers Want to Know," *Milwaukee Sentinel,* November 2, 1893, p. 1.

131 "PABST Milwaukee Beer WINS": *Milwaukee Sentinel,* November 17, 1893, p. 9.

131 "digest the voluminous evidence": "The Beer Award Contest," *Milwaukee Sentinel,* November 29, 1893, p. 10.

132 "fine diplomatic talk": Quoted in Peter Hernon and Terry Ganey, *Under the Influence: The Unauthorized Story of the Anheuser-Busch Dynasty* (New York: Simon & Schuster, 1991), 51.

133 "are not given to the goods": Ibid., 52.

133 "You ask me Gustav": Quoted in Cochran, *Pabst Brewing Company,* 191.

134 "I can truly say": "Spreads Sorrow in the City," *Milwaukee Sentinel,* January 2, 1904, p. 3.

134 "Let us meet": Adolphus Busch to Charles Nagel, April 18, 1910; Nagel Papers, Box 3/Folder 40. I supplied periods, commas, and capitals to this otherwise mostly unpunctuated telegram.

134 "[Y]ou are such": Quoted in Giersch, *Gussie,* 27.

135 "world wide fame": Ibid., 26.

CHAPTER FOUR
The Enemy at the Gates

PAGE

140 "[t]he constant use": Quoted in G. Thomann, *The Effects of Beer Upon Those Who Make It and Drink It* (New York: The United States Brewers' Association, 1886), 3.

141 "the filthiest fats": George T. Angell, *Autobiographical Sketches and Personal Recollections* (Boston: American Humane Education Society, [1892]), 60.

142 "It is well known": "Beer Substitutes," *Milwaukee Daily News,* September 22, 1878, p. 4.

143 "spurious beer": "Rice Beer," *Milwaukee Daily News,* September 26, 1878, p. 4.

143 "temporary insanity": "A Sad Example," *Milwaukee Daily News,* October 9, 1878, p. 4.

143 "[W]e have constantly aimed": "Ph. Best Brewing Co.," *Milwaukee Daily News,* September 25, 1878, p. 4.

144 "mental disturbance": Department of Agriculture, Division of Chemistry, Bulletin No. 13, *Food and Food Adulterants. Part Third: Fermented Alcoholic Beverages, Malt Liquors, Wine, and Cider,* by C. A. Crampton (Washington, D.C.: Government Printing Office, 1887), 311.

144 *"Acid in the Beer"*: "Acid in the Beer," *Milwaukee Sentinel,* January 8, 1888, p. 2.

148 "In those first few years": Quoted in Justin Steuart, *Wayne Wheeler Dry Boss* (1928; reprint Westport, CT: Greenwood Press, 1970), 50.

149 *"I stand for prohibition"*: Quoted in Andrew Sinclair, *Prohibition: The Era of Excess* (Boston: Little, Brown and Co., 1962), 113.

149 "The Headquarters for Murderers": Peter H. Odegard, *Pressure Politics; The Story of the Anti-Saloon League* (New York: Columbia University Press, 1928): 43.

149 "[W]hen the saloon": Ibid., 59.

150 "Liquor is responsible": Ibid., 60.

150 "create the appetite": Ibid., 41.

150 "is the most autocratic": Ibid., 23.

150 "run over": Ibid.

151 "Uncle Sam": Quoted in Richard F. Hamm, *Shaping the Eighteenth Amendment: Temperance Reform, Legal Culture, and the Polity, 1880–1920* (Chapel Hill: University of North Carolina Press, 1995), 96.

152 "tyrrany, idiocy, fanaticism": Quoted in *The Brewers and Texas Politics* (San Antonio, TX: Passing Show Print Co., 1916), 151.

152 "He recommends and speaks": Adolphus Busch to Charles Nagel, July 29, 1911; Charles Nagel Papers, Box 6/Folder 84, Manuscripts and Archives, Yale University. Hereafter cited as Nagel Papers.

152 "It is my aim": Quoted in *Brewers and Texas Politics,* 92.

153 "As you are aware": Quoted in ibid., 579.

153 "We have about arranged": Quoted in ibid., 258.

154 "the young, lawless element": Quoted in ibid., 696–97.

154 "low dives": Quoted in Senate Committee on the Judiciary, *Brewing and Liquor Interests and German Propaganda: Hearings Before a Subcommittee of the Committee on the Judiciary.* 65th Cong., 2d sess., 1918, 1117.

155 "The Salt Lake Brewing Company": Quoted in ibid., 1115.

155 "the object of severest criticism": Charles Nagel to August A. Busch, November 26, 1907, Nagel Papers, microfilm set. Nagel wrote this letter less than a week after the Busches finally took his advice and agreed to close lawless saloons affiliated with Anheuser-Busch. The letter's text makes it clear that Nagel was only restating on paper arguments he had made verbally in the preceding months.

155 "the suppression": "Busch Firm Declares War on Evil Saloons," *St. Louis Post-Dispatch,* November 15, 1907, p. 9.

156 "110 saloons": "Busch Defied to 'Make Good' in Belleville," *St. Louis Post-Dispatch,* November 17, 1907, p. 4.

157 "[H]ow many thousands": "Fanatical Envy!," *American Brewer* 33, no. 4 (April 1, 1910): 167.

157 "devotion and love": "13,000 Attend Busch Wedding Jubilee," *St. Louis Republican,* March 8, 1911, p. 4.

158 "I . . . wish to know": Quoted in Stanley Baron, *Brewed in America: A History of Beer and Ale in the United States* (Boston: Little, Brown and Co., 1962), 289.

158 "promote": "Wilson Speaks to Brewers," *New York Times,* October 19, 1911, p. 7.

158 "If Mr. Farwell will call": Ibid.

158 "[T]here was nothing else": Quoted in Baron, *Brewed in America,* 299.

159 "Well, they couldn't have": Adolphus Busch to Charles Nagel, March 7, 1912; Nagel Papers, Box 7/Folder 102.

159 "I have a kind of feeling": Adolphus Busch to Charles Nagel, August 2, 1912; Nagel Papers, Box 8/Folder 114.

160 "giant among men": Charles Nagel, "Adolphus Busch: A Great Life Understood," *Western Brewer* 41 (November 1913): 231.

160 "Our song to-day": " 'Loved Busch, Not His Riches,' Says Bartholdt," *St. Louis Globe-Democrat,* October 26, 1913, 8.

160 "Kings inherit their realms": "Busch Body Moves Thro' Silent Throng to Resting Place," *St. Louis Republic,* October 26, 1913, II:1.

160 "Temperance Crank": Adolphus Busch to Charles Nagel, March 7, 1912, Nagel Papers, Box 7/Folder 102.

161 "Prohibition is no longer": Quoted in K. Austin Kerr, *Organized for Prohibition: A New History of the Anti-Saloon League* (New Haven, CT: Yale University Press, 1985), 179.

162 "You may exercise": Quoted in David E. Kyvig, *Repealing National Prohibition,* 2d ed. (Kent, OH: The Kent State University Press, 2000), 9.

163 "the progress of every fight": Wayne B. Wheeler, "The Inside Story of Prohibition's Adoption. Article II: Organizing for National Prohibition," *New York Times,* March 29, 1926, p. 21.

164 "breed deceit, hypocrisy": *Congressional Record,* 63rd Cong., 3rd sess., 1914, 52, pt. 2: 544.

164 "Crime is caused by drink": "Prohibition is Beaten in House," *New York Times,* December 23, 1914, p. 7.

165 "exceedingly gratifying": "Keeps Up Liquor Fight," *New York Times,* December 24, 1914, p. 4.

168 "Just think": *Congressional Record,* 65th Cong., 1st sess., 1917, 55, pt. 1:4727.

168 "no patriotism among": Ibid., 4724.

168 "praying": Ibid., 4711, 4712.

169 "We cannot tell": "Change in Beer to Save Grain Here Worth $1,675,000," *St. Louis Post-Dispatch,* December 12, 1917, p. 1.

169 "I do not think": Ibid.

170 "indefatigable and shrewd": Quoted in Steuart, *Wayne Wheeler,* 73.

170 "cohabit with the devil": Quoted in Norman H. Clark, *Deliver Us From Evil: An Interpretation of American Prohibition* (New York: W. W. Norton, 1976), 114.

171 "a red-hot": Quoted in Steuart, *Wayne Wheeler,* 51.

172 "We could not have": Ibid., 118.

172 "Was the National Association": Senate Committee on the Judiciary, *National German-American Alliance: Hearings Before the Subcommittee of the Committee on the Judiciary.* 65th Cong., 2d sess., February 23–April 13, 1918, 216.

172 "It may have been": Ibid., 206.

173 "German enemies": "Pabst Charge is Filed," *Milwaukee Journal,* February 13, 1918, p. 6. Not long after the speech, Gustav Pabst sued Strange for slander and defamation of character, asking $25,000 in damages (about $300,000 today). Strange defended himself by arguing that at the time he made the speech, he was not acquainted with Pabst and so had not made any kind of personal attack; nor, he

claimed, did anyone in the audience interpret his words as a personal attack. The judge dismissed the case.

173 "organization of power": "The Brewers' Campaign of Righteousness," *The Literary Digest* 56, no. 2 (January 12, 1918): 57.

173 "German breweries": Ibid., 58.

173 "The unthinkable barbarism": Ibid.

174 "part of the deliberate plan": Quoted in Stanley Coben, *A. Mitchell Palmer: Politician* (New York: Columbia University Press, 1963), 137–38.

174 "Believing with many others": Lilly Busch sworn affidavit, June 29, 1918, p. 4; File 193959, Box 2925, at AII loc: 230/7/24/6, Department of Justice, National Archives at College Park, College Park, MD.

175 "If Mr. Ehret": "Nation Gets Ehret Property," *New York Times,* May 4, 1918, p. 1.

175 "I am informed": Quoted in Steuart, *Wayne Wheeler,* 121–22.

176 "prominent in German court": "Kaiser Seizes Busch Estate in Germany," *St. Louis Globe-Democrat,* June 17, 1918, p. 1.

176 "Mrs. Bush has relatives": Jay Adams to Department of Justice, March 14, 1918; File 193959, Box 2925, at AII loc: 230/7/24/6, Department of Justice, National Archives at College Park, College Park, MD.

177 "Question, Search, and report": Josephus Daniels to [Thomas W. Gregory], August 12, 1918; File 193959, Box 2925, at AII loc: 230/7/24/6, Department of Justice, National Archives at College Park, College Park, MD.

177 "entire estate": "Busch Property Seized By Nation," *New York Times,* June 18, 1918, p. 1.

177 "August": "Mrs. Busch Detained By U.S. at Key West," *St. Louis Globe-Democrat,* June 18, 1918, p. 1.

178 "the person and effects": Josephus Daniels to [Thomas W. Gregory], August 12, 1918.

178 "laid the old lady": Harry Hawes to Thomas W. Gregory, July 2, 1918, p. 5; File 193959, Box 2925, at AII loc: 230/7/24/6, Department of Justice, National Archives at College Park, College Park, MD.

178 "No person in the world": "Mrs. Busch Vindicated by U.S. Then Released and Starts for Home," *St. Louis Globe-Democrat,* June 20, 1918,
p. 1.

179 "From the day": Quoted in Senate Committee on the Judiciary,
Brewing and Liquor Interests, 736.

180 "*Enemy Propaganda*": "Enemy Propaganda Backed By Brewers," *New
York Times,* November 21, 1918, p. 14.

180 "Nobody at the meeting": "Brewers Undecided As to Their Future,
New York Times, September 10, 1918, p. 17.

181 "Give me a chance": "Busch Offers to Make Plant Munition Factory,"
St. Louis Post-Dispatch, September 22, 1918, p. 3.

181 "our men": "Brewers in a Quandary," *New York Times,* September 22,
1918, p. 4.

181 "We consider it": "Announcement by Anheuser-Busch Missouri's
Largest Industrial Institution," *St. Louis Post-Dispatch,* September 14,
1918, p. 10.

181 "false reports and statements": Ibid.

CHAPTER FIVE
Happy Days?

PAGE

184 "great indoor sport": August A. Busch, Jr., "As Beer Draws Near,"
American Legion Monthly 14 (January 1933): 20.

185 "Business is very, very poor": Quoted in Michael R. Worcester,
"Been A Long Time A-Brewing: A History of the Minneapolis Brewing Company, 1890–1975" (Master's thesis, Saint Cloud State University, 1993), 79.

186 "Wonderful Body Stimulants": Ibid., 80.

187 "sheer nerve": Alvin Griesedieck, *The Falstaff Story* [St. Louis], n.p.,
1951, 81.

192 "an outrage": Quoted in David E. Kyvig, *Repealing National Prohibition,* 2d ed. (Kent, OH: Kent State University Press, 2000), 82.

192 "Beer for Taxation": "All-Day Parade for Beer Jauntily Led By Walker;
Cheered by Gay Throngs," *New York Times,* May 15, 1932, p. 3.

193 "enemies of society": Quoted in Kyvig, *Repealing National Prohibition,*
166.

194 "Beer": Quoted in "Let Beer Be the Opiate of the People!," *Christian Century* 49, no. 50 (December 14, 1932): 1534.

194 "I want it": Quoted in House Committee on Ways and Means, *Modification of Volstead Act: Hearings on H. R. 13312,* 72d Cong., 2d sess., 1932, 57.

194 "Ho, ho": "Ruth Pins His Hope of Big Salary on Beer; Sees Ruppert 'Too Tickled' to Refuse Demand," *New York Times,* December 23, 1932, p. 24.

195 "character": House Committee on Ways and Means, *Modification of Volstead Act,* 41.

195 "would not hold anymore": Ibid., 44.

196 "In addition to that": Ibid., 33.

196 "parasitic": Ibid., 379.

197 "We have a large volume": "Breweries Swamped by Rush of Orders," *Milwaukee Sentinel,* March 21, 1933, p. 1.

197–198 "[O]rders are piling up": "Bottles, Kegs and Malt Put Kick in Trade," *Milwaukee Sentinel,* March 24, 1933, p. 3.

198 "It is quite possible": "City Beer Shortage Feared by Brewers," *New York Times,* March 26, 1933, p. 1.

198 "We have been swamped": Ibid.

198 "no nation ever drank itself": "Women Warned of Fattening Beer," *New York Times,* March 18, 1933, p. 2.

199 "personal liberty": "Crowds in Cafes, Hotels Give Beer Rousing Welcome," *St. Louis Post-Dispatch,* April 7, 1933, p. 2.

200 "Mr. President": "Roosevelt Gets First Cases of Capital's 3.2 Beer; Gov. Lehman Will Serve the Brew at Albany," *New York Times,* April 7, 1933, p. 1.

200 "Now that beer": "Mae West Taps Beer Bet and It's a Draw," *Milwaukee Sentinel,* April 10, 1933, p. 4.

200–1 "You jumped the gun": "Plane Rushes Special Cases to Roosevelt," *Milwaukee Sentinel,* April 7, 1933, p. 1.

201 "To President": Ibid.

201 "carnival": "City Regulations Ready," *New York Times,* April 6, 1933, p. 2.

202 "I have seen": "Six Big Horses Bring Smith a Case of Beer," *New York Times,* April 8, 1933, p. 3.

202 "We are begging": "Sunday Beer Is Legal But Supply Runs Low," *St. Louis Post-Dispatch,* April 9, 1933, p. 1.

204 "a foregone conclusion": Julius J. Schwarz, "Today's Brewing Industry—A Modern Tower of Babel," *Brewery Age* 2 (April 1934): 35.

206 "boys and girls": Joseph Dubin, "The Interlude," *Brewery Age* 1, no. 11
(November 1933): 7.

207 "[v]ery few people": R. J. Kaye, "Analyze and Dramatize Beer Advertising," *Brewery Age* 1, no. 11 (November 1933): 27.

207 "Munich matron": "Beer With A Collar," *Business Week* (January 4, 1936):
18.

209 "We had to forget": Neil M. Clark, "The Remarkable Come-Back of
Anheuser-Busch," *Forbes* 18 (December 1, 1926): 42.

209 "a long way": Ibid., 44.

209 "experience on which": Ibid., 46.

210 "sweetness of nature": "August A. Busch Funeral Is Held at Grant's
Farm," *St. Louis Post-Dispatch,* February 16, 1934, pp. 1, 3.

CHAPTER SIX
"You Have to Think About Growth"

PAGE

211 "so that if the US": Quoted in John Gurda, *Miller Time: A History of
Miller Brewing Company 1855–2005* ([Milwaukee, WI]: Miller Brewing Company, 2005): 102.

212 "beer should come back": Ibid., 108.

214 "KRUEGER'S": "Krueger Introduces Canned Beer," *Modern Brewer*
13 (March 1935): 33.

218 "When you share": Advertisement, *Modern Brewery Age* 29 (January
1943): 17.

219 "The big brewers": "Small Brewers Scan Wartime Outlook," *Modern
Brewery Age* 29 (June 1943): 24.

223 "What do you mean": Quoted in Tim John, *The Miller Beer Barons:
The Frederick J. Miller Family and Its Brewery* (Oregon, WI: Badger
Books Inc., 2005), 294.

229 "streamlined": "MBA Holds Reconversion Conference," *Modern
Brewery Age* 34 (November 1945): 60, 62.

229 "blandness": Robert I. Tenney, "In Beer Character—What Does the
Public Want?," *Modern Brewery Age* 46 (December 1951): 30.

229 "the dethronement": "What Has Happened to Flavor?," *Fortune* 45 (April 1952): 131.

230 "too bitter and strong": "Formula for Survival Unfolded at Annual BAA Enclave," *Modern Brewery Age* 50 (November 1953):34.

230 "a pale, dry": Untitled news item, *Modern Brewery Age* 47 (April 1952): 67.

230 "extra-dry": Untitled news item, *Modern Brewery Age* 47 (March 1952): 82.

230 "The full flavor": "Bock Gets Big Play in February–March Brewery Ads," *Modern Brewery Age* 49 (March 1953): 55.

231 "women and beginners": "The Rise of Miller High Life," *Fortune* 47 (February 1953): 133.

232 "Our goal": "Higher High Life," *Time* 61 (January 12, 1953): 83.

233 "radically influence": Quoted in Kirse Granat May, *Golden State, Golden Youth: The California Image in Popular Culture, 1955–1965* (Chapel Hill: University of North Carolina Press, 2002), 11.

234 "Being second": "Gussie," *St. Louis Post-Dispatch,* September 30, 1989, p. 10A.

234 "almost defiantly uninhibited": Ibid.

234 "He rarely talks": "The Baron of Beer," *Time* 66 (July 11, 1955): 83.

236 "worst mistake": "Marketing Briefs," *Business Week,* April 23, 1955, p. 44.

236 "When midnight came": "Baron of Beer," 83.

236 "We hope to make": " 'Sporting Venture,' " *Time* 61 (March 2, 1953): 46.

238 "voodoo rhythm": Lawrence E. Doherty, "Hamm Brewing Builds to National Brand by '70," *Advertising Age* 32, no. 3 (January 16, 1961): 66.

239 "You have to think": "Are the Drinkers Doing Their Part?," *Business Week,* April 13, 1963, p. 106.

240 "a sophisticated market": "More Than Ads Sell Rheingold," *Business Week,* September 21, 1957, p. 74.

240 "leisure and casualness": Ibid., 74, 76.

240 "It's Lucky": Ibid., 76.

241 "You don't sell": Ibid., 72.

247 "There is": Senate Committee on the Judiciary, *Distribution Problems*

Affecting Small Business: Hearings Before the Subcommittee on Antitrust and Monopoly, 89th Cong., 2d sess., January 18–20, 26–27, 1966, 595.

248 "big lion dozing": Jacques Neher, "What Went Wrong," *Advertising Age* 52, no. 16 (April 13, 1981): 62.

248 "genius-I.Q. types": William Bowen, "How They Put the 'Gusto' In Schlitz," *Fortune* 70, no. 4 (October 1964): 106.

249 "you imbibe the image": Ibid., 220.

249 "what makes the beer drinker": "Selling Suds Like Soap," *Business Week*, August 8, 1964, p. 62.

249 "It's the Procter & Gamble way": Bowen, "Gusto," 225.

249 "premiumness": Ibid., 220.

249 "lots of white": Ibid.

250 "Meet the beer": "The Introduction of Lite," *Brewers Digest* 42, no. 8 (August 1967): 70.

250 "save the bread": "Saving the Bread for the Sandwich," *Time* 90 (July 7, 1967): 75.

250 "It's fun when you have": "Snob Suds," *Newsweek* 63 (February 17, 1964): 80.

250 "It is particularly irritating": "Bidding for a Market with Growth Built In," *Business Week*, November 18, 1961, p. 45.

251 "fancy foods": "Everyone's in the Kitchen," *Time* (November 25, 1966): 74.

252 "anything was possible": Quoted in Timothy Miller, *The 60s Communes: Hippies and Beyond* (Syracuse, NY: Syracuse University Press, 1999), 33.

253 "are a puzzle to us": Robert N. Harris, "The Aware Generation," *Brewers Digest* 43, no. 1 (January 1968): 45.

253 "their own ideas": Ibid., 46.

253 "unpleasant or bitter": Ibid.

253 "spell[ed] disaster": "Marijuana Turning Some Youths Away From Beer," *New York Times*, August 9, 1970, p. 47.

253 "where it really swings": "Utica Club *is* where it really swings," *Brewers Digest* 43, no. 7 (July 1968): 30.

254 "Utica Club is where": Ibid.

256 "price promotion": Charles G. Burck, "While the Big Brewers Quaff, the Little Ones Thirst," *Fortune* 86 (November 1972): 107.

256 "Now no brewery": Senate Committee on the Judiciary, *Distribution Problems*, 591.

CHAPTER SEVEN
Make Mine Small, Pure, Real, and Lite

PAGE

258 "wore Levis to class": Lew Bryson, "Fritz Maytag," *Malt Advocate* 9, no. 3 (July 2000). Unpaginated copy provided to the author by Bryson.

259 "I would no more": Fritz Maytag, interview by Maureen Ogle, tape recording, April 20, 2005. Hereafter cited as Maytag interview.

259 "I wish I had": Ibid.

261 "No, no": Bryson, "Fritz Maytag."

262 "Ja, I know": Maytag interview.

262 "bible": Ibid.

262 "very, very quiet": Bill Leinenkugel, interview by Maureen Ogle, April 22, 2005. Hereafter cited as Bill Leinenkugel interview.

262 "listened like mad": Maytag interview.

263 "everything from enzymes": Ibid.

263 "Well, try five thousand": Dick Yuengling, Jr., interview by Maureen Ogle, May 10, 2005.

263 "cash surpluses": "Who Drinks? The Brewer's Dilemma," *Newsweek* 64 (August 24, 1963): 67.

263 "mock-Bavarian": Ibid.

264 "smoke a pipe": Maytag interview.

265 "exceptional respect": Curtis Hartman, "The Alchemist of Anchor Steam," *Inc.* 5, no. 1 (January 1983): 36.

266 "I have tried them all": Mike Royko, "Advertising vs. Flavor," *Chicago Daily News*, May 22, 1973, p. 3.

266 "Go to hell": Mike Royko, "Big Taste Test is Brewing," *Chicago Daily News*, July 6, 1973, p. 3.

267 "is proud about finding": Michael F. Jacobson, quoted at http://www.activistcash.com/biography.cfm/bid/1284.

267 "slick, multi-million dollar": Michael F. Jacobson and Joel Anderson, *Chemical Additives in Booze* (Washington, D.C.: Center for Science in the Public Interest, 1972), 1.

268 "At least with a horse": Mike Royko, "The Lowdown on U.S. Beer," *Chicago Daily News*, February 28, 1974, p. 3.

269 "a realm of intimate": "Purpose," *Whole Earth Catalog Access to Tools* ([Menlo Park, CA]: Portola Institute, Fall 1969), unpaginated title page.

271 "first-ever": Nathaniel Benchley, "Day Two: Cooling Off Period," *Esquire* 82 (July 1974): 86.

271 "Bill,": Bill Leinenkugel interview.

271 "Some people": Linda Hales, "Increased success seems to be brewing for Leinenkugel," *Chicago Tribune,* November 14, 1977, p. 6:12.

272 "everything was laid": Harry Hurt III, "Muscling In On Texas Beer," *Texas Monthly* 4 (March 1976): 177

272 "Cuero turkey trot": Ibid., 179.

274 "must be handled": John Porter, *All About Beer* (Garden City, NY: Doubleday & Co., 1975), 43.

274 "For many connoisseurs": "The Beer That Won the West," *Time* 103 (February 11, 1974): 73.

274 "Pleasure-loving parasites": Hurt, "Muscling In on Texas Beer," 75.

277 "[N]ow that growing your own": "Beer—Brew It Yourself," *Great Speckled Bird* (May 17, 1971): 22. This article appeared in multiple publications thanks to the Underground Press Syndicate, the hippies' version of the Associated Press.

278 "leave the beer-making": "Treasury Warns Home-Brewers," *Washington Post,* July 27, 1973, p. A3.

279 "this interpretation": Byron Burch, *Quality Brewing: A Guidebook for the Home Production of Fine Beers* (Richmond, CA: Joby Books, 1977), 2.

279 "Most of us": Mark Jones, "A Fine Froth For Those Who Brew Their Own Beer," *Washington Post,* July 2, 1978, p. H5.

280 "everybody": Raymond Mungo, *Cosmic Profit: How To Make Money Without Doing Time* (Boston: Little, Brown and Company, 1980), 90.

281 "expanded by leaps": Charlie Papazian, interview by Maureen Ogle, April 27, 2005. Hereafter cited as Papazian interview.

282 "an Olympic-class beer drinker": Quoted in Richard Kluger, *Ashes To Ashes: America's Hundred-Year Cigarette War, the Public Health, and the Unabashed Triumph of Philip Morris* (New York: Alfred A. Knopf, 1996), 403.

282 "country club": John Gurda, *Miller Time: A History of Miller Brewing 1855–2005* ([Milwaukee, WI]: Miller Brewing Company, 2005), 148.

283 "[a]fter all": Thomas O'Hanlon, "August Busch Brews Up a New Spirit in St. Louis," *Fortune* 99 (January 15, 1979): 93.

283 "convincing beer-drinking personalities": "How Miller Won a Market Slot for Lite beer," *Business Week,* October 13, 1975, p. 118.

283 "easy-opening": Gurda, *Miller Time,* caption on p. 152.

283 "so tough": "The Light Beer Game," *Forbes* 117 (January 15, 1976): 31.

283–84 "I've been in this business": "How Miller Won a Market Slot," 116.

284 "The whole light beer thing": "Giving the Light a Bit of Sight," *St. Louis Post-Dispatch,* August 12, 1979, 1F.

284 "Drink Joe's Beer,": Ibid.

285 "I could cut production": "A Struggle to Stay First in Brewing," *Business Week,* March 24, 1973, p. 46.

285 "You can be sure": Ibid., 49.

285 "Tell Miller": "Turmoil Among Brewers: Miller's Fast Growth Upsets the Beer Industry," *Business Week,* November 8, 1976, p. 58.

285 "This light stuff": "Beer: Let There Be Light," *Newsweek* 89 (June 6, 1977): 68.

286 "We didn't really": Gail Compton, "St. Louis Enters Great Light Beer Competition," *Milwaukee Journal,* August 3, 1977; Mercantile and Manufacturing file, Missouri Historical Society.

286 "It's an entirely organic": Ibid.

286 "non-natural additives": Eliot Marshall, "Frothing and Foaming," *New Republic* 179 (July 8 & 15, 1978): 19.

287 "We find it incredulous": "Lowenbrau Promotion Under Investigation By Trade Commission," *Washington Post,* July 23, 1978, p. A7.

287 "Miller people": Senate Committee on the Judiciary. *Mergers and Industrial Concentration: Hearings Before the Subcommittee on Antitrust and Monopoly.* 95th Cong., 2d sess., 1978, p. 67.

288 "We are the company": "Struggle to Stay First," 45.

288 "[T]hat board": Jacques Neher, "What Went Wrong," *Advertising Age* 52, no. 16 (April 13, 1981): 64.

288 "accelerated-batch": "Who Rules the Foam?," *Forbes* 110 (December 15, 1972): 36.

289 "When we want you": Neher, "What Went Wrong," 64.

290 "flat as apple cider": Jaques Neher, "Schlitz Lost At Sea," *Advertising Age* 52, no. 17 (April 20, 1981): 49.

290 "Here were three guys": Ibid., 52.

292 "very smart": Michael Lewis, interview by Maureen Ogle, May 18, 2005.

292 "acted like he was from Mars": Jack McAuliffe, interview by Maureen Ogle, February 10, 2004.

293 "with the approximate velocity": Douglas Bartholomew, "New Albion," *American Spectator* 14, no. 7 (July 1981): 24.

294 "sea captain": Nancy Vineyard, interview by Maureen Ogle, June 6, 2005.

294 "If you make": William Ristow and Michael E. Miller, "Brewing 'Real Ale' Is a Yeasty Business," *Washington Post,* July 9, 1978, p. G10.

295 "Get out": Don Barkley, interview by Maureen Ogle, May 8, 2005. Hereafter cited as Barkley interview.

295 "You have to be": Ristow and Miller, "Brewing 'Real Ale,'" G10.

296 "We knew we were": Barkley interview.

296 "what button to push": Ibid.

298 "lived like a spider": John R. McAuliffe, "Brewing On A Small Scale," *Amateur Brewer* (Winter 1986): 31.

298 "We knew": Barkley interview.

CHAPTER EIGHT
Something Old, Something New

PAGE

302 "came down out of the hills": Ken Grossman, interview by Maureen Ogle, April 7, 2005.

302 "hoppy": Ibid.

304 "We'll build it to here": Ibid.

304 "guru": Ibid.

304 "jump[ed] off the page": Nancy Vineyard, interview by Maureen Ogle, June 6, 2005.

306 "[h]omebrewing and brewing": Quoted in Stuart Harris, "Sierra Nevada Brewery," *Zymurgy* 4, no. 3 (Fall 1981): 19.

306 "It's the few": Ibid.

306 "I don't want to knock": Ibid.

307 "tremendous migration": Don Barkley, interview by Maureen Ogle, May 8, 2005.

307 "golden rolling hills": "The Redtail Hawk," music and lyrics by George Schroder, 1975.

309 "schlepping bags": Jim Koch, interview by Maureen Ogle, April 6, 2005.

309 "vocational school": Ibid.

310 "When you think": Ibid.

311 "marketing smoke and mirrors": Ibid.

312 "didn't feel the need": Ibid.

313 "Sales of 5,000 barrels": Prospectus quoted in Robert A. Mamis, "Market Maker," *Inc.* (December 1995), online edition at Expanded Academic ASAP.

313 "never sold anything": James Koch, "Portrait of the CEO as Salesman," *Inc. Magazine* (March 1988); online edition at Expanded Academic ASAP.

314 "I think contract brewers": Quoted in Daniel Bradford, "Contract Brewing," *New Brewer* 3, no. 6 (November–December 1986): 29.

314 "more interested": Suzanne Alexander, "Is a Beer Local If It's Produced Not So Locally?," *Wall Street Journal*, July 21, 1989, p. B1.

314 "I'm dripping wet": Ibid., B2.

315 "If a contract brewer": Quoted in Bradford, "Contract Brewing," 29.

315 "True Beer": Vince Cottone, *Good Beer Guide: Breweries and Pubs of the Pacific Northwest, British Columbia, Washington and Oregon* (Seattle, WA: Homestead Book Company, 1986), 10.

315 "to cheapen": Ibid., 11.

315 "It's not a new kind": Ibid., 10.

316 "True micros": Quoted in Terri Finnegan, "Microbrewing Comes of Age," *Modern Brewery Age,* magazine section 40, no. 19 (May 8, 1989): 12.

316 "technologically advanced": Peter Krebs, *Redhook: Beer Pioneer* (New York: Four Walls Eight Windows, 1998), 145.

316 "handcrafted": Quoted in ibid., 146.

317 "We need contract brewers": Fred Eckhardt, "The Budweiser Menace," *All About Beer* (March 1997); online at http://www.allaboutbeer.com/columns/fred4.html.

318 "pasteurized carbonated malt": Fred Eckhardt, "A Treatise on Lager Beers," (Portland, OR: Hobby Winemaker, 1970), 2 and [ii].

319 "uncomfortable": Charlie Papazian, interview by Maureen Ogle, April 27, 2005.

319 "extension of homebrewing": Charlie Papazian, "How Many Apples Does It Take to Make a Pie?," *Zymurgy* 5, no. 4 (Winter 1982): 2.

321 "I didn't do this": Edward A. Gargan, "Microbrewers Set the Pace, and Draw the Heat," *New York Times,* November 20, 1994, p. F12.

322 "responsible drinking": Dwight B. Heath, "The New Temperance Movement: Through the Looking-Glass," *Drugs and Society* 3 (1989): 153.

323 "stabilize per capita": Ibid., 154.

323 "It's not easy": Frank Rose, "If It Feels Good, It Must Be Bad," *Fortune* 124 (October 21, 1991): 92.

323 "The sixties generation": "Water, Water Everywhere," *Time* 125, no. 20 (May 20, 1985): 70.

325 "turn spring break": Teresa Riordan, "The Lites of Spring. Miller Guy Life," *New Republic* 200 (March 27, 1989): 16.

328 "Something": Jake Leinenkugel, interview by Maureen Ogle, April 22, 2005.

329 "are bored with": Quoted in Gherry Khermouch, "A Different Brew," *Brandweek* 36, no. 44 (November 20, 1995); online version from Expanded Academic ASAP.

329 "meddlesome thing": Quoted in ibid.

330 "We have people": Jack Kenny, "Macro Micros: Back To School," *All About Beer* 16, no. 5 (November 1995): 13.

330 "They will not say Coors": Ibid., 14.

330 "A big name": Quoted in Kermouch, "A Different Brew."

331 "fictitious": Jim Dorsch, "What's In a Micro? Label Flap Makes Strange Bedfellows," *Ale Street News* 4, no. 2 (April/May 1996): 7.

332 "100-percent mind share": Nigel Jacques, "Microblues: How Bud Is Smashing Local Breweries," *Willamette Week,* April 8, 1998; online at http://www.wweek.com/html/cover040898.html.

332 "expensive microbrews": "Can You Judge a Beer By Its Label?," *Consumer Reports* (June 1996): 10.

332 "Boston Beer": Reed Abelson, "Boston Beer: The Sad Fall of an I.P.O. Open to All," *New York Times,* November 24, 1996, p. F4.

EPILOGUE

341 "Craft beers have pushed": "Brewing Up a New Image," http://www.forbes.com/manufacturing/2006/01/23/budweiser-coors-beer-cx_0124wharton.html

BIBLIOGRAPHY

What follows is not intended to be a comprehensive bibliography; rather, it is limited to those works that I consulted and ones that would interest a general reader seeking more information.

BREWERS AND BREWING

Ackoff, Russell L., and James R. Emshoff. "Advertising Research at Anheuser-Busch, Inc. (1968–74)." *Sloan Management Review* 16, no. 3 (Spring 1975): 1–15.

Allison, Ralph I., and Kenneth P. Uhl. "Influence of Beer Brand Identification on Taste Perception." *Journal of Marketing Research* 1, no. 3 (August 1964): 36–39.

Anderson, Harry H. "The Women Who Helped Make Milwaukee Breweries Famous." *Milwaukee History* 4 (1981): 66–78.

Anderson, Will. *The Breweries of Brooklyn.* Croton Falls, NY: Anderson, 1976.

Appel, Susan Kay Bigley. "The Midwestern Brewery Before Prohibition: Development of an American Industrial Building Type." Ph.D. dissertation, University of Illinois at Urbana-Champaign, 1990.

Appel, Susan K. "Artificial Refrigeration and the Architecture of 19th-Century American Breweries." *IA: Journal of the Society for Industrial Archaeology* 16, no. 1 (1990): 21–38.

Appel, Susan K. "Building Milwaukee's Breweries: Pre-Prohibition Architecture in the Cream City." *Wisconsin Magazine of History* 78, no. 3 (Spring 1995): 163–99.

Appel, Susan K. "Chicago and the Rise of Brewery Architecture." *Chicago History* 24, no. 1 (1995): 4–19.

Apps, Jerry. *Breweries of Wisconsin*. Madison: University of Wisconsin Press, 1992.

Arnold, John P., and Frank Penman. *History of the Brewing Industry and Brewing Science in America*. Chicago: n.p., 1933.

Baluyut, Fernando de Lara. "Anheuser-Busch: A Study in Firm Growth." Master's thesis, St. Louis University, 1961.

Barbash, Walter V., and Timothy J. Dennee. "The First Lager Brewery in America." *American Breweriana*, January–February 1993, 10–11.

Baron, Stanley. *Brewed in America: A History of Beer and Ale in the United States*. Boston: Little, Brown and Company, 1962.

Baum, Dan. *Citizen Coors: An American Dynasty*. New York: William Morrow, 2000.

Blough, David Roy. "Applying Organizational Ecology to the Study of Regional Technical Change: Fitness and Competition in the American Brewing Industry." Ph.D. dissertation, University of Wisconsin–Madison, 2000.

Blum, Peter H. *Brewed in Detroit: Breweries and Beers Since 1830*. Detroit, MI: Wayne State University Press, 1999.

Bryson, Lew. *Pennsylvania Breweries*. Mechanicsburg, PA: Stackpole Books, 1998.

Budnick, Jason J. "The Cold Spring Brewing Company, 1874–1997: A History and Analysis of a Regional Brewery." Master's thesis, St. Cloud State University, 1998.

Burch, Byron. *Quality Brewing: A Guidebook for the Home Production of Fine Beers,* 2d ed. Richmond, CA: Joby Books, 1974.

Burgess, Robert J. *Silver Bullets: A Soldier's Story of How Coors Bombed in the Beer Wars*. New York: St. Martin's Press, 1993.

Calagione, Sam. *Brewing Up A Business: Adventures in Entrepreneurship from the Founder of Dogfish Head Craft Brewery*. Hoboken, NJ: John Wiley & Sons, Inc., 2005.

Carroll, Glenn R., and Anand Swaminathan. "The Organizational Ecology of Strategic Groups in the American Brewing Industry from 1975 to 1990." *Industrial and Corporate Change* 1, no. 1 (1992): 65–97.

Carroll, Glenn R., and Anand Swaminathan. "Why The Microbrewery Movement? Organizational Dynamics of Resource Partitioning in the U.S. Brewing Industry." *American Journal of Sociology* 106, no. 3 (November 2000): 715–62.

Ceccatti, John Simmons. "Science in the Brewery: Pure Yeast Culture and the Transformation of Brewing Practices in Germany at the End of the 19th Century." Ph.D. dissertation, University of Chicago, 2001.

Childs, Carl M. C. " 'Brewed and Aged the Old-Fashioned Way': Prohibition, Near Beer, and the Diversification of the D. G. Yuengling Brewery." Master's thesis, James Madison University, 1992.

Cochran, Thomas C. *The Pabst Brewing Company: The History of an American Business.* New York: New York University Press, 1948.

Cook, Stephen R. "The Historical and Economic Geography of the Brewing Industry in the Denver Region, 1859–1987." Master's thesis, University of Colorado, 1987.

Darlington, James. "Hops and Hop Houses in Upstate New York." *Material Culture* 16, no. 1 (1984): 25–42.

Dornbusch, Horst D. *Prost! The Story of German Beer.* Boulder, CO: Siris Books, 1997.

Downard, William L. *The Cincinnati Brewing Industry: A Social and Economic History.* Athens: Ohio University Press, 1973.

Downard, William L. *Dictionary of the History of the American Brewing and Distilling Industries.* Westport, CT: Greenwood Press, 1980.

Eastberg, John C. "The Paramour and the Press: Society, Scandal and the Schandeins." Master's essay, Marquette University, 2000.

Eckhardt, Fred. *A Treatise on Lager Beers: An Anthology of American and Canadian Lager Beer.* Portland, OR: Hobby Winemaker, 1970.

Ehret, George. *Twenty-five Years of Brewing with an Illustrated History of American Beer Dedicated to the Friends of George Ehret.* New York: Gast Lithograph and Engraving Co., 1891.

Fauntleroy, Phylicia Ann. "An Economic Analysis of the United States Demand for Distilled Spirits, Wine, and Beer Incorporating Taste Changes Through Demographic Factors, 1960–1981." Ph.D. dissertation, The American University, 1984.

Fix, George J. "Explorations in Pre-Prohibition American Lagers." *Brewing Techniques* 2 (May–June 1994): 28–31.

Flanagan, John T. *Theodore Hamm in Minnesota: His Family and His Brewery.* [St. Paul, MN]: Pogo Press, 1989.

Fogarty, David. "From Saloon to Supermarket: Packaged Beer and the Reshaping of the U.S. Brewing Industry." *Contemporary Drug Problems* 12, no. 4 (Winter 1985): 541–91.

Garwood, William L. "Coors and the Brewing Industry." M.B.A. thesis, University of Texas–Austin, 1987.

Gettelman, Nancy Moore. *The A. Gettelman Brewing Company: One-Hundred and Seven Years of a Family Brewery in Milwaukee.* Milwaukee, WI: Procrustes Press, 1995.

Giersch, Lottie Busch. *Gussie.* Privately printed, 1985; copy at Anheuser-Busch Corporate Library.

Glamann, Kristof. *Jacobsen of Carlsberg: Brewer and Philanthropist.* Translated by Geoffrey French. Copenhagan: Gyldendal, 1991.

Glamann, Kristof. "The Scientific Brewer: Founders and Successors During the Rise of the Modern Brewing Industry," in *Enterprise and History: Essays in Honour of Charles Wilson,* ed. D. C. Coleman and Peter Mathias. Cambridge: Cambridge University Press, 1984: 186–98.

Greer, Douglas F. "Product Differentiation and Concentration in the Brewing Industry." *Journal of Industrial Economics* 19, no. 3 (July 1971): 201–19.

Greer, Douglas F. "The Causes of Concentration in the US Brewing Industry." *Quarterly Review of Economics and Business* 21, no. 4 (Winter 1981): 87–106.

Gurda, John. *Miller Time: A History of Miller Brewing Company 1855–2005.* [Milwaukee, WI]: Miller Brewing Company, 2005.

Haag, Daniel Eric. "'Place' Bottled and Sold: A Case Study of Anheuser-Busch Advertisements, 1880–1916." Master's thesis, University of Illinois, 1995.

Hard, Mikael. *Machines Are Frozen Spirit: The Scientification of Refrigeration and Brewing in the 19th Century—A Weberian Tradition.* Boulder, CO: Westview Press, 1994.

Harris, Moira F. *The Paws of Refreshment: The Story of Hamm's Beer Advertising.* [St. Paul, MN]: Pogo Press, 1990.

Hernon, Peter, and Terry Ganey. *Under the Influence: The Unauthorized Story of the Anheuser-Busch Dynasty.* New York: Simon & Schuster, 1991.

Hindy, Steve, and Tom Potter. *Beer School: Bottling Success at the Brooklyn Brewery.* Hoboken, NJ: John Wiley & Sons, 2005.

Holian, Timothy J. *Over the Barrel: The Brewing History and Beer Culture of Cincinnati, Volume One: 1800–Prohibition.* St. Joseph, MO: Sudhaus Press, 2000.

Holtzman, Myron, as told by William J. Vollmar. "An Oral History of Anheuser-Busch." Photocopy, Anheuser-Busch Corporate Library.

Horowitz, Ira, and Ann R. Horowitz. "Firms in a Declining Market: The Brewing Case." *Journal of Industrial Economics* 13, no. 2 (March 1965): 129–53.

Hudepohl Brewing Company. *Brewing in Cincinnati, 1885–1985: 100 Years Hudepohl Brewing Company.* Cincinnati, OH: The Company, 1985.

Ingraham, Ankjen Tadema. "Henry Weinhard: Portland's Elusive Founding Father." Bachelor's thesis, Whitman College, 1998.

Jackson, Michael. "The Birth of Lager." *All About Beer* 17 (1996): 8–11, 29, 44.

Jones, Jay Edward. "The Restructuring of the U.S. Brewing Industry and Small Firm Survival." Ph.D. dissertation, Boston College, 1990.

Kostka, William. *The Pre-Prohibition History of Adolph Coors Company, 1873–1933.* n.p.

Krebs, Roland, with Percy J. Orthwein. *Making Friends Is Our Business: 100 Years of Anheuser-Busch.* [St. Louis, MO]: Anheuser-Busch Brewing Company, 1953.

Larsen, Carlton K. "Relax and Have a Homebrew: Beer, The Public Sphere, and (Re)Invented Traditions." *Food and Foodways* 7, no. 4 (1997): 265–88.

Leisy, Bruce R. *A History of the Leisy Brewing Companies.* North Newton, KS: Mennonite Press, 1975.

Lindhurst, James. "History of the Brewing Industry in St. Louis, 1804–1860." Master's thesis, Washington University, 1939.

Lisheron, Mark. "Capturing the Past: The Rebirth of Pre-Prohibition Lager." *Zymurgy* 20 (1997): 20–23, 82–86.

Lobbig, David. "Adam Lemp's Taste for Beer." *Gateway Heritage* 20, no. 2 (1999): 84–88.

Lynk, William J. "Interpreting Rising Concentration: The Case of Beer." *Journal of Business* 57 (January 1984): 43–55.

Maxwell, H. James, and Bob Sullivan. *Hometown Beer: A History of Kansas City's Breweries*. Kansas City, MO: Omega Innovative Marketing, 1999.

Mathias, Peter. *The Brewing Industry in England 1700–1830*. Cambridge: Cambridge University Press, 1959.

Mayer, James Douglas. "Bavarian Breweries and Brewmasters, 1871–1914: A Study of *Mittelstandspolitik* and German Economic Modernization." Ph.D. dissertation, Harvard University, 1982.

McBride, Robert. "Industry Structure, Marketing, and Public Health: A Case Study of the U.S. Beer Industry." *Contemporary Drug Problems* 12, no. 4 (Winter 1985): 593–620.

McGahan, A. M. "Cooperation in Prices and Capacities: Trade Associations in Brewing After Repeal." *Journal of Law and Economics* 38 (October 1995): 521–55.

McGahan, A. M. "The Emergence of the National Brewing Oligopoly: Competition in the American Market, 1933–1958." *Business History Review* 65, no. 2 (Summer 1991): 229–84.

McMillen, Harlow. "Staten Island's Lager Beer Breweries, 1851–1962." *The Staten Island Historian* 30 (July–September 1969): 15–21.

Miller, Carl H. *Breweries of Cleveland*. Cleveland: Schnitzelbank Press, 1998.

Nelson, James L. "Business History of San Antonio Brewing Association (Pearl Brewing Company) 1886–1933." Master's thesis, Trinity University, 1976.

Noon, Mark A. *Yuengling: A History of America's Oldest Brewery*. Jefferson, NC: McFarland & Company, 2005.

Norman, Donald Alan. "Structural Change and Performance in the U.S. Brewing Industry." Ph.D. dissertation, University of California, Los Angeles, 1975.

O'Bannon, Patrick W. "Inconsiderable Progress: Commercial Brewing in Philadelphia Before 1840," in *Early American Technology: Making and Doing Things from the Colonial Era to 1850*, ed. Judith A. McGaw. Chapel Hill: University of North Carolina, 1994, pp. 148–63.

One Hundred Years of Brewing. 1903, Reprint. New York: Arno Press, 1974.

Ornstein, Stanley I. "Antitrust Policy and Market Forces as Determinants of Industry Structure: Case Histories in Beer and Distilled Spirits." *The Antitrust Bulletin* 26, no. 2 (Summer 1981): 281–313.

Plavchan, Ronald Jan. "A History of Anheuser-Busch, 1852–1933." Ph.D. dissertation, St. Louis University, 1969.

Porter, John. *All About Beer.* New York: Doubleday & Company, 1975.

Powell, Stephen R. *Rushing the Growler: A History of Brewing in Buffalo.* Buffalo, NY: Apogee Design, 1996.

Rabin, Dan, and Carl Forget, comp. *The Dictionary of Beer and Brewing.* Boulder, CO: Brewers Publication, 1998.

Reilly, Michael R. Schlitz company history compiled at http://www.chiptin.com.

Renner, Jeff. "Reviving the Classic American Pilsner—A Shamefully Neglected Style." *Brewing Techniques* 3 (September–October 1995): 70–71.

Rhodes, Christine P., editor. *The Encyclopedia of Beer.* New York: Henry Holt, 1995.

Robertson, James D. *The Great American Beer Book.* Ottawa, IL: Caroline House Publishers, 1978.

Ronnenberg, Herman. *Beer and Brewing In the Inland Northwest, 1850 to 1950.* Moscow: University of Idaho Press, 1993.

Sandberg, Maxine Sylvia. "The Life and Career of Adolphus Busch." Master's thesis, University of Texas, 1951.

Schaefer, F. & M. Brewing Company. *Our One Hundredth Year, 1842–1942.* Brooklyn, NY: n.p., 1942.

Schnell, Steven M., and Joseph F. Reese. "Microbreweries as Tools of Local Identity." *Journal of Cultural Geography* 21, no. 1 (Fall–Winter 2003): 45–69.

Schoenknecht, John, and David Kapsos. *Brewed With Waukesha Water: The History of the Brewing Industry in Waukesha, Wisconsin.* [Waukesha, WI]: n.p., 1993.

Skilnik, Bob. *The History of Beer and Brewing in Chicago 1833–1978.* [St. Paul, MN]: Pogo Press, 1999.

Slosberg, Pete. *Beer for Pete's Sake: The Wicked Adventures of a Brewing Maverick.* Boulder, CO: Siris Books, 1998.

Smith, George Vinal. "History of Spokane Brewing and Malting Company, Spokane, Washington, 1887–1916." Master's thesis, Washington State University, 1967.

Smith, Gregg. *Beer: A History of Suds and Civilization from Mesopotamia to Microbreweries.* New York: Avon Books, 1995.

Smith, Michael Lee. "The Historical Geography of the United States Brewing Industry." Master's thesis, University of Vermont, 1990.

Smith, Robert J. *A History of the Halm Brewing Company, Bryan, Ohio, 1865–1908.* Bryan, OH: the author, 1992.

Stack, Martin Heidegger. "Liquid Bread: An Examination of the American Brewing Industry, 1865–1940." Ph.D. dissertation, University of Notre Dame, 1998.

Teich, Mikuláš. "A Case of Industrial Espionage in Brewing in 1833," in *A Special Brew: Essays in Honour of Kristof Glamann,* ed. Thomas Riis. [Odense, Denmark]: Odense University Press, 1993: 183–87.

Teich, Mikuláš. "Fermentation Theory and Practice: The Beginnings of Pure Yeast Cultivation and English Brewing, 1883–1913." *History of Technology* 8 (1893): 117–33.

Teich, Mikuláš. "The Industrialization of Brewing in Germany (1800–1914)," in *Production, Marketing and Consumption of Alcoholic Beverages Since the Late Middle Ages,* ed. Erik Aerts, Louis M. Cullen, and Richard G. Wilson. Leuven, Belgium: Leuven University Press, 1990, 102–13.

Thausing, Julius, et al. *The Theory and Practice of the Preparation of Malt and the Fabrication of Beer.* Philadelphia: Henry Carey Baird & Co., 1882.

Tilton, Alice Busch. *Remembering.* n.p. [1941].

Tremblay, Victor J. "A Reappraisal of Interpreting Rising Concentration: The Case of Beer." *Journal of Business* 58 (October 1985): 419–31.

Tritton, S. M. *Guide to Better Wine and Beer Making for Beginners.* New York: Dover Publications, 1965.

Uihlein, Edward G. "Memoir of Edward G. Uihlein," trans. Rosina L. Lippi and Jill D. Carlisle. Typed transcript, Edward G. Uihlein Reminiscences, 1917, Chicago Historical Society (n.b.: at the CHS, this document is listed only in the online catalog, and only under the name "Schlitz.").

Van Wieren, Dale P. *American Breweries II.* West Point, PA: Eastern Coast Breweriana Association, 1995.

Wahl, Robert, and Max Henius. *American Handy Book of Brewing, Malting and Auxiliary Trades,* 3d ed. Chicago: Wahl-Henius Institute, 1908.

Walker, Stephen P. *Lemp: The Haunting History.* Webster Groves, MO: The Lemp Preservation Society, 1988.

Wells, Robert W. "The Uihleins of Milwaukee." *Milwaukee Journal Insight* (Sunday magazine), April 23 and 30, 1972, and May 7, 1972.

Worcester, Michael R. "Been A Long Time A-Brewing: A History of the Minneapolis Brewing Company, 1890–1975." Master's thesis, Saint Cloud State University, 1993.

WPA biographies, State Historical Society of Wisconsin.

CITY HISTORIES

Bruce, William George. *History of Milwaukee City and County*. Chicago: S. J. Clarke Publishing Co., 1922.

Buck, James S. *Pioneer History of Milwaukee*, 2 vols., rev. ed. Milwaukee, WI: Swain and Tate, 1890.

Conard, Louis. *History of Milwaukee From Its First Settlement to the Year 1895*. Chicago: American Biographical Dictionary, 1895.

Conzen, Kathleen Neils. *Immigrant Milwaukee 1836–1860: Accommodation and Community in A Frontier City*. Cambridge, MA: Harvard University Press, 1976.

Dictionary of Wisconsin Biography. Madison: State Historical Society of Wisconsin, 1960.

Evening Wisconsin Newspaper Reference Book: Wisconsin and Milwaukee Men and Events. Milwaukee: Evening Wisconsin Co., 1914.

Flower, Frank Abial. *History of Milwaukee, Wisconsin*. Chicago: The Western Historical Co., 1881.

Gregory, John G. *History of Milwaukee, Wisconsin*. Chicago: S. J. Clarke Publishing Co., 1931.

Gurda, John. *The Making of Milwaukee*. Milwaukee, WI: County Historical Society, 1999.

Hyde, William, and Howard L. Conard. *Encyclopedia of the History of St. Louis*. New York: The Southern History Company, 1899.

Koss, Rudolf. *Milwaukee*, translated by Hans Ibsen. Typescript at State Historical Society of Wisconsin.

Primm, James Neal. *Lion of the Valley: St. Louis, Missouri, 1764–1980*. 3d ed. St. Louis: Missouri Historical Society Press, 1998.

Still, Bayard. *Milwaukee: The History of a City*. Madison: State Historical Society of Wisconsin, 1948.

United States Biographical Dictionary and Portrait Gallery of Eminent and Self-Made Men, Wisconsin volume. Chicago: American Biographical Publishing Co., 1877.

Usher, Ellis Baker. *Wisconsin: Its Story and Biography, 1848–1913.* Chicago: Lewis Publishing Co., 1914.

Wisconsin: Stability Progress Beauty, vol. 5: Wisconsin Biography. Chicago: Lewis Publishing Co., 1946.

IMMIGRATION AND NATIVISM

Baldwin, Thomas P. "The Public Image of Germans in Louisville and in Jefferson County, Kentucky, 1840–72." *Yearbook of German-American Studies* 29 (1994): 83–90.

Baughin, William A. "Bullets and Ballots: The Election Day Riots of 1855." *Bulletin of the Historical and Philosophical Society of Ohio* 21 (October 1963): 267–72.

Baughin, William A. "The Development of Nativism in Cincinnati." *Bulletin of the Cincinnati Historical Society* 22 (1964): 240–55.

Billington, Ray A. *The Protestant Crusade, 1830–1860.* New York: Macmillan, 1938.

Burnett, Robyn. *German Settlement in Missouri: New Land, Old Ways.* Columbia: University of Missouri Press, 1996.

Byrne, Frank L. "Cold Water Crusade: The Wisconsin Temperance Movement, 1832–1860." Master's thesis, University of Wisconsin, 1951.

Byrne, Frank L. "Maine Law Versus Lager Beer: A Dilemma of Wisconsin's Young Republican Party." *Wisconsin Magazine of History* 42 (Winter 1958–59): 115–20.

Dannenbaum, Jed. "Immigrants and Temperance: Ethnocultural Conflict in Cincinnati, 1845–1860." *Ohio History* 87 (Spring 1978): 125–39.

Deusner, Charles E. "The Know Nothing Riots in Louisville." *Register of the Kentucky Historical Society* 61 (1963): 122–47.

Gerber, David A. "'The Germans Take Care of Our Celebrations': Middle-Class Americans Appropriate German Ethnic Culture in Buffalo in the 1850s," in *Hard At Play: Leisure In America, 1840–1940,* ed.

Kathryn Grover. Amherst: University of Massachusetts Press for the Strong Museum, 1992: 39–60.

Gerber, David A. *The Making of an American Pluralism: Buffalo, New York, 1825–60.* Urbana: University of Illinois Press, 1989.

Glasco, Laurence A. *Ethnicity and Social Structure: Irish, Germans, and Native-Born of Buffalo, New York, 1850–1860.* (1973; reprint ed., New York: Arno Press, 1980).

Kargau, Ernst D. *The German Element in St. Louis.* Translated by William G. Bek, ed. Don Heinrich Tolzmann. 1893; reprint ed., Baltimore, MD: Clearfield Publishing, 2000.

Kellner, George Helmuth. "The German Element on the Urban Frontier: St. Louis 1830–1860." Ph.D. dissertation, University of Missouri, 1973.

Knobel, Dale T. *'America for the Americans': The Nativist Movement in the United States.* New York: Twayne, 1996.

Knobel, Dale T. "To Be an American: Ethnicity, Fraternity, and the Improved Order of Red Men." *Journal of American Ethnic History* 4 (Fall 1984): 62–87.

Lindberg, Richard C. *To Serve and Collect: Chicago Politics and Police Corruption from the Lager Beer Riot to the Summerdale Scandal.* New York: Praeger, 1991.

Maizlish, Stephen E. "The Meaning of Nativism and the Crisis of the Union: The Know-Nothing Movement in the Antebellum North," in *Essays on American Antebellum Politics, 1840–1869,* ed. Stephen E. Maizlish. College Station: Texas A&M University Press for the University of Texas at Arlington, 1982: 166–98.

McCrossen, Alexis. *Holy Day, Holiday: The American Sunday.* Ithaca, NY: Cornell University Press, 2000.

Mintz, Steven. *Moralists and Modernizers: America's Pre-Civil War Reformers.* Baltimore, MD: The Johns Hopkins University Press, 1995.

Olson, Audrey L. "St. Louis Germans, 1850–1920: The Nature of an Immigrant Community and Its Relation to the Assimilation Process." Ph.D. dissertation, University of Kansas, 1970.

O'Toole, William G., Jr., and Charles E. Aebersold, trans. "Louisville's Bloody Monday Riots from a German Perspective." *Filson Club History Quarterly* 70 (October 1996): 419–25.

Pettibone, Dennis Lynn. "Caesar's Sabbath: The Sunday-Law Controversy in the United States, 1879–1892." Ph.D. dissertation, University of California, Riverside, 1979.

Renner, Richard Wilson. "In a Perfect Ferment: Chicago, the Know-Nothings, and the Riot for Lager Beer." *Chicago History* 5 (Fall 1976): 161–70.

Rorabaugh, W. J. "Rising Democratic Spirits: Immigrants, Temperance, and Tammany Hall, 1854–1860." *Civil War History* 22 (June 1976): 138–57.

Ross, Steven J. *Workers on the Edge: Work, Leisure, and Politics in Industrializing Cincinnati, 1788–1890.* New York: Columbia University Press, 1985.

Schafer, Joseph. "Know-Nothingism in Wisconsin." *Wisconsin Magazine of History* 8 (September 1924): 3–21.

Sullivan, Margaret Lo Piccolo. *Hyphenism in St. Louis, 1900–1921: The View From the Outside.* New York: Garland, 1990.

Wittke, Carl. "The Germans of Cincinnati." *Bulletin of the Historical and Philosophical Society of Ohio* 20 (January 1962): 3–14.

ALCOHOL AND DRINKING CULTURE

Barrows, Susanna, Robin Room, and Jeffery Verhey. *The Social History of Alcohol: Drinking and Culture in Modern Society.* Berkeley, CA: Alcohol Research Group, 1987.

Blocker, Jack S., Jr. "Artisan's Escape: A Profile of the Postbellum Liquor Trade in a Midwestern Small Town." *Essays in Economic and Business History* 12 (1994): 335–46.

Burnham, John C. *Bad Habits: Drinking, Smoking, Taking Drugs, Gambling, Sexual Misbehavior, and Swearing in American History.* New York: New York University Press, 1993.

Carnes, Mark C., and Clyde Griffen, eds. *Meanings for Manhood: Constructions of Masculinity in Victorian America.* Chicago: University of Chicago Press, 1990.

Duis, Perry R. *The Saloon: Public Drinking in Chicago and Boston 1880–1920.* Urbana: University of Illinois Press, 1983.

Engleman, Larry. "Old Saloon Days in Michigan." *Michigan History* 61, no. 2 (Summer 1977): 99–134.

Grimes, William. *Straight Up or On the Rocks: A Cultural History of American Drink.* New York: Simon & Schuster, 1993.

Jacobson, Michael, Robert Atkins, and George Hacker. *The Booze Merchants: The Inebriating of America.* Washington, D.C.: CSPI Books, 1983.

Kingsdale, Jon M. "The 'Poor Man's Club': Social Functions of the Urban Working-Class Saloon," in *The American Man,* ed. Elizabeth H. Pleck and Joseph H. Pleck. Englewood Cliffs, NJ: Prentice-Hall, 1980: 255–83.

Lender, Mark Edward, and James Kirby Martin. *Drinking in America: A History.* 1982; rev. exp. ed., New York: The Free Press, 1987.

Levine, Harry Gene. "The Discovery of Addiction: Changing Conceptions of Habitual Drunkenness in America." *Journal of Studies on Alcohol* 39 (January 1978): 143–74.

Lukacs, Paul. *American Vintage: The Rise of American Wine.* Boston: Houghton Mifflin, 2000.

McNamara, Brooks. *The New York Concert Saloon: The Devil's Own Nights.* New York: Columbia University Press, 2002.

Murdock, Catherine Gilbert. *Domesticating Drink: Women, Men, and Alcohol in America, 1870–1940.* Baltimore, MD: The Johns Hopkins University Press, 1998.

Noel, Thomas J. *The City and the Saloon: Denver 1858–1916.* Lincoln: University of Nebraska Press, 1982.

Park, Peter. "The Supply Side of Drinking: Alcohol Production and Consumption in the United States Before Prohibition." *Contemporary Drug Problems* 12 (Winter 1985): 473–509.

Parsons, Elaine Frantz. *Manhood Lost: Fallen Drunkards and Redeeming Women in the Nineteenth-Century United States.* Baltimore, MD: The Johns Hopkins University Press, 2003.

Parsons, Elaine Frantz. "Risky Business: The Uncertain Boundaries of Manhood in the Midwestern Saloon." *Journal of Social History* 34, no. 2 (Winter 2000): 283–307.

Powers, Madelon. *Faces Along the Bar: Lore and Order in the Workingman's Saloon, 1870–1920.* Chicago: University of Chicago Press, 1998.

Room, Robin. "The Movies and the Wettening of America: The Media as Amplifiers of Cultural Change." *British Journal of Addiction* 83, no. 1 (January 1988): 11–18.

Rorabaugh, W. J. *The Alcoholic Republic: An American Tradition.* New York: Oxford University Press, 1979.

Rorabaugh, W. J. "Beer, Lemonade, and Propriety in the Gilded Age," in *Dining in America, 1850–1900,* ed. Kathryn Grover. Amherst: University of Massachusetts Press and the Margaret Woodbury Strong Museum, 1987: 24–46.

Rosenzweig, Roy. *Eight Hours For What We Will: Workers and Leisure in an Industrial City, 1870–1920.* Cambridge: Cambridge University Press, 1983.

Rotskoff, Lori. *Love On the Rocks: Men, Women, and Alcohol in Post–World War II America.* Chapel Hill: University of North Carolina Press, 2002.

Rubin, Jay L. "The Wet War: American Liquor Control, 1941–1945," in *Alcohol, Reform and Society,* ed. Jack S. Blocker, Jr. Westport, CT: Greenwood Press, 1979.

Slout, William, ed. *Broadway Below the Sidewalk: Concert Saloons of Old New York.* San Bernardino, CA: The Borgo Press, 1994.

Wells, Ken. *Travels With Barley: A Journey Through Beer Culture in America.* New York: Free Press, Wall Street Journal Books, 2004.

Zellers, Parker. "The Cradle of Variety: The Concert Saloon." *Educational Theatre Journal* 20 (December 1968): 578–85.

TEMPERANCE AND PROHIBITION

Blocker, Jack S. *'Give to the Winds Thy Fears': The Women's Temperance Crusade, 1873–1874.* Westport, CT: Greenwood Press, 1985.

Bradley, Claire Lucile. "The Prohibition Movement: Dramshop Law Enforcement in Missouri, 1887–1910." Master's thesis, Washington University, 1941.

Cherrington, E. H. *The Evolution of Prohibition in the United States of America.* Westerville, OH: American Issues Press, 1920.

Clark, Norman H. *Deliver Us From Evil: An Interpretation of American Prohibition.* New York: W. W. Norton & Co., 1976.

Dannenbaum, Jed. *Drink and Disorder: Temperance Reform in Cincinnati from* the *Washingtonian Revival to the WCTU*. Urbana: University of Illinois Press, 1984.

Drescher, Nuala McGann. "The Opposition to Prohibition, 1900–1919: A Social and Institutional Study." Ph.D. dissertation, University of Delaware, 1964.

Hamm, Richard F. *Shaping the Eighteenth Amendment: Temperance Reform, Legal Culture, and the Polity, 1880–1920*. Chapel Hill: University of North Carolina Press, 1995.

Heath, Dwight B. "The New Temperance Movement: Through the Looking-Glass." *Drugs and Society* 3 (1989): 143–68.

Hogan, Charles Marshall. "Wayne B. Wheeler: Single Issue Exponent." Ph.D. dissertation, University of Cincinnati, 1986.

Kerr, K. Austin. *Organized for Prohibition: A New History of the Anti-Saloon League*. New Haven, CT: Yale University Press, 1985.

Kobler, John. *Ardent Spirits: The Rise and Fall of Prohibition*. New York: Putnam, 1973.

Kyvig, David E. *Repealing National Prohibition*, 2d ed. Kent, OH: The Kent State University Press, 2000.

Lender, Mark Edward. *Dictionary of American Temperance Biography: From Temperance Reform to Alcohol Research, the 1600s to the 1980s*. Westport, CT: Greenwood Press, 1984.

Levine, Harry Gene. "The Birth of American Alcohol Control: Prohibition, the Power Elite, and the Problem of Lawlessness." *Contemporary Drug Problems* 12 (Spring 1985): 63–115.

Meyer, Paul R. "The Transformation of American Temperance: The Popularization and Radicalization of a Reform Movement, 1813–1860." Ph.D. dissertation, University of Iowa, 1976.

Miron, Jeffrey A., and Jeffrey Zwiebel. *Alcohol Consumption During Prohibition*. Cambridge, MA: National Bureau of Economic Research, 1991.

Pegram, Thomas R. *The Struggle for a Dry America, 1800–1933*. Chicago: Ivan R. Dee, 1998.

Renner, C. K. "Prohibition Comes to Wisconsin, 1910–1919." *Missouri Historical Review* 62 (1968): 363–97.

Robert, Anthony. "The Brewing Interests and the Coming of National Prohibition: A Study in Defeat." Master's thesis, University of Texas, 1965.

Roberts, James S. *Drink, Temperance and the Working Class in Nineteenth-Century Germany.* Boston: George Allen & Unwin, 1984.

Schafer, Joseph. "Prohibition in Early Wisconsin." *Wisconsin Magazine of History* 8 (March 1925): 281–99.

Sinclair, Andrew. *Era of Excess: A Social History of the Prohibition Movement.* New York: Harper and Row, 1964.

Sponholtz, Lloyd. "The Politics of Temperance in Ohio." *Ohio History* 84 (Winter 1975): 4–27.

Steuart, Justin. *Wayne Wheeler Dry Boss.* 1928; reprint ed., Westport, CT: Greenwood Press, 1970.

Thelen, David P. "La Follette and the Temperance Crusade." *Wisconsin Magazine of History* 47 (1963–64): 291–300.

Timberlake, James H. *Prohibition and the Progressive Movement, 1900–1920.* Cambridge, MA: Harvard University Press, 1963.

Turner, James Ross. "The American Prohibition Movement, 1865–1897." Ph.D. dissertation, University of Wisconsin, 1972.

Tyrell, Ian R. *Sobering Up: From Temperance to Prohibition in Antebellum America, 1800–1860.* Westport, CT: Greenwood Press, 1979.

Warburton, Clark. *The Economic Results of Prohibition.* 1932; reprint ed., New York: AMS Press, 1968.

Weisensel, Peter R. "The Wisconsin Temperance Crusade to 1919." Master's thesis, University of Wisconsin, 1965.

CIVIL WAR

Anderson, Galusha. *A Border City During the Civil War.* Boston: Little, Brown & Co., 1908.

Blum, Virgil C. "Political and Military Activities of the German Element in St. Louis, 1859–1861." *Missouri Historical Review* 42 (January 1948): 103–29.

Boernstein, Henry. *Memoirs of a Nobody: The Missouri Years of An Austrian Radical, 1849–1866.* Translated by Steven Rowan. St. Louis: Missouri Historical Society Press, 1987.

Carson, William G. B. "Secesh." *Missouri Historical Society Bulletin* 23 (January 1967): 119–45.

Dorpalen, Andreas. "The German Element and the Issues of the Civil War." *Mississippi Valley Historical Review* 29 (June 1942): 55–76.

Goodrich, James W., ed. "The Civil War Letters of Bethiah Pyatt Mc-Kown." *Missouri Historical Review* 67 (January 1973): 227–44.

Guese, Lucius E. "St. Louis and the Great Whiskey Ring." *Missouri Historical Review* 36 (January 1942): 160–83.

Hu, Tun-Yuan. *The Liquor Tax in the United States 1791–1947.* New York: Columbia University Press, 1950.

Irwin, Ray W., ed. "Missouri in Crisis: The Journal of Captain Albert Tracy." *Missouri Historical Review* 51 (October 1956): 20–21.

Josyph, Peter. *The Wounded River: The Civil War Letters of John Vance Lauderdale, M.D.* East Lansing: Michigan State University Press, 1993.

Mittelman, Amy. "The Politics of Alcohol Production: The Liquor Industry and the Federal Government 1862–1900." Ph.D. dissertation, Columbia University, 1986.

Richard, Patricia. " 'A Great Crying Evil': Civil War Soldiers' Experiences in Milwaukee, Wisconsin." *Milwaukee History* 22 (1991): 16–32.

Rombauer, Robert J. *The Union Cause in St. Louis in 1861.* St. Louis: Nixon-Jones Printing Co., 1906.

Smith, Harry Edwin. *The United States Internal Tax History from 1861 to 1871.* Boston: Houghton Mifflin, 1914.

Van Ravenswaag, Charles. "Years of Turmoil, Years of Growth: St. Louis in the 1850s." *Missouri Historical Society Bulletin* 23 (1967): 303–24.

Winter, William C. *The Civil War in St. Louis.* St. Louis: Missouri Historical Society Press, 1994.

INDUSTRY AND INDUSTRIALIZATION

Atack, Jeremy. "Industrial Structure and the Emergence of the Modern Industrial Corporation." *Explorations in Economic History* 22 (1985): 29–52.

Chandler, Alfred D., Jr. *The Visible Hand: The Managerial Revolution in American Business.* Cambridge, MA: The Belknap Press of Harvard University, 1977.

Cohen, Ruth Schwartz. *A Social History of American Technology*. New York: Oxford University Press, 1997.

Cross, Gary, and Rick Szostak. *Technology and American Society: A History*. Englewood Cliffs, NJ: Prentice Hall, 1995.

Cummings, Richard Osborn. *The American Ice Harvests: A Historical Study in Technology, 1800–1918*. Berkeley: University of California Press, 1949.

Hall, Henry. "Ice Industry in the United States; with a Brief Sketch of Its History and Estimate of Production in the Different States," in *Tenth Census of the United States, 1880*. Washington, D.C.: Government Printing Office, 1883.

Hurt, R. Douglas. "Cold Comfort: Harvesting Natural Ice." *Timeline* 3 (February–March 1986): 38–49.

Lawrence, Lee E. "The Wisconsin Ice Trade." *Wisconsin Magazine of History* 48 (1965): 257–67.

Licht, Walter. *Industrializing America: The Nineteenth Century*. Baltimore, MD: The Johns Hopkins University Press, 1995.

Nelson, Daniel, ed. *A Mental Revolution: Scientific Management Since Taylor*. Columbus: Ohio State University Press, 1992.

Porter, Glenn. *The Rise of Big Business, 1860–1910*, 2d ed. Arlington Heights, IL: Harlan Davidson, 1992.

Ronnenberg, Herman. "Idaho on the Rocks: The Ice Business in the Gem State." *Idaho Yesterdays* 33 (Winter 1990): 2–8.

Smith, Philip Chadwick Foster. "Crystal Blocks of Yankee Coldness: The Development of the Massachusetts Ice Trade from Frederick Tudor to Wenham Lake 1806–1886." *Essex Institute Historical Collections* 97 (July 1961): 197–232.

Weightman, Gavin. *The Frozen-Water Trade: A True Story*. New York: Hyperion, 2003.

FOOD AND DRINK

Anderson, Oscar. *The Health of A Nation: Harvey W. Wiley and the Fight for Pure Food*. Chicago: University of Chicago Press, 1958.

Angell, George T. *Autobiographical Sketches and Personal Recollections*. Boston: American Humane Education Society, [1892].

Belasco, Warren J. *Appetite for Change: How the Counterculture Took on the Food Industry, 1966–1988.* New York: Pantheon Books, 1989.

Berrett, Jesse. "Feeding the Organization Man: Diet and Masculinity in Postwar America." *Journal of Social History* 30 (Summer 1997): 805–25.

Goodwin, Lorine Swainston. *The Pure Food, Drink, and Drug Crusaders, 1879–1914.* Jefferson, NC: McFarland & Co., 1999.

Hamilton, Shane. "The Economies and Conveniences of Modern-Day Living: Frozen Foods and Mass Marketing, 1945–1965." *Business History Review* 77 (Spring 2003): 33–60.

Hayenga, Elizabeth Sharon. "Dieting Through the Decades: A Comparative Study of Weight Reduction in America as Depicted in Popular Literature and Books from 1940 to the Late 1980's." Ph.D. dissertation, University of Minnesota, 1988.

Levenstein, Harvey. *Paradox of Plenty: A Social History of Eating in Modern America.* New York: Oxford University Press, 1993.

Murdock, Catherine Gilbert. *Domesticating Drink: Women, Men, and Alcohol in America, 1870–1940.* Baltimore, MD: The Johns Hopkins University Press, 1998.

Okun, Mitchell. *Fair Play in the Marketplace: The First Battle for Pure Food and Drugs.* Dekalb: Northern Illinois University, 1986.

Riley, John. *A History of the American Soft Drink Industry.* Washington, D.C.: American Bottlers of Carbonated Beverages, 1958.

Wilden, Mark W. "Industrialization of Food Processing in the United States, 1860–1960." Ph.D. dissertation, University of Delaware, 1988.

Young, James Harvey. *Pure Food: Securing the Federal Food and Drugs Act of 1906.* Princeton, NJ: Princeton University Press, 1989.

FAIRS AND EXPOSITIONS

Birchall, Emily, and David Verey. *Wedding Tour: January–June 1873 and Visit to the Vienna Exhibition.* New York: St. Martin's Press, 1985.

Downey, Dennis B. *A Season of Renewal: The Columbian Exposition and Victorian America.* Westport, CT: Praeger Publishing, 2002.

Harris, Neil. *Grand Illusions: Chicago's World's Fair of 1893.* Chicago: Chicago Historical Society, 1993.

Hill, Hamilton Andrews. *Reports of the Massachusetts Commissioners to the Exposition at Vienna, 1873*. Boston: Wright & Potter, 1875.

Larson, Erik. *The Devil in the White City: Murder, Magic, and Madness at the Fair That Changed America*. New York: Crown Publishers, 2003.

McCabe, James D. *The Illustrated History of the Centennial Exhibition*. 1876; reprint ed., Philadelphia: National Publishing Co., 1975.

Muccigrosso, Robert. *Celebrating the New World: Chicago's Columbian Exposition of 1893*. Chicago: Ivan R. Dee, 1993.

Report of the Philadelphia Commission to Vienna, to the Select and Common Councils of the City of Philadelphia. Philadelphia: E. C. Markley & Son, 1874.

Reports on the Vienna Universal Exhibition of 1873: Presented to both Houses of Parliament by Command of Her Majesty. London: G. E. Eyre and W. Spottiswoode, 1874.

Russell, Fred W. "The Use of Wine and Beer at Vienna: With Some Account of the Drinking Places," in *Reports of the Massachusetts Commissioners to the Exposition at Vienna, 1873. With Special Reports Prepared for the Commission,* ed. Hamilton A. Hill. Boston: Wright & Potter, 1875.

Rydell, Robert W. *All the World's a Fair: Visions of Empire at American International Expositions*. Chicago: University of Chicago Press, 1984.

Rydell, Robert W. *World of Fairs: The Century-of-Progress Expositions*. Chicago: University of Chicago Press, 1993.

Thurston, Robert H. *Reports of the Commissioners of the United States to the International Exhibit at Vienna, 1873*. Washington, D.C.: Government Printing Office, 1875–1876.

United States Secretary of State. *Reports of the United States Commissioners to the Paris Universal Exposition, 1878*. Washington, D.C.: Government Printing Office, 1880.

[United States Brewers' Association]. *Essays on the Malt Liquor Question*. New York: Francis Hart & Co., 1876.

WORLD WAR I

Child, Clifton J. *The German-Americans in Politics, 1914–1917.* 1939; reprint ed., New York: Arno Press and the New York Times, 1970.

Christensen, Lawrence O. "Prelude to World War I in Missouri." *Missouri Historical Review* 89, no. 1 (1994): 1–16.

Coben, Stanley. *A. Mitchell Palmer, Politician*. New York: DaCapo Press, 1963.

Crighton, John C. *Missouri and the World War, 1914–1917: A Study in Public Opinion*. Columbia: University of Missouri Press, 1947.

Detjen, David W. *The Germans in Missouri, 1900–1918: Prohibition, Neutrality, and Assimilation*. Columbia: University of Missouri Press, 1985.

Dobbert, G. A. "German-Americans Between New and Old Fatherland, 1870–1914." *American Quarterly* 19 (Winter 1967): 663–80.

Keller, Phyllis. "German-America and the First World War." Ph.D. dissertation, University of Pennsylvania, 1969.

Kennedy, David. *Over Here: The First World War and American Society*. New York: Oxford University Press, 1980.

Luebke, Frederick C. *Bonds of Loyalty: German-Americans and World War I*. Dekalb: Northern Illinois University Press, 1974.

Luebke, Frederick C. "The German-American Alliance in Nebraska, 1910–1917," in Frederick C. Luebke, *Germans in the New World: Essays in the History of Immigration*. Urbana: University of Illinois Press, 1990: 14–30.

Scheiber, Clara Eve. *The Transformation of American Sentiment Toward Germany, 1870–1914*. 1923; reprint ed., New York: Russell and Russell, 1973.

Small, Melvin. "The American Image of Germany, 1906–1914." Ph.D. dissertation, University of Michigan, 1965.

Wittke, Carl Frederick. *The German-Language Press in America*. 1957; reprint ed., New York: Haskell House, 1973.

THE TWENTIES, THIRTIES AND WORLD WAR II

Cohen, Lizabeth. *Making a New Deal: Industrial Workers in Chicago, 1919–1939*. Cambridge: Cambridge University Press, 1990.

Dumenil, Lynn. *The Modern Temper: American Culture and Society in the 1920s*. New York: Hill and Wang, 1995.

Erenberg, Lewis A. "From New York to Middletown: Repeal and the Legitimization of Nightlife in the Great Depression." *American Quarterly* 38 (Winter 1986): 761–78.

Fox, Stephen. *The Mirror Makers: A History of American Advertising and Its Creators*. New York: William Morrow, 1984.

Kyvig, David E. *Daily Life in the United States, 1920–1939: Decades of Promise and Pain*. Westport, CT: Greenwood Press, 2002.

Marchand, Roland. *Advertising the American Dream: Making Way for Modernity, 1920–1940*. Berkeley: University of California Press, 1985.

May, Lary. *Screening Out the Past: The Birth of Mass Culture and the Motion Picture Industry*. New York: Oxford University Press, 1980.

Miller, Nathan. *New World Coming: The 1920s and the Making of Modern America*. New York: Scribner, 2003.

Morris, Sam. *Booze and the War*. Grand Rapids, MI: Zondervan Publishing, 1944.

Pope, Daniel. *The Making of Modern Advertising*. New York: Basic Books, 1983.

Parrish, Michael E. *Anxious Decades: America in Prosperity and Depression, 1920–1941*. New York: W.W. Norton, 1992.

Rusco, Elmer Ritter. "Machine Politics, California Model: Arthur H. Samish and the Alcoholic Beverages Industry." Ph.D. dissertation, University of California, Berkeley, 1960.

Strasser, Susan. *Satisfaction Guaranteed: The Making of the American Mass Market*. New York: Pantheon Books, 1989.

Tedlow, Richard S. *New and Improved: The Story of Mass Marketing in America*. New York: Basic Books, 1990.

Walker, Pamela Laird. *Advertising Progress: American Business and the Rise of Consumer Marketing*. Baltimore, MD: The Johns Hopkins University Press, 1998.

POSTWAR AMERICA

Armstrong, David. *A Trumpet to Arms: Alternative Media in America*. Los Angeles: J. P. Tarcher, 1981.

Bawer, Bruce. "The Other Sixties." *The Wilson Quarterly* (Spring 2004).

Bennett, Amanda. *The Death of the Organization Man*. New York: William Morrow and Company, 1990.

[Campaign for Real Ale]. *Whose Pint Is It Anyway?* St. Albans, England: Campaign for Real Ale, 1979.

Cavanagh, John, and Frederick F. Clairmonte. *Alcoholic Beverages: Dimensions of Corporate Power*. London: Croom & Helm, 1985.

Chafe, William H. *The Unfinished Journey: America Since World War II,* 5th ed. New York: Oxford University Press, 2003.

Cullman, Joseph F. 3rd. *I'm A Lucky Guy.* n.p.: Joseph F. Cullman 3rd, [1998].

Eisner, Marc Allen. "Institutional History and Policy Change: Exploring the Origins of the New Antitrust." *Journal of Policy History* 2, no. 3 (1990): 261–89.

Farber, David R. *The Age of Great Dreams: America in the 1960s.* New York: Hill and Wang, 1994.

Flack, Wes. "American Microbreweries and Neolocalism: 'Ale-ing' for a Sense of Place." *Journal of Cultural Geography* 16, no. 2 (1997): 37–53.

Frank, Robert H. *Luxury Fever: Why Money Fails to Satisfy in an Era of Excess.* New York: The Free Press, 1999.

Givens, Richard A. "The Milwaukee Brewery Strike of 1953." Master's thesis, University of Wisconsin, 1954.

Klugar, Richard. *Ashes to Ashes: America's Hundred-Year Cigarette War, the Public Health, and the Unabashed Triumph of Philip Morris.* New York: Alfred A. Knopf, 1996.

Kovacic, William E., and Carl Shapiro. "Antitrust Policy: A Century of Economic and Legal Thinking." *Journal of Economic Perspectives* 14, no. 1 (Winter 2000): 43–60.

Lebergott, Stanley. *Pursuing Happiness: American Consumers in the Twentieth Century.* Princeton, NJ: Princeton University Press, 1993.

Lee, Martin A., and Bruce Shlain. *Acid Dreams: The Complete Social History of LSD: The CIA, the Sixties, and Beyond.* New York: Grove Weidenfeld, 1992.

Leinberger, Paul, and Bruce Tucker. *The New Individualists: The Generation After the Organization Man.* New York: HarperCollins Publishers, 1991.

Makower, Joel. *Woodstock: The Oral History.* New York: Doubleday, 1989.

Markoff, John. *What the Dormouse Said: How the Sixties Counterculture Shaped the Personal Computer Industry.* New York: Viking, 2005.

May, Kirse Granat. *Golden State, Golden Youth: The California Image in Popular Culture, 1955–1966.* Chapel Hill: University of North Carolina Press, 2002.

Miles, Barry. *Zappa: A Biography.* New York: Grove Press, 2004.

Nelson, Daniel. *Shifting Fortunes: The Rise and Decline of American Labor, from the 1820s to the Present.* Chicago: Ivan R. Dee, 1997.

Nelson, Jon P. "Broadcast Advertising and U.S. Demand for Alcoholic Beverages." *Southern Economic Journal* 65, no. 4 (1999): 774–90.

Patterson, James T. *Grand Expectations: The United States, 1945–1974.* New York: Oxford University Press, 1996.

Peck, Abe. *Uncovering the Sixties: The Life and Times of the Underground Press.* New York: Pantheon Books, 1985.

Perry, Charles. *The Haight-Ashbury: A History.* New York: Random House, 1984.

Perry, Paul. *On the Bus: The Complete Guide to the Legendary Trip of Ken Kesey and the Merry Pranksters and the Birth of the Counterculture.* New York: Thunder's Mouth Press, 1990.

Postman, N., C. Nystrom, L. Strate, and C. Weingartner. *Myths, Men, & Beer: An Analysis of Beer Commercials on Broadcast Television, 1987.* Falls Church, VA: AAA Foundation for Traffic Safety, n.d.

Protz, Roger, and Tony Millns, eds. *Called to the Bar: An Account of the First 21 Years of the Campaign for Real Ale.* St. Albans, England: CAMRA Ltd., 1992.

Rawls, James J., and Walton Bean. *California: An Interpretive History,* 8th ed. Boston: McGraw Hill, 2002.

Rice, Richard B., William A. Bullough, and Richard J. Orsi. *The Elusive Eden,* 3rd ed. Boston: McGraw Hill, 2002.

Sobel, Robert. *The Great Boom 1950–2000: How A Generation of Americans Created the World's Most Properous Society.* New York: St. Martin's Press, 2000.

Spitz, Robert Stephen. *Barefoot In Babylon: The Creation of the Woodstock Music Festival, 1969.* New York: The Viking Press, 1979.

Stevens, Jay. *Storming Heaven: LSD and the American Dream.* New York: Atlantic Monthly Press, 1987.

Takebayashi, Shuichi. "The *Whole Earth Catalog* and the San Francisco Hippies: A Study of Counterculture Business." Master's thesis, Pennsylvania State University, 2001.

INDEX

at World's Columbian Exposition,
125–26, 129
anti-Prohibition movement,
emergence of, 190–91
Anti-Saloon League (ASL). *See also*
prohibition movement; Russell,
Howard Hyde; Wheeler, Wayne
brewers mount opposition to,
152–54, 165–66, 167
budget of, 150
coercive political methods,
162–64
creation of, 148
opposition to, lack of, 151–52
political strategy of, 163–64
power struggle within, 191
prohibition amendment presented
to Congress by, 161–62
propaganda published by, 149–50
success of, 150, 154, 156
structure of, 148–49
tactics of, 148–49, 150, 156–57,
158
tests strength in Congress,
164–65
Arizona Brewing Company, 245
Armadillo World Headquarters
(Austin), 272
Armstrong, Sue F. (Mrs.), 157–58
Association Against the Prohibition
Amendment (AAPA), 191–92
Association of Brewers, 320, 321
Atlantic Garden, 88–89
Austin City Limits, 272
Aztec Brewing Company, 233

Baker, Patrick, 279, 281
Ballantine Brewing Company, 225,
232, 241, 245
Balling, Karl, 74–75

Barkley, Don, 295, 296, 298, 307.
See also Mendocino Brewing
Company; New Albion Brewing
Company
barley, 70–71, 74
Bartholdt, Richard, 159, 160
Bartholomay Brewing Company, 125
Bass Ale, 266
Bates, Tom, 297
Baumann, Ruby, 176, 178
Bavarian Brewery. *See* Anheuser-
Busch Brewing Association
Beecher, Lyman, 25
beer, American preferences in,
72–73, 78, 85, 229. *See also*
lager, Bohemian
beer, bland. *See* beer, American
preferences in
beer can. *See* packaged beer
beer, changing attitudes toward. *See
also* homebrewing,
microbrewing
in 1850s, 30–31, 33–34
in 1920s, 206, 207
in 1950s, 226, 227, 228–29
in 1960s, 253
in 1970s, 266, 269–79
beer, consumption of, per capita
in 1840s, 151
in 1890s, 151
in 1915, 190
in 1934, 190
in 1960s, 226–27
in 1981, 322
in 1985; 322
in 2000, 322
beer gardens, 21, 86, 89. *See also*
saloons
beerhalls, 20, 21, 86, 88–89. *See also*
saloons